CICERO

V

LCL 342

Lineberger Memorial Library

Lutheran Theological Southern Seminary   Columbia, S. C.

CICERO

BRUTUS

WITH AN ENGLISH TRANSLATION BY

G. L. HENDRICKSON

ORATOR

WITH AN ENGLISH TRANSLATION BY

H. M. HUBBELL

HARVARD UNIVERSITY PRESS

CAMBRIDGE, MASSACHUSETTS

LONDON, ENGLAND

First published 1939
Reprinted 1942, 1952
Revised 1962
Reprinted 1971, 1988, 1997

LOEB CLASSICAL LIBRARY® is a registered trademark
of the President and Fellows of Harvard College

ISBN 0-674-99377-2

Printed in Great Britain by St Edmundsbury Press Ltd,
Bury St Edmunds, Suffolk, on acid-free paper.
Bound by Hunter & Foulis Ltd, Edinburgh, Scotland.

CONTENTS

BIBLIOGRAPHICAL ADDENDUM (1987)

Editions

A. E. Douglas, *Brutus*, Oxford 1966
Otto Seel, *Orator*, Heidelberg 1962

Index

W. A. Oldfather, W. V. Canter, and K. M. Abbott, *Index Verborum in Ciceronis Rhetorica*, Urbana, Ill. 1964

Studies

F. Portalupi, *Bruto e i neo-atticisti*, Turin 1955
A. E. Douglas, 'The Intellectual Background of Cicero's Rhetorica,' ANRW, Berlin 1973
G. V. Sumner, *The Orators in Cicero's Brutus: Prosopography and Chronology* (Phoenix Suppl. 11), Toronto 1973

General

M. L. Clarke, *Rhetoric at Rome: a historical survey*, London 1953
G. Kennedy, *The art of rhetoric in the Roman world*, Princeton 1972

LIST OF CICERO'S WORKS

SHOWING THEIR DIVISION INTO VOLUMES IN THIS EDITION

LIST OF CICERO'S WORKS

LIST OF CICERO'S WORKS

LIST OF CICERO'S WORKS

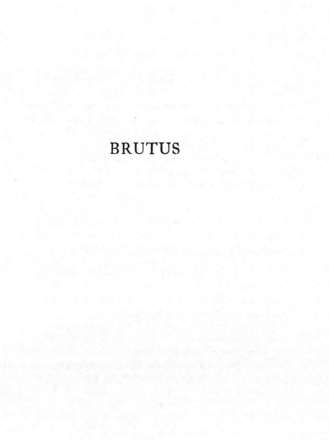

BRUTUS

INTRODUCTION

In the series of the more important rhetorical writings of Cicero the *Brutus* occupies a place intermediate in point of time between the *de Oratore* and the *Orator*. Cicero in the *de Divinatione* [a] alludes to these three works as a corpus of five books, which he ventures to compare with the writings of Aristotle and Theophrastus on the same subject. On this hint some modern scholars have constructed a doctrine of unity of plan, designating the three books *de Oratore* as the foundation of theory, the *Brutus* as the historical exemplification, and the *Orator* as the delineation of the ideal. This looks attractive and is not without some elements of truth. But, in fact, of the three works the *de Oratore* is the only one of spontaneous origin, written with a desire to present abstractly a theory of oratory and the portrait of the perfect orator. The *Brutus* and the *Orator* on the contrary, of later date, are controversial treatises, looking to the support of one side of a debate which had not yet arisen to general consciousness when the *de Oratore* was composed.

The general point of view of the *de Oratore* is an adaptation to Roman conditions and experience of doctrines which were entertained by recent or contemporary Greek philosophers, such as Philo and

[a] *De Div.* 2. 4.

Antiochus. Their aim seems to have been to effect a truce between the opposing factions of rhetoric and philosophy, which had waged war upon each other since Socrates' challenge to the assumptions of the sophists. Thus in Cicero the orator is at once philosopher and orator, the speaker who is able to draw upon universals for the elucidation and presentation of particular questions. From a stylistic point of view Cicero's " orator " (who is none other than himself) has his roots in the copiousness, not to say grandiloquence, of the Asiatic rhetoric, which had furnished instruction and example to Roman oratory from the time of its first conscious study.

But at the very time when Cicero was composing the *de Oratore* (55 B.C.) there existed at Rome a coterie of younger men who had begun to revolt from the manner represented by Cicero and Hortensius, and from the recognized Roman tradition in general. It would seem that Calidius, who is characterized as elegant but lifeless, justified his restraint by deliberate antithesis to what seemed to him " the bacchanalian frenzy " (*Brutus* 276) of current oratory. But the first specific evidence of a school and a tendency relates to Gaius Licinius Calvus, who called himself " Attic," and from Cicero's point of view " erred himself and caused others to err " (284). This is apparently the first emergence in ancient literature of that movement of revolt called Atticism, which was destined to have an enormous influence on subsequent times, and even upon the selection and preservation of Greek (and in some degree of Latin) literature for posterity. Roman " Atticism " we think of most commonly as an antithesis to " Asiatic " rhetoric ; but in truth it is probable that in origin the

3

movement was rather grammatical than rhetorical, and aimed to set up a standard of correctness for the Greek common tongue against foreign and alien corruption. But in the train of grammatical purity based upon earlier Attic models went a plea for return to Attic simplicity and artlessness of expression.

For Calvus to call himself " Attic " was of course only to use the term as designation of an analogous movement in Latin. His use of the Greek term seems to imply a well-recognized school of Atticism in Greek, the origins of which are, however, lost in the meagre record of the Hellenistic period. We have no definite record of the followers, whom (as Cicero complains) Calvus had misled, but apart from Calidius, already mentioned, we cannot err in assigning to this new heresy two of Cicero's younger friends, Brutus and Caelius, with whom Caesar, with his plea for cultivation of correctness and elegance in the speech of everyday life (253), was certainly in full sympathy. Thus at the very time when Cicero believed that his own reputation as an orator was most deserving of recognition, and when too he had formulated his creed in large outlines, he found himself confronted by a younger generation, which he himself had helped to train, looking with scepticism upon his life-work. Evidence of concern for this rebellion is to be found in scattered allusions in the correspondence of the years which followed the *de Oratore,*[a] but the first considerable protest and defence of his own camp is contained in this dialogue, dedicated to Brutus and bearing his name.

The date of composition can be placed within

[a] *Cf.* " Cicero's Correspondence with Brutus and Calvus on Oratorical Style," in *Am. Journ. Phil.* 1926, pp. 234 ff.

narrow limits.   Caesar is abroad completing the
destruction of the Pompeian opposition in Africa,
under the leadership of Cato and Scipio.   The final
battle of Thapsus has not yet taken place, but Rome
is tense and eager to learn the outcome of the final
struggle.[a]   Cato and Scipio are both alluded to as
still living (118 and 212).   Brutus, already designated as governor of Gaul, is still in Rome, but con-
templates early departure (171).   The scene of the
dialogue and the composition are co-incident, and
may therefore be placed at some point in the first
quarter of the year 46 B.C., before Thapsus (April 6),[b]
or before the news of it had reached Rome.

The primary motive for writing has been indicated
above, that is, by appeal to the record of Roman practice to demonstrate the correctness of the writer's
point of view concerning effective oratory.   But this
main purpose, even though it colours and sometimes
distorts the record, is not inconsistent with a real
historical and curious interest in the professed subject matter itself.   To write a history involving the
names and relationships of many individuals of an
earlier time was for a Roman of this period a difficult thing ; a chronology based upon the names of
consuls, pontifices, and lesser magistrates, was awkward, and from repetitions of the same or very similar
names often confusing.   Cicero was no archivist to
search the public records, and the *Brutus* would never
have been produced in the present form had not the

[a] The nervous anxiety with which news of the situation in
Africa was awaited is set forth vividly in Cicero's letter to
Mescinius Rufus, *Fam.* 5. 21.
[b] That is, of the pre-Julian calendar, which had out-
stripped the solar year by more than two months.

appearance of the *Liber Annalis* of Atticus made the
historical task possible and inviting, as he himself
says (15). This work made available to wider circles
the studies of professed scholars and antiquarians,
like Varro and others ; it gave careful lists of
magistrates, of laws, of all important events of
peace and war in their chronological relation to
each other, and especially the history of important
families through successive generations, as Nepos,
in his life of Atticus, records. From allusions at the
beginning of our dialogue it appears that the work
of Atticus had but recently appeared and was dedicated to Cicero. We may surmise from what he says
of its salutary effect upon him in the midst of deep
depression that it reached him in his unhappy
sojourn at Brindisi in the summer of 47. As the
work of Atticus made the *Brutus* possible, so to him
he assigns a rôle in the dialogue beside that of
Brutus. But to Brutus also acknowledgement is
made for a literary indebtedness. It is referred to
as a letter from Asia (11), which Atticus had read
with great pleasure, and its nature is suggested by
his comment, that " it admonished you with wise
counsel and consoled you affectionately." Its effect,
Cicero rejoins, was to call him back to life and
to look upon the sunlight once more, as if from a
long and desperate illness. It is probable that this
composition, named with much emphasis at the
beginning of the treatise and again at the end, was
something more than a private letter. There is,
in fact, reason to suspect that it was the epistolary
essay *de Virtute*, which is known to us from Seneca's
allusion and citation. Its argument, we may conjecture, was an exposition of the sufficiency of virtue
6

for the wise man, and it instanced the serenity and peace of mind which Brutus had found in Marcellus, living in exile at Mytilene.[a]

To these two compositions, the historical manual of Atticus and the consolatory essay of Brutus, Cicero acknowledges his indebtedness, and discharges it by making them the interlocutors in his dialogue. Titus Pomponius Atticus (born in 109, died in 32 B.C.) is the old and faithful friend of Cicero, to whom his most intimate letters are addressed. Marcus Junius Brutus, the character so familiar to us from Plutarch and Shakespeare, belongs to a generation younger. Born probably in 85,[b] he took his own life upon the defeat at Philippi in 42 B.C. In the Civil War he had supported the senatorial cause and participated in the defeat at Pharsalus. Reconciliation with Caesar followed, and from him he had received appointment as governor of Cisalpine Gaul for the year 46, whither he is about to go at the time of this dialogue (171).

The historical importance of the *Brutus*, as an early and often a contemporary witness, is very great. To many minor figures, who otherwise would have been no more than a name or would have been completely lost, it gives outline and sometimes even life. Cicero's attitude toward the men and measures of an earlier time is in harmony with the tradition of the optimates, but he recognizes statesmanlike ability and oratorical skill in men of whatever party. In allusion to the contemporary political scene Cicero is

[a] Cf. Seneca, *ad Helviam matrem* 8. 1 and 9. 4, together with the remarks of Brutus on Marcellus in *Brutus* 250, which clearly are drawn from the treatise to which Seneca refers.   [b] See note on section 324.

7

unreconciled and expresses openly his present despair
and forebodings for the future. Toward Caesar the
orator, writer, and scholar he is generous and almost
excessive in flattery, but he seems deliberately to
avoid confessing any debt to him for his present
restoration to a place in the senate and in the state.
He represents Atticus and Brutus as in complete
agreement with his despair, though Atticus strove to
be neutral, and Brutus was at the moment one of the
chief lieutenants of Caesar, and holder of high office
as governor of Cisalpine Gaul. This may not have
been entirely agreeable to Brutus, and when a little
later, after the death of Cato, he pressed Cicero to
write an eulogy of the defeated hero, he suggested
that Cicero use more restraint than he had done in the
Brutus. Caesar's magnanimity toward the defeated
Pompeians was great, but it balked at public defence
and eulogy of the lost cause. The severe censorship
which Caesar imposed is told vividly in the unhappy
letter of Aulus Caecina (*Fam.* 6. 7), but considerations
of policy made it wise to overlook the offences of
Cicero's pen. Soon after the death of Caesar, in
complaining to Atticus of the present check upon free
speech, Cicero contrasts it with Caesar's indulgence :
" for of me at all events, from whatever cause, he was
extraordinarily tolerant " (*Att.* 14. 17. 6).

The dialogue as a literary form was primarily a
vehicle of inquiry, reflecting debate and conversation upon some problem of common interest to the
speakers. In its earlier form it aimed to reproduce
the actual steps of such inquiry in the questions and
answers of the interlocutors. The procedure even
at the hands of Plato seems often slow, and may
become tedious and artificial. In the course of time

its inconvenience was felt, with the result that Aristotle and his school modified the Socratic form by assigning to a leading speaker a larger and more continuous rôle, lightened by interludes, interruptions, and transitions, shared in by other speakers. Through this device the dialogue was made serviceable, not only for dialectical inquiry, but also for continuous presentation of almost any subject matter.

This is the manner of the Ciceronian dialogue in general, which in a letter to Atticus (13. 19. 4) is designated specifically as Aristotelian. In the complete loss of the dialogues of Aristotle and his school, this form was known to us only from Cicero (and some later imitators), until the recent discovery of a considerable fragment of a dialogue by the Peripatetic Satyrus (of the third century B.C.). It was published by Hunt in the ninth volume of the *Oxyrhynchus Papyri* (No. 1176) from a papyrus of the second century of our era. The original work presented in dialogue form the lives of Aeschylus, Sophocles, and Euripides, of which only the last is preserved. The discovery was of no small value from every point of view, but for our *Brutus* its interest is peculiar. Here is an inquiry and exposition *de poetis* exactly analogous to Cicero's *de oratoribus*. In both there are three speakers, one of whom carries the principal part and rests his exposition on the inquiries of the minor characters. To follow out other resemblances in detail is an inviting study, but not appropriate to this place.[a]

The *Brutus* is not a carefully elaborated work,

---

[a] *Cf.* F. Leo, in *Nachrichten d. Götting. Akad.* 1912, pp. 273 ff., and D. Stuart, *Epochs of Greek and Roman Biography*, pp. 179 ff.

9

comparable for example to the *de Oratore*. It bears many marks of hasty composition and of lack of revision. It conveys the impression of rapid dictation, moving forward as one point suggests another, and frequently recalling itself to a sequence or a promised treatment overpassed. It may be urged with some plausibility that such features, if not deliberately designed, were at all events not avoided, but careful study in comparison with other work of Cicero's will scarcely support this view. It is much more probable that some circumstance of the time turned Cicero at a given moment to a defence of his threatened position in oratory, and that under stress of emotion and some resentment he threw off quickly an apologia for his own oratorical creed against a background of Roman practice. While the resulting defects of symmetry and careful plan may qualify somewhat our estimate of the work, yet they serve to give a reality and vivacity to the *Brutus* which is lacking to some of Cicero's other dialogues, and relate it more nearly to the intimacies of the *Letters*.

The many characterizations of orators which our dialogue presents afford unusual opportunities for observing the method and procedure of literary criticism as practised in Cicero's time. Formal characterization is, however, meagre and disappointing. Its captions are afforded by the divisions of rhetorical theory, some knowledge of which is necessary to an adequate understanding of Cicero's criticism. Against the division of rhetoric into its five parts (invention, arrangement, diction, action, memory) the accomplishments of speakers are checked off, though even in this arid scheme there is considerable opportunity for originality and picturesqueness of

observation. Then there are the divisions of the functions of the orator: to teach, to please, to move, and the classifications of style: the plain, the grand, etc. But apart from such schematism, the aridity of which Cicero recognizes, there are many passages of narrative and illustrative episode, which reveal a sensitive feeling for individuality, and a recognition that vitality of portraiture is to be found rather in particular incident than in abstract analysis. Thus, for example, the description of Laelius and Galba as advocates (85–89), the story of Crassus's treatment of a case involving a contested will against the severe legalism of Scaevola (195–198), the refutation of Calidius in an accusation of attempted poisoning (277), the account of Hortensius's rise to fame, partial eclipse, and return (301 ff.), and most of all, the interesting autobiographical sketch of Cicero's own training and early career (313 ff.) with which the work closes.[a]

The *Brutus* has come down to us by a single thread of tradition, a manuscript of Lodi, containing all of the more important rhetorical works of Cicero, discovered in 1421. Some four years later this codex disappeared, but not until one or more copies of it had been made. This parent-manuscript is designated as *L(audensis)*. It is a matter of dispute among critics as to how many of the manuscripts written before the disappearance of *L* were made directly from it. Of these there is general agree-

---

[a] The subject deserves a more sympathetic and intelligent treatment than it has received. *Cf*. P. R. Haenni, *Die literarische Kritik in Ciceros Brutus*, Freiburg (Switzerland) diss. 1905. Saintsbury (*Lit. Crit.* i. p. 218) alludes to the *Brutus* in a single sentence which says nothing.

ment that *F*(lorentinus) is the most faithful representative of the archetype. *O*(ttobonianus 2057) and *B* (Ottobonianus 1592), while apparently written from a copy, were corrected by comparison with *L*. *G* (Neapolitanus IV A 44), although it bears the name of Barzizza, the Milanese scholar to whom the *Laudensis* was first submitted, while early, does not appear to be a direct copy. These four manuscripts therefore represent the most reliable sources for the reconstruction of the archetype, and their consensus is designated as *L*.

[A most exact discussion of the sources of our text is contained in the preface to the edition of P. Reis, Teubner, which presents also a very complete critical apparatus accompanying the text. Of annotated editions most useful are the text and commentary of Jules Martha, Paris, 1892 (2nd ed. 1907), and his text and translation with brief notes (Budé), Paris, 1923, and the 6th edition of O. Jahn and W. Kroll's work by B. Kytzler, Berlin, 1962. Note also the edition by A. Douglas, Oxford, 1966 ; the edition by E. Malcovati, Leipzig, Teubner, 1965 ; the edition and translation by E. V. d'Arbela, Milan, 1968 ; and *Opere Retoriche*, vol. 1 ed. and trans. by G. Norcio, Turin, 1970 (*de Oratore, Brutus, Orator*). Important also are the biographical studies in the *Realencyclopädie* (Pauly-Wissowa), especially those of F. Münzer.]

The only earlier translation of the *Brutus* into English appears to be that of E. Jones, London, 1776. It was reprinted in Harper's Classical Library in 1890. The general editor of the volume characterizes the translation of Jones as one " which has long had the deserved reputation of combining

fidelity with elegance." It is however for the most part little more than a free paraphrase, with occasional happy renderings which may justify the title of elegant.

The present edition does not profess to give a complete record of the text as it has been transmitted. Orthographical variations, and slight but obvious corrections, which were made in early manuscript copies or by early printers and scholars, have not for the most part been recorded in the critical notes. For such information readers are referred to the edition of P. Reis named above. The text on the whole is well preserved and scarcely merits the complaints of corruption which editors have bestowed on it. Words believed to be additions or glosses of readers upon the archetype *L* are, in accordance with prevailing usage, enclosed in brackets [. . .]; words added by modern editors as necessary or desirable to complete the thought are indicated by pointed brackets ⟨. . .⟩.

SUMMARY OF CONTENTS

PROOEMIUM. The opening sections of the *Brutus* constitute a general preface to the reader, noting the coincidence of the death of Hortensius with the civil strife which had put an end to a free and unconstrained eloquence. Sections 1-6, reflections on the death of Hortensius and on Cicero's long association with him, and 7-9, on the unworthy position to which civil strife has consigned Cicero himself.

Dialogue setting, introduction of the interlocutors, Titus Pomponius Atticus and Marcus Junius Brutus, and of the theme of discussion (*de oratoribus, quando esse coepissent, qui etiam et quales fuissent*), 10-24.

Treatment of the subject (*laudare eloquentiam*, etc.) 25-330.

Survey of the Greek origins of oratory 25-52.

Résumé of Roman tradition concerning early oratory down to the first definitely attested Roman orator, Marcus Cornelius Cethegus (cos. 204 B.C.), 53-60.

Marcus Porcius Cato (cos. 194 B.C.) 61-76, contemporaries 77-80, younger contemporaries 81, with special mention of Gaius Laelius (cos. 140 B.C.), and of Publius Cornelius Scipio (Minor, cos. 147 B.C.).

Servius Sulpicius Galba (cos. 144 B.C.) 82-94. Galba, in comparison and contrast with Laelius, is named with special emphasis as the first Roman to

and Gaius Licinius Calvus (82–47 B.C., poet and friend of Catullus) 279-283.

The mention of Calvus, leader of the neo-Attic oratorical movement, leads to a lively critique of the revolt of this group from the abundance and elaboration of style characteristic of Hortensius and Cicero 284-291.

In the form of a protest in the mouth of Atticus, Cicero makes correction of the too laudatory account of early Roman oratory 292-300.

He returns finally to Hortensius 301-307, and interweaves with the career of Hortensius his own beginnings 308-316. Their association and rivalry, the decline of Hortensius and Cicero's own progress 317-324, reasons for the waning reputation of Hortensius 325-328, final tribute to him 329.

Epilogue 330-333.

M. TULLI CICERONIS

BRUTUS

1 I. Cum e Cilicia decedens Rhodum venissem et eo
mihi de Q. Hortensi morte esset allatum, opinione
omnium maiorem animo cepi dolorem. Nam et
amico amisso cum consuetudine iucunda tum multorum officiorum coniunctione me privatum videbam et
interitu talis auguris dignitatem nostri collegi demi-
nutam dolebam. Qua in cogitatione et cooptatum me
ab eo in collegium recordabar, in quo iuratus iudicium
dignitatis meae fecerat, et inauguratum ab eodem,
ex quo augurum institutis in parentis eum loco colere
2 debebam. Augebat etiam molestiam quod magna
sapientium civium bonorumque penuria vir egregius
coniunctissimusque mecum consiliorum omnium socie-
tate alienissimo rei publicae tempore exstinctus et
auctoritatis et prudentiae suae triste nobis desiderium
reliquerat, dolebamque quod non, ut plerique puta-

---

^a Quintus Hortensius Hortalus, born 114 B.C., died in
June or July 50. Cicero, proconsul of Cilicia 51–50 B.C., on
returning from his province learned of his death at Rhodes,
probably in August. Their relation to each other and
common activities are set forth at the end of the *Brutus*,
sections 317-330.

^b Cicero was made a member of the augural college in the
year 53, succeeding Publius Crassus, son of the triumvir
(*cf.* 281).

MARCUS TULLIUS CICERO

BRUTUS

WHEN on leaving Cilicia I had come to Rhodes, and 1
word was there brought me of the death of Quintus
Hortensius, I was more deeply affected by it than anyone suspected.[a] For I saw myself bereft of a friend
who was bound to me by ties of pleasant companionship and by exchange of many friendly offices, and I
grieved that in the death of so distinguished an augur
the dignity of our college had suffered loss. Thinking
of this, I recalled that I had been elected to that body
on his nomination and sworn statement of my worth,
and that by him I had been inducted into its ranks, so
that, in accordance with augural tradition, it was my
duty to regard him as a father.[b] It distressed me 2
too, that in the great dearth of wise and patriotic
citizens there had gone from us a great man, in fullest
sympathy with me on all questions of public policy,[c]
at a time most alien to the interests of the state,
leaving us to lament the loss of his authority and wise
experience. I grieved moreover to have lost in him,

---

[a] Cicero alludes often to the political principles (*consilia*)
which had guided his conduct. He defended them in a
special treatise which later writers refer to as *de Consiliis
suis*, perhaps identical with the *Liber* Ἀνέκδοτος mentioned
in *Att.* 14. 17, 6 (*cf.* Drumann, vol. vi. p. 360).

bant, adversarium aut obtrectatorem laudum mearum
sed socium potius et consortem gloriosi laboris amise-
3 ram.   Etenim si in leviorum artium studio memoriae
proditum est poetas nobilis poetarum aequalium
morte doluisse, quo tandem animo eius interitum
ferre debui, cum quo certare erat gloriosius quam
omnino adversarium non habere ? cum praesertim
non modo numquam sit aut illius a me cursus impedi-
tus aut ab illo meus, sed contra semper alter ab altero
adiutus et communicando et monendo et favendo.
4   Sed quoniam perpetua quadam felicitate usus ille
cessit e vita suo magis quam suorum civium tempore
et tum occidit cum lugere facilius rem publicam
posset, si viveret, quam iuvare, vixitque tam diu
quam licuit in civitate bene beateque vivere, nostro
incommodo detrimentoque, si est ita necesse, dolea-
mus, illius vero mortis opportunitatem benevolentia
potius quam misericordia prosequamur, ut, quotiens-
cumque de clarissimo et beatissimo viro cogitemus,
illum potius quam nosmet ipsos diligere videamur.
5 Nam si id dolemus, quod eo iam frui nobis non licet,
nostrum est id malum, quod modice feramus, ne id
non ad amicitiam sed ad domesticam utilitatem
referre videamur; sin tamquam illi ipsi acerbitatis
aliquid acciderit angimur, summam eius felicitatem
6 non satis grato animo interpretamur. II. Etenim si
viveret Q. Hortensius, cetera fortasse desideraret

---

* Perhaps with reference to the story of Sophocles' mani-
festation of grief on the death of Euripides (*Vita Eurip.* 10).

not, as some may have thought, a rival jealous of my
forensic reputation, but rather a comrade and fellow-
worker in the same field of glorious endeavour. If 3
in arts of lesser moment history records that famous
poets have manifested grief for the death of fellow
poets,[a] how much more must I have felt the death
of one with whom rivalry was more glorious than to
have been quite without a rival ?—the more so since
his official career was never challenged nor crossed by
me, nor mine by him. Quite the contrary; each of
us was helped by the other with exchange of suggestion, admonition, and friendly offices.

His life was one of uninterrupted felicity, and he 4
departed it more opportunely for himself than for his
fellow countrymen. He fell at a time when, had he
lived, he would have found himself able only to lament
the fate of his country, not to help it. He lived as
long as it was possible for a good citizen to live an
honourable and happy life. To our own misfortune and
loss, then, let us confine our grief, if grieve we must;
but as for him, let us not think of his death with pity,
but rather with gratitude for its timeliness, and as
often as we recall this illustrious and truly happy man,
let our thoughts be fixed with affection upon him, and
not with self-love upon ourselves. For if this is our 5
grief, that we can no longer enjoy his presence, it is a
sorrow which it behooves us to bear with reason, and
to beware lest we entertain it, not out of love for him,
but from loss of some advantage to ourselves. If on
the other hand our hearts are troubled as though he
had suffered some calamity we fail to recognize with
adequate gratitude the supreme felicity of his life and
death. For were Hortensius alive to-day he would 6
doubtless have occasion, along with other good and

21

una cum reliquis bonis et fortibus civibus, hunc aut praeter ceteros aut cum paucis sustineret dolorem, cum forum populi Romani, quod fuisset quasi theatrum illius ingeni, voce erudita et Romanis Graecisque auribus digna spoliatum atque orbatum videret.

7 Equidem angor animo non consili, non ingeni, non auctoritatis armis egere rem publicam, quae didiceram tractare quibusque me assuefeceram quaeque erant propria cum praestantis in re publica viri tum bene moratae et bene constitutae civitatis. Quod si fuit in re publica tempus ullum, cum extorquere arma posset e manibus iratorum civium boni civis auctoritas et oratio, tum profecto fuit cum patrocinium pacis exclusum est aut errore hominum aut

8 timore. Ita nobismet ipsis accidit ut, quamquam essent multo magis alia lugenda, tamen hoc doleremus quod, quo tempore aetas nostra perfuncta rebus amplissimis tamquam in portum confugere deberet non inertiae neque desidiae sed oti moderati atque honesti, cumque ipsa oratio iam nostra canesceret haberetque suam quandam maturitatem et quasi senectutem, tum arma sunt ea sumpta, quibus illi ipsi, qui didicerant eis uti gloriose, quem ad

9 modum salutariter uterentur, non reperiebant. Itaque ei mihi videntur fortunate beateque vixisse cum in ceteris civitatibus tum maxime in nostra, quibus cum auctoritate rerumque gestarum gloria tum etiam sapientiae laude perfrui licuit.

---

[a] The dictatorship of Caesar was felt as a restriction upon freedom of speech, not only in the senate and popular assemblies, but even in the courts of criminal and private justice.

[b] The abrupt transition from Hortensius to himself reveals that the essential motive of this preface is to set forth Cicero's

loyal men, to mourn the loss of many things ; but one pang he would feel beyond the rest, or with few to share it : the spectacle of the Roman forum, the scene and stage of his talents, robbed and bereft of that finished eloquence worthy of the ears of Rome or even of Greece.[a]

For me too[b] it is a source of deep pain that the state 7 feels no need of those weapons of counsel, of insight, and of authority, which I had learned to handle and to rely upon,—weapons which are the peculiar and proper resource of a leader in the commonwealth and of a civilized and law-abiding state. Indeed if there ever was a time in the history of the state when the authority and eloquence of a good citizen might have wrested arms from the hands of angry partisans, it was exactly then when through blindness or fear the door was abruptly closed upon the cause of peace. Thus, amidst other things far more deplor- 8 able, it was to me a peculiar sorrow, that after a career of conspicuous achievements, at an age when it was my right to take refuge in a harbour, not of indolence and sloth, but of honourable and well-ordered ease, when my oratory too had attained a certain ripeness and maturity of age,—it was, I say, a peculiar sorrow that at that moment resort was had to arms, which those who had learned to use them gloriously did not find a way to use them beneficently. Those men therefore appear to me to have 9 lived fortunate and happy lives, in other states and especially in our own, whom fate permitted to enjoy to the end the authority acquired by the renown of their deeds, and the esteem earned by their wisdom.

own tragedy and the collapse of his career as orator and statesman.

Quorum memoria et recordatio in maximis nostris
gravissimisque curis iucunda sane fuit, cum in eam
10 nuper ex sermone quodam incidissemus. III. Nam
cum inambularem in xysto et essem otiosus domi,
M. ad me Brutus, ut consueverat, cum T. Pomponio
venerat, homines cum inter se coniuncti tum mihi ita
cari itaque iucundi, ut eorum aspectu omnis quae me
angebat de re publica cura consederit. Quos post-
quam salutavi :

Quid vos, inquam, Brute et Attice ? numquid
tandem novi ?

Nihil sane, inquit Brutus, quod quidem aut tu
audire velis aut ego pro certo dicere audeam.

11 Tum Atticus : Eo, inquit, ad te animo venimus, ut
de re publica esset silentium et aliquid audiremus
potius ex te quam te afficeremus ulla molestia.

Vos vero, inquam, Attice, et praesentem me cura
levatis et absenti magna solacia dedistis. Nam ves-
tris primum litteris recreatus me ad pristina studia
revocavi.

Tum ille : Legi, inquit, perlibenter epistulam quam

---

^a Presumably his residence at Rome, since he refers later
to possible resumption of the discussion at one of his country
villas (cf. 300).

^b Referring to news of the war in Africa. The final defeat
of the Pompeian army at Thapsus (Apr. 6, 46 B.C. of the pre-
Julian calendar) has not yet taken place ; both Cato (118)
and Scipio (212), in command of the senatorial forces, are
spoken of as still living.

To recall the memory of such men in the midst of the grievous anxieties of the present was an agreeable relief, when recently we chanced upon the subject in the course of a conversation. For one day **10** when I was at home [a] and was leisurely pacing up and down my garden walk, Marcus Brutus dropped in upon me, as he often did, and brought with him Titus Pomponius, both of them close friends to each other, and so dear to me and so welcome, that at sight of them all the anxiety which weighed upon me for the state of public affairs quite subsided. I greeted them and began abruptly :

" How now, Brutus, and you, Atticus ? Any news yet ? " [b]

" No, nothing," replied Brutus ; " nothing at least that you would wish to hear or that I should venture to report as certain."

Here Atticus broke in : " It was precisely our **11** thought in coming, to avoid talk about public affairs, and to hear something from you, rather than to distress you with words of ours."

" Distress me ? Quite the contrary, my dear Atticus," I replied ; " for your presence lightens my care, and when absent too you afforded me great solace. For your letters [c] first restored my spirits and recalled me to my former studies."

" The letter which Brutus wrote you from Asia," he replied, " I have read with the keenest interest,

[c] The word " letters " is confusing to the modern reader, since the letters in question are considerable books or treatises dedicated to Cicero. The distinction between a personal letter and a treatise was by no means sharp ; so for example the *Orator*, which maintains throughout the form of an epistle to Brutus.

ad te Brutus misit ex Asia, qua mihi visus est et
monere te prudenter et consolari amicissime.

12 Recte, inquam, est visus ; nam me istis scito litteris
ex diuturna perturbatione totius valetudinis tamquam ad aspiciendam lucem esse revocatum. Atque
ut post Cannensem illam calamitatem primum Marcelli ad Nolam proelio populus se Romanus erexit
posteaque prosperae res deinceps multae consecutae
sunt, sic post rerum nostrarum et communium gravis-
simos casus nihil ante epistulam Bruti mihi accidit
quod vellem aut quod aliqua ex parte sollicitudines
allevaret meas.

13 Tum Brutus : Volui id quidem efficere certe et
capio magnum fructum, si quidem quod volui tanta
in re consecutus sum. Sed scire cupio, quae te
Attici litterae delectaverint.

Istae vero, inquam, Brute, non modo delectationem mihi sed etiam, ut spero, salutem attulerunt.

Salutem ? inquit ille. Quodnam tandem genus
istuc tam praeclarum litterarum fuit ?

An mihi potuit, inquam, esse aut gratior ulla salu-
tatio aut ad hoc tempus aptior quam illius libri quo
me hic affatus quasi iacentem excitavit ?

14 Tum ille : Nempe eum dicis, inquit, quo iste
omnem rerum memoriam breviter et, ut mihi quidem
visum est, perdiligenter complexus est ?

---

^a This " letter of Brutus from Asia " (perhaps more
exactly from Mytilene or Samos in the province of Asia)
was apparently what is known to us from other sources as
the treatise of Brutus *de Virtute* (see Introd. p. 6). The
present work is regarded as an immediate acknowledgement
and return-offering to Brutus ; to Atticus as well for his
recent treatise, the *Liber Annalis*, mention of which follows.
^b It is difficult to render aptly the play upon the double

and it seemed to me that in it he gave you at once good advice and affectionate solace." [a]

" Yes, you are quite right, and I assure you that 12 after long perturbation of spirit, which even affected my physical health, that letter of his brought me back as if to look once more upon the light of day. You will recall how after the defeat at Cannae the Roman people first took heart again with the victory of Marcellus at Nola, and that from that time on a continuous series of successes followed ; well, in some such way, after all the disasters which had befallen me, and the state no less, there was nothing before the letter of Brutus which roused my interest or which in any way eased the anxieties of my spirit."

" That certainly was what I hoped to accomplish," 13 replied Brutus, " and I have abundant reward if in fact at such a crisis I did attain my end. But I am eager to know what writing of Atticus gave you such pleasure."

" Pleasure indeed, Brutus, it brought me, but more than that, health and salvation, if I do not exaggerate."

" Salvation ? " said he ; " that must be an extraordinary kind of writing ; what can it have been ? "

" What salutation [b] could have given me greater pleasure or have come more opportunely than that book, in which our Atticus here addressed me and, like one lying prostrate on the ground, raised me up ? "

" Ah yes," he replied, " you mean that work in 14 which he sets forth all history so briefly, and, if I may venture to judge, so faithfully." [c]

meaning of *salus*, " health " and " greeting." It is found not infrequently, as in Plautus, *Pseudolus* 709.
  [c] The *Liber Annalis* (see Introd. p. 6).

Istum ipsum, inquam, Brute, dico librum mihi saluti fuisse.

iv. Tum Atticus : Optatissimum mihi quidem est quod dicis ; sed quid tandem habuit liber iste quod tibi aut novum aut tanto usui posset esse ?

15 Ille vero et nova, inquam, mihi quidem multa et eam utilitatem quam requirebam, ut explicatis ordinibus temporum uno in conspectu omnia viderem. Quae cum studiose tractare coepissem, ipsa mihi tractatio litterarum salutaris fuit admonuitque, Pomponi, ut a te ipso sumerem aliquid ad me reficiendum teque remunerandum si non pari, at grato tamen munere; quamquam illud Hesiodium laudatur a doctis,[a] quod eadem mensura reddere iubet quae acceperis 16 aut etiam cumulatiore, si possis. Ego autem voluntatem tibi profecto emetiar, sed rem ipsam nondum posse videor, idque ut ignoscas, a te peto.[b] Nec enim ex novis, ut agricolae solent, fructibus est, unde tibi reddam quod accepi, sic omnis fetus repressus exustusque flos siti veteris ubertatis exaruit ; nec ex conditis, qui iacent in tenebris et ad quos omnis nobis aditus, qui paene solis patuit, obstructus est. Seremus igitur aliquid tamquam in inculto et derelicto solo ; quod ita diligenter colemus, ut impendiis etiam augere possimus largitatem tui muneris, modo idem noster animus efficere possit quod ager, qui cum multos annos quievit uberiores efferre fruges solet.

17 Tum ille : Ego vero et exspectabo ea quae polli-

---

a *Works and Days* 349-350.

b It is most probable that Cicero alludes to some historical subject such as Atticus (as interlocutor in *de Legibus* 1. 6) exhorts him to undertake.

" Yes, Brutus, that is the book, and I say again it was my salvation."

" What you say is the kind of praise I most covet," said Atticus, " but what did that book of mine contain that could have been to you either novel or so helpful ? "

" Much indeed that was novel," I replied, " and it 15 afforded me exactly the help that I required, to survey in one comprehensive view the whole course of things in the order of their times. I began to study it attentively, and the very act of study was health-giving and awakened in me the idea, Pomponius, of taking something from you for my own refreshment, and for making repayment to you, which however acceptable cannot be equal. Scholars cite the admonition of Hesiod to repay with what measure you have received, or if possible with larger.[a] I am pre- 16 pared to make payment of goodwill in full measure, but the debt itself I do not now seem able to pay and for this I ask your forbearance. I cannot undertake to repay you out of the new crop, as farmers do, for all new growth has been checked within me, and drought has burned and withered all that flowering which once promised abundance. Nor can I repay you from the garnered grain of my storehouse ; it lies there in darkness and I who alone have the key find every approach to it cut off. I must therefore sow something in soil uncultivated and abandoned, and by careful cultivation make it possible to increase with interest the generosity of your gift; that is if my mind can respond as well as a field, which after lying fallow for many years generally yields a richer harvest." [b]

" Be sure that I shall await with eagerness what 17

ceris, nec exigam nisi tuo commodo et erunt mihi pergrata si solveris.

Mihi quoque, inquit Brutus, exspectanda sunt ea quae Attico polliceris, etsi fortasse ego a te huius voluntarius procurator petam, quod ipse, cui debes, incommodo exacturum negat.

18 v. At vero, inquam, tibi ego, Brute, non solvam, nisi prius a te cavero amplius eo nomine neminem, cuius petitio sit, petiturum.

Non me hercule, inquit, tibi repromittere istuc quidem ausim. Nam hunc, qui negat, video flagitatorem non illum quidem tibi molestum, sed assiduum tamen et acrem fore.

Tum Pomponius : Ego vero, inquit, Brutum nihil mentiri puto. Videor enim iam te ausurus esse appellare, quoniam longo intervallo modo primum 19 animadverti paulo te hilariorem. Itaque quoniam hic quod mihi deberetur se exacturum professus est, quod huic debes ego a te peto.

Quidnam id ? inquam.

Ut scribas, inquit, aliquid ; iam pridem enim conticuerunt tuae litterae. Nam ut illos de re publica libros edidisti, nihil a te sane postea accepimus eisque nosmet ipsi ad rerum et magistratuum[1] memoriam comprehendendam impulsi atque incensi sumus.

[1] et magistratuum *Reis (coll. Nep. Att. 18. 1)* ; naturalium *L.*

---

[a] Cicero has expressed obligation to both Atticus and Brutus. He has now made promise to reimburse Atticus at some future time, and now Atticus calls for repayment to Brutus (*quod huic debes*). The allusion following, *ut scribas aliquid,* is to the *Brutus* itself, which is not excluded by the words *sed illa cum poteris.* For the request that follows, *nunc vero expone nobis,* conceives of the present task as a living current conversation, not as a literary composition.

you promise," he replied, " nor shall I require it of you except at your convenience, however grateful I shall be for the discharge of your debt."

" I too," said Brutus, " shall look forward to the fulfilment of your promise to Atticus, though perchance as his agent I shall demand of you, his debtor, what he himself says he will not exact except at your convenience."

" But, my dear Brutus, you may rest assured," said 18 I, " that I will not make payment to you until I first have your pledge that the one whose agent you are shall not seek payment a second time on the same account."

" Pledge indeed ! " said Brutus. " No, I would not venture to give you that, for I can see that our friend here, though he denies it, will dun you for his debt, if not offensively, at least sharply and insistently."

" Yes," said Pomponius, " I suspect that Brutus is not far from right. In fact at this very moment I find myself making bold to demand payment, since now for the first time after so long an interval of despondency I find you in a more cheerful mood. So then, since Brutus here has promised that he will 19 exact what you owe me, I on my part make demand on you for what you owe him."

" What, pray, do you mean by that ? " I replied.

" That you write something ; for it is a long time now that your pen has lain silent.[a] Indeed since you brought out your books *On the State* we have had nothing whatever from you, and it was by that work that I too was fired with ambition to put together a

When it has been reproduced as a published record of that conversation it will be the writing which repays Brutus for his letter from Asia and will bear his name.

31

20 Sed illa, cum poteris atque ut possis, rogo ; nunc vero, inquit, si es animo vacuo, expone nobis quod quaerimus.

Quidnam est id ? inquam.

Quod mihi nuper in Tusculano incohavisti de oratoribus : quando esse coepissent, qui etiam et quales fuissent. Quem ego sermonem cum ad Brutum tuum, vel nostrum potius, detulissem, magno opere hic audire se velle dixit. Itaque hunc elegimus diem, cum te sciremus esse vacuum. Qua re, si tibi est commodum, ede illa quae coeperas et Bruto et mihi.

21 Ego vero, inquam, si potuero, faciam vobis satis.

Poteris, inquit : relaxa modo paulum animum aut sane, si potes, libera.

Nempe igitur hinc tum, Pomponi, ductus est sermo, quod erat a me mentio facta causam Deiotari fidelissimi atque optimi regis ornatissime et copiosissime a Bruto me audisse defensam.

VI. Scio, inquit, ab isto initio tractum esse sermonem teque Bruti dolentem vicem quasi deflevisse iudiciorum vastitatem et fori.

22 Feci, inquam, istuc quidem et saepe facio. Nam mihi, Brute, in te intuenti crebro in mentem venit vereri, ecquodnam curriculum aliquando sit habitura tua et natura admirabilis et exquisita doctrina et singularis industria. Cum enim in maximis causis

---

ª Deiotarus, tetrarch of Galatia, a partisan of Pompey, for whom Brutus interceded before Caesar at Nicaea in the summer of 47. It may be presumed that the speech of Brutus in written form was in the hands of Cicero not long afterward. With the words *me audisse* Cicero observes the fiction of oral communication for knowledge derived from a written source. *Cf.* 85 and note.

record of public men and events. But I do not insist **20**
on that now ; when you can, and as you can, is all
that I crave. Now, however, if you are free and in
the mood for it, set forth to us the subject about
which we came to ask you."

"What, pray, is that," said I.

"I mean the matter which you began with me
recently at your house in Tusculum about orators :
when they first made their appearance, and who, and
of what sort they were. When I reported that talk
to your—I should say rather, our Brutus here, he said
that he was very eager to hear it, and therefore we
have chosen to-day knowing that you were free. So
then, if it suits your convenience, go on now and tell
us what you then began, for the benefit of Brutus as
well as for me."

"Very well," I replied, "I will try to satisfy your **21**
curiosity if I can."

"You can certainly ; only relax a little, or, if you
can, set your mind quite free."

"If I am not mistaken it was from this starting-
point, Pomponius, that our discussion at that time
arose : I had made mention of having heard with
what superb eloquence Brutus defended the cause
of the good and loyal king Deiotarus." [a]

"Yes," said Atticus, "I recall that our talk started
from that point, and that you, grieving for the lot of
Brutus, fairly shed tears over the desolation of the
courts and the forum."

"I did, it is true," I replied, "and I still do. For **22**
when I look on you, Brutus, it crosses my mind constantly to fear and wonder what career lies open to
your remarkable natural gifts, your thorough training
and unique industry ; for just at the time when you

versatus esses et cum tibi aetas nostra iam cederet
fascisque summitteret, subito in civitate cum alia
ceciderunt tum etiam ea ipsa, de qua disputare
ordimur, eloquentia obmutuit.

23   Tum ille : Ceterarum rerum causa, inquit, istuc et
doleo et dolendum puto ; dicendi autem me non tam
fructus et gloria quam studium ipsum exercitatioque
delectat, quod mihi nulla res eripiet te praesertim
tam studiosum et . . .[1] Dicere enim bene nemo
potest nisi qui prudenter intellegit ; qua re qui
eloquentiae verae dat operam, dat prudentiae, qua
ne maximis quidem in bellis aequo animo carere
quisquam potest.

24   Praeclare, inquam, Brute, dicis eoque magis ista
dicendi laude delector, quod cetera, quae sunt quondam habita in civitate pulcherrima, nemo est tam
humilis qui se non aut posse adipisci aut adeptum
putet ; eloquentem neminem video factum esse victoria. Sed quo facilius sermo explicetur, sedentes,
si videtur, agamus.

Cum idem placuisset illis, tum in pratulo propter
Platonis statuam consedimus.

25   Hic ego : Laudare igitur eloquentiam et quanta vis
sit eius expromere quantamque eis qui sint eam
consecuti dignitatem afferat, neque propositum nobis

---

[1] studiosum et ⟨optumarum artium cupidum intuenti⟩
Kroll.

---

[a] A slight lacuna in the manuscript at this point must
have contained some such thought as the words in brackets.
[b] *Prudentia* is here used in the meaning of philosophy.
It represents the point of view set forth in the *de Oratore*,
that the ideal orator must be a philosopher. The same
scholastic claim, here implied, for a military leader is alluded
to with ridicule in *de Oratore* 2. 75.

were beginning to be engaged in cases of great significance, and when I, because of advancing age, was
giving way to you and laying down my sceptre, there
came a sudden collapse in other fields of public life,
and eloquence, the theme of our present discussion,
became mute."

Here Brutus interposed : " For other reasons 23
I share your grief and I recognize that it is a thing
to be deplored ; but so far as eloquence is concerned, my pleasure is not so much in its rewards
and the renown that it confers, as in the study
and training which it involves. Nothing can deprive
me of that, especially when I have before me the
example of your unflagging devotion to [the pursuit
of all liberal studies].[a] For no one can be a good
speaker who is not a sound thinker. Thus whoever
devotes himself to true eloquence, devotes himself to sound thinking,[b] which even in the conduct
of great wars cannot reasonably be dispensed
with."

" Well said, Brutus," I replied, " and the more 24
therefore I delight in your reputation for eloquence,
because any man however humble may fancy that he
could obtain, or has obtained, other rewards which
have ever been esteemed the fairest in public life, but
a man made eloquent by victory in war I have yet to
see. But that our conversation may proceed more
comfortably, let us sit down if you like and take up
our subject."

This was agreeable to them, and we sat down on
the lawn near the statue of Plato.

" Well then," I began, " to praise eloquence, to 25
set forth its power and the honours which it brings
to those who have it, is not my present purpose, nor

est hoc loco neque necessarium. Hoc vero sine ulla dubitatione confirmaverim, sive illa arte pariatur aliqua sive exercitatione quadam sive natura, rem unam esse omnium difficillimam. Quibus enim ex quinque rebus constare dicitur, earum una quaeque est ars ipsa magna per sese. Qua re quinque artium concursus maximarum quantam vim quantamque difficultatem habeat existimari potest.

26 VII. Testis est Graecia, quae cum eloquentiae studio sit incensa iamdiuque excellat in ea praestetque ceteris, tamen omnis artis vetustiores habet et multo ante non inventas solum sed etiam perfectas, quam haec est a Graecis elaborata dicendi vis atque copia. In quam cum intueor, maxime mihi occurrunt, Attice, et quasi lucent Athenae tuae, qua in urbe primum se orator extulit primumque etiam monumentis et litteris oratio est coepta mandari.

27 Tamen ante Periclem, cuius scripta quaedam feruntur, et Thucydidem, qui non nascentibus Athenis sed iam adultis fuerunt, littera nulla est quae quidem ornatum aliquem habeat et oratoris esse videatur. Quamquam opinio est et eum, qui multis annis ante hos fuerit, Pisistratum et paulo seniorem etiam Solonem posteaque Clisthenem multum ut temporibus

28 illis valuisse dicendo. Post hanc aetatem aliquot annis, ut ex Attici monumentis potest perspici, Themistocles fuit, quem constat cum prudentia tum etiam eloquentia praestitisse ; post Pericles, qui cum floreret omni genere virtutis, hac tamen fuit laude

---

[a] The importance of a subject matter and praise of it is the conventional opening of a discussion. Thus also *de Inv.* 1. 2 and *de Oratore* 1. 30.

[b] Invention, arrangement, diction, action, memory.

[c] In the *Liber Annalis.* See section 14 above.

is it necessary.[a] However, this one thing I venture
to affirm without fear of contradiction, that whether
it is a product of rules and theory, or a technique
dependent on practice, or on natural gifts, it is one
attainment amongst all others of unique difficulty.
For of the five elements of which, as we say, it is made
up, each one is in its own right a great art.[b] One
may guess therefore what power is inherent in an art
made up of five great arts, and what difficulty it
presents.

" Witness to this is Greece, which was fired with 26
a passion for eloquence, and long has excelled in it
beyond other states ; and yet all other arts she had
discovered, and even brought to perfection long
before this art of effective and eloquent speech was
developed. And when I think of Greece it is especially your Athens which comes to my mind, Atticus,
and shines out like a beacon. It was there that the
orator first made his appearance, and there first that
oratory began to be consigned to written records.
However, before Pericles, to whom some writings are 27
attributed, and Thucydides, who do not belong to the
cradle of Athens but to her maturity, there is not a
vestige of the written word, at all events nothing
which reveals any elaboration and resembles the
work of an orator. Yet it is believed that Pisistratus,
who lived long before them, and Solon too somewhat earlier than Pisistratus, and Clisthenes afterward, were for their time very effective speakers.
Some years later than their period, as can be seen 28
from the tables of Atticus,[c] Themistocles lived, whom
we know to have been pre-eminent in eloquence as
well as in political shrewdness. Then followed
Pericles, distinguished in every form of excellence,

37

clarissimus. Cleonem etiam temporibus illis tur-
bulentum illum quidem civem, sed tamen eloquen-
29 tem constat fuisse. Huic aetati suppares Alcibiades
Critias Theramenes ; quibus temporibus quod dicendi
genus viguerit ex Thucydidi scriptis, qui ipse tum
fuit, intellegi maxime potest. Grandes erant verbis,
crebri sententiis, compressione rerum breves et ob
eam ipsam causam interdum subobscuri.

30 VIII. Sed ut intellectum est quantam vim haberet
accurata et facta quodam modo oratio, tum etiam
magistri dicendi multi subito exstiterunt. Tum
Leontinus Gorgias, Thrasymachus Calchedonius, Protagoras Abderites, Prodicus Cius, Hippias Elius in
honore magno fuit ; aliique multi temporibus eisdem
docere se profitebantur, arrogantibus sane verbis,
quem ad modum causa inferior—ita enim loque-
31 bantur—dicendo fieri superior posset. His opposuit
sese Socrates, qui subtilitate quadam disputandi
refellere eorum instituta solebat. verbis.[1] Huius ex
uberrimis sermonibus exstiterunt doctissimi viri,
primumque tum philosophia non illa de natura, quae
fuerat antiquior, sed haec in qua de bonis rebus et
malis deque hominum vita et moribus disputatur,
inventa dicitur. Quod quoniam genus ab hoc quod
proposuimus abhorret, philosophos aliud in tempus
reiciamus ; ad oratores, a quibus digressi sumus,
revertamur.

32 Exstitit igitur iam senibus illis quos paulo ante
diximus Isocrates, cuius domus cunctae Graeciae

---

[1] verbis *secl. Wetzel*, acerbius *Madvig*, urbanius *Vitelli*.

---

[a] The pre-Socratics (Heraclitus, Democritus, Anaxagoras,
Empedocles and others), who were more concerned with the

and especially illustrious in this art. At the same time we know that Cleon, for all his turbulence as a citizen, was a man of eloquence. Almost contemporary with Cleon were Alcibiades, Critias, Theramenes. The style of eloquence that flourished in their time may be learned best from the writings of Thucydides, their contemporary. They were stately in the choice of words, rich in thought, from compression of matter brief, and for this reason sometimes obscure. 29

" But when it was recognized what power lay in speech carefully prepared and elaborated as a work of art, then suddenly a whole host of teachers of oratory arose : Gorgias of Leontini, Thrasymachus of Calchedon, Protagoras of Abdera, Prodicus of Ceos, Hippias of Elis, all of whom enjoyed great honour in their day. They and many others of the same time professed, not without arrogance to be sure, to teach how by the force of eloquence the worse (as they called it) could be made the better cause. Opposed to them was Socrates, who with characteristic adroitness of argumentation made it a practice to refute their doctrines. Out of the wealth of his discourses there emerged a group of men of great learning, and to them is attributed the first discovery of the philosophy which deals with good and evil, with human life and society, as distinguished from the philosophy of nature, which belonged to an earlier time.[a] But, since this field of knowledge is alien to our present purpose, I relegate philosophers to another time and return to orators, from whom I have digressed. 30 31

" In the old age of those whom I have just mentioned Isocrates came forward, whose house became a 32

nature of the universe and the character of matter than with man and his ethical and social problems.

quasi ludus quidam patuit atque officina dicendi,
magnus orator et perfectus magister, quamquam
forensi luce caruit intraque parietes aluit eam gloriam
quam nemo meo quidem iudicio est postea consecutus.
Is et ipse scripsit multa praeclare et docuit alios ; et
cum cetera melius quam superiores tum primus intel-
lexit etiam in soluta oratione, dum versum effugeres,
modum tamen et numerum quendam oportere ser-
33 vari.   Ante hunc enim verborum quasi structura et
quaedam ad numerum conclusio nulla erat aut, si
quando erat, non apparebat eam dedita opera esse
quaesitam—quae forsitan laus sit,   verum tamen
natura magis tum casuque nonnumquam, quam aut
34 ratione aliqua aut ulla observatione fiebat.   Ipsa
enim natura circumscriptione quadam verborum
comprehendit concluditque sententiam, quae cum
aptis constricta verbis est, cadit etiam plerumque
numerose.   Nam et aures ipsae quid plenum, quid
inane sit iudicant et spiritu quasi necessitate aliqua
verborum comprehensio terminatur ; in quo non
modo defici sed etiam laborare turpe est.
35   ix. Tum fuit Lysias, ipse quidem in causis forensibus non versatus, sed egregie subtilis scriptor atque
elegans, quem iam prope audeas oratorem perfectum
dicere.   Nam plane quidem perfectum et quoi[1] nihil
admodum desit Demosthenem facile dixeris.   Nihil
acute inveniri potuit in eis causis quas scripsit, nihil,
ut ita dicam, subdole, nihil versute, quod ille non

------

[1] quoi *cod. Laur. 50. 31, Friedrich,* quo *L,* cui *vulg.*

------

[a] The introduction of the periodic sentence and the rhythmical cadence of its conclusion is credited to Isocrates,
doubtless a claim of the Isocratean school.

veritable training-school or studio of eloquence open to all Greece. He was a great orator and an ideal teacher, but he shrank from the broad daylight of the forum, and within the walls of his school brought to fullness a renown such as no one after him has in my judgement attained. He wrote much of surpassing excellence and taught others. He was in other respects superior to his predecessors, and particularly he was the first to recognize that even in prose, while strict verse should be avoided, a certain rhythm and measure should be observed. Before 33 him there was nothing structure-like, so to speak, in the joining of words, and no rhythmical rounding out of the sentence,[a] or, if it did occur, it was not apparent that it was deliberately intended. That may perhaps be a matter of praise, but in any case it came about then at times from natural feeling and chance, rather than by rule or design. For it is true that by some 34 natural instinct the expression of a thought may fall into a periodic form and conclusion, and when it is thus gathered up in fitting words it ends often with a rhythmical cadence. The reason is that the ear itself judges what is complete, what is deficient, and the breath by natural compulsion fixes a limit to the length of the phrase. If the breath labours, not to say fails utterly, the effect is painful.

" At the same time Lysias lived, not himself en- 35 gaged in forensic cases, but a writer of extraordinary refinement and elegance, whom you might almost venture to call a perfect orator. For the perfect orator and the one who lacks absolutely nothing you would without hesitation name Demosthenes. Ingenuity however acute, however subtle, however shrewd would fail to discover any point in the orations

41

viderit ; nihil subtiliter dici, nihil presse, nihil enucleate, quo fieri possit aliquid limatius ; nihil contra
grande, nihil incitatum, nihil ornatum vel verborum
gravitate vel sententiarum, quo quicquam esset
36 elatius.   Huic Hyperides proximus et Aeschines fuit
et Lycurgus et Dinarchus et is, cuius nulla exstant
scripta, Demades aliique plures.   Haec enim aetas
effudit hanc copiam ; et, ut opinio mea fert, sucus ille
et sanguis incorruptus usque ad hanc aetatem oratorum fuit, in qua naturalis inesset, non fucatus nitor.
37 Phalereus enim successit eis senibus adulescens eruditissimus ille quidem horum omnium, sed non tam
armis institutus quam palaestra.   Itaque delectabat
magis Atheniensis quam inflammabat.   Processerat
enim in solem et pulverem, non ut e militari taberna-
culo, sed ut e Theophrasti doctissimi hominis umbra-
38 culis.   Hic primus inflexit orationem et eam mollem
teneramque reddidit et suavis, sicut fuit, videri maluit
quam gravis ; sed suavitate ea, qua perfunderet
animos, non qua perfringeret, [et][1] tantum ut memoriam concinnitatis suae, non, quem ad modum de
Pericle scripsit Eupolis, cum delectatione aculeos
etiam relinqueret in animis eorum a quibus esset
auditus.
39   x. Videsne igitur, Brute,[2] in ea ipsa urbe, in qua
et nata et alta sit eloquentia, quam ea sero prodie-
rit in lucem ? si quidem ante Solonis aetatem et
Pisistrati de nullo ut diserto memoriae proditum est.
At hi quidem, ut populi Romani aetas est, senes,

[1] et secl. *Manutius.*
[2] Brute *Martha,* ut *L.*

---

[a] *Cf.* Kock, *Comic. Att. Fragmenta,* i. (p. 281), frag. 94: τὸ
κέντρον ἐγκατέλειπε τοῖς ἀκροωμένοις.

from his hand which he has overlooked ; in diction
nothing more finished than the simplicity, the compression, the directness of his style ; and again
nothing more elevated than the sublimity, the passion,
the dignity and beauty, whether of his words or of his
sentiments. Next to him in point of time and rank 36
were Hyperides and Aeschines, Lycurgus and Dinarchus, Demades (of whom no writings are extant) and
several others. So prodigal was this age in its out-
put ; and, as I hold, the sap and blood of oratory
remained fresh and uncorrupted down to this time,
and retained a natural colour that required no rouge.
To the old age of these men succeeded the youthful 37
Demetrius of Phaleron, and though perhaps the most
accomplished of them all, yet his training was less for
the field than for the parade-ground. He entertained
rather than stirred his countrymen ; for he came
forth into the heat and dust of action, not from
a soldier's tent, but from the shady retreat of the
great philosopher Theophrastus. He was the first 38
to modulate oratory and to give it softness and pli-
ability. He chose to use charm, as was his nature,
rather than force, a charm which diffused itself
through the minds of his listeners without overwhelm-
ing them. His oratory left behind a memory of
elegance, but did not, as Eupolis said of Pericles,
leave, along with delight, a sting in the minds of his
hearers.[a]

" You see thus, Brutus, even in that city where 39
eloquence was born and grew to maturity, how late
it stepped forth into the light of day, since before
the age of Solon and Pisistratus there is no record of
any notable speaker. These men are, to be sure, as
Roman chronology goes, early ; but in the reckoning

ut Atheniensium saecula numerantur, adulescentes
debent videri.   Nam etsi Servio Tullio regnante
viguerunt, tamen multo diutius Athenae iam erant
quam est Roma ad hodiernum diem.   Nec tamen
dubito quin habuerit vim magnam semper oratio.
40 Neque enim iam Troicis temporibus tantum laudis in
dicendo Ulixi tribuisset Homerus et Nestori, quorum
alterum vim habere voluit, alterum suavitatem, nisi
iam tum esset honos eloquentiae ; neque ipse poeta
hic tam [idem]¹ ornatus in dicendo ac plane orator fuisset.   Cuius etsi incerta sunt tempora, tamen annis
multis fuit ante Romulum ; si quidem non infra superiorem Lycurgum fuit, a quo est disciplina Lacedae-
41 moniorum astricta legibus.   Sed studium eius generis
maiorque vis agnoscitur in Pisistrato.   Denique hunc
proximo saeculo Themistocles insecutus est, ut apud
nos, perantiquus, ut apud Atheniensis, non ita sane
vetus.   Fuit enim regnante iam Graecia, nostra
autem civitate non ita pridem dominatu regio libe-
rata.   Nam bellum Volscorum illud gravissimum, cui
Coriolanus exsul interfuit, eodem fere tempore quo
Persarum bellum fuit, similisque fortuna clarorum
42 virorum ; si quidem uterque cum civis egregius fuisset,
populi ingrati pulsus iniuria se ad hostis contulit

¹ idem *secl. Koch.*

ᵃ This first sketch of Greek oratory is followed curiously
by a second which takes up the same subject and most of the
same names from the point of view of the origins of rhetorical
theory and instruction.   For this second treatment Cicero
was doubtless indebted to Aristotle, whom he cites in 46.
His Συναγωγὴ τεχνῶν was a repository of information concerning all earlier rhetorical doctrine.   Cicero alludes to it
with high praise in *de Inv.* 2. 6 and again briefly in *de Or.*
2. 160.

ᵇ *Iliad* 3. 221-222 (Ulysses), 1. 248-249 (Nestor).

of Athenian history they must appear very late ; for though they flourished as far back as the reign of Servius Tullius, yet Athens even then had existed much longer than Rome has down to the present day. And yet I do not doubt that oratory always exercised great influence.[a] Surely even in Trojan times Homer **40** would not have allotted such praise to Ulysses and Nestor for their speech unless even then eloquence had enjoyed honour—to the one, you will recall, he attributed force, to the other charm [b]—nor indeed otherwise had the poet himself been so accomplished in utterance and so completely the orator. Though his time is quite uncertain, still it was many years before Romulus ; certainly he was not later than the first Lycurgus,[c] who fixed the Spartan way of life by the enactment of his laws. But the deliberate culti- **41** vation of this art and its greater influence become recognizable in Pisistratus. In the next generation he was succeeded by Themistocles,—for us a very early figure, but for Athens by no means remote. He lived when Greece was already at its height as a ruling power, when our state however had but recently freed itself from the rule of kings. For the greatest of the Volscian wars, the one which Coriolanus took part in as an exile from Rome, was fought at about the same time as the Persian War, and the fortunes of these two famous men were not unlike. For **42** both, though great men in their respective states, were unjustly exiled by an ungrateful people, and, going over to the enemy, made an end to their plans of

[c] Cicero alludes apparently to the view of Timaeus (Plut. *Lyc.* 1. 4) that there were two early kings of Sparta of thi name, of whom the elder was contemporary with Homer, or not much later.

conatumque iracundiae suae morte sedavit. Nam
etsi aliter apud te est, Attice, de Coriolano, concede
tamen ut huic generi mortis potius assentiar.

XI. At ille ridens : Tuo vero, inquit, arbitratu,
quoniam quidem concessum est rhetoribus ementiri
in historiis, ut aliquid dicere possint argutius. Ut
enim tu nunc de Coriolano, sic Clitarchus, sic Stra-
43 tocles de Themistocle finxit. Nam quem Thucydides,
qui et Atheniensis erat et summo loco natus sum-
musque vir et paulo aetate posterior, tantum mortuum scripsit et in Attica clam humatum, addidit
fuisse suspicionem veneno sibi conscivisse mortem,
hunc isti aiunt, cum taurum immolavisset, excepisse
sanguinem patera et eo poto mortuum concidisse.
Hanc enim mortem rhetorice et tragice ornare
potuerunt, illa mors vulgaris nullam praebebat
materiem ad ornatum. Qua re quoniam tibi ita
quadrat omnia fuisse Themistocli[1] paria et Coriolano,
pateram quoque a me sumas licet, praebebo etiam
hostiam, ut Coriolanus sit plane alter Themistocles.
44 Sit sane, inquam, ut libet, de isto ; et ego cautius
posthac historiam attingam te audiente, quem
rerum Romanarum auctorem laudare possum reli-
giosissimum.

Sed tum fere Pericles Xanthippi filius, de quo ante
dixi, primus adhibuit doctrinam ; quae quamquam
tum nulla erat dicendi, tamen ab Anaxagora physico
eruditus exercitationem mentis a reconditis abstrusis-

---

[1] Themistocli *cod. Laur. 50. 19*, Themistocle *L.*

revenge by a voluntary death. I know, Atticus, that in your book the story of Coriolanus is related otherwise, but grant me the privilege of giving my assent rather to a death of this kind."

At this he smiled and said : " As you like, since the privilege is conceded to rhetoricians to distort history in order to give more point to their narrative. Like your story of Coriolanus's death, Clitarchus and Stratocles both have invented an account of the death of Themistocles. But Thucydides, a native Athenian 43 of high birth and distinction, and only a little later in time, merely says that he died a natural death and was buried secretly in Attic soil, adding that rumour said he had taken his own life by poison. The others say that on sacrificing a bullock, he drank a bowl of its blood and from that draught fell dead. That's a kind of death that gave them the chance for rhetorical and tragic treatment ; the ordinary natural death gave them no such opportunity. So then, since it squares with your taste to make everything the same in the careers of Themistocles and Coriolanus, take the bowl too with my leave—I will even provide a sacrificial victim—in order to make of Coriolanus a second Themistocles."

" Very well, as for him let it be as you will," I 44 replied, " but hereafter I shall touch on history with more caution when you are present, an historian of Rome whom I can commend as most scrupulous.

" But to return : At about the same time Pericles, son of Xanthippus, of whom I spoke before, was the first orator to be influenced by theoretical study. There was, to be sure, then nothing of the sort for oratory, but having been trained by Anaxagoras, the natural philosopher, he found it easy to transfer that

que rebus ad causas forensis popularisque facile
traduxerat. Huius suavitate maxime hilaratae
Athenae sunt, huius ubertatem et copiam admiratae,
eiusdem vim dicendi terroremque timuerunt.

45 XII. Haec igitur aetas prima Athenis oratorem
prope perfectum tulit. Nec enim in constituenti-
bus rem publicam nec in bella gerentibus nec in impe-
ditis ac regum dominatione devinctis nasci cupiditas
dicendi solet. Pacis est comes otique socia et iam
bene constitutae civitatis quasi alumna quaedam
46 eloquentia. Itaque ait Aristoteles, cum sublatis in
Sicilia tyrannis res privatae longo intervallo iudiciis
repeterentur, tum primum, quod esset acuta illa gens
et controversa[1] natura, artem et praecepta Siculos
Coracem et Tisiam conscripsisse, nam antea neminem
solitum via nec arte, sed accurate tamen et discripte[2]
plerosque dicere ; scriptasque fuisse et paratas a
Protagora rerum illustrium disputationes, qui nunc
47 communes appellantur loci ; quod idem fecisse Gorgiam, cum singularum rerum laudes vituperationes-
que conscripsisset, quod iudicaret hoc oratoris esse
maxime proprium, rem augere posse laudando vitu-
perandoque rursus affligere ; huic Antiphontem
Rhamnusium similia quaedam habuisse conscripta,
quo neminem umquam melius ullam oravisse capitis
causam, cum se ipse defenderet, se audiente locuples

---

[1] controversa *edd. vet.*, controversia *L, edd. rec. alii alia
tempt.*
[2] discripte *Eberhard*, descripto *L.*

---

[a] This view of the origin of eloquence (repeated elsewhere
by Cicero) is derived from Aristotle, who apparently con-
templated only forensic or judicial oratory, from which
rhetorical theory proceeded. With extension to public and

mental discipline from obscure and abstruse problems to the business of the forum and the popular assembly. With the charm of his oratory Athens was vastly pleased, its wealth and fluency it admired, before its power and terrors it trembled.

"This age therefore first produced at Athens an 45 orator all but perfect. For the ambition to speak well does not arise when men are engaged in establishing government, nor occupied with the conduct of war, nor shackled and chained by the authority of kings. Upon peace and tranquillity eloquence attends as their ally, it is, one may say, the offspring of well-established civic order.[a] Thus Aristotle says that in 46 Sicily, after the expulsion of tyrants, when after a long interval restitution of private property was sought by legal means, Corax and Tisias the Sicilians, with the acuteness and controversial habit of their people, first put together some theoretical precepts; that before them, while many had taken pains to speak with care and with orderly arrangement, no one had followed a definite method or art. He says further that Protagoras wrote out and furnished discussions of certain large general subjects such as we now call commonplaces[b]; that Gorgias did the same, writing 47 particularly in praise or in censure of given things, since he held that it was the peculiar function of oratory to magnify a thing by praise, or again by disparagement to belittle it; that Antiphon of Rhamnus produced some similar writings, concerning whom we have the trustworthy assurance of Thucydides that

political oratory the view is disputed by Tacitus, *Dialogus* 40 (with possible reference to this passage).

[b] Topics of a general character, such as patriotism, justice, avarice, ready for use as occasion might suggest.

48 auctor scripsit Thucydides ; nam Lysiam primo pro-
fiteri solitum artem esse dicendi ; deinde, quod
Theodorus esset in arte subtilior, in orationibus
autem ieiunior, orationes eum scribere aliis coepisse,
artem removisse ; similiter Isocratem primo artem
dicendi esse negavisse, scribere autem aliis solitum
orationes, quibus in iudiciis uterentur ; sed cum ex
eo, quia quasi committeret contra legem quo quis
iudicio circumveniretur, saepe ipse in iudicium
vocaretur, orationes aliis destitisse scribere totumque
se ad artes componendas transtulisse.

49 XIII. Et Graeciae quidem oratorum partus atque
fontis vides, ad nostrorum annalium rationem veteres,
ad ipsorum sane recentes. Nam ante quam delectata
est Atheniensium civitas hac laude dicendi, multa
iam memorabilia et in domesticis et in bellicis rebus
effecerat. Hoc autem studium non erat commune
50 Graeciae, sed proprium Athenarum. Quis enim aut
Argivum oratorem aut Corinthium aut Thebanum
scit fuisse temporibus illis ? nisi quid de Epaminonda
docto homine suspicari libet. Lacedaemonium vero
usque ad hoc tempus audivi fuisse neminem. Mene-
laum ipsum dulcem illum quidem tradit Homerus, sed
pauca dicentem. Brevitas autem laus est interdum
in aliqua parte dicendi, in universa eloquentia laudem
non habet.

ª A section of Sulla's comprehensive *lex (Cornelia) de
sicariis*, which in addition to crimes of violence embraced
" judicial murder," through bribery, conspiracy, perjury, etc.,
looking to the circumvention of justice. *Cf.* Marcianus, *Dig.*
48. 8, 1 ; *pro Cluent.* 151. There was not in fact at Athens
any such prohibition of composing speeches for others as
Cicero implies. Quintilian (2. 15, 30) assumes that such a
law existed, but was consistently violated.

no man ever pleaded his case better, when in his hearing Antiphon defended himself on a capital charge ; that as to Lysias, it was only in the be- 48 ginning of his career that he professed the art of rhetoric, but afterwards, seeing that Theodorus was a more skilful theorist and teacher, though dry as a speaker, he began to compose speeches for others and abandoned the profession of teacher. He tells also how Isocrates with similar alternation at first denied that there was an art of speaking, while at the same time he was writing speeches for others to use in court ; but when it happened repeatedly that he was summoned as having violated a law like ours[a] 'providing against circumvention or chicanery by judicial process,' he ceased to write speeches for others and devoted himself wholly to the composition of theory and models of oratory.

" Thus, as regards Greece, you see the birth and 49 origins of oratory, early from the standpoint of our chronology, but from theirs quite recent. For long before Athens found pleasure in the art of speaking and in the glory of its exercise, it had accomplished many memorable things both in peace and in war. The pursuit of oratory however was not shared in by Greece as a whole, but was peculiar to Athens. Who 50 ever heard of an orator of Argos or Corinth or Thebes of that period, unless perhaps you entertain a suspicion in regard to Epaminondas, who was a man of some training ? As for a Spartan orator, I have never down to the present day heard of one. Menelaus, even, Homer refers to as an agreeable speaker, but a man of few words, and while brevity in oratory is a thing to praise in some places, yet in eloquence as a whole it is not a merit.

51 At vero extra Graeciam magna dicendi studia fuerunt maximique huic laudi habiti honores illustre oratorum nomen reddiderunt. Nam ut semel e Piraeo eloquentia evecta est, omnis peragravit insulas atque ita peregrinata tota Asia est, ut se externis oblineret[1] moribus omnemque illam salubritatem Atticae dictionis et quasi sanitatem perderet ac loqui paene dedisceret. Hinc Asiatici oratores non contemnendi quidem nec celeritate nec copia, sed parum pressi et nimis redundantes ; Rhodii saniores 52 et Atticorum similiores. Sed de Graecis hactenus ; etenim haec ipsa forsitan fuerint non necessaria.

Tum Brutus : Ista vero, inquit, quam necessaria fuerint non facile dixerim ; iucunda certe mihi fuerunt neque solum non longa, sed etiam breviora quam vellem.

Optime, inquam, sed veniamus ad nostros, de quibus difficile est plus intellegere quam quantum ex 53 monumentis suspicari licet. XIV. Quis enim putet aut celeritatem ingeni L. Bruto illi nobilitatis vestrae principi defuisse ? qui de matre savianda ex oraculo Apollinis tam acute arguteque coniecerit ; qui summam prudentiam simulatione stultitiae texerit ; qui potentissimum regem clarissimi regis filium expulerit civitatemque perpetuo dominatu liberatam magistratibus annuis legibus iudiciisque devinxerit ; qui collegae suo imperium abrogaverit, ut e civitate regalis nominis memoriam tolleret ; quod certe effici

---

[1] oblineret *cod. Ven.*, obtineret *L.*

ᵃ The oracle, consulted by the sons of Tarquin and by Brutus, had said that " supreme power at Rome was destined to the one who should first kiss his mother. Brutus, suspecting that the Pythian response had another meaning, making as if to fall kissed the earth," Livy 1. 56.

" But outside of Greece proper eloquence was 51
cultivated with great ardour, and the honours awarded
to excellence in this art gave distinction to the name
of orator. For when once eloquence had sailed forth
from Piraeus it traversed all the islands and visited
every part of Asia, but in this process it contracted
some stain from foreign ways and lost that wholesomeness, and what one might call the sound health,
of Attic diction ; indeed it almost unlearned the art
of natural speech. From this source came the
Asiatic orators, not to be despised whether for their
readiness or their abundance, but redundant and
lacking conciseness. The school of Rhodes however
retained more sanity and more similarity to the Attic
source. So much then for the Greeks, and even this 52
perchance was superfluous."

" How far from superfluous," rejoined Brutus, " I
cannot easily tell you. Certainly I found it interesting, and far from being too much, it was even briefer
than I could have wished."

" You're very kind," I replied ; " but now let us
come to our early orators, about whom it is hard
to know more than can be inferred from historical
records. Who, for example, can suppose that Lucius 53
Brutus, the founder of your noble family, was lacking
in ready wit, who interpreted so acutely and shrewdly
the oracle of Apollo about kissing his mother [a] ; who
concealed under the guise of stupidity great wisdom ;
who drove from the state a powerful king, son of a
famous king, and freeing it from the domination of an
absolute ruler fixed its constitution by establishing
annual magistrates, laws, and courts ; who abrogated
the authority of his colleague so that the very memory
of the regal name might be obliterated ? All this

54 non potuisset, nisi esset oratione persuasum. Videmus item paucis annis post reges exactos, cum plebes
prope ripam Anionis ad tertium miliarium consedisset
eumque montem qui Sacer appellatus est occupa-
visset, M. Valerium dictatorem dicendo sedavisse dis-
cordias eique ob eam rem honores amplissimos habitos
et eum primum ob eam ipsam causam Maximum esse
appellatum. Ne L. Valerium quidem Potitum arbitror non aliquid potuisse dicendo, qui post decem-
viralem invidiam plebem in patres incitatam legibus
55 et contionibus suis mitigaverit. Possumus Appium
Claudium suspicari disertum, quia senatum iam-
iam inclinatum a Pyrrhi pace revocaverit; possumus
C. Fabricium, quia sit ad Pyrrhum de captivis recu-
perandis missus orator; Ti. Coruncanium, quod ex
pontificum commentariis longe plurimum ingenio valuisse videatur; M'. Curium, quod is tribunus plebis
interrege Appio Caeco diserto homine comitia contra
leges habente, cum de plebe consulem non accipiebat,
patres ante auctores fieri coegerit; quod fuit per-
56 magnum nondum lege Maenia lata. Licet aliquid
etiam de M. Popili ingenio suspicari, qui cum consul
esset eodemque tempore sacrificium publicum cum
laena faceret, quod erat flamen Carmentalis, plebei

---

[a] Senatorial ratification of acts of the *comitia* was necessary to give them validity, but the people had wrested from
the patricians the rule that such ratification should actually
precede the voting in the *comitia*. The *lex Maenia* of
287 B.C. reaffirmed older enactments and usage looking to
this end.

certainly could not have been accomplished without the persuasion of oratory. We see again a few years 54 after the expulsion of the kings, when the plebeians had withdrawn to the third milestone near the Anio, and occupied the eminence which thereafter was called the Sacred Mount, that Marcus Valerius the dictator appeased their discord by his eloquence. For this success we learn that the most distinguished honours were conferred upon him, and that for the same reason he was the first to be called Maximus. Nor do I think that Lucius Valerius Potitus was without capacity as an orator, since by his laws and public harangues he succeeded in assuaging the passions of the common people against the patricians after the odium aroused by the rule of the decemvirs. We may suspect that Appius Claudius too was a ready 55 speaker, since he recalled the wavering senate from concluding peace with Pyrrhus ; so also Gaius Fabricius, since he was sent as ambassador to Pyrrhus in the matter of exchanging prisoners ; Tiberius Coruncanius, since the pontifical records make it plain that his character and intelligence gave him great authority ; Manius Curius, who as tribune of the people overcame the opposition of the eloquent Appius Caecus—as interrex and director of the election, Appius had refused, in defiance of the law, to accept a plebeian candidate for consul—and compelled the senators to pledge beforehand ratification of their choice ; it was a great thing to have carried through before the passage of the *lex Maenia.*[a] One may also 56 infer something about the oratorical talent of Marcus Popilius ; while as consul he was engaged in performing a public sacrifice, robed in the vestments of his office as flamen Carmentalis, word was brought him

55

contra patres concitatione et seditione nuntiata, ut
erat laena amictus ita venit in contionem seditionem-
que cum auctoritate tum oratione sedavit. Sed eos
oratores habitos esse aut omnino tum ullum eloquentiae praemium fuisse nihil sane mihi legisse
videor ; tantum modo coniectura ducor ad suspican-
57 dum. Dicitur etiam C. Flaminius, is qui tribunus
plebis legem de agro Gallico et Piceno viritim divi-
dundo tulerit, qui consul apud Trasumennum sit
interfectus, ad populum valuisse dicendo. Q. etiam
Maximus Verrucosus orator habitus est temporibus
illis et Q. Metellus, is qui bello Punico secundo cum
L. Veturio Philone consul fuit.

xv. Quem vero exstet et de quo sit memoriae
proditum eloquentem fuisse et ita esse habitum,
primus est M. Cornelius Cethegus, cuius eloquentiae
est auctor et idoneus quidem mea sententia Q. Ennius,
praesertim cum et ipse eum audiverit et scribat de
mortuo, ex quo nulla suspicio est amicitiae causa esse
58 mentitum. Est igitur sic apud illum in nono ut opinor
annali :

> additur orator Cornelius suaviloquenti
> ore Cethegus Marcus Tuditano collegae[1]
> Marci filius.

[1] Marcus Tuditano collega *Schütz*, Marcus studio collegam *L*.

---

[a] Cicero's contention throughout the *Brutus* is that
oratory is late in its origins and development. He is at
pains to point out that the existence of an effective early
oratory is merely an inference from episodes in Roman

of riot and conflict of the people with the patricians ;
clad in his priestly robe, just as he was, he hurried to
the assembly, and by the authority of his presence as
well as by his words allayed the tumult.   But that
these men were accounted orators, or that at that
time eloquence held out any prize to be coveted, I
cannot recall ever having read ;   I am only led by
conjecture to suspect it was so.[a]   It is reported too 57
that Gaius Flaminius, the tribune of the plebs who
carried through the law authorizing the distribution
of the land of Hither Gaul and of Picenum to individual settlers, and who as consul lost his life at
Trasumenus, was a valiant speaker before the people.
Also Quintus Maximus Verrucosus was by the standards of that time accounted an orator, and Quintus
Metellus as well, I mean the one who was consul
during the second Punic War with Lucius Veturius
Philo.

"But the first Roman concerning whom there is
extant record of his eloquence, and evidence of his
recognition for it, is Marcus Cornelius Cethegus. The
authority for this statement, and an adequate one
I fancy, is Quintus Ennius, especially since he had
heard him speak and writes of him after his death, so
that no suspicion of distortion because of friendship
can arise.   The passage of Ennius, if I recall aright, 58
is found in the ninth book of the *Annals* and runs as
follows :

> To his colleague Tuditanus was added the orator
> Marcus Cornelius Cethegus, of the sweet-speaking tongue,
> Son of Marcus.

---

history, in which certain men are reported to have accomplished results by the influence and persuasion of their
personality.   Record of their oratory did not exist.

Et oratorem appellat et suaviloquentiam tribuit, quae nunc quidem non tam est in plerisque—latrant enim iam quidam oratores, non loquuntur ; sed est ea laus eloquentiae certe maxima :

> is dictust ollis popularibus olim,
> qui tum vivebant homines atque aevum agitabant,[1]
> flos delibatus populi—

59 probe vero ; ut enim hominis decus ingenium, sic ingeni ipsius lumen est eloquentia, qua virum excellentem praeclare tum illi homines florem populi esse dixerunt

> Suadai[2] . . . medulla.

Πειθώ quam vocant Graeci, cuius effector est orator, hanc Suadam appellavit Ennius ; eius autem Cethegum medullam fuisse vult, ut quam deam in Pericli labris scripsit Eupolis sessitavisse, huius hic medullam nostrum oratorem fuisse dixerit.

60 At hic Cethegus consul cum P. Tuditano fuit bello Punico secundo quaestorque his consulibus M. Cato modo plane annis CXL ante me consulem; et id ipsum nisi unius esset Enni testimonio cognitum, hunc vetustas, ut alios fortasse multos, oblivione obruisset. Illius autem aetatis qui sermo fuerit ex Naevianis scriptis intellegi potest. His enim consulibus, ut in veteribus commentariis scriptum est, Naevius est

---

[1] agitabant *Gellius 12. 2, 3*, agebant *L.*
[2] suadai *L* (suadai, *F in marg.*, suadat *F¹ GB*, sua dat *O*).

---

[a] Cicero, perhaps unwittingly, distorts the evidence of Ennius, since *orator* is here used in the sense of ambassador. *Cf.* also 55 above, *missus orator*. The word *orator*, as applied to the pleader or public speaker of whatever type (ῥήτωρ), seems to be scarcely earlier than the first century B.C.
[b] *Cf.* Plato, *Gorg.* 453 A, " rhetoric the artificer of persuasion," πειθοῦς δημιουργός (*effector*). For the saying of

He calls him orator[a] and adds the attribute of sweetness of speech, a thing you do not find nowadays in most of them—more barking in some than speaking ; but what follows is certainly the greatest title to praise in eloquence :

> He used to be called by his fellows of that time,
> The men who then lived and passed their restless days,
> The choice flower of the people—

and well said indeed ; for as reason is the glory of 59 man, so the lamp of reason is eloquence, for preeminence in which the men of that time did well to call such a man the flower of the people,

> the marrow of Persuasion.

Πειθώ the Greek term, which it is the business of the orator to effect,[b] Ennius calls Persuasion, the very marrow of which Cethegus was, he claims ; so that of that goddess, which according to Eupolis ever sat on the lips of Pericles, our orator was, he said, the very marrow.

" Now this Cethegus was consul with Publius Tudi- 60 tanus in the second Punic War, while Marcus Cato was quaestor with the same consuls, only one hundred and forty years, to be exact, before my consulship[c] ; and unless the knowledge of his eloquence were known to us by the sole testimony of Ennius, time would have consigned him to oblivion as it has doubtless many others. The language of that period can be learned from the writings of Naevius, for in the consulship of those two, as early records show, Naevius died ;

Eupolis *cf.* reference in note on 38 above : πειθώ τις ἐπεκάθιζεν ἐπὶ τοῖς χείλεσιν.

[c] From 204 b.c. to the end of 64. Cicero does not in his reckoning include the year of his consulship, 63 b.c.

mortuus; quamquam Varro noster diligentissimus
investigator antiquitatis putat in hoc erratum vitam-
que Naevi producit longius. Nam Plautus P. Claudio L. Porcio viginti annis post illos quos ante dixi
consulibus mortuus est, Catone censore.

61   Hunc igitur Cethegum consecutus est aetate Cato,
qui annis VIIII post eum fuit consul. Eum nos ut
perveterem habemus, qui L. Marcio M'. Manilio
consulibus mortuus est, annis LXXXVI ipsis ante me
consulem. XVI. Nec vero habeo, quemquam antiqui-
orem, cuius quidem scripta proferenda putem, nisi
quem Appi Caeci oratio haec ipsa de Pyrrho et non
62 nullae mortuorum laudationes forte delectant. Et
hercules eae quidem exstant; ipsae enim familiae
sua quasi ornamenta ac monumenta servabant et ad
usum, si quis eiusdem generis occidisset, et ad memoriam laudum domesticarum et ad illustrandam
nobilitatem suam. Quamquam his laudationibus historia rerum nostrarum est facta mendosior. Multa
enim scripta sunt in eis quae facta non sunt, falsi
triumphi, plures consulatus, genera etiam falsa et
ad plebem transitiones, cum homines humiliores in
alienum eiusdem nominis infunderentur genus; ut
si ego me a M'. Tullio esse dicerem, qui patricius cum
Servio Sulpicio consul anno x post exactos reges fuit.
63   Catonis autem orationes non minus multae fere

ª The most common reason for transition from patrician
to plebeian status was to gain the right to stand for the
tribuneship, as in the case of Clodius, Cicero's enemy. See
also Suetonius, *Aug.* 2. Thus a plebeian family might
boast that it had originally belonged to some distinguished
patrician family of the same name.

though our friend Varro, with his thoroughness of investigation into early history, thinks this date erroneous and makes the life of Naevius somewhat longer. His reason is that Plautus, his contemporary, did not die until the consulship of Publius Claudius and Lucius Porcius, twenty years after the consuls named above, when Cato was censor.

" But to resume, Cethegus was followed next in 61 point of time by Cato, who was consul nine years after him. Cato we look upon as very early ; he died in the consulship of Lucius Marcius and Manius Manilius, exactly eighty-six years before my consulship, and yet, recent as that is, I cannot name anyone earlier whose writings can be adduced, unless perchance one find pleasure in the speech of Appius Caecus concerning Pyrrhus, to which I have just referred, or in some funeral orations. Of these some 62 are, to be sure, extant, which the families of the deceased have preserved as trophies of honour and for use on the death of a member of the same family, whether to recall the memory of past glories of their house, or to support their own claims to noble origins. Yet by these laudatory speeches our history has become quite distorted ; for much is set down in them which never occurred, false triumphs, too large a number of consulships, false relationships and transitions of patricians to plebeian status,[a] in that men of humbler birth professed that their blood blended with a noble family of the same name, though in fact quite alien to them ; as if I, for example, should say that I was descended from Manius Tullius the patrician, who was consul with Servius Sulpicius ten years after the expulsion of the kings.

" But to come back to Cato ; his orations are 63

sunt quam Attici Lysiae, cuius arbitror plurimas esse
—est enim Atticus, quoniam certe Athenis est et
natus et mortuus et functus omni civium munere,
quamquam Timaeus eum quasi Licinia et Mucia lege
repetit Syracusas—et quodam modo est non nulla in
eis etiam inter ipsos similitudo. Acuti sunt, elegantes
faceti breves; sed ille Graecus ab omni laude felicior.
64 Habet enim certos sui studiosos, qui non tam habitus
corporis opimos quam gracilitates consectentur, quos,
valetudo modo bona sit, tenuitas ipsa delectat—
quamquam in Lysia sunt saepe etiam lacerti, sic ut
eo[1] fieri nihil possit valentius, verum est certe genere
toto strigosior; sed habet tamen suos laudatores,
qui hac ipsa eius subtilitate admodum gaudeant.
65 XVII. Catonem vero quis nostrorum oratorum, qui
quidem nunc sunt, legit? aut quis novit omnino? At
quem virum, di boni! mitto civem aut senatorem aut
imperatorem—oratorem enim hoc loco quaerimus;
quis illo gravior in laudando acerbior in vituperando,
in sententiis argutior in docendo edisserendoque subtilior? Refertae sunt orationes amplius centum
quinquaginta, quas quidem adhuc invenerim et
legerim, et verbis et rebus illustribus. Licet ex his
eligant ea quae notatione et laude digna sint; om-
66 nes oratoriae virtutes in eis reperientur. Iam vero
Origines eius quem florem aut quod lumen eloquentiae non habent? Amatores huic desunt, sicuti

---

[1] ut eo *Manutius*, ut et L.

---

[a] A law of 95 B.C. which relegated to the place of their
birth non-Roman Italians who by long residence had
assumed the rights of Roman citizenship (Asconius, *ed. K-S*,
p. 60). Lysias, though born in Athens, was the son of a
Syracusan father, and did not enjoy full Attic citizenship.

scarcely less numerous than those of Lysias the
Athenian, and to him far too many I am sure are
assigned ;—I call him Athenian since he was certainly
born at Athens, died there, and performed all the
offices of citizenship, though Timaeus, as if in accordance with an Athenian law like our Licinian and
Mucian,[a] remands him to Syracuse. Between the
two men there is in some sense a likeness : both are
acute, precise, clever, brief. But in respect of fame
the Greek has been altogether more fortunate. He 64
has his devotees who cultivate a lean rather than a
full habit of body, and within the limits of health even
admire spareness. And yet, while in Lysias there is
often a muscular vigour of the most effective kind,
still it is quite true that in his style as a whole he
belongs to the more meagre type, and, as I have said,
has his admirers who have their special delight in
this very slightness. As for Cato, who of our orators 65
living to-day reads him or has any acquaintance with
him ? And yet, good heavens, what a man ! I do
not now refer to the citizen, the senator, the commander ; we seek now only the orator. Whom will
you find more weighty in commendation, sharper in
censure, shrewder in aphorism, more subtle in presentation and proof ? His orations, more than one
hundred and fifty in number so far as I have yet found
and read them, are packed with brilliant diction and
matter. Select from them the passages which deserve to be marked for special praise ; you will find
there every oratorical excellence. His *Origines* too 66
—what flower, what lustre of eloquence do they not
contain ! But ardent admirers he lacks, just as some

Timaeus, a Sicilian, probably with patriotic pride, claimed
him for Sicily.

CICERO

multis iam ante saeculis et Philisto Syracusio et
ipsi Thucydidi. Nam ut horum concisis sententiis,
interdum etiam non satis [autem] apertis cum
brevitate tum nimio acumine, officit Theopompus
elatione atque altitudine orationis suae (quod idem
Lysiae Demosthenes), sic Catonis luminibus obstruxit
haec posteriorum quasi exaggerata altius oratio.
67 Sed ea in nostris inscitia est, quod hi ipsi, qui in
Graecis antiquitate delectantur eaque subtilitate,
quam Atticam appellant, hanc in Catone ne nove-
runt quidem. Hyperidae volunt esse et Lysiae ; laudo,
68 sed cur nolunt Catones ? Attico genere dicendi se
gaudere dicunt ; sapienter id quidem, atque utinam
imitarentur nec ossa solum sed etiam sanguinem !
gratum est tamen quod volunt. Cur igitur Lysias
et Hyperides amatur, cum penitus ignoretur Cato ?
Antiquior est huius sermo et quaedam horridiora
verba. Ita enim tum loquebantur ; id muta, quod
tum ille non potuit, et adde numeros et ut aptior
sit oratio, ipsa verba compone et quasi coagmenta,
quod ne Graeci quidem veteres factitaverunt, iam
69 neminem anteponas Catoni. Ornari orationem
Graeci putant, si verborum immutationibus utantur,
quos appellant τρόπους, et sententiarum orationisque
formis, quae vocant σχήματα ; non veri simile est
quam sit in utroque genere et creber et distinctus
Cato. XVIII. Nec vero ignoro nondum esse satis

---

a Dryden's preface to *Translations from Chaucer and
Boccaccio* has some curious and entertaining parallels to
this judgement of Cato: *e.g.* " I have added somewhat of my
own where . . . he had not given the thoughts their true
lustre, for want of words in the beginning of our language."
" The words are given up as a post not to be defended (in
Chaucer), because he wanted the modern art of fortifying."

centuries earlier Philistus of Syracuse and even Thucydides lacked them. For just as their concise, pungent, and often obscure brevity was eclipsed by Theopompus with his high-flown, elevated style (as befell Lysias also compared with Demosthenes), so this language of succeeding writers, built up like some tall structure, has cut off the light from Cato. But **67** observe the ignorance of our Romans ! The very men who find such pleasure in the early period of Greek letters, and in that simplicity which they call Attic, have no knowledge of the same quality in Cato. Their aim is to be like Hyperides and Lysias ; laudable certainly, but why not like Cato ? They profess to **68** have delight in the Attic style, and in that they show sound sense ; but I would that they might imitate not its bones only, but its flesh and blood as well. Still their aim is good ; but why then are Lysias and Hyperides loved, while Cato is wholly unknown ? His language is archaic, and some of his words are quite uncouth. Yes, for that was how they spoke in his day ; change that, which in his time he could not change, add rhythm and, to fit his language together more smoothly, rearrange his words, cement them as it were together (what even the older Greeks did not do), and behold, you will not find anyone to place before Cato.[a] The Greeks consider that language is **69** embellished if such changes in the use of words are employed as they call tropes, and such figures of thought and language as they call postures ; you will scarcely believe how rich and pointed Cato is in the employment of both these features of style. I am not of course unaware that he is not yet an orator of

Would an oration of Cato's thus " fortified " by Cicero have fared better than the *Knight's Tale* in the hands of Dryden?

politum hunc oratorem et quaerendum esse aliquid
perfectius, quippe cum ita sit ad nostrorum temporum rationem vetus, ut nullius scriptum exstet
dignum quidem lectione quod sit antiquius. Sed
maiore honore in omnibus artibus quam in hac una
arte dicendi versatur antiquitas.

70　Quis enim eorum qui haec minora animadvertunt
non intellegit Canachi signa rigidiora esse quam ut
imitentur veritatem ; Calamidis dura illa quidem, sed
tamen molliora quam Canachi ; nondum Myronis
satis ad veritatem adducta, iam tamen quae non
dubites pulchra dicere ; pulchriora etiam Polycliti et
iam plane perfecta, ut mihi quidem videri solent ?
Similis in pictura ratio est ; in qua Zeuxim et Poly-
gnotum et Timanthem et eorum, qui non sunt usi plus
quam quattuor coloribus, formas et liniamenta lauda-
mus ; at in Aetione Nicomacho Protogene Apelle iam
71 perfecta sunt omnia.　Et nescio an reliquis in rebus
omnibus idem eveniat ; nihil est enim simul et inven-
tum et perfectum ; nec dubitari debet quin fuerint
ante Homerum poetae, quod ex eis carminibus intellegi potest, quae apud illum et in Phaeacum et in
procorum epulis canuntur. Quid, nostri veteres
versus ubi sunt ?

> quos olim Fauni vatesque canebant
> cum neque Musarum scopulos
> nec dicti studiosus quisquam erat ante hunc,

ait ipse de se nec mentitur in gloriando ; sic enim

---

a Ennius, born 239 B.C. The lines are given after Vahlen,
Annales 214-216. They are obviously incomplete, but it

sufficient finish, and that something more perfect is to
be desired. Nor is it strange, since according to our
chronology he is so early that we have no piece of
writing before him that is worth reading. But early
periods of culture awarded greater honour to all other
forms of art than to this one art of discourse.

" What critic who devotes his attention to the lesser 70
arts does not recognize that the statues of Canachus
are too rigid to reproduce the truth of nature ? The
statues of Calamis again are still hard, and yet more
lifelike than those of Canachus. Even Myron has
not yet fully attained naturalness, though one would
not hesitate to call his works beautiful. Still more
beautiful are the statues of Polyclitus, and indeed in
my estimation quite perfect. The same development
may be seen in painting. In Zeuxis, Polygnotus,
Timanthes, and others, who used only four colours,
we praise their outline and drawing ; but in Aetion,
Nicomachus, Protogenes, Apelles, everything has
been brought to perfection. The same thing I take 71
it is true of all the other arts ; nothing is brought to
perfection on its first invention. We cannot doubt
that there were poets before Homer, as we may infer
from the songs which he introduces into the feasts of
the Phaeacians and of the suitors. And what of our
own history ? Where are our early verses,

> which Fauns and native bards once sang
> When yet the Muse's heights [no one had scaled],
> Nor studious of the word was any man before me,

as says our poet of himself ? [a] Nor is he false in his

seems more likely that Cicero himself selected from familiar
verses brief suggestion of the ideas which he wished to
convey, rather than that the missing words have been lost.

sese res habet, nam et Odyssia Latina est sic[1] tamquam opus aliquod Daedali et Livianae fabulae
72 non satis dignae quae iterum legantur. Atqui hic
Livius [qui] primus fabulam C. Claudio Caeci filio et
M. Tuditano consulibus docuit anno ipso ante quam
natus est Ennius, post Romam conditam autem
quartodecimo et quingentensimo, ut hic ait, quem
nos sequimur ; est enim inter scriptores de numero
annorum controversia. Accius autem a Q. Maximo
quintum consule captum Tarento scripsit Livium,
annis xxx post quam eum fabulam docuisse et Atticus
scribit et nos in antiquis commentariis invenimus,
73 docuisse autem fabulam annis post xi C. Cornelio Q.
Minucio consulibus ludis Iuventatis, quos Salinator
Senensi proelio voverat. In quo tantus error Acci
fuit, ut his consulibus xl annos natus Ennius fuerit ;
quoi[2] aequalis fuerit Livius : minor fuit aliquanto
is, qui primus fabulam dedit, quam ei, qui multas
docuerant ante hos consules, et Plautus et Naevius.
74 xix. Haec si minus apta videntur huic sermoni,

---

[1] sic in *L*, sic incondita *Reis*.
[2] quoi *Wilkins*, *Martha*, quod *L*.

---

[a] Livius Andronicus, presumably a freedman in the family
of the Livii, translated the *Odyssey* into the old national
verse called the Saturnian. It probably antedated his plays,
and was accounted the earliest monument of Latin literature.

[b] Livius produced his first play, and the first recorded
play of the Roman theatre, at the *Ludi Romani* in September
240 B.C., the year following the conclusion of the First Punic
War. The poet and scholar Accius, toward the end of the
second century B.C., was apparently the first historian of the
Roman drama, in his *Didascalica*. Believing, or perhaps
knowing, that Livius was of Tarentine origin, he assumed

vaunt ; it is as he says, for the Latin *Odyssey*[a] is as it were a statue of Daedalus, and the plays of Livius are not worth a second reading.   And yet this Livius 72 produced his first play in the consulship of Gaius Claudius, son of Caecus, and Marcus Tuditanus, as late as the very year before the birth of Ennius, five hundred and fourteen years after the founding of Rome, according to the authority whom I follow ; for there is a dispute among writers about the chronology.   Accius however stated that Livius was taken captive from Tarentum by Quintus Maximus in his fifth consulship, thirty years after Livius had produced his first play, according to Atticus, whose statement I find confirmed by early records.[b]   Accius goes 73 on to say that Livius produced his first play eleven years after the date (of his capture) in the consulship of Gaius Cornelius and Quintus Minucius at the Ludi Iuventatis, which Livius Salinator had vowed at the battle of Sena.   In this the error of Accius is so great that in the consulship of these men Ennius was already forty years of age.   But suppose that Livius was his contemporary : it will appear then that the first one to produce a play at Rome was somewhat younger than the two who had already produced many plays before this date, Plautus and Naevius. If this discussion seems ill-suited to our conversation, 74

that he was a captive from Tarentum, taken by Q. Maximus in 209 B.C.   The first play of Livius (and in view of the traditional priority of Livius also the first Roman play) he assigned to the year 197 B.C., and thus distorted the whole early chronology of Roman literature by more than forty years. Varro from public records was able to correct the error, and from him Atticus, whom Cicero follows, presented the correct chronology and refutation of Accius's error.   *Cf.* the translator's discussion in *Am. Journ. Phil.* xix. (1898), p. 289.

Brute, Attico assigna, qui me inflammavit studio
illustrium hominum aetates et tempora persequendi.

Ego vero, inquit Brutus, et delector ista quasi
notatione temporum et ad id quod instituisti, oratorum genera distinguere aetatibus, istam diligentiam
esse accommodatam puto.

75 Recte, inquam, Brute, intellegis. Atque utinam
exstarent illa carmina, quae multis saeculis ante
suam aetatem in epulis esse cantitata a singulis con-
vivis de clarorum virorum laudibus in Originibus
scriptum reliquit Cato ! Tamen illius, quem in vati-
bus et Faunis annumerat Ennius, bellum Punicum
76 quasi Myronis opus delectat. Sit Ennius sane, ut est
certe, perfectior ; qui si illum, ut simulat, contemneret, non omnia bella persequens primum illud
Punicum acerrimum bellum reliquisset. Sed ipse
dicit cur id faciat : ' scripsere,' inquit, ' alii rem
vorsibus '—et luculente quidem scripserunt, etiam
si minus quam tu polite, nec vero tibi aliter videri
debet, qui a Naevio vel sumpsisti multa, si fateris,
vel, si negas, surripuisti.

77 Cum hoc Catone grandiores natu fuerunt C. Flami-
nius C. Varro Q. Maximus Q. Metellus P. Lentulus
P. Crassus, qui cum superiore Africano consul fuit.
Ipsum Scipionem accepimus non infantem fuisse.
Filius quidem eius, is qui hunc minorem Scipionem a

---

* This spirited form of literary criticism, addressing itself
to the author as if a living person and present, is not uncommon in early Latin literature. The comment of Caesar
on Terence will be recalled, *tu quoque tu in summis, o dimi-
diate Menander,* and Horace's *Lucili, quam sis mendosus,*
etc. There are numerous examples in the literary epigrams
of the Greek Anthology.

Brutus, put the blame on Atticus, who has inspired me with interest in tracing out the successive generations of famous men and their time in relation to one another."

"On the contrary," replied Brutus, "I am deeply interested in that sort of chronological treatment, and I consider that accuracy such as yours is entirely suited to the task you have undertaken, of distinguishing the characteristics of orators within their respective periods."

"That was my thought, Brutus, as you say; and 75 would there were still extant those songs, of which Cato in his *Origines* has recorded, that long before his time the several guests at banquets used to sing in turn the praise of famous men! For all that Ennius counts Naevius among primitive bards and fauns, his *Bellum Punicum*, like a work of Myron, still yields pleasure. Grant that Ennius is more finished, as 76 undoubtedly he is; yet if Ennius had really scorned him, as he professes, he would not in undertaking to describe all our wars have passed over that stubbornly contested first Punic War. But he tells us himself why he does so : ' Others,' he says, ' have written the theme in verse '—yes, and brilliantly too they wrote, even if with less polish than you, sir ; and surely you ought not to think otherwise, you who from Naevius have taken much, if you confess the debt, or if you deny it, much have stolen.[a]

"Older contemporaries of Cato were Gaius 77 Flaminius, Gaius Varro, Quintus Maximus, Quintus Metellus, Publius Lentulus, Publius Crassus, the one who was consul with the elder Africanus. Scipio himself we learn was not without some gift of speech ; and his son, the one who adopted the younger Scipio,

Paullo adoptavit, si corpore valuisset, in primis
habitus esset disertus ; indicant cum oratiunculae
tum historia quaedam Graeca scripta dulcissime.
78 xx. Numeroque eodem fuit Sex. Aelius, iuris quidem civilis omnium peritissimus, sed etiam ad dicendum paratus.

De minoribus autem C. Sulpicius Gallus, qui
maxime omnium nobilium Graecis litteris studuit ;
isque et oratorum in numero est habitus et fuit
reliquis rebus ornatus atque elegans.   Iam enim erat
unctior quaedam splendidiorque consuetudo loquendi.   Nam hoc praetore ludos Apollini faciente cum
Thyesten fabulam docuisset, Q. Marcio Cn. Ser-
79 vilio consulibus mortem obiit Ennius.   Erat isdem
temporibus Ti. Gracchus P. f., qui bis consul et
censor fuit, cuius est oratio Graeca apud Rhodios ;
quem civem cum gravem tum etiam eloquentem
constat fuisse.   P. etiam Scipionem Nasicam, qui est
Corculum appellatus, qui item bis consul et censor
fuit, habitum eloquentem aiunt, illius qui sacra acceperit filium ; dicunt etiam L. Lentulum, qui cum
C. Figulo consul fuit.   Q. Nobiliorem M. f. iam
patrio instituto deditum studio litterarum—qui etiam
Q. Ennium, qui cum patre eius in Aetolia militaverat,
civitate donavit, cum triumvir[1] coloniam deduxisset
—et T. Annium Luscum huius Q. Fulvi collegam non

---

[1] triumvir *codd. det.*, iiivirum *L*, tresvir *Eberhard.*

---

[a] Publius Cornelius Scipio Nasica, Corculum, " the dar-
ling of the people," consul in 162 B.C. and 155, son of the
P. Cornelius Scipio Nasica who was chosen by the senate as
" the best man of the state," and so accounted worthy to receive the Great Mother (*Magna Mater*), whose statue and
cult were brought to Rome in 204 B.C. (Livy 39. 14).

the son of Paulus, would have been accounted eloquent among the first had he possessed health and vigour. Some slight orations show it, and especially a piece of historical narrative written in Greek with great charm. To the same group belongs Sextus 78 Aelius, the most learned man of his time in the civil law, but also a ready speaker.

" Of younger contemporaries there was Gaius Sulpicius Gallus, who of all the nobility was the profoundest student of Greek letters. He was accounted an orator, and in other respects was a man of culture and refinement. Now by this time a richer and more brilliant habit of speaking had arisen ; for when Gallus as praetor conducted the games in honour of Apollo, Ennius at that festival presented the tragedy of *Thyestes*, and died in the year of the consuls Quintus Marcius and Gnaeus Servilius. To the same 79 time belonged Tiberius Gracchus, son of Publius, who was twice consul and censor. We have his oration, written in Greek, before the people of Rhodes, and we know that he was eloquent as well as a man of influence. Publius Scipio Nasica also, the one called familiarly Corculum,[a] like the foregoing twice consul and censor, son of the famous Scipio who was chosen to receive the sacred relics, was, they say, accounted eloquent. The same is said of Lucius Lentulus, who was consul with Gaius Figulus. Quintus Nobilior, son of Marcus, trained by his father from boyhood to the study of letters, is reported to have been not without readiness in discourse. It was he who, using his privilege as triumvir in establishing a colony, bestowed citizenship upon Quintus Ennius, who had campaigned with his father in Aetolia. The same report is made of Titus Annius Luscus, colleague

80 indisertum dicunt fuisse ; atque etiam L. Paullus
Africani pater personam principis civis facile dicendo
tuebatur.

Et vero etiam tum Catone vivo, qui annos quinque
et octoginta natus excessit e vita, cum quidem eo
ipso anno contra Ser. Galbam ad populum summa
contentione dixisset, quam etiam orationem scriptam
reliquit—sed vivo Catone minores natu multi uno
81 tempore oratores floruerunt. XXI. Nam et A. Albinus,
is qui Graece scripsit historiam, qui consul cum L.
Lucullo fuit, et litteratus et disertus fuit ; et tenuit
cum hoc locum quendam etiam Ser. Fulvius et una
Ser.[1] Fabius Pictor et iuris et litterarum et antiquitatis
bene peritus ; Quinctusque[2] Fabius Labeo fuit ornatus
isdem fere laudibus. Nam Q. Metellus, is cuius
quattuor filii consulares fuerunt, in primis est habitus
eloquens, qui pro L. Cotta dixit accusante Africano ;
cuius et aliae sunt orationes et contra Ti. Gracchum
82 exposita est in C. Fanni annalibus. Tum ipse L. Cotta
est veterator habitus ; sed C. Laelius et P. Africanus
in primis eloquentes, quorum exstant orationes, ex
quibus existimari de ingeniis oratorum potest. Sed
inter hos aetate paulum his antecedens sine controversia Ser. Galba eloquentia praestitit ; et nimirum
is princeps ex Latinis illa oratorum propria et quasi

[1] una Ser. (Serius *F*) *L*, Numerius *Martha*.
[2] Quinctus *FO* (*cf. Marx, Rh. Mus. lxxxi.* (*1932*) *304*).

---

[a] Consul 143 B.C. A stereotyped example in Roman
tradition of a life crowned with perfect good fortune. His
speech on the duty of rearing children for the state (*de prole
augenda*) was read to the senate by Augustus (*Suet.* 89).
[b] Publius Scipio Aemilianus, grandson (by adoption) of
the great Scipio Africanus, consul in 147 B.C., destroyer of

of the Quintus Fulvius (Nobilior) just mentioned.
Lucius Paullus also, the father of Africanus, sustained 80
easily by his eloquence the rôle of first citizen.

" Still in the lifetime of Cato, who died at the
advanced age of eighty-five and in the very year of
his death delivered before the people that vehement
indictment of Servius Galba, which he left too in
written form—still in his lifetime, I say, there
flourished many younger orators. Thus Aulus 81
Albinus, the writer of a history in Greek, consul with
Lucius Lucullus, was not only a man of letters but a
good speaker as well. A similar position was held by
Servius Fulvius and with him Servius Fabius Pictor, a
man learned in law, in letters, and in our history.
Quintus Fabius Labeo enjoyed somewhat the same
reputation. As for Quintus Metellus, whose four
sons attained to consular rank, you are of course
aware that he was esteemed one of the most eloquent
men of his time.[a] He spoke in behalf of Lucius Cotta
against the indictment of him brought by Africanus.
This and other of his orations are extant besides the
one against Tiberius Gracchus, which is set forth in
the Annals of Gaius Fannius. Lucius Cotta himself 82
was esteemed a practised speaker, but of routine
type. Gaius Laelius and Publius Africanus [b] however were in the first rank of orators ; their speeches
are extant, from which one may judge of their
oratorical genius. But among all of these, preceding
them a little in point of time, Servius Galba stood
out beyond question as pre-eminent in eloquence.
And in fact of Latin orators he was the first to employ
those resources which are the proper and legitimate

Carthage 146, and called Africanus Minor, about whom was
grouped the so-called Scipionic Circle.

legitima opera tractavit, ut egrederetur a proposito ornandi causa, ut delectaret animos, ut permoveret, ut augeret rem, ut miserationibus, ut communibus locis uteretur. Sed nescio quo modo huius, quem constat eloquentia praestitisse, exiliores orationes sunt et redolentes magis antiquitatem quam aut Laeli ⟨aut⟩ Scipionis aut etiam ipsius Catonis, itaque exaruerunt vix iam ut appareant.

83 De ipsius Laeli et Scipionis ingenio quamquam ea est fama,[1] ut plurimum tribuatur ambobus, dicendi tamen laus est in Laelio illustrior. At oratio Laeli de collegiis non melior quam de multis quam voles Scipionis ; non quo illa Laeli quicquam sit dulcius aut quo de religione dici possit augustius, sed multo tamen vetustior et horridior ille quam Scipio ; et, cum sint in dicendo variae voluntates, delectari mihi magis antiquitate videtur et libenter verbis 84 etiam uti paulo magis priscis Laelius. Sed est mos hominum, ut nolint eundem pluribus rebus excellere. Nam ut ex bellica laude aspirare ad Africanum nemo potest, in qua ipsa egregium Viriathi bello reperimus fuisse Laelium, sic ingeni litterarum eloquentiae sapientiae denique, etsi utrique primas, priores tamen libenter deferunt Laelio. Nec mihi ceterorum iudicio solum videtur, sed etiam ipso- 85 rum inter ipsos concessu ita tributum fuisse. Erat omnino tum mos, ut in reliquis rebus melior, sic

---

[1] fama *Baiter*, iam *L*.

functions of the orator—to digress from the business
in hand for embellishment, to delight his listeners, to
move them, to amplify his theme, to use pathos and
general topics. But for whatever cause, though his
pre-eminence in eloquence is well attested, his
orations are more meagre and savour more of
antiquity than those of Laelius or Scipio, or even of
Cato himself. Their colours have become so much
faded that they are scarcely still visible.

" Concerning the talent of Laelius and Scipio, 83
while both enjoy the highest reputation, yet in
eloquence the fame of Laelius is the brighter. However, the speech of Laelius concerning the priestly
colleges is no better than any one of the many
speeches of Scipio. Not that anything could be more
pleasing than that speech of Laelius, nor that anything more impressive and solemn could be uttered
on religion, yet he is much harsher and more archaic
than Scipio ; and indeed, as in habits of speech and
style there are varying likes and dislikes, it would
seem that Laelius had a greater fondness for the
antique and took pleasure in using words of older stamp.
But it is the way of human nature not to concede 84
pre-eminence to the same person in several fields.
Thus, as no one could aspire to the military glory of
Africanus, though we know that Laelius won distinction in the war against Viriathus, so for intellect,
letters, eloquence, philosophy in fine, while first rank
was awarded to both, yet people liked to assign the
higher place to Laelius. Nor, I suspect, did this
allotment of distinction exist only in the judgement
of others, but was allowed as between the two men
themselves. Speaking generally, there was in those 85
days a habit of mind, better in all other respects,

77

in hoc ipso humanior, ut faciles essent in suum
cuique tribuendo.

XXII. Memoria teneo Smyrnae me ex P. Rutilio
Rufo audivisse, cum diceret adulescentulo se accidisse, ut ex senatus consulto P. Scipio et D. Brutus, ut opinor, consules de re atroci magnaque
quaererent. Nam cum in silva[1] Sila facta caedes
esset notique homines interfecti insimulareturque
familia, partim etiam liberi societatis eius quae pi-
carias de P. Cornelio L. Mummio censoribus rede-
misset, decrevisse senatum ut de ea re cognoscerent
86 et statuerent consules. Causam pro publicanis
accurate, ut semper solitus esset, eleganterque
dixisse Laelium. Cum consules re audita ' amplius '
de consili sententia pronuntiavissent, paucis interpositis diebus iterum Laelium multo diligentius
meliusque dixisse iterumque eodem modo a consulibus rem esse prolatam. Tum Laelium, cum
eum socii domum reduxissent egissentque gratias et
ne defatigaretur oravissent, locutum esse ita : se
quae fecisset honoris eorum causa studiose accu-
rateque fecisse, sed se arbitrari causam illam a
Ser. Galba, quod is in dicendo ardentior[2] acriorque

---

[1] in silva Sila *Turnebus*, in sivas ita *F* (*similiter alii*).
[2] ardentior *Corradus*, adhortor *L*.

---

[a] It is the habit of dialogue to observe the fiction of
communication by word of mouth (*cf.* 21 above). The
following narrative was however most probably taken from
the *Memoirs* of Rutilius, which existed in a Latin version
(*de Vita sua*) and in a Greek form, which is cited as *Histories*.
(*Cf.* the translator's " Literary Sources in the Brutus, etc.,"

and in this one thing worthier of our human nature, of granting readily to each his own particular excellence.

" I still remember an anecdote which I heard from Publius Rutilius at Smyrna[a]: how in his early youth the consuls Publius Scipio and Decimus Brutus, I believe, were instructed by a resolution of the senate to investigate a great and shocking crime. It seems that in the forest of Sila murder had been committed, resulting in the death of well-known men ; and that slaves of the company's household were under accusation, as well as some free members of the corporation which had leased the pine-pitch product from the censors Publius Cornelius and Lucius Mummius. The senate therefore had decreed that the consuls should make investigation of the charges and pass judgement. The case in behalf of the 86 corporation was presented by Laelius with great thoroughness, as was his wont, and with finish and precision. When at the end of the hearing the consuls announced, that on the advice of their counsel the question should be postponed to a further hearing, after a few days' recess Laelius spoke again with greater pains and more effectively, and again as before the case was continued. Thereupon, when the members of the corporation had escorted him to his house and had thanked him, and begged him not to relax his efforts in their behalf, Laelius spoke thus : that what he had done he had done with studious care, out of regard and honour for them, but that he believed their case could be defended with greater force and effect by Servius Galba, because of his more

Am. Journ. Phil. xxvii. (1906), 184, and " Memoirs of Rutilius Rufus," *Cl. Phil.* xxviii. (1933), 153.)

esset, gravius et vehementius posse defendi. Itaque
auctoritate C. Laeli publicanos causam detulisse
87 ad Galbam ; illum autem, quod ei viro succeden-
dum esset, verecunde et dubitanter recepisse.
Unum quasi comperendinatus medium diem fuisse,
quem totum Galbam in consideranda causa com-
ponendaque posuisse ; et cum cognitionis dies esset
et ipse Rutilius rogatu sociorum domum ad Galbam
mane venisset, ut eum admoneret et ad dicendi
tempus adduceret, usque illum, quoad ei nuntia-
tum esset consules descendisse, omnibus exclusis
commentatum in quadam testudine cum servis
litteratis fuisse, quorum aliud dictare eodem alii[1]
tempore solitus esset. Interim cum esset ei nuntia-
tum tempus esse, exisse in aedis eo colore et eis
oculis ut egisse causam, non commentatum putares.
88 Addebat etiam idque ad rem pertinere putabat,
scriptores illos male mulcatos exisse cum Galba ;
ex quo significabat illum non in agendo solum, sed
etiam in meditando vehementem atque incensum
fuisse. Quid multa ? magna exspectatione, plurimis audientibus, coram ipso Laelio sic illam causam tanta vi tantaque gravitate dixisse Galbam
ut nulla fere pars orationis silentio praeteriretur.
Itaque multis querellis multaque miseratione adhi-

----

[1] alii *Reis*, a *L.*

ardent and more pungent style of speaking. Therefore on the advice of Laelius the corporation carried
its case to Galba. He, however, as succeeding a man 87
such as Laelius, took it over with scruples and hesitation. Only one day before the final hearing inter-
vened (analogous to our present rule of adjournment
for final hearing to the third day succeeding), and
this whole time Galba devoted to consideration of
the case and shaping it for presentation. When the
day of the hearing came, Rutilius, at the request
of members of the corporation, went himself at an
early hour to the house of Galba to remind him and
to conduct him to the court in good season. But until
word should be brought him of the presence of the
consuls in court, Galba continued his preparation of
the case, working in a vaulted room of his house from
which everyone was excluded, and surrounded by
lettered slaves, to whom after his habit he was dictating memoranda now to one and now to another at one
and the same time. Presently, when informed that
it was time to go, he came out into the hall with
flushed face and flashing eyes, like one, you would think,
who had already conducted, and not merely prepared
his case. Rutilius added as a relevant circumstance, 88
that the scribes who came out with him were badly
used up, an indication he thought of the vehemence
and temper of Galba in preparation as well as in action.
But to make a long story short : with expectation raised
to the highest pitch, before a great audience, and in
the presence of Laelius himself, Galba pleaded this
famous case so forcibly and so impressively that
almost no part of his oration was passed over in
silence. Thus, with many moving appeals to the
mercy of the court, the associates in the corporation

bita socios omnibus approbantibus illa die quaestione liberatos esse.

89 XXIII. Ex hac Rutili narratione suspicari licet, cum duae summae sint in oratore laudes, una subtiliter disputandi ad docendum, altera graviter agendi ad animos audientium permovendos, multoque plus proficiat is qui inflammet iudicem quam ille qui doceat, elegantiam in Laelio, vim in Galba fuisse. Quae quidem vis tum maxime cognita est, cum Lusitanis a Ser. Galba praetore contra interpositam, ut existimabatur, fidem interfectis L. Libone tribuno plebis populum incitante et rogationem in Galbam privilegi similem ferente, summa senectute, ut ante dixi, M. Cato legem suadens in Galbam multa dixit; quam orationem in Origines suas rettulit, paucis ante quam mortuus est [an] 90 diebus an mensibus. Tum igitur ⟨nihil⟩[1] recusans Galba pro sese, et populi Romani fidem implorans, cum suos pueros tum C. Galli etiam filium flens commendabat, cuius orbitas et fletus mire miserabilis fuit propter recentem memoriam clarissimi patris; isque se tum eripuit flamma, propter pueros misericordia populi commota, sicut idem scriptum

---

[1] nihil *ante* recusans *add. Corradus ex Val. Max. 8. 1, 2.*

---

[a] It is probable that Cicero has distorted the account of Rutilius for the sake of his argument. Praise of Galba and of his type of oratory cannot easily be credited to Rutilius, the austere Roman and devout Stoic. See the discussion referred to in the note preceding.

[b] The *rogatio* of Libo, without naming Galba, sought to redress a wrong done by him, and is for this reason compared to a *privilegium*, a law apparently general, but in fact aiming at an individual (*in privum*). Its passage would have been

were that day acquitted of the charge, with the approbation of everyone present.[a]

" From this story of Rutilius one may conclude, 89 that of the two chief qualities which the orator must possess, accurate argument looking to proof and impressive appeal to the emotions of the listener, the orator who inflames the court accomplishes far more than the one who merely instructs it ; that in short Laelius possessed precision, Galba power. This same power was most strikingly recognized again when Servius Galba was accused of massacring surrendered Lusitanians in violation (as was believed) of his pledged faith. To protest against this perfidy Lucius Libo, tribune of the commons, incited the people, and introduced a measure directed in effect at Galba in person, which Marcus Cato in extreme old age (as I have said before) pressed, with vigorous attack upon Galba. (His speech, on this occasion, he incorporated into his *Origines* only a few days or months before his death.) Thereupon Galba, asking 90 no favour for himself, but appealing to the loyalty of the Roman people, with tears in his eyes commended to their protection his own children as well as the young son of Gaius Gallus. The presence of this orphan and his childish weeping excited great compassion because of the memory still fresh of his illustrious father. Thus Galba by stirring the pity of the populace for little children snatched himself from the flames, as Cato wrote and has left recorded.[b]

in effect a condemnation of the perpetrator of the wrong. Galba in self-defence made no denial of the act, submitted extenuating circumstances, and threw himself on the mercy of the court, which in this case was the popular assembly. The bill (*rogatio*) was not passed. Its failure constituted a pardon rather than an acquittal.

reliquit Cato. Atque etiam ipsum Libonem non
infantem video fuisse, ut ex orationibus eius intellegi
potest.

91 Cum haec dixissem et paulum interquievissem :

Quid igitur, inquit, est causae, Brutus, si tanta
virtus in oratore Galba fuit, cur ea nulla in orationibus eius appareat ? quod mirari non possum in
eis qui nihil omnino scripti reliquerunt.

XXIV. Nec enim est eadem, inquam, Brute, causa
non scribendi et non tam bene scribendi quam
dixerint. Nam videmus alios oratores inertia nihil
scripsisse, ne domesticus etiam labor accederet ad
forensem—pleraeque enim scribuntur orationes habi-
92 tae iam, non ut habeantur ; alios non laborare,
ut meliores fiant—nulla enim res tantum ad dicendum proficit quantum scriptio ; memoriam autem
in posterum ingeni sui non desiderant, cum se
putant satis magnam adeptos esse dicendi gloriam
eamque etiam maiorem visum iri, si in existimantium
arbitrium sua scripta non venerint ; alios, quod
melius putent dicere se posse quam scribere, quod
peringeniosis hominibus neque satis doctis plerumque
93 contingit, ut ipsi Galbae. Quem fortasse vis non
ingeni solum sed etiam animi et naturális quidam
dolor dicentem incendebat efficiebatque ut et incitata et gravis et vehemens esset oratio ; dein
cum otiosus stilum prenderat motusque omnis
animi tamquam ventus hominem defecerat, flac-
cescebat oratio. Quod eis qui limatius dicendi
consectantur genus accidere non solet, propterea
quod prudentia numquam deficit oratorem, qua
ille utens eodem modo possit et dicere et scribere ;

This Libo, also, just referred to, was not, I observe, an unskilled speaker, as may be gathered from his speeches."

I ceased speaking and paused for a little.　　91

" Why is it then," asked Brutus, " if Galba possessed such skill as an orator, that nothing of it appears in his orations—a contrast which cannot surprise us in those who have left nothing written ? "

" The reasons for not writing at all, Brutus," I replied, " and for not writing as well as one speaks, are by no means identical. Some orators merely out of inertia have left nothing written, not being inclined to add a task at home to their exertions in the forum— for of course most orations are written after, and not for, delivery. Others do not strive to improve their 92 style (and there is nothing you know that contributes so much to good speaking as writing), and do not crave a memorial of their skill for posterity. They are satisfied with the renown they have, and judge that it will appear greater if their writings do not come into the hands of critics. Still others do not write because they are aware that they speak better than they write—the case frequently with men of unusual talent but insufficient training, like Galba. In his case it 93 would seem that when he spoke, in addition to vigorous intellectual grasp, he was fired by a kind of innate emotion, which produced a style of speaking earnest, passionate, and vehement ; then when he took up his pen at leisure and all that storm of emotion had subsided, his language lost its vigour. That would not happen naturally to those who follow a more concise style of speaking, because reason and judgement need not desert the orator at any time, and relying upon them he may write in the same

ardor animi non semper adest, isque cum consedit,
omnis illa vis et quasi flamma oratoris exstinguitur.
94 Hanc igitur ob causam videtur Laeli mens spirare
etiam in scriptis, Galbae autem vis occidisse.

xxv. Fuerunt etiam in oratorum numero mediocrium L. et Sp. Mummii fratres, quorum exstant
amborum orationes ; simplex quidem Lucius et
antiquus, Spurius autem nihilo ille quidem ornatior,
sed tamen astrictior ; fuit enim doctus ex disciplina
Stoicorum.   Multae sunt Sp. Albini orationes.   Sunt
etiam L. et C. Aureliorum Orestarum, quos aliquo
95 video in numero oratorum fuisse.   P. etiam Popilius
cum civis egregius tum non indisertus fuit ; Gaius
vero filius eius disertus, Gaiusque Tuditanus cum
omni vita atque victu excultus atque expolitus,
tum eius elegans est habitum etiam orationis genus.
Eodemque in genere est habitus is qui iniuria ac-
cepta fregit Ti. Gracchum patientia, civis in rebus
optimis constantissimus M. Octavius.

At vero M. Aemilius Lepidus, qui est Porcina
dictus, isdem temporibus fere quibus Galba, sed
paulo minor natu et summus orator est habitus et
fuit, ut apparet ex orationibus, scriptor sane bonus.
96 Hoc in oratore Latino primum mihi videtur et
levitas apparuisse illa Graecorum et verborum com-
prensio et iam artifex, ut ita dicam, stilus.   Hunc
studiose duo adulescentes ingeniosissimi et prope

manner as he speaks ; but powerful emotion is not
always present, and when it has subsided, all that force
and fire of oratory goes out.   This then is the reason 94
why the mind of Laelius still breathes in his writings,
the force of Galba has vanished.

" Reckoned in the ranks of orators of moderate
ability were also the two brothers Lucius and Spurius
Mummius, from both of whom there are orations
extant ; Lucius, simple and archaic, Spurius no more
elaborated, but more concise, since he was trained
in the school of Stoicism.   The orations of Spurius
Albinus are numerous ; numerous also the orations
of Lucius and Gaius Aurelius Orestes, who, I find,
held a modest place in the ranks of orators.   Publius 95
Popilius too was at once an outstanding figure in
public life and a speaker not unskilled ; his son
Gaius however was a really able speaker.   Gaius
Tuditanus in his whole personality and way of life
was a man of culture and polish, with which his
finished style of oratory was felt to be in agreement.
Of similar type was esteemed the man who, after
suffering affront at the hands of Tiberius Gracchus,
persisted until he broke him,—Marcus Octavius, a
patriot unswerving in his loyalty to the cause of the
best.

" But more significant was Marcus Aemilius
Lepidus, called Porcina, a contemporary of Galba,
though somewhat younger.   He was accounted a
great orator, and, as appears from his speeches, was
in fact a good writer.   In him appears, I think, for 96
the first time that smoothness of diction and periodic
sentence-form which is characteristic of Greek models,
and in fine the artistic pen, if I may so call it.   Devoted auditors of his were two young men of almost

aequales C. Carbo et Ti. Gracchus audire soliti sunt;
de quibus iam dicendi locus erit cum de senioribus
pauca dixero. Q. enim Pompeius non contemptus
orator temporibus illis fuit, qui summos honores
homo per se cognitus sine ulla commendatione
97 maiorum est adeptus. Tum L. Cassius multum
potuit non eloquentia, sed dicendo tamen; homo
non liberalitate, ut alii, sed ipsa tristitia et severitate
popularis, cuius quidem legi tabellariae M. Antius
Briso[1] tribunus plebis diu restitit, M. Lepido consule
adiuvante; eaque res P. Africano vituperationi fuit,
quod eius auctoritate de sententia deductus Briso[1]
putabatur. Tum duo Caepiones multum clientes
consilio et lingua, plus auctoritate tamen et gratia
sublevabant. Sex. Pompei sunt scripta nec nimis
extenuata, quamquam veterum est similis, et plena
98 prudentiae. xxvi. P. Crassum valde probatum oratorem isdem fere temporibus accepimus, qui et
ingenio valuit et studio et habuit quasdam etiam
domesticas disciplinas. Nam et cum summo illo
oratore Ser. Galba, cuius Gaio filio filiam suam col-
locaverat, affinitate sese devinxerat et cum esset
P. Muci filius fratremque haberet P. Scaevolam,
domi ius civile cognoverat. In eo industriam constat
summam fuisse maximamque gratiam, cum et con-
99 suleretur plurimum et diceret. Horum aetatibus

---

[1] Briso *L*, Restio *Martha.*

equal age and both of surpassing talent, Gaius Carbo
and Tiberius Gracchus, of whom I shall find a place to
speak presently, after I have said a little about their
seniors. Of these Quintus Pompeius was for his
time no mean orator, a man who gained recognition
on his own merits, and with no recommendation of
ancestry attained to the highest honours. Of the 97
same time was Lucius Cassius, whose words, though
he was not eloquent, exercised great influence. He
was a favourite of the people, not because of a free
and genial disposition, but for his very harshness and
severity. His ballot law was long opposed by the
tribune Marcus Antius Briso with the help of Marcus
Lepidus, then consul, and it became a matter of
reproach to Publius Africanus that Briso was believed
to have withdrawn his opposition to it through the
influence of Africanus. Then also the two Caepiones
served ably the needs of their clients with their
advice and with their pleas in court, and still more by
their influence and standing. Of Sextus Pompeius
there are writings extant, not too bald, though they
suggest an earlier time, and full of sound sense. Pub- 98
lius Crassus at about the same time was, we are told,
an orator highly esteemed, who to native ability added
zealous study, and some disciplines he possessed too
as by right of birth and family. For on the one hand
he had established family ties with the famous orator
Servius Galba, to whose son Gaius he had given
his daughter in marriage, and on the other, as being
the son of Publius Mucius and brother of Publius
Scaevola, he had learned the civil law in his own
home. He was clearly a man of remarkable industry
and of great popularity, much in demand for his
legal advice and active as a pleader. Associated in 99

adiuncti duo C. Fannii C. et M. filii fuerunt ; quorum
Gai filius, qui consul cum Domitio fuit, unam orationem de sociis et nomine Latino contra Gracchum
reliquit sane et bonam et nobilem.

Tum Atticus : Quid ergo ? estne ista Fanni ?
nam varia opinio pueris nobis erat. Alii a C. Persio
litterato homine scriptam esse aiebant, illo quem
significat valde doctum esse Lucilius ; alii multos
nobilis, quod quisque potuisset, in illam orationem
contulisse.

100 Tum ego : Audivi equidem ista, inquam, de
maioribus natu, sed numquam sum adductus ut
crederem ; eamque suspicionem propter hanc causam credo fuisse, quod Fannius in mediocribus oratoribus habitus esset, oratio autem vel optima esset
illo quidem tempore orationum omnium. Sed nec
eiusmodi est ut a pluribus confusa videatur—unus
enim sonus est totius orationis et idem stilus—nec
de Persio reticuisset Gracchus, cum ei[1] Fannius de
Menelao Maratheno et de ceteris obiecisset ; praesertim cum Fannius numquam sit habitus elinguis.
Nam et causas defensitavit et tribunatus eius arbitrio
et auctoritate P. Africani gestus non obscurus fuit.

101 Alter autem C. Fannius M. filius, C. Laeli gener, et
moribus et ipso genere dicendi durior. Is soceri
instituto, quem, quia cooptatus in augurum col-

---

[1] ei *Gruter*, et *L.*

---

[a] Cicero in two letters to Atticus (12. 5, 3 and 16. 13 c)
asks for clarification concerning the Fannii. See Tyrrell's
note, vol. v. p. 100. There was in fact but one C. Fannius,
son of Marcus (*CIL*, i. 650).

time with these were the two Fannii, both with the
surname Gaius, sons of Gaius and Marcus.[a] Of them
the son of Gaius, who was consul with Domitius, has
left one oration concerning the allies and the Latin
name against Gracchus, which is very good and well
known."

Here Atticus interrupted : " How about that ?
Is it really the work of Fannius ? For I recall that in
my boyhood there were various opinions concerning
it. Some held that it was written by Gaius Persius,
the grammarian and scholar, the one to whom
Lucilius refers as a man of vast learning ; others that
many of the nobles contributed what each one could
to its composition."

" Yes, I have heard that story from our elders," I 100
replied, " but I never could be persuaded to believe
it, and I surmise that the suspicion arose for the
reason that Fannius was accounted only a mediocre
orator, whereas the oration is quite the best of all of
that time. But neither is it of such character that it
could plausibly have been a composite product (for
the tone and style of the oration is uniform throughout), nor would Gracchus have been silent about
Persius when Fannius reproached him with using the
help of Menelaus of Marathus and other teachers.
No, I cannot believe it, especially since Fannius was
never regarded as without a ready tongue. He
defended cases in the courts, and his tribuneship,
carried through under the patronage and authority
of Publius Africanus, was in no wise obscure. The 101
other Gaius Fannius, son of Marcus, son-in-law of
Gaius Laelius, was a man of more severity both of
character and of oratorical style. Following the
suggestion and example of his father-in-law, of whom

legium non erat, non admodum diligebat, praesertim
cum ille Q. Scaevolam sibi minorem natu generum
praetulisset, cui tamen Laelius se excusans non
genero minori dixit se illud, sed maiori filiae detulisse,
is tamen instituto Laeli Panaetium audiverat. Eius
omnis in dicendo facultas historia ipsius non inele-
ganter scripta perspici potest, quae neque nimis est
102 infans neque perfecte diserta. Mucius autem augur,
quod pro se opus erat, ipse dicebat, ut de pecuniis
repetundis contra T. Albucium. Is oratorum in
numero non fuit, iuris civilis intellegentia atque
omni prudentiae genere praestitit. L. Coelius Antipater scriptor, quem ad modum videtis, fuit ut
temporibus illis luculentus, iuris valde peritus,
multorum etiam ut L. Crassi magister.

103   xxvii. Utinam in Ti. Graccho Gaioque Carbone
talis mens ad rem publicam bene gerendam fuisset,
quale ingenium ad bene dicendum fuit ; profecto
nemo his viris gloria praestitisset. Sed eorum alter
propter turbulentissimum tribunatum, ad quem ex
invidia foederis Numantini bonis iratus accesserat,

---

a Concerning Panaetius see 114 and note. The structure
of this sentence with its ambiguous pronominal relations is
commented on by Quint. 7. 9, 12. It is a nice example
of language following loosely the suggestions of the thought
as they occur to the writer, probably dictating to a secretary.
To punctuate the Latin text with dashes and marks of

however he was not particularly fond, because he had
not been elected to the college of augurs on his
nomination, more especially since Laelius had preferred his younger son-in-law Quintus Scaevola to him,
—a choice for which, by the way, Laelius made
jesting excuse that he had proffered that honour not
to his younger son-in-law, but to his elder daughter
—this Fannius, I say, following nevertheless the
suggestion and example of Laelius, had listened to
the instruction of Panaetius.[a] His abilities as a
speaker may be discerned from his history written
with considerable finish ; it is not devoid of art nor
again really eloquent. As for Mucius the Augur, his 102
oratory was adequate for his own defence, as for
example in his reply to Titus Albucius on the charge
of extortion. He was not reckoned among orators,
but in understanding of the civil law and in all
statesmanlike wisdom he was supreme. Lucius
Coelius Antipater was, as you are aware, a writer
accounted brilliant for his time, a man deeply learned
in the law and the teacher of many, as for instance of
Lucius Crassus.[b]

" Would that Tiberius Gracchus and Gaius Carbo 103
had possessed minds as well disposed to the right
conduct of affairs of state as they possessed genius for
eloquence ; surely none would have surpassed them
in renown. The one, because of his revolutionary
tribuneship, to which office he came in anger at the
nobility because of the animosities provoked by
rejection of the treaty with the Numantines, was put

parenthesis conveys a false sense of order and plan. Similar
examples in 106 and 140.
[b] The orator, principal interlocutor in the *de Oratore*,
discussed below in 143.

ab ipsa re publica est interfectus; alter propter
perpetuam in populari ratione levitatem morte
voluntaria se a severitate iudicum vindicavit. Sed
104 fuit uterque summus orator. Atque hoc memoria
patrum teste dicimus; nam et Carbonis et Gracchi
habemus orationes nondum satis splendidas verbis,
sed acutas prudentiaeque plenissimas. Fuit Gracchus diligentia Corneliae matris a puero doctus et
Graecis litteris eruditus. Nam semper habuit ex-
quisitos e Graecia magistros, in eis iam adulescens
Diophanem Mytilenaeum Graeciae temporibus illis
disertissimum. Sed ei[1] breve tempus ingeni augendi
et declarandi fuit.
105 Carbo, quoi[2] vita suppeditavit, est in multis
iudiciis causisque cognitus. Hunc qui audierant
prudentes homines, in quibus familiaris noster L.
Gellius, qui se illi contubernalem in consulatu fuisse
narrabat, canorum oratorem et volubilem et satis
acrem atque eundem et vehementem et valde dulcem
et perfacetum fuisse dicebat; addebat industrium
etiam et diligentem et in exercitationibus commenta-
tionibusque multum operae solitum esse ponere.

---

[1] ei *Lambinus*, et *L.*
[2] quoi *Friedrich*, quo *L.*

---

[a] The consul C. Hostilius Mancinus, in order to save his
army from annihilation, had signed a humiliating treaty with
the people of Numantia in Spain (137 B.C.), which the senate
annulled. Gracchus as quaestor had negotiated the treaty
and had in fact saved from destruction the whole Roman
force.

In saying that Tiberius was put to death " by the state
itself " Cicero, with gross partisanship, adopts the view that
the violence and lawless activity of the senatorial party, led
by Scipio Nasica, represented the true ultimate state (*ipsa*

to death by uprising of the state itself.[a] The other
paid the penalty for a consistent record of frivolous
demagogy with a self-inflicted death, which alone
saved him from the severity of a court of justice.
Both were orators of the first rank, a judgement 104
which I base on the evidence of our fathers who heard
them; for the orations which we possess of both
Carbo and Gracchus do not yet attain to any brilliancy of language, but they are acute and thoughtful.   Gracchus, thanks to the affectionate pains of
his mother Cornelia, had been trained from boyhood
and was thoroughly grounded in Greek letters. He
had always enjoyed the instruction of Greek teachers
carefully chosen, among whom from his early manhood was Diophanes of Mytilene, accounted the ablest
speaker of Greece in that day.[b] But his time for
developing his talent and for showing it was short.

" Carbo, who lived a longer life, came to be known 105
by participation in many public trials and civil suits.
Men who had heard him speak and were competent
to judge, such as my friend Lucius Gellius, who used
to refer to himself as an aide-de-camp to Carbo in his
consulship, characterized him as an orator of good
voice, ready, and with considerable vigour of manner,
and that furthermore along with vehemence he
possessed much charm and an engaging humour.
He said too that he was industrious, painstaking, and
in the habit of devoting much attention to declama-

republica), as contrasted with the established and legal
government of the moment, which had refused to take any
extraordinary measures against Tiberius (Plut. *Tib.* 19).
  [b] For the development of Roman oratory it is significant
that the teachers of the Gracchi, Diophanes here mentioned,
and the teacher of C. Gracchus, Menelaus of Marathus
(100), were both Asiatic Greeks.

106 Hic optimus illis temporibus est patronus habitus
eoque forum tenente plura fieri iudicia coeperunt.
Nam et quaestiones perpetuae hoc adulescente constitutae sunt quae antea nullae fuerunt—L. enim
Piso tribunus plebis legem primus de pecuniis repetundis Censorino et Manilio consulibus tulit ; ipse
etiam Piso et causas egit et multarum legum aut
auctor aut dissuasor fuit, isque et orationes reliquit,
quae iam evanuerunt, et annalis sane exiliter scriptos
—et iudicia populi, quibus aderat Carbo, iam magis
patronum desiderabant, tabella data ; quam legem
L. Cassius Lepido et Mancino consulibus tulit.

107 XXVIII. Vester etiam D. Brutus M. filius, ut ex
familiari eius L. Accio poeta sum audire solitus, et
dicere non inculte solebat et erat cum litteris Latinis
tum etiam Graecis ut temporibus illis eruditus.
Quae tribuebat idem Accius etiam Q. Maximo L.
Paulli nepoti ; et vero ante Maximum illum Scipionem, quo duce privato Ti. Gracchus occisus esset,
cum omnibus in rebus vehementem tum acrem
108 aiebat in dicendo fuisse. Tum etiam P. Lentulus
ille princeps ad rem publicam dumtaxat quod opus
esset satis habuisse eloquentiae dicitur ; isdemque

---

[a] The *quaestiones perpetuae* was a standing court for the
investigation and trial of cases involving the sovereignty cf
the state (*delicta publica*). Before its establishment in
149 B.C. each case had been brought before the assembly of
the people or had been referred to a specially appointed
commission or court. *Cf.* Madvig, *Verfassung*, ii. p. 306.

tory exercises and compositions. He was accounted 106
the best advocate of his time. During his supremacy
in the forum there was a marked increase in the
number of cases coming to trial. This was due in
part to the establishment in his youth of the standing
court for criminal cases, which had not existed
before [a];—for it was Lucius Piso who as tribune of
the people first passed the law of procedure in cases
of maladministration and extortion, in the consulship
of Censorinus and Manilius. Piso himself, I should
say in passing, was the advocate or opponent of many
measures, and left orations which have now quite
faded from memory, as well as Annals written in a
bald dry style;—in part also it was due to the circumstance that criminal trials before the people, in
which Carbo was often retained, made the assistance
of an attorney more important, now that verdicts
were rendered by secret ballot, a provision which
Lucius Cassius passed in the consulship of Lepidus
and Mancinus.

" Your relative too, Decimus Brutus, son of Marcus, 107
as I used to hear from his friend Lucius Accius the
poet, was a speaker not without finish, and was for his
time well versed in both Latin and Greek letters.
The same praise Accius accorded to Quintus Maximus,
grandson of Lucius Paullus. Earlier in point of time
than Maximus, that scion of the Scipios, who without
holding public office headed the movement leading to
the assassination of Tiberius Gracchus, was, he said,
as in other respects a man of strong feeling and
action, so also in speaking sharp and vigorous. Then 108
too, Publius Lentulus, the famous chief of the senate,
is reported to have possessed an eloquence adequate
at least for his participation in affairs of state. Lucius

97

temporibus L. Furius Philus perbene Latine loqui
putabatur litteratiusque quam ceteri ; P. Scaevola
valde prudenter et acute ; paulo etiam copiosius
nec multo minus prudenter M'. Manilius. Appi
Claudi volubilis, sed paulo fervidior oratio. Erat in
aliquo numero etiam M. Fulvius Flaccus et C. Cato,
Africani sororis filius, mediocres oratores ; etsi Flacci
scripta sunt, sed ut studiosi litterarum. Flacci
autem aemulus P. Decius fuit, non infans ille
quidem, sed ut vita sic oratione etiam turbulentus.
109 M. Drusus C. f., qui in tribunatu C. Gracchum
collegam iterum tribunum fregit,[1] vir et oratione
gravis et auctoritate, eique proxime adiunctus
C. Drusus frater fuit. Tuus etiam gentilis, Brute,
M. Pennus facile[2] agitavit in tribunatu, paulum[3]
C. Gracchum aetate antecedens ; fuit enim M.
Lepido et L. Oreste consulibus quaestor Gracchus,
tribunus Pennus, illius Marci filius, qui cum Q.
Aelio consul fuit ; sed is omnia summa sperans
aedilicius est mortuus. Nam de T. Flaminino,
quem ipse vidi, nihil accepi nisi Latine diligenter
locutum.

[1] fregit *Pisanus*, fecit *L*.
[2] facile *L*, facete *Lambinus*.
[3] paulum C. Gracchum *L*, C. Gracchum paulum *vulg.*

---

[a] The mention of this earlier representative of the Junian
family and the precise fixing of his time and parentage are
a complimentary gesture to Brutus, his kinsman. Editors,
down to the most recent, have emended and transposed in
order to put more meaning into it, but it is hazardous to
touch the well-attested idiom *facile agitare*. In two other
examples (Porcius Licinus in *Vita Terenti*, and Terence,
Adelph. 501) it means " to live easily," " to be prosperous,"
and here with slight transference, " to be successful." As
an orator Pennus is characterized only by the implications

Furius Philus of the same period was considered a
speaker very choice in his Latinity and of more
scholarly training than others. Publius Scaevola
spoke with great legal and political wisdom and
was acute in argument. More abundant in expression and not much inferior in knowledge and
experience was Manius Manilius. The oratory of
Appius Claudius was fluent but rather too fervid. A
certain place too was granted to Marcus Fulvius
Flaccus, and to Gaius Cato, son of the sister of
Africanus, both orators of very moderate gifts.
There are, to be sure, extant writings of Flaccus, but
they show the student of letters rather than the
orator. His political rival was Publius Decius, not
without some gift of eloquence, but as in his life so
in his language he was undisciplined and turbulent.
Marcus Drusus, son of Gaius, who as tribune frus- 109
trated the designs of his colleague Gaius Gracchus in
his second tribuneship, was a man of weight and
influence both in speech and in personality. Closely
associated with him in rank was his brother Gaius
Drusus. Your kinsman too, Brutus, Marcus (Junius)
Pennus made a successful record in his tribuneship[a];
he was a little older than Gaius Gracchus, who was
quaestor in the consulship of Marcus Lepidus and
Lucius Orestes, when Pennus, son of the Marcus
Pennus who was consul with Quintus Aelius, was
tribune ; but with prospect of attaining all the
highest honours he died after his aedileship. As for
Titus Flamininus, whom I myself have seen, I know
nothing more than that he was accounted a painstaking user of the mother tongue.

of a successful tribunate, the great promise of which was
frustrated by an untimely death.

110 XXIX. His adiuncti sunt C. Curio M. Scaurus P.
Rutilius C. Gracchus. De Scauro et Rutilio breviter
licet dicere, quorum neuter summi oratoris habuit
laudem, et uterque in multis causis versatus. Erat
in quibusdam laudandis viris, etiam si maximi
ingeni non essent, probabilis tamen industria;
quamquam his quidem non omnino ingenium,
sed oratorium ingenium defuit. Neque enim refert
videre quid dicendum sit, nisi id queas solute et
suaviter dicere; ne id quidem satis est, nisi id
quod dicitur fit voce voltu motuque conditius.
111 Quid dicam opus esse doctrina? sine qua etiam
si quid bene dicitur adiuvante natura, tamen id,
quia fortuito fit, semper paratum esse non potest.
In Scauri oratione, sapientis hominis et recti, gravitas summa et naturalis quaedam inerat auctoritas, non ut causam, sed ut testimonium dicere
112 putares cum pro reo diceret. Hoc dicendi genus
ad patrocinia mediocriter aptum videbatur, ad
senatoriam vero sententiam, cuius erat ille princeps,
vel maxime; significabat enim non prudentiam
solum, sed quod maxime rem continebat, fidem.
Habebat hoc a natura ipsa, quod a doctrina non
facile posset; quamquam huius quoque ipsius rei,
quem ad modum scis, praecepta sunt. Huius et
orationes sunt et tres ad L. Fufidium libri scripti

" Associated with the foregoing were Gaius Curio, 110
Marcus Scaurus, Publius Rutilius, Gaius Gracchus.
Concerning Scaurus and Rutilius let me speak briefly.
Neither enjoyed a reputation for great oratory,
though both were active in many private suits.
There were, then as now, some men of high reputation who, lacking great talent, yet through their
industry won for themselves recognition. I do not
say that these two were quite without talent, but
they lacked talent for oratory. For it is not enough
to discern what is to be said unless you have the
ability to say it fluently and with some charm ;
nor even is this enough unless what is said is recom-
mended by some grace of voice, facial expression,
and action. Need I speak also of the need of 111
theoretical training ? For even if without it one succeeds in saying something good with nature's help,
yet because this is fortuitous it cannot always
be at one's disposal. In the oratory of Scaurus, a
wise man and upright, there was great dignity and
a certain innate authority, so that when he spoke
for a client you had the feeling of one giving testimony, not of one pleading a case. His manner 112
of speaking seemed little suited to the part of a
pleader at the bar, though for the expression of an
opinion in the senate, where his place was first, it
was perfect. It conveyed the impression not only
of experience and wisdom, but of that quality which
holds the secret of success, trustworthiness. Thus
he possessed by nature that which art could not
easily lend, although as you know the books give
precepts for that too. We have orations of his and
the three books about his own life addressed to
Lucius Fufidius ; very well worth reading, though

de vita ipsius acta sane utiles, quos nemo legit ; at
Cyri vitam et disciplinam legunt, praeclaram illam
quidem, sed neque tam nostris rebus aptam nec
113 tamen Scauri laudibus anteponendam. xxx. Ipse
etiam Fufidius in aliquo patronorum numero fuit.

Rutilius autem in quodam tristi et severo genere
dicendi versatus est. Erat uterque natura vehemens et acer ; itaque cum una consulatum petivis-
sent, non ille solum, qui repulsam tulerat, accusavit
ambitus designatum competitorem, sed Scaurus
etiam absolutus Rutilium in iudicium vocavit.
Multaque opera multaque industria Rutilius fuit,
quae erat propterea gratior, quod idem magnum
114 munus de iure respondendi sustinebat. Sunt eius
orationes ieiunae ; multa praeclara de iure ; doctus
vir et Graecis litteris eruditus, Panaeti auditor,
prope perfectus in Stoicis ; quorum peracutum et
artis plenum orationis genus scis tamen esse exile
nec satis populari assensioni accommodatum. Itaque illa, quae propria est huius disciplinae, philosophorum de se ipsorum opinio firma in hoc viro et
115 stabilis inventa est. Qui cum innocentissimus in
iudicium vocatus esset, quo iudicio convulsam penitus scimus esse rem publicam, cum essent eo tempore eloquentissimi viri L. Crassus et M. Antonius
consulares, eorum adhibere neutrum voluit. Dixit

---

[a] The *Cyropedia* of Xenophon, which is thought of loosely
as a biography analogous to Scaurus's life of himself. As an
example and model of early Attic style the young Roman
Atticists, who are dealt with later on, had given it a new
vogue.
[b] The famous Stoic, associate of the younger Scipio and
his circle, whose treatise of ethics formed the basis of Cicero's
de Officiis. In this form it has exercised a great and

no one reads them. They prefer nowadays to read
the life and training of Cyrus,[a] a splendid book no
doubt, but not so suited to our conditions and not
deserving to be preferred to Scaurus's encomium of
himself. This Fufidius too had some place in the 113
ranks of advocates.

" As for Rutilius, he kept to a style of speaking
sombre and severe. Both men were by nature intense in feeling and sharp. They showed it when
they were candidates at the same time for the consulship ; for not only did Rutilius, who was defeated,
accuse his rival, the consul elect, of bribery, but
Scaurus on acquittal brought similar suit against
Rutilius. Rutilius was a man of many engagements
and of much forensic activity, which was the more
appreciated because at the same time he gave his
services generously as a consulting jurist. His 114
orations are dry ; many admirable passages on
questions of law ; a man of learning and wide reading in Greek ; a pupil of Panaetius,[b] all but perfectly trained in the doctrines of the Stoics. Their
style of oratory is acute and systematic, as you
know, but meagre and not well suited to winning
the assent of a popular audience. That familiar
dogma of self-sufficiency which is characteristic of
this sect of philosophy was in him exemplified in its
firmest and most unswerving form ; so that when, 115
though perfectly innocent, he was brought to that
trial which fairly rent the state in twain, he refused
to invoke the aid of either of the two greatest orators
of the time, Lucius Crassus and Marcus Antonius,
both of consular rank. He spoke himself in his own

incalculable effect upon conduct and upon ethical theory.
Cf. Zielinski, *Cicero im Wandel d. Jahrhunderte.*

ipse pro sese et pauca C. Cotta, quod sororis erat
filius—et is quidem tamen ut orator, quamquam
erat admodum adulescens—et Q. Mucius enucleate
ille quidem et polite, ut solebat, nequaquam autem
ea vi atque copia quam genus illud iudici et magni-
116 tudo causae postulabat. Habeamus[1] igitur in Stoicis
oratoribus Rutilium, Scaurum in antiquis ; utrumque
tamen laudemus, quoniam per illos ne haec quidem
in civitate genera hac oratoria laude caruerunt.
Volo enim ut in scaena sic etiam in foro non eos
modo laudari, qui celeri motu et difficili utantur,
sed eos etiam quos statarios appellant, quorum sit
illa simplex in agendo veritas, non molesta.

117 XXXI. Et quoniam Stoicorum est facta mentio,
Q. Aelius Tubero fuit illo tempore, L. Paulli nepos ;
nullo in oratorum numero, sed vita severus et congruens cum ea disciplina quam colebat, paulo etiam
durior ; qui quidem in triumviratu iudicaverit contra
P. Africani avunculi sui testimonium vacationem
augures quo minus iudiciis operam darent non habere ;
sed ut vita sic oratione durus incultus horridus ; itaque honoribus maiorum respondere non potuit. Fuit
autem constans civis et fortis et in primis Graccho
molestus, quod indicat Gracchi in eum oratio. Sunt

[1] habeamus *Madvig (cf. 146)*, habemus *L.*

defence, and Gaius Cotta, the son of his sister, added a few words—the latter to be sure as an orator, though then very young. Quintus Mucius also spoke, simply but with finish, as was his wont, but with nothing of that fire and fullness which a trial of that kind and the importance of the case demanded. To conclude then, let us regard Rutilius as a repre- 116 sentative of the Stoic, Scaurus of the old Roman school of oratory, and let us bestow praise upon both as showing that these two types of oratory have not been without a place of distinction in our public life. In dwelling upon them it has been my desire to do for the forum what is done for the stage, that is to award praise not only to those whose acting is marked by rapid movement and complicated effects, but also to those who are called 'stationary,' whose performance displays a simple realism, free from exaggeration.

"While we are on the Stoics mention should be 117 made of Quintus Aelius Tubero of the same period, the grandson of Lucius Paullus. He had no place in the ranks of orators, but his way of life was severe and congruent with that philosophy which he cherished, even somewhat more rigid. It was a mark of his character, that as triumvir presiding in court, he rendered decision against the testimony of his uncle, Publius Africanus, that the augurs had no right of exemption from service as judges in the courts of law. But like his life, so his language was harsh, untrained, and rough, so that in the career of office he did not attain to the rank of his ancestors. He was, however, a bold and steadfast patriot, and a constant source of irritation to Gracchus, as the speech of Gracchus against him shows. There are

etiam in Gracchum Tuberonis ; is fuit mediocris in dicendo, doctissimus in disputando.

118   Tum Brutus : Quam hoc idem in nostris contingere intellego quod in Graecis, ut omnes fere Stoici prudentissimi in disserendo sint et id arte faciant sintque architecti paene verborum, idem traducti a disputando ad dicendum inopes reperiantur.   Unum excipio Catonem, in quo perfectissimo Stoico summam eloquentiam non desiderem ; quam exiguam in Fannio, ne in Rutilio quidem magnam, in Tuberone nullam video fuisse.

119   Et ego : Non, inquam, Brute, sine causa, propterea quod istorum in dialecticis omnis cura consumitur ; vagum illud orationis et fusum et multiplex non adhibetur genus.   Tuus autem avunculus, quem ad modum scis, habet a Stoicis id quod ab illis petendum fuit, sed dicere didicit a dicendi magistris eorumque more se exercuit.   Quod si omnia a philosophis essent petenda, Peripateticorum institutis commodius

120 fingeretur oratio.   Quo magis tuum, Brute, iudicium probo, qui eorum [id est ex vetere Academia][1] philosophorum sectam secutus es, quorum in doctrina atque praeceptis disserendi ratio coniungitur cum suavitate dicendi et copia ; quamquam ea ipsa Peripateticorum Academicorumque consuetudo in ratione dicendi talis est ut nec perficere oratorem possit ipsa per sese nec sine ea orator esse perfectus. Nam ut Stoicorum astrictior est oratio aliquantoque

[1] *secl. Lambinus.*

---

  a Cato, the younger, who was, or at the time of writing was believed to be, still living. He took his own life after the victory of Caesar at Thapsus in the adjacent city of Utica (April, 46 b.c.).

  b On the philosophy of Brutus see 149 and note there.

also speeches of Tubero against Gracchus. They reveal him as a mediocre speaker, but very able in argument."

Thereupon Brutus : " Remarkable how one ob- 118 serves the same thing in our countrymen as in the Greeks, that practically all adherents of the Stoic school are very able in precise argument ; they work by rule and system and are fairly architects in the use of words ; but transfer them from discussion to oratorical presentation, and they are found poor and unresourceful. One exception I make, that is Cato, in whom, though a Stoic through and through, I feel no craving for more perfect eloquence.[a] In Fannius it was slight, even in Rutilius not great, in Tubero nothing whatever."

" There is good reason for it, Brutus," I replied, 119 " because all their attention is absorbed in dialectic ; they pay no attention to the qualities of style which range freely, which are discursive and varied. Your uncle, as you know, took from Stoicism that which it had to offer, but he learned to speak from masters of speaking and trained himself in their methods. If however one were to seek all his training from philosophy he would shape his style more effectively by the precepts of the Peripatetic school. The more therefore I praise your judgement, Brutus, 120 who have followed that school of philosophers in whose teaching and precepts the method of logical discussion is joined with charm and fullness of presentation.[b] However, the actual habit of Peripatetics and Academics with respect to oratorical discourse is such that it could never produce the perfect orator, nor on the other hand could the perfect orator be produced without it. Stoic oratory

contractior quam aures populi requirunt, sic illorum
liberior et latior quam patitur consuetudo iudiciorum
et fori. Quis enim uberior in dicendo Platone?
121 Iovem sic [ut]¹ aiunt philosophi, si Graece loquatur,
loqui. Quis Aristotele nervosior, Theophrasto dulcior? Lectitavisse Platonem studiose, audivisse
etiam Demosthenes dicitur idque apparet ex genere
et granditate verborum; dicit etiam in quadam
epistula hoc ipse de sese; sed et huius oratio in
philosophiam tralata pugnacior, ut ita dicam, videtur
et illorum in iudicia pacatior.
122 XXXII. Nunc reliquorum oratorum aetates, si placet, et gradus persequamur.

Nobis vero, ⟨inquit⟩ Atticus, et vehementer quidem, ut pro Bruto etiam respondeam.

Curio fuit igitur eiusdem aetatis fere sane illustris
orator, cuius de ingenio ex orationibus eius existimari potest; sunt enim et aliae et pro Ser. Fulvio
de incestu nobilis oratio. Nobis quidem pueris haec
omnium optima putabatur, quae vix iam comparet
in hac turba novorum voluminum.
123 Praeclare, inquit Brutus, teneo qui istam turbam
voluminum effecerit.

Et ego, inquam, intellego, Brute, quem dicas;
certe enim et boni aliquid attulimus iuventuti,
magnificentius quam fuerat genus dicendi et orna-

---

¹ *secl. Schütz,* sic ut ⟨illum⟩ *Reis.*

ᵃ The writer of the fifth letter attributed to Demosthenes
(Bekker, ii. p. 307) poses as a pupil of Plato. The letter
is certainly not by Demosthenes, whether a genuine letter
or not. The controversies between rhetoricians and philosophers yielded many spurious documents to support one
side or the other (*cf.* Blass, *Attische Beredsamkeit,* iii. p.
454).

is too closely knit and too compact for a popular audience ; theirs again is too free and discursive for the usage of court and forum. Where will you find a writer of greater richness than Plato ? Jupiter 121 would speak with his tongue, they say, if he spoke Greek. Where will you find a style more vigorous than Aristotle's, more charming than that of Theophrastus ? It is reported that Demosthenes read Plato diligently, even that he was his pupil—and this too is apparent from the character and sublimity of his vocabulary ; in fact he himself is authority for the statement in one of his letters.[a] But his style, if transferred to philosophy, would seem too pugnacious, if I may use the word ; theirs, transferred to the courts, too pacific.

"Now let me go on, if you like, to review the 122 periods and ranks of the orators that still remain."

"By all means," said Atticus ; "it is most emphatically what we want, if I may speak for Brutus as well as for myself."

"Well then, Curio was an orator of about the same time and quite a distinguished one too. His talent can be judged from his orations, among which stands out as particularly well-known his speech for Servius Fulvius on the charge of incest. In my boyhood this was considered a masterpiece, though it has almost disappeared from sight in the mass of new volumes of to-day."

"I can make a brilliant guess," said Brutus, "who 123 it is that is responsible for that mass (as you call it) of new volumes."

"I recognize very well, Brutus, to whom you refer. I have, I am sure, contributed some benefit to the rising generation in showing them a more elevated

tius ; et nocuimus fortasse, quod veteres orationes post nostras, non a me quidem—meis enim illas antepono—sed a plerisque legi sunt desitae.

Me numera,[1] inquit, in plerisque ; quamquam video mihi multa legenda iam te auctore, quae antea contemnebam.

124 Atqui haec, inquam, de incestu laudata oratio puerilis est locis multis—de amore, de tormentis, de rumore loci sane inanes, verum tamen nondum tritis nostrorum hominum auribus nec erudita civitate tolerabiles. Scripsit etiam alia non nulla et multa dixit et illustria et in numero patronorum fuit, ut eum mirer, cum et vita suppeditavisset et splendor ei non defuisset, consulem non fuisse.

125 XXXIII. Sed ecce in manibus vir et praestantissimo ingenio et flagranti studio et doctus a puero C. Gracchus. Noli enim putare quemquam, Brute, pleniorem aut uberiorem ad dicendum fuisse.

Et ille : Sic prorsus, inquit, existimo atque istum de superioribus paene solum lego.

Immo plane, inquam, Brute, legas censeo. Damnum enim illius immaturo interitu res Romanae 126 Latinaeque litterae fecerunt. Utinam non tam fratri pietatem quam patriae praestare voluisset ! Quam ille facile tali ingenio, diutius si vixisset, vel paternam esset vel avitam gloriam consecutus !

---

[1] me numera *Weidner*, enumera *L.*

and more elaborated style, and perhaps too some harm, in that the older orations in comparison with mine have ceased to be read by the majority ; not by me however, since I prefer them to my own."

" Place me among that majority," replied Brutus, " though I recognize now, in view of what you have told us, that I have much to read which I looked down upon before."

" But to come back : This much praised oration on 124 incest is in many places puerile ; whole sections about love, about torture, about rumour, quite inane ; and yet then to our unpractised ears and to the taste of an untrained public they were tolerable. Curio wrote not a little besides ; he was in much demand as a speaker, and prominent in the ranks of pleaders. One must wonder, since he enjoyed long life and was by no means obscure, that he never was consul.

" But now at length we come to a man of pre- 125 eminent talent, of intense application, of careful training from childhood, Gaius Gracchus. Do not imagine, Brutus, that anyone was ever more completely or more richly endowed for a career of eloquence than he."

" Yes," he replied, " that is exactly my judgement, and of our earlier orators he is almost the only one I read."

" Say not almost, but quite the only one, dear Brutus, and I shall approve your judgement. In his untimely death the Roman state and Latin letters suffered irreparable loss. Would that he had shown as 126 much loyalty to his country as to the memory of his brother. Had he lived longer, how easily with such talent would he have equalled the glory of his father

111

Eloquentia quidem nescio an habuisset parem
neminem. Grandis est verbis, sapiens sententiis,
genere toto gravis. Manus extrema non accessit
operibus eius ; praeclare incohata multa, perfecta
non plane. Legendus, inquam, est hic orator,
Brute, si quisquam alius, iuventuti ; non enim solum acuere sed etiam alere ingenium potest.

127 Huic successit aetati C. Galba, Ser. illius[1] eloquentissimi viri filius, P. Crassi eloquentis et iuris periti
gener. Laudabant hunc patres nostri, favebant
etiam propter patris memoriam, sed cecidit in cursu.
Nam rogatione Mamilia, Iugurthinae coniurationis
invidia, cum pro sese ipse dixisset, oppressus est.
Exstat eius peroratio, qui epilogus dicitur ; qui tanto
in honore pueris nobis erat ut eum etiam edisceremus.
Hic, qui in collegio sacerdotum esset, primus post
Romam conditam iudicio publico est condemnatus.

128 xxxiv. P. Scipio, qui est in consulatu mortuus, non
multum ille quidem nec saepe dicebat, sed et Latine
loquendo cuivis erat par et omnis sale facetiisque
superabat. Eius collega L. Bestia ⟨a⟩ bonis initiis
orsus tribunatus—nam P. Popilium vi C. Gracchi
expulsum sua rogatione restituit—vir et acer et non
indisertus, tristis exitus habuit consulatus. Nam

---

[1] Ser. illius *Reis*, Seruilius *L*.

---

[a] Cicero says later in the work (319) that he desires to give
advice and precept as well as an historical record. This
passage and some others savour of the treatises *de Imitatione*
such as we have in the fragments of Dionysius of Halicarnassus and in Quintilian 10. 1.

[b] A vivid account of popular resentment at this venal
jobbery is given by Sallust, *Jugurtha* 40. Cicero's
judgement (*invidia* and *invidiosa lege* just below) is sadly
partisan. It is well rebuked by Niebuhr (*Vorlesungen*, ii.
p. 313).

or grandfather! In eloquence at least, he would I think have found no equal. In diction he is elevated, in ideas wise and thoughtful, in his whole style earnest and impressive ; his writings have not received the last touch ; much shows brilliant beginnings, but lacks final perfection. Yes, Brutus, he if anyone is an orator for our youth to read.[a] He can give not only edge to their wits, but sustenance as well.

" Upon this period followed Gaius Galba, son of 127 the eloquent Servius, and son-in-law of Publius Crassus, who himself was eloquent and an able jurist. Galba's oratory received the praise of our fathers ; they liked him too for the memory of his father ; but he fell in the race. For brought to trial under the proposal of Mamilius, outgrowth of the invidious charges of conspiracy with Jugurtha, though he spoke in his own defence, he was convicted.[b] His peroration at that time, the so-called *Epilogue*, is still extant, and in my boyhood it was in such honour that I learned it by heart. In the whole history of Rome he was the first man belonging to a priestly college to be tried and found guilty by a public criminal court. Publius 128 Scipio,[c] the one who died in his consulship, did not speak much nor often, but in the purity of his Latinity he was the equal of anyone, and in wit and pleasantry he surpassed all. His colleague (in the consulship), Lucius Bestia, made a good beginning with his tribuneship—for by the measure which bears his name he recalled Publius Popilius, banished by the violence of Gaius Gracchus—a man of keen mind and not without skill as a speaker, but his consulship came to a melancholy end. For by that

[c] P. Scipio Nasica, cos. 111 B.C. son of the slayer of Tiberius Gracchus.

invidiosa lege Mamilia quaestorium[1] C. Galbam sacer-
dotem et quattuor consularis L. Bestiam C. Catonem
Sp. Albinum civemque praestantissimum L. Opimium,
Gracchi interfectorem, a populo absolutum, cum is
contra populi studium stetisset, Gracchani iudices
129 sustulerunt.   Huius dissimilis in tribunatu reliquaque
omni vita civis improbus C. Licinius Nerva non
indisertus fuit.   C. Fimbria temporibus isdem fere,
sed longius aetate provectus, habitus est sane, ut ita
dicam, truculentus[2] patronus asper maledicus ; genere
toto paulo fervidior atque commotior, diligentia
tamen et virtute animi atque vita bonus auctor in
senatu ; idem tolerabilis patronus nec rudis in iure
civili et cum virtute tum etiam ipso orationis genere
liber ; cuius orationes pueri legebamus, quas iam
130 reperire vix possumus.   Atque etiam acri ingenio et
sermone eleganti, valetudine incommoda C. Sextius
Calvinus fuit ; qui etsi, cum remiserant dolores
pedum, non deerat in causis, tamen id non saepe
faciebat.   Itaque consilio eius cum volebant homines
utebantur, patrocinio cum licebat.   Isdem temporibus M. Brutus, in quo magnum fuit, Brute, dedecus[3]
generi vestro, qui, cum tanto nomine esset patremque optimum virum habuisset et iuris peritissimum,
accusationem factitaverit, ut Athenis Lycurgus.   Is

[1] quaestorium *Kroll*, quaestio *L*.
[2] truculentus *Ernesti* (*cf. Quint. 11. 1, 3 trux atque
violentum genus dicendi*), luculentus *L*.
[3] dedecus *codd. det.*, genus *L*, decus *cod. Neapol. IV B 36*.

[a] Cicero does injustice to Lycurgus, a true patriot and,
like Demosthenes, a pillar of the anti-Macedonian party at
Athens.   The bitterness of his invective became traditional :
" he dipped his pen not in ink, but in blood " ($\theta\alpha\nu\acute{\alpha}\tau\varphi$).

invidious law of Mamilius, not only Gaius Galba, ex-quaestor of sacerdotal station, but also four ex-consuls, Lucius Bestia, Gaius Cato, Spurius Albinus, and most distinguished of all, Lucius Opimius, the slayer of Gracchus, who, though he had taken a stand against the popular cause, yet was absolved by the people—all these were deprived of civic rights by a court made up of the Gracchan judges. Wholly unlike Bestia in his tribuneship, and indeed 129 in every other aspect of his life, was Gaius Licinius Nerva, a bad citizen, though not unskilled as a speaker. Gaius Fimbria, at about the same time with these, though he lived much longer, was accounted a pleader of the truculent type, if I may use the word, harsh, abusive, and in his whole style and manner too fervid and excited; yet by reason of his thoroughness, the vigour of his mind and the purity of his life he was held in high esteem in the counsels of the senate. As a pleader he was tolerable, and not unlearned in the law; as in his character, so also in his style of speaking he was frank and open. In my boyhood we used to read his orations, which now one can scarcely find. Another man of keen 130 mind and careful speech, but of indifferent health, was Gaius Sextius Calvinus. Though he would not fail a client if his gout relaxed its tortures, yet he did not do it often, with the result that people availed themselves of his counsel when they would, of his help in court when they could. To the same time belonged Marcus Brutus, who was a blot on your family name, Brutus, in that, like Lycurgus at Athens,[a] he made a regular profession of prosecution, in spite of his distinguished name and father, who was so good a man and so able a jurisconsult. He never sought public office,

magistratus non petivit, sed fuit accusator vehemens
et molestus, ut facile cerneres naturale quoddam stir-
pis bonum degeneravisse vitio depravatae voluntatis.
131 Atque eodem tempore accusator de plebe L. Caesulenus fuit, quem ego audivi iam senem, cum ab L.
Sabellio[1] multam lege Aquilia damni iniuria[2] petivis-
set.   Non fecissem hominis paene infimi mentionem,
nisi iudicarem qui suspiciosius aut criminosius diceret
audivisse me neminem.   xxxv. Doctus etiam Graecis
T. Albucius vel potius paene Graecus.   Loquor ut
opinor; sed licet ex orationibus iudicare; fuit autem
Athenis adulescens, perfectus Epicurius evaserat,
minime aptum ad dicendum genus.
132 Iam Q. Catulus non antiquo illo more, sed hoc
nostro, nisi quid fieri potest perfectius, eruditus.
Multae litterae, summa non vitae solum atque
naturae sed orationis etiam comitas, incorrupta
quaedam Latini sermonis integritas; quae perspici
cum ex orationibus eius potest tum facillime ex
eo libro quem de consulatu et de rebus gestis suis
conscriptum molli et Xenophontio genere sermonis
misit ad A. Furium poetam, familiarem suum; qui
liber nihilo notior est quam illi tres, de quibus
ante dixi, Scauri libri.
133   Tum Brutus : Mihi quidem, inquit, nec iste notus
est nec illi; sed haec mea culpa est, numquam

---

[1] Sabellio *vulg.*, Sauelio *L*, Saufeio *Martha*.
[2] damni iniuria *Hotomann*, de iustitia *L* (*corruptela ex
compendio D I orta.   Cf. Gaium 3. 210*).

but as a prosecuting lawyer he was sharp-tongued and ugly. You could readily see how superior natural gifts derived from his stock had degenerated through a depraved choice of career. Another prosecutor of 131 this time, but of humble origin, was Lucius Caesulenus, whom in his old age I heard once when he brought suit for amercement against Lucius Sabellius, under the provisions of the *lex Aquilia* ' for damages and restitution.' I should scarcely have mentioned a man so nearly from the dregs of the profession were it not to say that I have never heard anyone who could make insinuation of guilt more cleverly and drive it home more effectively. Titus Albucius was learned in all things Greek, or rather you could call him almost a real Greek. I give you my opinion, but you may form your own judgement from his orations ; he spent his youth at Athens and turned out a complete Epicurean, a creed ill-suited to public speaking.

" I come now to Quintus Catulus, a man trained, 132 not in the old Roman style, but in our modern fashion, or if possible even more perfectly. He possessed wide reading, a natural courtesy, which showed itself in his style as well as in his life, an untainted purity of Latin diction. It can be seen in his orations, and especially in the book on his consulship and his own deeds, written in a smooth Xenophontean style and dedicated to his friend, the poet Aulus Furius,—a book unfortunately no better known than the three of Scaurus to which I alluded before."

Thereupon Brutus : " I must confess that I do not 133 know it, nor the work of Scaurus either. But I acknowledge that is my fault, though in fact neither one

enim in manus inciderunt. Nunc autem et a te
sumam et conquiram ista posthac curiosius.

Fuit igitur in Catulo sermo Latinus, quae laus
dicendi non mediocris ab oratoribus plerisque
neglecta est. Nam de sono vocis et suavitate
appellandarum litterarum, quoniam filium cognovisti, noli exspectare quid dicam. Quamquam
filius quidem non fuit in oratorum numero, sed non
deerat ei tamen in sententia dicenda cum prudentia
tum elegans quoddam et eruditum orationis genus.

134 Nec habitus est tamen pater ipse Catulus princeps
in numero patronorum, sed erat talis ut, cum quosdam audires qui tum erant praestantes, videretur
esse inferior, cum autem ipsum audires sine comparatione, non modo contentus esses, sed melius
non quaereres.

135 Q. Metellus Numidicus et eius collega M. Silanus
dicebant de re publica quod esset illis viris et consulari dignitati satis. M. Aurelius Scaurus non
saepe dicebat sed polite ; Latine vero in primis
est eleganter locutus. Quae laus eadem in A.
Albino bene loquendi fuit ; nam flamen Albinus
etiam in numero est habitus disertorum. Q. etiam
Caepio, vir acer et fortis, cui fortuna belli crimini,

136 invidia populi calamitati fuit. xxxvi. Tum etiam
C. L. Memmii fuerunt oratores mediocres, accusa-
tores acres atque acerbi ; itaque in iudicium capitis

118

ever chanced to come into my hands. Now, however, at your suggestion, I shall hunt them out more
carefully."

" As I was saying then, Catulus had a pure Latin
diction, no small merit of style, to which most
orators pay little attention. Concerning his voice
and the charm of his enunciation, you will not expect me to speak since you knew his son. The
latter to be sure was never esteemed an orator,
though he too in expressing himself in the senate
lacked neither practical wisdom nor a refined and
cultivated manner of speech. Nor was the father, 134
Catulus himself, accounted first in the ranks of
pleaders. He was one who might give you the impression of inferiority to other outstanding speakers
when you heard them speak together, but when
you heard him alone without opportunity of comparison, you would be more than satisfied and ask
for nothing better.

" Quintus Metellus Numidicus and his colleague 135
Marcus Silanus in deliberations of state spoke in
a manner befitting their character and the dignity
of their consular rank. Marcus Aurelius Scaurus
spoke with finish, but not often. For purity of
language he ranked among the first. A similar
reputation for excellence of diction was enjoyed by
Aulus Albinus. As for the flamen Albinus, he too
held a place in the ranks of eloquent speakers, as did
also Quintus Caepio, a brave and energetic man,
to whom the fortunes of war were imputed as a
crime against the state, and popular odium brought
him ruin. Of this time too were the brothers Gaius 136
and Lucius Memmius, mediocre orators ; as prosecutors keen and unsparing. They brought to trial

119

multos vocaverunt, pro reis non saepe dixerunt. Sp. Thorius satis valuit in populari genere dicendi, is qui agrum publicum vitiosa et inutili lege vectigali levavit. M. Marcellus Aesernini pater non ille quidem in patronis, sed et in promptis tamen et non inexercitatis ad dicendum fuit, ut filius eius
137 P. Lentulus. L. etiam Cotta praetorius in mediocrium oratorum numero dicendi non ita multum laude processerat, sed de industria cum verbis tum etiam ipso sono quasi subrustico persequebatur atque imitabatur antiquitatem.

Atque ego et in hoc ipso Cotta et in aliis pluribus intellego me non ita disertos homines et rettulisse in oratorum numerum et relaturum. Est enim propositum colligere eos qui hoc munere in civitate functi sint, ut tenerent oratorum locum ; quorum quidem quae fuerit ascensio et quam in omnibus rebus difficilis optimi perfectio atque absolutio ex eo
138 quod dicam existimari potest. Quam multi enim iam oratores commemorati sunt et quam diu in eorum enumeratione versamur, cum tamen spisse atque vix, ut dudum ad Demosthenem et Hyperidem, sic nunc ad Antonium Crassumque pervenimus ! Nam ego sic existimo, hos oratores fuisse maximos et in his primum cum Graecorum gloria Latine dicendi copiam aequatam.

---

[a] This seems to be the natural interpretation of Cicero's words, which make allusion to the agrarian law of Tiberius (Sempronius) Gracchus (133 b.c.), as modified by Spurius Thorius, trib. pleb. *circa* 118 b.c. The original measure was passed over the *intercessio* of the tribune M. Octavius (*cf.* 95) and hence *vitiosa*. *Cf.* Madvig, *Verfassung*, ii. p. 380, and H. Last, in *Camb. Anc. Hist.* ix. p. 100.
[b] L. Aurelius Cotta, distinguished thus from the consul

many on capital charges ; for defendants they seldom
spoke. Spurius Thorius had considerable ability as a
speaker before the people, and it was he who freed
the state lands from the tax burdens of the (Sem-
pronian) law, a measure at once unconstitutional and
ineffective.[a] Marcus Marcellus, the father of (Marcellus) Aeserninus, was not esteemed a pleader, but
was a ready and not unpractised speaker, as was also
his son Publius Lentulus. Lucius Cotta too, the prae- 137
torian,[b] held a place in the ranks of orators of moderate ability. He did not advance far on the road to
oratorical renown, but he is remembered because of
his deliberate affectation of archaic speech in choice
of words and in a rustic habit of enunciation.

" I am aware that in the case of this Cotta, and
some others as well, I have put into the ranks of
orators men who were not very good speakers, and
I shall continue to do so. For it is my purpose to
put together those who have made it their business
in civic life to be regarded as orators. What their
progress was and how difficult in every art is final
attainment of the best, may be judged from what
I have to say. How many orators have already 138
been named and how long I have been occupied
in enumeration of them ! And yet in spite of this
slow and laborious progress we have only come,
as before to Demosthenes and Hyperides, so now to
Antonius and Crassus. I suggest the comparison
because in my judgement these two men were orators
of the first rank, and in them for the first time Latin
eloquence attained a level comparable to the glory
of Greece.

(119 B.C.) of the same name, was tribune in 95 B.C. He is
alluded to again in 259.

139 xxxvii. Omnia veniebant Antonio in mentem eaque suo quaeque loco, ubi plurimum proficere et valere possent, ut ab imperatore equites pedites levis armatura, sic ab illo in maxime opportunis orationis partibus collocabantur. Erat memoria summa, nulla meditationis suspicio ; imparatus semper aggredi ad dicendum videbatur, sed ita erat paratus ut iudices illo dicente non numquam vide-

140 rentur non satis parati ad cavendum fuisse. Verba ipsa non illa quidem elegantissimo sermone, itaque diligenter loquendi laude caruit ; neque tamen est admodum inquinate locutus, sed illa, quae propria laus oratoris est in verbis. Nam ipsum Latine loqui est illud quidem, ut paulo ante dixi, in magna laude ponendum, sed non tam sua sponte quam quod est a plerisque neglectum ; non enim tam praeclarum est scire Latine quam turpe nescire, neque tam id mihi oratoris boni quam civis Romani proprium videtur. Sed tamen Antonius in verbis et eligendis, neque id ipsum tam leporis causa quam ponderis, et collocandis et comprehensione devinciendis nihil non ad rationem et tamquam ad artem dirigebat ; verum multo magis hoc idem in

141 sententiarum ornamentis et conformationibus. Quo genere quia praestat omnibus Demosthenes, idcirco a doctis oratorum est princeps iudicatus ; σχήματα

" As for Antonius, nothing relevant escaped his 139
attention, and it was all set in proper place for
greatest force and effectiveness. Like a general with
his cavalry, infantry, and skirmishers, he knew how
to place his material in the most opportune parts of
his discourse. His memory was perfect, there was
no suggestion of previous rehearsal; he always
gave the appearance of coming forward to speak
without preparation, but so well prepared was he
that when he spoke it was the court rather that
often seemed ill prepared to maintain its guard.
His words were not chosen with excessive care, and 140
thus he lacked the distinction of painstaking diction; not that his language was markedly impure,
but I mean he lacked that distinction in the use of
words which is proper and peculiar to the orator.
As for purity of diction, it is (as I have said before)
a quality deserving of high praise, and yet not so
much for its own sake as because it is commonly
neglected. It isn't so admirable a thing to know
good Latin as it is disgraceful not to know it, and it
is not, I think, so much the mark of a good orator as
it is of a true Roman.[a] But to return : In the matter
of choosing words (and choosing them more for weight
than for charm), in placing them and tying them
into compact sentences, Antonius controlled everything by purpose and by something like deliberate
art. This same quality was still more noticeable in
the embellishment which he gave to his thought by
figurative expression. It is because in this respect 141
Demosthenes surpasses all others that critics have
adjudged him the first of orators. For what the

[a] On the punctuation of the Latin text see note on 101
above.

enim quae vocant Graeci, ea maxime ornant oratorem eaque non tam in verbis pingendis habent pondus quam in illuminandis sententiis. XXXVIII. Sed cum haec magna in Antonio tum actio singularis ; quae si partienda est in gestum atque vocem, gestus erat non verba exprimens, sed cum sententiis congruens — manus umeri latera supplosio pedis status incessus omnisque motus cum verbis sententiisque consentiens ; vox permanens, verum subrauca natura. Sed hoc vitium huic uni in bonum
142 convertebat ; habebat enim flebile quiddam in questionibus aptumque cum ad fidem faciendam tum ad misericordiam commovendam ; ut verum videretur in hoc illud, quod Demosthenem ferunt ei, qui quaesivisset quid primum esset in dicendo, actionem, quid secundum idem, et idem tertium respondisse. Nulla res magis penetrat in animos eosque fingit format flectit talisque oratores videri facit, qualis ipsi se videri volunt.
143 Huic alii parem esse dicebant, alii anteponebant L. Crassum. Illud quidem certe omnes ita iudicabant, neminem esse qui horum altero utro patrono cuiusquam ingenium requireret. Equidem quamquam Antonio tantum tribuo quantum supra dixi, tamen Crasso nihil statuo fieri potuisse perfectius. Erat summa gravitas, erat cum gravitate iunctus

---

^a Figures (σχήματα) are of two kinds : figures of language or words, such as alliteration, rhyming or assonant pairs ; and figures of thought, in which an idea is given force or vividness by the form in which it is cast, as when a simple statement is put in the form of a rhetorical question, an appeal, a wish, a prayer, an oath (like the famous oath, in the oration *On the Crown*, by those who fought and fell at Marathon, etc.).

^b The Latin " action " (ὑπόκρισις) seems to render the

Greeks call postures or figures are the greatest ornaments of oratory.[a] They are not so important in
heightening the colour of words, as in throwing ideas
into a stronger light. In all these respects Antonius
was great, and combined with them a delivery of
peculiar excellence. If we divide delivery into gesture and voice, his gesture did not seek to reflect
words, but agreed with the course of his thought—
hands, shoulders, chest, stamp of the foot, posture in
repose and in movement, all harmonizing with his
words and thoughts ; voice sustained, but with a
touch of huskiness. This defect however, he had
the unique skill to turn into a merit. For in pass- 142
ages of pathos it had a touching quality well-suited
to winning confidence and to stirring compassion.
You can see by his example how all this bears out
the truth of the dictum attributed to Demosthenes ;
who when asked what was first in oratory replied to
his questioner, ' action,' what second, ' action,' and
again third, ' action.'[b] Nothing else so penetrates
the mind, shapes, moulds, turns it, and causes the
orator to seem such a man as he wills to seem.

" Equal in rank with him some placed Lucius 143
Crassus, others assigned to Crassus a higher place.
But in one thing the judgement of all was in agreement, that no one who could employ the services of
either of these as advocate required the help of any
other man's talent. For my part, though I assign to
Antonius all that I have pointed out above, yet I
hold that nothing could have been more perfect than
Crassus. He possessed great dignity, and combined

saying of Demosthenes more effectively than our more
precise equivalent " delivery." We have preserved the
Latin usage in " actor " (ὑποκριτής).

facetiarum et urbanitatis oratorius, non scurrilis
lepos ; Latine loquendi accurata et sine molestia diligens elegantia ; in disserendo mira explicatio ; cum
de iure civili, cum de aequo et bono disputaretur,
144 argumentorum et similitudinum copia. XXXIX. Nam
ut Antonius coniectura movenda aut sedanda su-
spicione aut excitanda incredibilem vim habebat,
sic in interpretando, in definiendo, in explicanda
aequitate nihil erat Crasso copiosius ; idque cum
saepe alias tum apud centumviros in M'. Curi causa
145 cognitum est.   Ita enim multa tum contra scriptum
pro aequo et bono dixit, ut hominem acutissimum
Q. Scaevolam et in iure, in quo illa causa vertebatur,
paratissimum obrueret argumentorum exemplorumque copia ; atque ita tum ab his patronis aequalibus et iam consularibus causa illa dicta est, cum
uterque ex contraria parte ius civile defenderet,
ut eloquentium iuris peritissimus Crassus, iuris
peritorum eloquentissimus Scaevola putaretur.

Qui quidem cum peracutus esset ad excogitandum
quid in iure aut in aequo verum aut esset aut non
esset, tum verbis erat ad rem cum summa brevitate
146 mirabiliter aptus.   Qua re sit nobis orator in hoc
interpretandi explanandi edisserendi genere mira-
bilis, sic ut simile nihil viderim ; in augendo, in

126

with dignity a pleasantry and wit, not smart nor
vulgar, but suited to the orator ; his Latinity was
careful and well chosen, but without affected pre-
ciseness ; in presentation and argument his lucidity
was admirable ; in handling questions whether of the
civil law or of natural equity and justice he was fertile
in argument and in analogies.   As Antonius possessed 144
incredible skill in creating a presumption of probability, in allaying or in provoking a suspicion, so in
interpretation, in definition, in unfolding the implications of equity no one could surpass the resourcefulness of Crassus. I could illustrate this by other
examples, but I will take especially the case of Manius
Curius before the centumvirs. Crassus there spoke 145
so well against the written word in behalf of general
considerations of equity and justice that Quintus
Scaevola, with all his acuteness and readiness in
technical law (the interpretation of which was the
question at issue in that case), was completely over-
whelmed by the wealth of arguments and precedents
adduced by his opponent. The handling of the case
by these two pleaders of like age and like consular
rank, each upholding the law from opposite points of
view, was such that Crassus was allowed to be the
ablest jurist in the ranks of orators, Scaevola the best
orator in the ranks of jurists.

  " As for Scaevola, he was at once very shrewd in
getting at the true significance and applicability of
principles of civil law or natural equity, and remark-
ably adept at finding the precise words suited to the
thing in question with greatest brevity. Therefore 146
let him stand for us, in respect of interpretation,
elucidation, and general exposition, as an orator
worthy of our highest admiration ; in this I have

127

ornando, in refellendo magis existimator metuendus quam admirandus orator. Verum ad Crassum revertamur.

147 XL. Tum Brutus : Etsi satis, inquit, mihi videbar habere cognitum Scaevolam ex eis rebus quas audiebam saepe ex C. Rutilio, quo utebar¹ propter familiaritatem Scaevolae nostri, tamen ista mihi eius dicendi tanta laus nota non erat ; itaque cepi voluptatem tam ornatum virum tamque excellens ingenium fuisse in nostra re publica.

148 Hic ego : Noli, inquam, Brute, existimare his duobus quicquam fuisse in nostra civitate praestantius. Nam ut paulo ante dixi consultorum alterum disertissimum, disertorum alterum consultissimum fuisse, sic in reliquis rebus ita dissimiles erant inter sese, statuere ut tamen non posses, utrius te malles similiorem. Crassus erat elegantium parcissimus, Scaevola parcorum elegantissimus ; Crassus in summa comitate habebat etiam severitatis satis, Scaevolae multa in severitate non deerat tamen

149 comitas. Licet omnia hoc modo ; sed vereor ne fingi videantur haec, ut dicantur a me quodam modo ; res se tamen sic habet. Cum omnis virtus sit, ut vestra, Brute, vetus Academia dixit, mediocritas, uterque horum medium quiddam volebat sequi ; sed

---

¹ utebar *codd. det.*, utebatur *L*.

ᵃ C. Rutilius, perhaps the son of P. Rutilius Rufus (113), in whose defence Q. Mucius Scaevola spoke (115). *Noster Scaevola* here mentioned was tribune of the people in 54 B.C., a friend and contemporary of Brutus. His exact relation to the pontifex and jurist under discussion is uncertain.

never seen his equal. In amplification, in embellishment, in refutation, he was rather the critic to be feared than the orator to be admired. But let us come back to Crassus."

Here Brutus remarked: "Though I thought that 147 I knew Scaevola adequately from what I used to hear from Gaius Rutilius,[a] whom I met often at the house of my friend Scaevola, yet I did not know that his reputation as a speaker was so great. It is a pleasure to learn that we have had in our public life a man so accomplished and of such distinguished ability."

"Do not question, Brutus, that our state has never 148 produced more distinguished talent than these two men. As a moment ago I called one the ablest speaker of jurisconsults, the other the ablest jurisconsult of speakers, so their differences in other respects were such that you could hardly choose which one you would rather be like. Crassus was most frugal of the elegant; Scaevola most elegant of the frugal; Crassus along with kindliness and affability had a certain severity; Scaevola with much severity was not without kindliness and affability. You could go on in this way no end, but I fear 149 that I should seem to have invented all this for the sake of saying it in a certain way; still the fact was so. All virtue, Brutus, according to your school of the Old Academy,[b] consists in the mean, and thus both these men made it a guiding principle to follow a middle course; but it fell out so that while each one

[b] By the "Old Academy" Cicero means the recent school of Antiochus (and his brother Aristus, *cf.* 332) who revolted from the "New Academy" of Carneades and Philo, and professed to revert to the original Academy of Plato. In fact his teaching was a rather loose synthesis of Platonic, Peripatetic, and especially Stoic ideas.

ita cadebat ut alter ex alterius laude partem, uterque
autem suam totam haberet.

150   Tum Brutus : Cum ex tua oratione mihi videor,
inquam, bene Crassum et Scaevolam cognovisse, tum
de te et de Ser. Sulpicio cogitans esse quandam
vobis cum illis similitudinem iudico.

    Quonam, inquam, istuc modo ?

    Quia mihi et tu videris, inquit, tantum iuris civilis
scire voluisse quantum satis esset oratori, et Servius
eloquentiae tantum assumpsisse ut ius civile facile
possit tueri ; aetatesque vestrae, ut illorum, nihil
aut non fere multum differunt.

151   XLI. Et ego : De me, inquam, dicere nihil est
necesse ; de Servio autem et tu probe dicis et ego
dicam quod sentio. Non enim facile quem dixerim
plus studi quam illum et ad dicendum et ad omnis
bonarum rerum disciplinas adhibuisse. Nam et in
isdem exercitationibus ineunte aetate fuimus et
postea una Rhodum ille etiam profectus est, quo melior esset et doctior ; et inde ut rediit, videtur mihi
in secunda arte primus esse maluisse quam in prima
secundus. Atque haud scio an par principibus esse
potuisset ; sed fortasse maluit, id quod est adeptus,
longe omnium non eiusdem modo aetatis sed eorum
etiam qui fuissent in iure civili esse princeps.

152   Hic Brutus : Ain tu ? inquit. Etiamne Q. Scaevolae Servium nostrum anteponis ?

    Sic enim, inquam, Brute, existimo, iuris civilis
magnum usum et apud Scaevolam et apud multos

---

    a Distinguished jurist, consul 51 B.C. See note, p. 134.

possessed a part of the other's characteristic merit, both had their own undivided."

"From what you have said," replied Brutus at this 150 point, "I think I have gained a good idea of Crassus and of Scaevola. In like manner, thinking of you and of Servius Sulpicius,[a] I venture to believe that as between you two there exists a somewhat similar relation."

"How do you mean?" I asked.

"Because," said he, "you seem to have made it your aim to know as much of the civil law as was requisite for an orator, and Servius to have acquired as much eloquence as was necessary to make himself a ready guardian of the law. Your relative ages too, like theirs, differ little if at all."

"Concerning myself," I replied, "there is no need 151 to speak. But about Servius you say well, and I will tell you what I think. I could not easily name any-one who has devoted more attention to the art of speaking and to all other subjects of liberal study than he. As young men we pursued the same rhetorical studies here, and afterwards he went with me to Rhodes to acquire a more perfect technical training. Returning from there he gave the impression of having chosen to be first in the second art rather than second in the first. In fact I'm not sure that he might not have been the equal of orators of the first rank; but perhaps he preferred, what he did attain, to be first, not only of his own time but of those who had gone before, in mastery of the civil law."

At this Brutus said: "Do you mean to say that 152 you place our Servius even above Quintus Scaevola?"

"Yes, Brutus," I replied, "I would put it this way: Scaevola, and many others too, had great practical

fuisse, artem in hoc uno ; quod numquam effecisset ipsius iuris scientia, nisi eam praeterea didicisset artem quae doceret rem universam tribuere in partis, latentem explicare definiendo, obscuram explanare interpretando, ambigua primum videre, deinde distinguere, postremo habere regulam qua vera et falsa iudicarentur et quae quibus propositis essent quae-
153 que non essent consequentia. Hic enim attulit hanc artem omnium artium maximam quasi lucem ad ea quae confuse ab aliis aut respondebantur aut agebantur.

XLII. Dialecticam mihi videris dicere, inquit.

Recte, inquam, intellegis ; sed adiunxit etiam et litterarum scientiam et loquendi elegantiam, quae ex scriptis eius, quorum similia nulla sunt, facil-
154 lime perspici potest. Cumque discendi causa duobus peritissimis operam dedisset, L. Lucilio Balbo C. Aquilio Gallo, Galli hominis acuti et exercitati promptam et paratam in agendo et in respondendo celeritatem subtilitate diligentiaque superavit ; Balbi docti et eruditi hominis in utraque re consideratam tarditatem vicit expediendis conficiendisque rebus. Sic et habet quod uterque eorum habuit,
155 et explevit quod utrique defuit. Itaque ut Crassus mihi videtur sapientius fecisse quam Scaevola—hic enim causas studiose recipiebat, in quibus a Crasso superabatur ; ille se consuli nolebat, ne qua in re

---

[a] The primacy of dialectic among the other " arts " is developed more fully in *de Or.* 1. 186-188. The position here claimed for it was assigned to philosophy in general by Aristotle (*Metaph.* 1. 2), and late sources attribute to him the definition of dialectic as " the art of arts, the science of sciences " (τέχνη τεχνῶν, ἐπιστήμη ἐπιστημῶν), of which the words here, *artem omnium artium maximam*, seem to be an echo. Besides διαλεκτική, Servius possessed *litterarum*

knowledge of the civil law ; Servius alone made of it
an art. This he could never have attained through
knowledge of the law alone had he not acquired in
addition that art which teaches the analysis of a
whole into its component parts, sets forth and defines
the latent and implicit, interprets and makes clear
the obscure ; which first recognizes the ambiguous
and then distinguishes ; which applies in short a rule
or measure for adjudging truth and falsehood,
for determining what conclusions follow from what
premises, and what do not. This art, the mistress of 153
all arts,[a] he brought to bear on all that had been put
together by others without system, whether in the
form of legal opinions or in actual trials."

" The art of logic I suppose you mean," said he.

" Quite right," I replied ; " but to this he joined a
knowledge of letters and a finished style of speaking,
as can be seen from his writings, which are quite
unique. For the sake of learning his profession he 154
had devoted himself to two of the ablest jurists,
Lucius Lucilius Balbus and Gaius Aquilius Gallus.
The acute and ready quickness of Gallus, whether at
the bar or in consultation, he surpassed in penetra-
tion and in accuracy ; to the erudite and well considered deliberateness of Balbus he was superior in
expedition and efficiency. He thus had what both
of them possessed, and supplied what each of them
lacked. And just as Crassus acted more prudently 155
than Scaevola—for Scaevola was quite willing to
undertake cases in which he was surpassed by
Crassus, while Crassus made it a point not to give
consultations, that he might in no respect be inferior

scientia (γραμματική) and *loquendi elegantia* (ῥητορική),
the three " logical " arts.

inferior esset quam Scaevola—sic Servius sapien
tissime, cum duae civiles artes ac forenses plurimum
et laudis haberent et gratiae, perfecit ut altera
praestaret omnibus, ex altera tantum assumeret
quantum esset et ad tuendum ius civile et ad
obtinendam consularem dignitatem satis.

156   Tum Brutus : Ita prorsus, inquit, et antea putabam
—audivi enim nuper eum studiose et frequenter
Sami, cum ex eo ius nostrum pontificium, qua ex
parte cum iure civili coniunctum esset, vellem cognoscere—et nunc meum iudicium multo magis con-
firmo testimonio et iudicio tuo ; simul illud gaudeo,
quod et aequalitas vestra et pares honorum gradus et
artium studiorumque quasi finitima vicinitas tantum
abest ab obtrectatione ⟨et⟩ invidia, quae solet lace-
rare plerosque, uti[1] ea non modo non exulcerare ves-
tram gratiam sed etiam conciliare videatur.   Quali
enim te erga illum perspicio, tali illum in te volun-
157 tate iudicioque cognovi.   Itaque doleo et illius consilio et tua voce populum Romanum carere tam
diu ; quod cum per se dolendum est tum multo
magis consideranti ad quos ista non tralata sint, sed
nescio quo pacto devenerint.

Hic Atticus : Dixeram, inquit, a principio, de re
publica ut sileremus ; itaque faciamus.   Nam si isto
modo volumus singulas res desiderare, non modo
querendi sed ne lugendi quidem finem reperiemus.

---

[1] uti *Manutius*, ut in *L.*

---

[a] On Brutus's return from Asia in the summer of 47.
See note, p. 26.   Sulpicius had been with Pompey at
Pharsalus, and after the defeat withdrew to Samos, where
he seems to have remained until his pardon and reconciliation
with Caesar.   Cicero writing in September 46 praises the

to Scaevola—so Servius, seeing that these two civic
and forensic arts led to fame and favour, very wisely
conducted himself so as to be supreme in the one,
and from the other to borrow as much as was needful
to sustain the honour of the civil law and to advance
himself to consular dignity."

Here Brutus interposed : " That is precisely the 156
opinion of him which I had already formed ; for only
recently at Samos,*a* when I was bent on learning in
how far our pontifical law was related to the civil law,
I listened with great interest to his replies to my
many questions. Now I have greater confidence in
the opinion I had formed, seeing it confirmed by
your testimony. It is a pleasure too to note that,
as peers in official honours and as neighbours so to
speak in arts and studies, such vicinity, far from the
detraction and envy which commonly poisons the
relations of rivals, has with you promoted mutual
regard rather than disturbed it. For I know that
toward you he entertains the same esteem and goodwill which I find in you towards him. I cannot but 157
grieve therefore that the Roman people have so long
been deprived of his counsel and of your voice,—a
thing to deplore in itself, and much more when one
considers into what hands those functions, I will not
say have been transferred, but somehow or other have
merely drifted."

At this point Atticus interrupted : " I said in the
beginning that we should not touch on politics.
Let us keep to that ; for if in this fashion we should
go on to recount our losses one by one we should
never come to an end of sighs and complaints."

magnanimity of Caesar as shown in the honours and position bestowed upon his former enemies (*ad Fam.* 6. 6, 10).

158 XLIII. Pergamus ergo, inquam, ad reliqua et
institutum ordinem persequamur. Paratus igitur
veniebat Crassus, exspectabatur, audiebatur ; a
principio statim, quod erat apud eum semper ac-
curatum, exspectatione dignus videbatur. Non
multa iactatio corporis, non inclinatio vocis, nulla
inambulatio, non crebra supplosio pedis ; vehemens
et interdum irata et plena iusti doloris oratio, multae
et cum gravitate facetiae ; quodque difficile est,
159 idem et perornatus et perbrevis ; iam in altercando
invenit parem neminem. Versatus est in omni fere
genere causarum ; mature in locum principum oratorum venit. Accusavit C. Carbonem eloquentis-
simum hominem admodum adulescens ; summam
ingeni non laudem modo sed etiam admirationem est
160 consecutus. Defendit postea Liciniam virginem,
cum annos XXVII natus esset. In ea ipsa causa fuit
eloquentissimus orationisque eius scriptas quasdam
partis reliquit. Voluit adulescens in colonia Nar-
bonensi causae popularis aliquid attingere eamque
coloniam, ut fecit, ipse deducere ; exstat in eam
legem senior, ut ita dicam, quam aetas illa ferebat
oratio. Multae deinde causae ; sed ita tacitus
tribunatus ut, nisi in eo magistratu cenavisset apud
praeconem Granium idque nobis bis narravisset
Lucilius, tribunum plebis nesciremus fuisse.

" Let us go on then," I replied, " to the orators who 158
remain and continue the enumeration we began.
Crassus then came always prepared and ready, he was
waited for eagerly and listened to with attention.
From the very exordium, which with him was always
carefully prepared, he rewarded expectation abun-
dantly ; no violent movements of the body, no sudden
variation of voice, no walking up and down, no frequent stamping of the foot ; his language vehement,
sometimes angry and filled with righteous indignation;
much wit but always dignified, and, what is most difficult, he was at once ornate and brief; finally, in the 159
give and take of altercation he was unequalled. He
appeared in cases of almost every type ; he came early
to an acknowledged rank among the first orators.
When still a mere lad he conducted the indictment
against Gaius Carbo, one of the best speakers of his
time. Through this he won not only the highest
reputation for talent, but also great applause. Later 160
at the age of twenty-seven he defended the vestal
virgin Licinia. In this case he was particularly eloquent, and he has left some parts of his speech in
writing. While still young he chose to ingratiate himself with the popular party in the matter of the colony
of Narbo, and strove to make himself the leader of that
colony, as in fact he succeeded in doing. In favour of
the law establishing it his speech is extant, somewhat older in tone than his youthful years would
suggest. Then followed a multitude of cases. However, his tribuneship passed with so little mention,
that, had he not during his term of office dined with
Granius the crier, and had not Lucilius twice told the
story of that dinner, we should never know that he
had been tribune of the people at all."

161 Ita prorsus, inquit Brutus ; sed ne de Scaevolae quidem tribunatu quicquam audivisse videor et eum collegam Crassi credo fuisse.

Omnibus quidem aliis, inquam, in magistratibus, sed tribunus anno post fuit eoque in rostris sedente suasit Serviliam legem Crassus ; nam censuram sine Scaevola gessit ; eum enim magistratum nemo umquam Scaevolarum petivit. Sed haec Crassi cum edita oratio est, quam te saepe legisse certo scio, quattuor et triginta tum habebat annos totidemque annis mihi aetate praestabat. His enim consulibus eam legem suasit quibus nati sumus, cum ipse esset Q. Caepione consule natus et C. Laelio, triennio ipso minor quam Antonius. Quod idcirco posui ut dicendi Latine prima maturitas in qua aetate exstitisset posset notari et intellegeretur iam ad summum paene esse perductam, ut eo nihil ferme quisquam addere posset, nisi qui a philosophia, a iure civili, ab historia fuisset instructior.

162 XLIV. Erit, inquit [M.] Brutus, aut iam est iste quem exspectas ?

Nescio, inquam. Sed est etiam L. Crassi in consulatu pro Q. Caepione defensione iuncta,[1] non brevis ut laudatio, ut oratio autem brevis ; postrema censoris oratio, qua anno duodequinquagesimo usus est. In his omnibus inest quidam sine ullo

[1] defensione iuncta *L* (*sc. oratio defensione ipsius Caepionis iunctă) loc. fort. corrupt.*

"Quite true," said Brutus, "but neither do I 161 recall hearing anything about the tribuneship of Scaevola, and I assume that he was Crassus's colleague in that office."

"In all other offices, yes," I replied, "but Scaevola was tribune in the year following, and while he was on the platform as presiding officer, Crassus urged the passage of the *lex Servilia*. The censorship, to be sure, he did hold without Scaevola, for no Scaevola ever stood for that one office. But the published speech of Crassus on this occasion, which I am sure you must have read often, he delivered when he was thirty-four, and exactly that number of years older than I. For he urged the passage of that law under the same consuls as the consuls of my birth, while he himself was born in the consulship of Quintus Caepio and Gaius Laelius, three years younger than Antonius. I set this down precisely for this reason, that the time when Latin eloquence first came to maturity may be marked, and that it·may be made clear that it now had been brought to all but the highest perfection. Henceforth no one could expect to add anything considerable to it unless he should come better equipped in philosophy, in law, in history."

"Shall we ever find such a one as you contemplate," 162 said Brutus, "or is he indeed already here?"

"I cannot say," I replied. "But to return: There is extant also from the consulship of Crassus an encomium in behalf of Quintus Caepio, which formed a part of his defence of Caepio, for its laudatory purpose long enough, but as a whole oration very brief. Last of all his speech as censor, which he delivered in his forty-eighth year. In all these there is

fuco veritatis color ; quin etiam comprehensio et ambitus ille verborum, si sic περίοδον appellari placet, erat apud illum contractus et brevis, et in membra quaedam, quae κῶλα Graeci vocant, dispertiebat orationem libentius.

163 Hoc loco Brutus : Quando quidem tu istos oratores, inquit, tanto opere laudas, vellem aliquid Antonio praeter illum de ratione dicendi sane exilem libellum, plura Crasso libuisset scribere ; cum enim omnibus memoriam sui tum etiam disciplinam dicendi nobis reliquissent. Nam Scaevolae dicendi elegantiam satis ex eis orationibus quas reliquit, habemus cognitam.

164 Et ego : Mihi quidem a pueritia quasi magistra fuit, inquam, illa in legem Caepionis oratio ; in qua et auctoritas ornatur senatus, quo pro ordine illa dicuntur, et invidia concitatur in iudicum et in accusatorum factionem, contra quorum potentiam populariter tum dicendum fuit. Multa in illa oratione graviter, multa leniter, multa aspere, multa facete dicta sunt ; plura etiam dicta quam scripta, quod ex quibusdam capitibus expositis nec explicatis intellegi potest. Ipsa illa censoria contra Cn. Domitium collegam non est oratio, sed quasi

---

[a] The *lex Servilia iudiciaria*, introduced by Servilius Caepio, sought to deprive the equites of their exclusive right to serve as *iudices* in the courts. It was defended by Crassus, but unsuccessfully, in a speech of which portions are given in *de Or.* 1. 225 ff. *Cf.* translator's discussion in *Cl. Phil.* xxviii. (1933), p. 156.

present what we may call a natural complexion free from make-up. Even that grouping and rounding out of words, if we may thus render the Greek word *period*, with him was compact and short, and he preferred rather to break up his language into members, or parts of the whole, such as the Greeks call *colons*."

At this point Brutus interrupted : " Considering 163 the great praise you bestow upon these two orators one cannot but wish that Antonius had cared to write something besides the meagre little treatise *On Rhetoric*, and that Crassus too had chosen to write more. Had they done so they would have left a monument to their own memory for all men to read, and to us valuable lessons in the art of speaking. As for Scaevola, the simple directness of his oratory is adequately known from the speeches which he left."

" For me at any rate," I replied, " that speech in 164 favour of the law of Caepio was from my boyhood in some sort a textbook.[a] In it the dignity of the senate was upheld, in behalf of which its most famous passages were spoken, and it sought to inspire hatred of the group from which both judges and prosecutors were drawn, against whose influence it was necessary to speak in such a manner as to win popular favour. In that speech there is much that is said with earnestness, much lightly and with charm, much with bitterness, much with wit and pleasantry. More too was spoken than the written text contains, as can be discerned from certain headings which are indicated but not developed. Even the speech of his censorship, against his colleague Gnaeus Domitius, is not properly a discourse but scarcely more

141

capita rerum et orationis commentarium paulo plenius. Nulla est enim altercatio clamoribus um-
165 quam habita maioribus. Et vero fuit in hoc etiam popularis dictio excellens ; Antoni genus dicendi multo aptius iudiciis quam contionibus.

XLV. Hoc loco ipsum Domitium non relinquo. Nam etsi non fuit in oratorum numero, tamen pono satis in eo fuisse orationis atque ingeni quo et magistratus personam et consularem dignitatem tueretur ; quod idem de C. Caelio dixerim, industriam in eo summam fuisse summasque virtutes, eloquentiae tantum quod esset in rebus privatis amicis eius,
166 in re publica ipsius dignitati satis. Eodem tempore M. Herennius in mediocribus oratoribus Latine et diligenter loquentibus numeratus est ; qui tamen summa nobilitate hominem, cognatione sodalitate collegio, summa etiam eloquentia, L. Philippum in consulatus petitione superavit. Eodem tempore C. Claudius, etsi propter summam nobilitatem et singularem potentiam magnus erat, tamen etiam
167 eloquentiae quandam mediocritatem afferebat. Eiusdem fere temporis fuit eques Romanus C. Titius, qui meo iudicio eo pervenisse videtur quo potuit fere Latinus orator sine Graecis litteris et sine multo usu pervenire. Huius orationes tantum argutiarum, tantum exemplorum,[1] tantum urbanitatis habent, ut

---

[1] exemplorum *L*, leporum *Simon*.

---

[a] The pleasant story of the aristocrat's effort to play the benefactor to the humble *praeco* Volteius Mena, in Horace (*Epp.* 1. 7), will be recalled. His family, the Marcii, claimed descent from Ancus Marcius.

than a table of contents and a somewhat extended outline. This is evident, since no encounter of rival orators was ever delivered with greater applause. He possessed besides a manner of speaking admir- 165 ably adapted to an audience of the people ; Antonius's manner was better suited to the courts than to popular assemblages.

" Domitius too, while we are speaking of him, I should not pass over ; for though he did not enjoy the title of orator, yet I hold that he had natural ability and spoke well enough to sustain the character of magistrate and of his consular station. I may say the same of Gaius Caelius; he was a man of great industry and of the highest qualities ; his eloquence in questions of private law was adequate to succour his friends, and in affairs of state to sustain his senatorial rank. In the same time Marcus Herennius was 166 numbered among the orators of only moderate ability, and as one who used a pure and painstaking Latinity ; and yet, as candidate for the consulship, he defeated Lucius Philippus, a man of the highest nobility, commended by family connexions, by membership in guilds and priestly colleges, and possessing in addition outstanding eloquence.[a] Another contemporary, Gaius Claudius, though conspicuous chiefly for the distinction of his family and his social position, yet showed some moderate talent for oratory. Of about the same time was Gaius 167 Titius, of equestrian rank, who in my judgement would seem to have gone as far as any Latin orator could go without acquaintance with Greek letters and without long practical experience. His orations have such refinements of expression, such wealth of anecdote and example, such urbanity, that they

paene Attico stilo scriptae esse videantur. Easdem argutias in tragoedias satis ille quidem acute,
sed parum tragice transtulit. Quem studebat imitari L. Afranius poeta, homo perargutus, in fabulis
168 quidem etiam, ut scitis, disertus. Fuit etiam Q.
Rubrius Varro, qui a senatu hostis cum C. Mario
iudicatus est, acer et vehemens accusator, in eo
genere sane probabilis. Doctus autem Graecis
litteris propinquus noster, factus ad dicendum,
M. Gratidius M. Antoni perfamiliaris, cuius prae-
fectus cum esset in Cilicia est interfectus, qui accusavit C. Fimbriam, M. Mari Gratidiani pater.

169   XLVI. Atque etiam apud socios et Latinos oratores
habiti sunt Q. Vettius Vettianus e Marsis, quem
ipse cognovi, prudens vir et in dicendo brevis;
Q. D. Valerii Sorani, vicini et familiares mei, non
tam in dicendo admirabiles quam docti et Graecis
litteris et Latinis; C. Rusticelius Bononiensis, is
quidem et exercitatus et natura volubilis; omnium
autem eloquentissimus extra hanc urbem T. Betutius
Barrus Asculanus, cuius sunt aliquot orationes
Asculi habitae; illa Romae contra Caepionem
nobilis sane, quoi[1] orationi Caepionis ore respondit
Aelius, qui scriptitavit orationes multis, orator ipse
170 numquam fuit. Apud maiores autem nostros video
disertissimum habitum ex Latio L. Papirium Fre-

---

[1] quo L, cui *vulg.*

would seem almost to have been written by an Attic pen. These same refinements he carried over into his tragedies, where they seem clever, but scarcely tragic. Upon him the poet Lucius Afranius strove to pattern himself, a man of cunning wit and, as you know, in his plays really eloquent. There 168 was also Quintus Rubrius Varro (whom the senate pronounced a public enemy along with Gaius Marius), a sharp and aggressive prosecutor, and in that type of activity an acceptable speaker. A man thoroughly trained in Greek letters was my relative Marcus Gratidius, a born orator, the intimate friend of Marcus Antonius, whose prefect he was in Cilicia, where he lost his life. He will be recalled as the one who brought accusation against Gaius Fimbria, and as the father of Marcus Marius Gratidianus.

" Among the allies and Latins there were also some 169 who were esteemed orators, such as Quintus Vettius Vettianus, of the Marsi, whom I knew personally, a man of wisdom and experience and brief of speech; Quintus and Decimus Valerius of Sora, neighbours and friends of mine, not so much admired for their eloquence as for their acquaintance with Greek and Latin letters; Gaius Rusticelius of Bologna, a trained and practised speaker, with a natural gift of readiness. But the most eloquent of all outside of the city was Titus Betutius Barrus of Asculum, some of whose orations delivered there are extant. Very well known too is his speech delivered at Rome against Caepio, to which reply was made through the mouth of Caepio by Aelius, a writer of speeches for many, though no orator himself. Of an earlier 170 generation I note that from Latium Lucius Papirius of Fregellae was considered the best speaker, a con-

gellanum Ti. Gracchi P. f. fere aetate ; eius etiam oratio est pro Fregellanis colonisque Latinis habita in senatu.

Tum Brutus : Quid tu igitur, inquit, tribuis istis externis quasi oratoribus ?

Quid censes, inquam, nisi idem quod urbanis ? praeter unum, quod non est eorum urbanitate quadam quasi colorata oratio.

171 Et Brutus : Qui est, inquit, iste tandem urbanitatis color ?

Nescio, inquam ; tantum esse quendam scio. Id tu, Brute, iam intelleges, cum in Galliam veneris ; audies tum quidem etiam verba quaedam non trita Romae, sed haec mutari dediscique possunt ; illud est maius, quod in vocibus nostrorum oratorum retinnit quiddam et resonat urbanius. Nec hoc in 172 oratoribus modo apparet sed etiam in ceteris. Ego memini T. Tincam Placentinum hominem facetissimum cum familiari nostro Q. Granio praecone dicacitate certare.

Eon', inquit Brutus, de quo multa Lucilius ?

Isto ipso ; sed Tincam non minus multa ridicule dicentem Granius obruebat nescio quo sapore vernaculo ; ut ego iam non mirer illud Theophrasto accidisse, quod dicitur, cum percontaretur ex anicula

---

^a Before his departure for Africa at the end of 47 Caesar had named Brutus as governor (*propraetore*) of Cisalpine Gaul. His departure, to which Cicero here alludes, was imminent. Even if the time of our dialogue could be fixed as only a little before Thapsus (as may be suggested by the words of section 10), the presence of Brutus still in Rome need cause no surprise, since according to the true seasonal calendar the battle took place more than two months earlier

temporary approximately of Tiberius Gracchus, son of Publius. From him also we have a speech delivered in the senate, in behalf of the people of Fregellae and the Latin colonists in general."

"What characteristics," inquired Brutus at this point, "do you assign to these orators, who are in a sense foreigners ? "

"Why, no others," I replied, "than those we have ascribed to our city orators ; except in one respect, that their oratory lacks what I venture to call a certain urban colouring."

"What do you mean by an urban colouring ? " 171 asked Brutus.

"I can't exactly say," I replied ; "I only know that it exists. You will understand presently what I mean, Brutus, when you come to Gaul.[a] There you will hear some words which are not current at Rome, but these could be unlearned and exchanged for Roman words. It is much more significant that in the words and pronunciation of our orators there is a certain intonation and quality which is characteristic of the city, and this is recognizable not in orators only but in others. I recall hearing Titus Tinca of 172 Placentia, a very amusing fellow, engaged in a bout of wit with my friend Quintus Granius the crier."

"You mean the one of whom Lucilius says so much ? "

"Yes, the very same. But Tinca, for all that what he said was quite as funny, was completely worsted by Granius through some indescribable vernacular flavour. I'm not surprised therefore about the story told of Theophrastus, who asked an old market

than April 6, its date by the pre-Julian calendar (see Introd. p. 5).

quadam quanti aliquid venderet et respondisset
illa atque addidisset ' hospes, non pote minoris,'
tulisse eum moleste se non effugere hospitis speciem,
cum aetatem ageret Athenis optimeque loqueretur
omnium. Sic, ut opinor, in nostris est quidam
urbanorum, sicut illic Atticorum sonus.

Sed domum redeamus, id est ad nostros reverta-
173 mur. XLVII. Duobus igitur summis, Crasso et Antonio, L. Philippus proximus accedebat, sed longo
intervallo tamen proximus. Itaque eum, etsi nemo
intercedebat qui se illi anteferret, neque secundum
tamen neque tertium dixerim. Nec enim in quadrigis eum secundum numeraverim aut tertium qui
vix e carceribus exierit, cum palmam iam primus
acceperit, nec in oratoribus qui tantum absit a
primo, vix ut in eodem curriculo esse videatur. Sed
tamen erant ea in Philippo, quae qui sine comparatione illorum spectaret, satis magna diceret: summa
libertas in oratione, multae facetiae, satis creber in
reperiendis, solutus in explicandis sententiis; erat
etiam in primis, ut temporibus illis, Graecis doctrinis institutus; in altercando cum aliquo aculeo et
maledicto facetus.

174 Horum aetati prope coniunctus L. Gellius non tam
vendibilis orator, quamvis[1] nescires quid ei deesset;
nec enim erat indoctus nec tardus ad excogitandum
nec Romanarum rerum immemor et verbis solutus
satis; sed in magnos oratores inciderat eius aetas;

---

[1] quamvis *Jeep*, quam ut *L.*

---

[a] Quintilian (8. 1, 2) embellishes the same story with the
inept addition that the woman on being asked how she had
detected his foreign origin replied, "because your speech is
too Attic."

woman the price of something. She named it and
added : ' Yes, kind stranger, not a farthing less.' It
vexed him that she had detected his foreign birth,
although he had lived long at Athens and was
accounted the most perfect speaker of his time.[a] In
like manner I take it there is in our urban speakers
a characteristic accent analogous to that peculiar to
Athens.

" But let us come back home, that is let us return
to our urban orators. While then Crassus and 173
Antonius were the leaders, Lucius Philippus held the
place next to them, but next after a long interval.
Thus, though no one who could claim to surpass him
stood between him and them, yet I would not place
him second or third in rank. In a chariot race I
should not name as second or third one who has
barely crossed the starting line when the leader has
already been awarded the prize, nor in orators, one
who is so far from the leader that he scarcely seems
to be in the same race. But yet there were those
qualities in Philippus, which, looked at without comparison with those two, one could call very considerable. He was notably free and outspoken in his
language, with a large fund of humour ; resourceful
in invention, and in exposition unconstrained and
facile ; for his time conspicuously versed in Greek
learning ; clever in the give and take of debate with
a certain pungent and personal wit.

" Nearly contemporary with these was Lucius 174
Gellius, an orator who did not greatly commend himself, though it would be hard to say what he lacked.
He was not untrained, nor slow in invention, nor
unresourceful in Roman precedents and examples,
while his diction was facile and adequate ; but his

multam tamen operam amicis et utilem praebuit,
atque ita diu vixit ut multarum aetatum oratoribus
175 implicaretur. Multum etiam in causis versabatur[1]
isdem fere temporibus D. Brutus, is qui consul cum
Mamerco fuit, homo et Graecis doctus litteris et
Latinis. Dicebat etiam L. Scipio non imperite
Gnaeusque Pompeius Sex. f. aliquem numerum
obtinebat. Nam Sex. frater eius praestantissimum
ingenium contulerat ad summam iuris civilis et ad
perfectam geometriae et rerum Stoicarum scientiam.
†itam in iure et[2] . . . . . ante hos M. Brutus et paulo
post eum C. Billienus homo per se magnus prope simili
ratione summus evaserat ; qui consul factus esset, nisi
in Marianos consulatus et in eas petitionis angustias
176 incidisset. Cn. autem Octavi eloquentia, quae fuerat
ante consulatum ignorata, in consulatu multis
contionibus est vehementer probata. Sed ab eis, qui
tantum in dicentium numero, non in oratorum
fuerunt, iam ad oratores revertamur.

Censeo, inquit Atticus ; eloquentis enim videbare,
non sedulos velle conquirere.

177 XLVIII. Festivitate igitur et facetiis, inquam, C.
Iulius L. f. et superioribus et aequalibus suis omnibus
praestitit oratorque fuit minime ille quidem vehemens, sed nemo umquam urbanitate, nemo lepore,
nemo suavitate conditior. Sunt eius aliquot orationes,

---

[1] versabatur *correx. et distinx. Kayser*, versaretur *L.*
[2] *sic L (relicto spatio quinque litt.).*

---

[a] Gaius Julius Caesar Strabo (of uncertain relationship
with the dictator), who as interlocutor in the *de Oratore* sets
forth the doctrine of wit and humour (2. 235 ff.). Suetonius
(*Caes.* 55) says that his style influenced the youthful Julius
Caesar.

time had fallen upon an age of great orators. However, he performed much useful service for his friends, and lived so long that he came into contact with orators of quite different periods. At about the 175 same time Decimus Brutus, the one I mean who was consul with Mamercus, was very active in private cases, a man well trained in Greek and Latin letters. Lucius Scipio likewise was a speaker not without skill, and Gnaeus Pompeius, son of Sextus, was held in some esteem. As for his brother Sextus, he had devoted his extraordinary talent to a mastery of civil law and to the attainment of a perfect knowledge of geometry and of Stoic philosophy. Likewise in knowledge of the law and . . . . . before them Marcus Brutus and soon after him Gaius Billienus, a self-made man of great distinction, along a similar path attained to almost the highest recognition. He would have become consul had he not chanced on the period of the successive consulships of Marius and the limitations of candidacy that arose from them. The eloquence of Gnaeus Octavius, which before his 176 consulship had not been recognized, found high favour through many public harangues in the course of his consulship. But now let me come back from men who were accounted only competent speakers to the real orators."

" Yes," said Atticus, " I think it is time ; for it was I thought your purpose to muster examples of eloquence, not of diligence and perseverance."

" For gaiety and cleverness of wit," I continued, 177 " Gaius Julius, son of Lucius, surpassed all his predecessors and contemporaries.[a] His oratory was entirely lacking in force, but in its humour, its grace, and its general charm it was incomparable. Some

151

ex quibus sicut ex eiusdem tragoediis lenitas eius
178 sine nervis perspici potest. Eius aequalis P. Cethegus, cui de re publica satis suppeditabat oratio;
totam enim tenebat eam penitusque cognoverat;
itaque in senatu consularium auctoritatem asseque-
batur, sed in causis publicis nihil, ⟨in⟩ privatis satis
veterator videbatur. Erat in privatis causis Q. Lucretius Vespillo et acutus et iuris peritus; nam Ofella [1]
contionibus aptior quam iudiciis. Prudens etiam T.
Annius Velina et in eius generis causis orator sane
tolerabilis. In eodem genere causarum multum
erat T. Iuventius nimis ille quidem lentus in dicendo et paene frigidus, sed et callidus et in capiendo
adversario versutus et praeterea nec indoctus et
179 magna cum iuris civilis intellegentia. Cuius auditor
P. Orbius meus fere aequalis in dicendo non nimis
exercitatus, in iure autem civili non inferior quam
magister fuit. Nam T. Aufidius, qui vixit ad summam senectutem, volebat esse similis horum eratque
et bonus vir et innocens, sed dicebat parum; nec
sane plus frater eius M. Vergilius, qui tribunus plebis L. Sullae imperatori diem dixit. Eius collega
180 P. Magius in dicendo paulo tamen copiosior. Sed
omnium oratorum sive rabularum, qui et plane
indocti et inurbani aut rustici etiam fuerunt, quos

[1] Ofella *Pisanus*, a filia *L.*

of his orations are extant, from which, as from his
tragedies, an idea may be gained of his smooth, somewhat nerveless style. Publius Cethegus was his con- 178
temporary, who possessed an oratory adequate for
the treatment of affairs of state. Of these he had
complete mastery and profound understanding, and
thus in the senate he obtained an influence equal
to that of men of consular rank. In criminal cases
he was nothing at all ; in private suits he was an
adequate routine pleader. In private suits Quintus
Lucretius Vespillo was shrewd and well versed in the
law. As for (Lucretius) Ofella, he was better suited
to popular harangues than to private trials. Titus
Annius of the tribus Velina was a man of sound
attainments in the law, and in cases of this latter type
a very tolerable pleader. With similar cases Titus
Juventius was much occupied, and though much too
slow and almost cold in his way of speaking, still he
was shrewd and clever in trapping his opponent, and
besides not untrained, and recognized for his remarkable grasp of the civil law. His pupil was Publius 179
Orbius, a man of about my own age, with no great
experience in speaking, but in knowledge of the civil
law he was not inferior to his master. As for Titus
Aufidius, who lived to an advanced age, he strove to
be as like these last two as possible. He lived a good
and blameless life, but his reputation as a speaker was
slight. His brother too, Marcus Vergilius, who as
tribune of the people instituted proceedings against
Sulla, then commanding the army (in Asia), was not
much more of a speaker. His colleague, Publius
Magius, however was somewhat more voluble. But 180
of all that class of orators, or rather ranters, who were
quite without training, without manners, or flatly

153

quidem ego cognoverim, solutissimum in dicendc
et acutissimum iudico nostri ordinis Q. Sertorium,
equestris C. Gargonium. Fuit etiam facilis et
expeditus ad dicendum et vitae splendore multo et
ingenio sane probabili T. Iunius L. f. tribunicius,
quo accusante P. Sextius praetor designatus damnatus est ambitus ; is processisset honoribus longius,
nisi semper infirma atque etiam aegra valetudine
fuisset.

181 XLIX. Atque ego praeclare intellego me in eorum
commemoratione versari qui nec habiti sint oratores
neque fuerint, praeteririque a me aliquot ex veteribus
commemoratione aut laude dignos. Sed hoc quidem
ignoratione ; quid enim est superioris aetatis quod
scribi possit de eis, de quibus nulla monumenta
loquuntur nec aliorum nec ipsorum ? de his autem,
quos ipsi vidimus, neminem fere praetermittimus
182 eorum quos aliquando dicentis audivimus.[1] Volo
enim sciri in tanta et tam vetere re publica maximis
praemiis eloquentiae propositis omnis cupisse dicere,
non plurimos ausos esse, potuisse paucos. Ego tamen
ita de uno quoque dicam ut intellegi possit quem
existimem clamatorem, quem oratorem fuisse.

Isdem fere temporibus aetate inferiores paulo
quam Iulius, sed aequales propemodum fuerunt
C. Cotta P. Sulpicius Q. Varius Cn. Pomponius
C. Curio L. Fufius M. Drusus P. Antistius ; nec
183 ulla aetate uberior oratorum fetus fuit. Ex his Cotta

---

[1] audivimus *Ruhnken*, vidimus *L*.

---

[a] Partisan of Marius, who withdrew to Spain and for
more than ten years defied the power of Sulla and Roman
rule. An interesting and somewhat romantic adventurer,
whose life Plutarch wrote.

uncouth, I hold Quintus Sertorius [a] of our order, and
Gaius Gargonius of the equestrian, to have been the
readiest and shrewdest I have ever known. A man
who was an easy and fluent speaker, distinguished by
birth and social position, and of recognized talent, was
Titus Junius, son of Lucius, whose career did not go
beyond the tribuneship. It was through his prosecution that the praetor elect Publius Sextius was convicted of bribery. He would have gone farther in
public office had he not always suffered from unstable
and even bad health.

" I recognize very well that I have been occupied 181
with the enumeration of many who never were
esteemed and in fact never were orators, and that
some earlier names have been passed over who
deserved laudable mention. But if so, it was from
ignorance ; for what can one write of men of an
earlier time when no records of others or works of
their own speak concerning them ? But of those
whom I myself have seen I pass over scarcely anyone
whom I ever heard speak. For it is my wish to make 182
it plain that in an old and great state like ours, where
eloquence has held out the greatest rewards, all men
have desired to be speakers, no great number have
ventured to try, few have been successful. Concerning each one I shall speak so that you may know
whom I consider to have been a mere declaimer, and
whom an orator.

" To about the same time, but somewhat younger
than Julius, yet essentially contemporary, belong
Gaius Cotta, Publius Sulpicius, Quintus Varius,
Gnaeus Pomponius, Gaius Curio, Lucius Fufius,
Marcus Drusus, Publius Antistius ; no period of our
history ever produced a more numerous progeny of

et Sulpicius cum meo iudicio tum omnium facile
primas tulerunt.

Hic Atticus : Quo modo istuc dicis, inquit, cum tuo
iudicio tum omnium ? Semperne in oratore probando aut improbando vulgi iudicium cum intellegentium iudicio congruit ? An alii probantur ⟨a⟩
multitudine, alii autem ab eis qui intellegunt ?

Recte requiris, inquam, Attice ; sed audies ex me
fortasse quod non omnes probent.

184 An tu, inquit, id laboras, si huic modo Bruto
probaturus es ?

Plane, inquam, Attice, disputationem hanc de
oratore probando aut improbando multo malim tibi
et Bruto placere, eloquentiam autem meam populo
probari velim. Etenim necesse est, qui ita dicat,
ut a multitudine probetur, eundem doctis probari.
Nam quid in dicendo rectum sit aut pravum ego
iudicabo, si modo is sum qui id possim aut sciam
iudicare ; qualis vero sit orator ex eo quod is dicendo
185 efficiet poterit intellegi. Tria sunt enim, ut quidem
ego sentio, quae sint efficienda dicendo : ut doceatur
is apud quem dicetur, ut delectetur, ut moveatur
vehementius. Quibus virtutibus oratoris horum
quidque efficiatur aut quibus vitiis orator aut non
assequatur haec aut etiam in his labatur et cadat,
artifex aliquis iudicabit. Efficiatur autem ab oratore

---

a The discussion which follows paves the way for the subsequent more specific attack upon the self-styled Atticists,
who we are told (289) could not hold the attention even of
the interested parties, much less of a miscellaneous and
curious audience. They arrogated to themselves, however,
a right of private judgement as *intellegentes* in contrast to
the *iudicium vulgi*.

orators. Of this number the first rank, in my judge- 183
ment and in the judgement of the public, was awarded
to Cotta and Sulpicius."

Here Atticus interposed : " What do you mean by
saying ' in your judgement and the judgement of the
public ' ? Is it always true that in the approval or
disapproval of an orator the judgement of the crowd
coincides with the judgement of experts ? Or is it not
rather true that some orators win the approbation of
the multitude, others of those qualified to judge ? " [a]

" Your question is a good one, Atticus," I replied,
" but you will get an answer from me which perhaps
everyone would not accept."

" Why," said Atticus, " should you be concerned 184
for general approbation if only you can win the
assent of Brutus here ? "

" You are quite right, Atticus," I replied. " This
discussion about the reasons for esteeming an orator
good or bad I much prefer should win the approval of
you and of Brutus, but as for my oratory I should
wish it rather to win the approval of the public. The
truth is that the orator who is approved by the multitude must inevitably be approved by the expert.
What is right or wrong in a man's speaking I shall
be able to judge, provided I have the ability and
knowledge to judge ; but what sort of an orator a
man is can only be recognized from what his oratory
effects. Now there are three things in my opinion 185
which the orator should effect : instruct his listener,
give him pleasure, stir his emotions. By what virtues
in the orator each one of these is effected, or from
what faults the orator fails to attain the desired
effect, or in trying even slips and falls, a master of
the art will be able to judge. But whether or not

necne ut ei qui audiunt ita afficiantur ut orator velit,
vulgi assensu et populari approbatione iudicari solet.
Itaque numquam de bono oratore aut non bono doctis
186 hominibus cum populo dissensio fuit. L. An censes,
dum illi viguerunt quos ante dixi, non eosdem gradus
oratorum vulgi iudicio et doctorum fuisse? De
populo si quem ita rogavisses : quis est in hac civitate
eloquentissimus? in Antonio et Crasso aut dubitaret
aut hunc alius, illum alius diceret. Nemone Philippum
tam suavem oratorem, tam gravem, tam facetum his
anteferret, quem nosmet ipsi, qui haec arte aliqua
volumus expendere, proximum illis fuisse diximus?
Nemo profecto ; id enim ipsum est summi oratoris
187 summum oratorem populo videri. Qua re tibicen
Antigenidas dixerit discipulo sane, frigenti ad populum, mihi cane et Musis ; ego huic Bruto, dicenti ut
solet apud multitudinem, mihi cane et populo, mi
Brute, dixerim, ut qui audient quid efficiatur, ego
etiam cur id efficiatur intellegam. Credit eis quae
dicuntur qui audit oratorem, vera putat, assentitur
probat, fidem facit oratio : tu artifex quid quaeris
188 amplius? Delectatur audiens multitudo et ducitur
oratione et quasi voluptate quadam perfunditur :
quid habes quod disputes? Gaudet dolet, ridet

the orator succeeds in conveying to his listeners the
emotions which he wishes to convey, can only be
judged by the assent of the multitude and the
approbation of the people. For that reason, as to
the question whether an orator is good or bad, there
has never been disagreement between experts and
the common people. Can you suppose that, in the 186
lifetime and activity of those whom I have named
above, the ranking of orators in the judgement of the
people and of experts was not the same ? If you had
put to any man of the common people this question :
' Who is the greatest orator in our commonwealth ? '
he might have hesitated as between Antonius or
Crassus, or one might have named Antonius, another
Crassus. Would no one have expressed a preference
to them for Philippus, with all his charm and dignity
and wit, whom I, deliberately weighing such qualities
in the scale of theory, have placed next to them ?
Certainly not ; for this is the very mark of supreme
oratory, that the supreme orator is recognized by
the people. Thus, while Antigenidas the flutist may 187
very well have said to a pupil, whom the public had
listened to coldly, ' play for me and for the Muses ' ;
I would say rather to our Brutus here, addressing as
he does commonly a great audience, ' play for me
and for the people, my dear Brutus.' They will
recognize the effect, I shall understand the reason for
it. When one hears a real orator he believes what
is said, thinks it true, assents and approves ; the
orator's words win conviction. You, sir, critic and
expert, what more do you ask ? The listening 188
throng is delighted, is carried along by his words, is
in a sense bathed deep in delight. What have you
here to cavil with ? They feel now joy now sorrow,

plorat, favet odit, contemnit invidet, ad misericordiam
inducitur, ad pudendum, ad pigendum ; irascitur
miratur, sperat timet ; haec perinde accidunt, ut
eorum qui adsunt mentes verbis et sententiis et
actione tractantur : quid est quod exspectetur docti
alicuius sententia ? Quod enim probat multitudo,
hoc idem doctis probandum est. Denique hoc
specimen est popularis iudici, in quo numquam fuit
189 populo cum doctis intellegentibusque dissensio : cum
multi essent oratores in vario genere dicendi, quis
umquam ex his excellere iudicatus est vulgi iudicio
qui non idem a doctis probaretur ? quando autem
dubium fuisset apud patres nostros eligendi cui
patroni daretur optio quin aut Antonium optaret aut
Crassum ? aderant multi alii ; tamen utrum de his
potius dubitasset aliquis, quin alterum nemo ; quid,
adulescentibus nobis cum esset Cotta et Hortensius,
num quis, quoi[1] quidem eligendi potestas esset,
quemquam his anteponebat ?

190   LI. Tum Brutus : Quid tu, inquit, quaeris alios ?
de te ipso nonne quid optarent rei, quid ipse Hortensius iudicaret videbamus ? qui cum partiretur tecum causas,—saepe enim interfui—perorandi locum,
ubi plurimum pollet oratio, semper tibi relinque-
bat.

    Faciebat ille quidem, inquam, et mihi benevolentia

<hr />

[1] quo *L*, cui *vulg.*

are moved now to laughter now to tears ; they show
approbation detestation, scorn aversion ; they are
drawn to pity to shame to regret ; are stirred to anger
wonder, hope fear ; and all these come to pass just
as the hearers' minds are played upon by word and
thought and action. Again, what need to wait for
the verdict of some critic ? It is plain that what the
multitude approves must win the approval of experts.
Take this finally as an illustration of the correctness of
popular judgement (wherein I repeat there never was
nor is any disagreement between the people and the
critic or expert) : There have been orators in great 189
number with many varied styles of speaking, but was
there ever among them all one who was adjudged
pre-eminent by the verdict of the masses who did not
likewise win the approval of the experts ? In our
fathers' day, for example, was there ever any doubt
that, if a man were free to choose his counsel, his
choice would fall upon either Antonius or Crassus ?
There were many others available, and yet, while as
between these two one might hesitate, as to selecting
the one or the other no one hesitated. Or again,
when in my youth Cotta and Hortensius were at the
bar, who, if he had freedom of choice, preferred
another to either of them ? ''

" Why," said Brutus at this point, " do you instance 190
others ? In your own case have we not often seen
the choice of clients, and the judgement of Hortensius
himself ? When he was associated in cases with you
(I know because I was often present in your con-
ferences) the concluding speech, where there was
the greatest opportunity for effect, he always left
to you."

" Yes, it is true," I replied ; " his kindliness of

credo, ductus tribuebat omnia. Sed ego quae de
me populi sit opinio nescio ; de reliquis hoc affirmo,
qui vulgi opinione disertissimi habiti sint, eosdem
intellegentium quoque iudicio fuisse probatissimos.
191 Nec enim posset idem Demosthenes dicere quod
dixisse Antimachum clarum poetam ferunt, qui cum
convocatis auditoribus legeret eis magnum illud
quod novistis volumen suum et eum legentem omnes
praeter Platonem reliquissent : legam, inquit, nihilo
minus ; Plato enim mihi unus instar est centum
milium.[1] Et recte ; poema enim reconditum paucorum approbationem, oratio popularis assensum
vulgi debet movere. At si eundem hunc Platonem
unum auditorem haberet Demosthenes, cum esset
192 relictus a ceteris, verbum facere non posset. Quid
tu, Brute ? possesne,[2] si te ut Curionem quondam
contio reliquisset ?

Ego vero, inquit ille, ut me tibi indicem, in eis
etiam causis, in quibus omnis res nobis cum iudicibus
est, non cum populo, tamen si a corona relictus sim,
non queam dicere.

Ita se, inquam, res habet. Ut, si tibiae inflatae
non referant sonum, abiciendas eas sibi tibicen putet,
sic oratori populi aures tamquam tibiae sunt ; eae
si inflatum non recipiunt aut si auditor omnino

[1] centum milium *Orelli*, omnium me illum *L.*
[2] posses nisi *L*, *corr. vulg.* (*cf. Ellendt ad loc.*).

---

[a] Antimachus of Colophon, epic poet of the period of the
Peloponnesian war, author of a long epic of the Theban cycle
(*Thebaïs*), which is probably the poem here referred to.

feeling toward me, I fancy, made him extravagant in doing me honour. What the popular judgement about me is I do not know; but of others I can affirm confidently, that those who in the opinion of the masses were accounted the best speakers are the very ones who have been most approved by trained critics. Demosthenes could never have said 191 what is reported of the famous poet Antimachus. When reading that long and well-known poem *a* of his before an assembled audience, in the very midst of his reading all his listeners left him but Plato: 'I shall go on reading,' he said, 'just the same; for me Plato alone is as good as a hundred thousand.' And quite right; for a poem full of obscure allusions can from its nature only win the approbation of the few; an oration meant for a general public must aim to win the assent of the throng. If Demosthenes on the other hand had held only Plato as his auditor and was deserted by the rest, he could not have uttered a single word. And you, Brutus? Could 192 you have done a thing if the whole assembly, as it did once with Curio, had deserted you?"

"I confess frankly," he replied, "that even in cases where I am only concerned with a bench of judges and not with the people, even so, if I am abandoned by the circle of listeners, I am quite unable to speak."

"Yes," I said, "that is inevitably the case. Thus, for example, if the wind instrument when blown upon does not respond with sound, the musician knows that the instrument must be discarded, and so in like manner the popular ear is for the orator a kind of instrument; if it refuses to accept the breath blown into it, or if, as a horse to the rein, the

163

tamquam equus non facit, agitandi finis faciendus
193 est. LII. Hoc tamen interest, quod vulgus interdum
non probandum oratorem probat, sed probat sine
comparatione ; cum a mediocri aut etiam malo
delectatur, eo est contentus ; esse melius non sentit,
illud quod est, qualecumque est, probat. Tenet enim
auris vel mediocris orator, sit modo aliquid in eo ;
nec res ulla plus apud animos hominum quam ordo
et ornatus orationis valet.

194 Qua re quis ex populo, cum Q. Scaevolam pro
M. Coponio dicentem audiret in ea causa de qua
ante dixi, quicquam politius aut elegantius aut
omnino melius aut exspectaret aut posse fieri
195 putaret ? Cum is hoc probare vellet, M'. Curium,
cum ita heres institutus esset, si pupillus ante
mortuus esset quam in suam tutelam venisset,
pupillo non nato heredem esse non posse, quid
ille non dixit de testamentorum iure, de antiquis
formulis ? quem ad modum scribi oportuisset, si
196 etiam filio non nato heres institueretur ? quam
captiosum esse populo, quod scriptum esset neglegi
et opinione quaeri voluntates et interpretatione
disertorum scripta simplicium hominum pervertere ?
197 Quam ille multa de auctoritate patris sui, qui semper
ius illud esse defenderat ? quam omnino multa de

164

listener does not respond, there is no use of urging
him. There is however this difference, that the 193
crowd sometimes gives its approval to an orator who
does not deserve it, but it approves without comparison. When it is pleased by a mediocre or even bad
speaker it is content with him ; it does not apprehend
that there is something better ; it approves what is
offered, whatever its quality ; for even a mediocre
orator will hold its attention, if only he amounts to
anything at all, since there is nothing that has so
potent an effect upon human emotions as well-
ordered and embellished speech.

" Thus, for example, what common man listening 194
to Quintus Scaevola in behalf of Marcus Coponius,
the case to which I referred before, would have expected, or indeed would have thought it possible, to
hear anything more finished or more nicely expressed
or in any respect better ? It was Scaevola's object 195
to prove that Manius Curius (who had been named as
heir in the event that an expected posthumous son
should die before said son had reached his majority)
could not become heir, because in fact no posthumous
son was born. How full and precise he was on
testamentary law, on ancient formulas, on the
manner in which the will should have been drawn
if Curius were to be recognized as heir even if no
son were born ; what a snare was set for plain people 196
if the exact wording of the will were ignored, and
if intentions were to be determined by guess-work,
and if the written words of simple-minded people
were to be perverted by the interpretation of clever
lawyers. How much he had to say about the 197
authority of his father, who had always upheld the
doctrine of strict interpretation, and in general how

conservando iure civili ? Quae quidem omnia cum
perite et scienter tum ita breviter et presse et satis
ornate et pereleganter diceret, quis esset in populo
qui aut exspectaret aut fieri posse quicquam melius
putaret ?

LIII. At vero, ut contra Crassus ab adulescente
delicato, qui in litore ambulans scalmum repperisset
ob eamque rem aedificare navem concupivisset, ex-
orsus est, similiter Scaevolam ex uno scalmo cap-
tionis centumvirale iudicium hereditatis effecisse—
hoc ille initio, consecutis multis eiusdem generis sententiis, delectavit animosque omnium qui aderant in
hilaritatem a severitate traduxit ; quod est unum
ex tribus quae dixi ab oratore effici debere. Deinde
hoc voluisse eum, qui testamentum fecisset, hoc
sensisse, quoquo modo filius non esset, qui in suam
tutelam veniret, sive non natus sive ante mortuus,
Curius heres ut esset ; ita scribere plerosque et id
valere et valuisse semper. Haec et multa eius modi
dicens fidem faciebat ; quod est ex tribus oratoris
198 officiis alterum. Deinde aequum bonum, testamentorum sententias voluntatesque tutatus est : quanta
esset in verbis captio cum in ceteris rebus tum in

---

* The usual order of the three functions of the orator is,
docere, delectare, movere. Here, following the order of Crassus's speech, he takes up *delectare* first, then *docere* (so that
it becomes necessary to translate *alterum* as " another "), and
finally *movere,* just below.

much concerning observance of the civil law as handed down ! In saying all this with mastery and knowledge, and again with his characteristic brevity and compactness, not without ornament and with perfect finish, what man of the people would have expected or thought that anything better could be said ?

" Crassus, however, in rebuttal began with a story of a boy's caprice, who while walking along the shore found a thole-pin, and from that chance became infatuated with the idea of building himself a boat to it. He urged that Scaevola in like manner, seizing upon no more than a thole-pin of fact and captious reason, had upon it made out a case of inheritance imposing enough to come before the centumviral court. From this beginning, and following it up with other suggestions of like character, he captivated the ears of all present and diverted their minds from earnest consideration of the case to a mood of pleasantry—one of the three things which I have said it was the function of the orator to effect. Thereupon he urged that the will, the real intention of the testator, was this : that in the event of no son of his surviving to the age of legal competence—no matter whether such a son was never born, or should die before that time—Curius was to be his heir ; that most people wrote their wills in this way and that it was valid procedure and always had been valid. With these and many similar arguments he won credence—which is another of the three functions of the orator.[a] He then passed over to general 198 right and equity ; defended observance of the manifest will and intention of the testator ; pointed out what snares lay in words, not only in wills but else-

testamentis, si neglegerentur voluntates ; quantam
sibi potentiam Scaevola assumeret, si nemo auderet
testamentum facere postea nisi de illius sententia.
Haec cum graviter tum ab exemplis copiose, tum
varie, tum etiam ridicule et facete explicans eam
admirationem assensionemque commovit, dixisse ut
contra nemo videretur ; hoc erat oratoris officium
partitione tertium, genere maximum. Hic ille de
populo iudex, qui separatim alterum admiratus esset,
idem audito altero iudicium suum contemneret ; at
vero intellegens et doctus audiens Scaevolam sentiret
esse quoddam uberius dicendi genus et ornatius.
Ab utroque autem causa perorata si quaereretur,
uter praestaret orator, numquam profecto sapientis
iudicium a iudicio vulgi discreparet.

199 LIV. Qui praestat igitur intellegens imperito ?
Magna re et difficili ; si quidem magnum est scire,
quibus rebus efficiatur amittaturve dicendo illud
quidquid est quod aut effici dicendo oportet aut
amitti non oportet. Praestat etiam illo doctus
auditor indocto, quod saepe, cum oratores duo aut
plures populi iudicio probantur, quod dicendi genus
optimum sit intellegit. Nam illud quod populo non
probatur ne intellegenti quidem auditori probari

where, if obvious intentions were ignored ; what
tyrannical power Scaevola was arrogating to himself
if no one hereafter should venture to make a will
unless in accordance with his idea. Setting forth
all this, at once with earnestness and abundant illustration, and with great variety of clever and amusing
allusion, he provoked such admiration and won such
assent that no opposition seemed possible. This
was an example of that function of the orator which
in my division was third, but in significance first and
greatest. Now that judge of ours, from the ranks
of the plain people, who had admired the one speaker
when heard by himself, on hearing the other would
abandon his first estimate as absurd. But the trained
critic on the other hand, listening to Scaevola, would
have recognized at once that his oratory lacked
something of richness and resourcefulness. If however when the case was over you had asked both of
our judges which of the two orators was superior,
you would find beyond a doubt that the judgement of
the expert was never at variance with the judgement
of the masses.

" Wherein then is the trained critic superior to 199
the untrained ? In respect of something which is
difficult to explain, and yet highly important ; since
it is certainly important to know how that, which
ought to be effected by eloquence or ought not
to fail of effect, is in fact effected or fails of effect.
The trained listener also has this advantage over
the untrained : that when two or more orators enjoy the favourable esteem of the people, the former
is often in position to recognize which style of
oratory is best. As for oratory which does not win
the approval of the people, it is quite unable to

potest.   Ut enim ex nervorum sono in fidibus quam
scienter et pulsi sint intellegi solet, sic ex animorum
motu cernitur quid tractandis his perficiat orator.
200 Itaque intellegens dicendi existimator, non assidens
et attente audiens, sed uno aspectu et praeteriens
de oratore saepe iudicat.   Videt oscitantem iudicem,
loquentem cum altero, non numquam etiam circu-
lantem, mittentem ad horas, quaesitorem ut dimittat
rogantem : intellegit oratorem in ea causa non adesse
qui possit animis iudicum admovere orationem tamquam fidibus manum.   Idem si praeteriens aspexerit
erectos intuentis iudices, ut aut doceri de re idque
etiam vultu probare videantur, aut ut avem cantu
aliquo sic illos viderit oratione quasi suspensos teneri,
aut, id quod maxime opus est, misericordia odio
motu animi aliquo perturbatos esse vehementius—
ea si praeteriens, ut dixi, aspexerit, si nihil audiverit, tamen oratorem versari in illo iudicio et opus
oratorium fieri aut perfectum iam esse profecto in-
telleget.

201   LV. Cum haec disseruissem, uterque assensus est,
et ego tamquam de integro ordiens :

Quando igitur, inquam, a Cotta et Sulpicio haec
omnis fluxit oratio, cum hos maxime iudicio illorum
hominum et illius aetatis dixissem probatos, revertar
ad eos ipsos ; tum reliquos, ut institui, deinceps per-

win the approval of the expert either. For just as from the sound of the strings on the harp the skill with which they are struck is readily recognized, so what skill the orator has in playing on the minds of his audience is recognized by the emotion produced. Thus the intelligent critic, not by patient 200 sitting and attentive listening, but by a single glance in passing can often form a correct judgement of an orator. He observes one of the judges yawning, talking to a fellow judge, sometimes even gossiping in a group, sending out to learn the time, asking the presiding judge to adjourn the court: he recognizes that in that case there is present no orator whose words can play on the minds of the court, as the hand of the musician plays upon the strings. Again, if in passing he notices that the judges are alert, attentive, and have the appearance whether of learning eagerly about the case in hand and of showing assent by their faces, or of hanging upon the words of the orator, like a bird lured by the trapper's notes, or (most of all) that they are stirred to pity, hate, or some like emotion—all these if he observe only in passing, without hearing a word, yet he will recognize inevitably that an orator is present in that court, and that the proper work of an orator is in process or is already accomplished."

To this exposition they both agreed, and I, as if 201 making a fresh start, continued :

" Well then, since all this talk started from Cotta and Sulpicius, who I said were the orators most esteemed in the judgement of such experts and by the general judgement of their time, I will come back to a consideration of those two men themselves, and then I shall proceed with the rest in order, as I

171

sequar. Quoniam ergo oratorum bonorum, hos enim
quaerimus, duo genera sunt, unum attenuate pres-
seque, alterum sublate ampleque dicentium, etsi
id melius est quod splendidius et magnificentius,
tamen in bonis omnia quae summa sunt iure lau-
202 dantur. Sed cavenda est presso illi oratori inopia
et ieiunitas, amplo autem inflatum et corruptum
orationis genus. Inveniebat igitur acute Cotta, dicebat pure ac solute ; et ut ad infirmitatem laterum per-
scienter contentionem omnem remiserat, sic ad
virium imbecillitatem dicendi accommodabat genus.
Nihil erat in eius oratione nisi sincerum, nihil nisi
siccum atque sanum, illudque maximum, quod,
cum contentione orationis flectere animos iudicum
vix posset nec omnino eo genere diceret, tractando
tamen impellebat ut idem facerent a se commoti
quod a Sulpicio concitati.

203 Fuit enim Sulpicius omnium[1] vel maxime, quos
quidem ego audiverim, grandis et, ut ita dicam,
tragicus orator. Vox cum magna tum suavis et
splendida ; gestus et motus corporis ita venustus
ut tamen ad forum, non ad scaenam institutus
videretur ; incitata et volubilis nec ea redundans

---

[1] omnium *om. L, add. B*[2].

---

[a] This is the only passage of the *Brutus* which alludes to
the so-called characters of style (χαρακτῆρες τῆς λέξεως).
They are usually referred to as three in number, the plain,
the middle, and the grand, and are discussed most fully in
the *Orator*. The twofold division here given, while adopted
for the characterization of the two orators in question, is in
fact closer to the original significance of this analysis than
the threefold. In origin this division marked merely the
contrast between language as a medium of communication,
and language as a means of producing an effect (emotional,

undertook to do. Since then there are two distinct types of good oratory [a]—and that is the only kind we are considering—one simple and concise, the other elevated and abundant, while naturally that is the better which is more brilliant and impressive, yet everything which falls under the category of good, and is supreme in its kind, wins a just praise. But 202 the concise orator must be on his guard against meagreness and emaciation, the abundant and elevated type against inflation and errors of taste. As for Cotta, he was acute in invention, pure and facile in diction ; lacking vigour of lungs and voice, he had very wisely learned to sacrifice vehemence, and to accommodate his style of speaking to his physical weakness. In his language everything was genuine, everything sane and healthy, and chiefest of all, since he could scarcely hope to move the judges by vehemence (and indeed never used that resource at all), he swayed them by artful management, and by leading accomplished the same result as Sulpicius by driving.

" Sulpicius indeed was of all orators whom I have 203 ever heard the most elevated in style, and, so to speak, the most theatrical. His voice was strong and at the same time pleasing and of brilliant timbre ; his gesture and bodily movement extraordinarily graceful, but with a grace that seemed made for the forum rather than for the stage ; his language was swift and of easy flow without being either redundant

aesthetic, etc.) upon the listener. This analysis is found first in Aristotle, and then more sharply formulated in Theophrastus. See the translator's discussion in *Am. Jour. Phil.* xxvi. (1905), pp. 249 ff., " Origin and Meaning of the Ancient Characters of Style."

tamen nec circumfluens oratio. Crassum hic volebat imitari ; Cotta malebat Antonium ; sed ab
hoc vis aberat Antoni, Crassi ab illo lepos.

204 O magnam, inquit, artem ! Brutus, si quidem istis,
cum summi essent oratores, duae res maximae
altera alteri defuit.

LVI. Atque in his oratoribus illud animadvertendum est, posse esse summos, qui inter se sint dissimiles. Nihil enim tam dissimile quam Cotta
Sulpicio, et uterque aequalibus suis plurimum
praestitit. Qua re hoc doctoris intellegentis est
videre, quo ferat natura sua quemque, et ea duce
utentem sic instituere, ut Isocratem in acerrimo
ingenio Theopompi et lenissimo Ephori dixisse tra-
ditum est, alteri se calcaria adhibere alteri frenos.

205 Sulpici orationes quae feruntur, eas post mortem
eius scripsisse P. Cannutius putatur aequalis meus,
homo extra nostrum ordinem meo iudicio disertissimus. Ipsius Sulpici nulla oratio est, saepeque
ex eo audivi, cum se scribere neque consuesse
neque posse diceret. Cottae pro se lege Varia quae
inscribitur, eam L. Aelius scripsit Cottae rogatu.
Fuit is omnino vir egregius et eques Romanus cum
primis honestus idemque eruditissimus et Graecis
litteris et Latinis, antiquitatisque nostrae et in

ᵃ *Antiquitas* embraces the record of historical facts (*actis*)
and of human discovery (*inventis*) in the devices and arts of
civilization, in customs, institutions, etc. The Greeks and
Romans attributed to discovery by some one at some exact
time (*qui primus*) much which was a development through
ages from undefinable beginnings. *Cf.* Pliny, *Nat. Hist.* 7.
191-215 (*indicare quae cuiusque inventa sint*), and contrast
Roger Bacon : "numquam in aliqua aetate inventa fuit
aliqua scientia, sed a principio mundi paulatim crevit
sapientia."

174

or verbose. He had fixed on Crassus as his model; Cotta had chosen rather Antonius. But Cotta lacked the force of Antonius, Sulpicius the charm of Crassus."

" Surely a marvellous art," said Brutus, " when 204 one considers that these were two of the greatest orators and yet that of two of its greatest qualifications each lacked one."

" Yes, and in both one thing is to be noticed, that orators may be supreme and yet unlike. No one could have been so unlike Sulpicius as Cotta, and yet both were far and away beyond their contemporaries. It is therefore the business of the discerning teacher to note the bent of each one's nature, and with that as his guide to train his pupils, as Isocrates is reported to have said of the high-spirited Theopompus and the gentle Ephorus, that with one he used the rein, to the other applied the spur. The orations of Sulpicius which are in circu- 205 lation are believed to have been written after his death by Publius Cannutius my contemporary, the most competent orator in my judgement outside the senatorial ranks. No oration from the hand of Sulpicius himself is extant. I often heard him comment on the fact that he had never cultivated the habit of writing and found it impossible. The oration entitled ' Cotta in his own defence under accusation by the terms of the Varian law ' was composed at Cotta's request by Lucius Aelius. This Aelius was in all respects an uncommon man, a Roman knight of highest integrity, and he was at the same time deeply read in Greek and Latin letters; with our early history, whether in respect of recorded facts or of discoveries and origins,[a] as well

175

inventis rebus et in actis scriptorumque veterum
litterate peritus. Quam scientiam Varro noster
acceptam ab illo auctamque per sese, vir ingenio
praestans omnique doctrina, pluribus et illustriori-
206 bus litteris explicavit. Sed idem Aelius Stoicus
⟨esse⟩[1] voluit, orator autem nec studuit umquam
nec fuit. Scribebat tamen orationes, quas alii
dicerent, ut Q. Metello . . .[2] f., ut Q. Caepioni,
ut Q. Pompeio Rufo, quamquam is etiam ipse
scripsit eas, quibus pro se est usus, sed non sine
207 Aelio. His enim scriptis etiam ipse interfui, cum
essem apud Aelium adulescens eumque audire
perstudiose solerem. Cottam autem miror summum ipsum oratorem minimeque ineptum Aelianas
levis oratiunculas voluisse existimari suas.

LVII. His duobus eiusdem aetatis annumerabatur
nemo tertius, sed mihi placebat Pomponius maxime,
vel dicam, minime displicebat. Locus erat omnino
in maximis causis praeter eos de quibus supra dixi
nemini, propterea quod Antonius, qui maxime ex-
petebatur, facilis in causis recipiendis erat; fasti-
diosior Crassus, sed tamen recipiebat. Horum
qui neutrum habebat, confugiebat ad Philippum
fere aut ad Caesarem; Cotta Sulpicius[3] expete-
bantur. Ita ab his sex patronis causae illustres
agebantur; neque tam multa quam nostra aetate
iudicia fiebant, neque hoc quod nunc fit, ut causae

---

[1] esse *add. codd. det.*
[2] ⟨Balearici⟩ f. *Lambinus*, L. f. *Martha.*
[3] Cotta Sulpicius *L*, post Cotta Sulpiciusque *Martha.*

as with all our early literature, he had the acquaintance of a professional scholar. All this field of knowledge our friend Varro, with superior capacity and wider learning, took over from him, and expanding it through his own study has set it forth in works surpassing Aelius in number and significance. Aelius was, besides, a professed Stoic and had no ambition to be an orator, and in fact never was one. However he wrote orations for others to deliver, as for example for Quintus Metellus, son of . . ., for Quintus Caepio, for Quintus Pompeius Rufus, though this last named himself wrote orations in his own defence, but not without the aid of Aelius. I know, because I had some knowledge of these compositions, as a young man in the house of Aelius, whose instruction I followed with great enthusiasm. I cannot but wonder too that Cotta, himself a great orator and far from devoid of taste, should have been willing to let the trivial speeches of Aelius be thought his own.

" With these two, Cotta and Sulpicius, no one of the same generation was associated as third in rank. However, Pomponius pleased me most, or rather displeased me least. In the most important cases there was in fact no place for anyone except those of whom I have spoken above ; for Antonius, who was most in demand, was always ready to undertake cases ; Crassus was somewhat more fastidious, and yet undertook them. Those who could get neither one of them had recourse generally to Philippus or to Caesar, and (after them) Cotta and Sulpicius were sought. Thus all the more prominent cases were handled by these six advocates. There were not then so many cases in court as in our time, nor was the

177

singulae defenderentur a pluribus, quo nihil est
208 vitiosius. Respondemus eis quos non audivimus,
in quo primum saepe aliter est dictum aliter ad nos
relatum ; deinde magni interest coram videre me
quem ad modum adversarius de quaque re asse-
veret, maxime autem, quem ad modum quaeque res
audiatur. Sed nil vitiosius quam, cum unum corpus
debeat esse defensionis, nasci de integro causam,
209 cum sit ab altero perorata. Omnium enim causarum unum est naturale principium, una peroratio ;
reliquae partes quasi membra suo quaeque loco
locata suam et vim et dignitatem tenent. Cum
autem difficile sit in longa oratione non aliquando
aliquid ita dicere ut sibi ipse non conveniat, quanto
difficilius cavere, ne quid dicas quod non conveniat
eius orationi qui ante te dixerit ? Sed quia et labor
multo maior est totam causam quam partem dicere
et quia plures ineuntur gratiae si uno tempore dicas
pro pluribus, idcirco hanc consuetudinem libenter
ascivimus.

210   LVIII. Erant tamen quibus videretur illius aetatis
tertius Curio, quia splendidioribus fortasse verbis
utebatur et quia Latine non pessime loquebatur,
usu, credo, aliquo domestico. Nam litterarum
admodum nihil sciebat ; sed magni interest quos
quisque audiat cotidie domi, quibuscum loquatur

178

present habit in vogue of employing several counsels for each case—a most vicious practice. We reply to 208 pleas which we have not heard, in which one thing was said and something quite different is reported to us. Then, further, it is important for me to see with my own eyes how and with what confidence each thing is urged by my opponent, and most of all how each thing is received. But most vicious of all is it, when a defence ought to be a whole, to have the case start all over again when it has already been concluded by one speaker. For there is one 209 natural beginning and one natural conclusion to all cases ; the remaining parts of the argument have their weight and their significance when placed in proper relation as members of a whole. It is difficult even in one long speech for the same speaker to avoid inconsistencies, and how much more difficult is it to guard against saying something which is inconsistent with the speech of a predecessor. But because much greater labour is involved in presenting a whole case than a part, and because you place a larger number under obligation to you with the same outlay of time if you speak in behalf of several clients, for this reason we have cheerfully accepted this usage.

" There were however some to whom Curio in that 210 time seemed to be a good third, after Cotta and Sulpicius ; probably because he employed a diction of superior brilliancy and used a Latin which was not so bad, by reason doubtless of his home training ; for he was absolutely without literary or theoretical training. It does certainly make a great difference what sort of speakers one is daily associated with at home, with whom one has been in the habit of talking

a puero, quem ad modum patres paedagogi
211 matres etiam loquantur. Legimus epistulas Corneliae matris Gracchorum; apparet filios non tam
in gremio educatos quam in sermone matris. Auditus est nobis Laeliae C. f. saepe sermo; ergo
illam patris elegantia tinctam vidimus et filias eius
Mucias ambas, quarum sermo mihi fuit notus, et
neptes Licinias, quas nos quidem ambas, hanc vero
Scipionis etiam tu, Brute, credo, aliquando audisti
loquentem.

Ego vero ac libenter quidem, inquit Brutus;
et eo libentius, quod L. Crassi erat filia.

212 Quid Crassum, inquam, illum censes, istius Liciniae
filium, Crassi testamento qui fuit adoptatus?

Summo iste quidem dicitur ingenio fuisse, inquit;
et vero hic Scipio, collega meus, mihi sane bene et
loqui videtur et dicere.

Recte, inquam, iudicas, Brute. Etenim istius
genus est ex ipsius sapientiae stirpe generatum.
Nam et de duobus avis iam diximus, Scipione et
Crasso, et de tribus proavis, Q. Metello, cuius
quattuor filii, P. Scipione, qui ex dominatu Ti.
Gracchi privatus in libertatem rem publicam vindi-

<a> The extravagant estimate which was placed upon purity
of diction (*Latine loqui*) goes back to grammatical studies
which were introduced into Rome by Greek scholars in
the Middle of the second century B.C. They were cultivated
by men in the Scipionic group, whose political and family
distinction lent to these studies an aristocratic glamour. In
many places of this treatise one discerns that purity of
speech had been used as a criterion of oratorical excellence
before Cicero's time (*cf.* 108).

<b> Quintus Caecilius Metellus Pius Scipio, colleague of
Brutus as pontifex, consul 52 B.C., at the time of writing in
command of Pompeian forces in Africa. After the defeat
at Thapsus, like Cato, he took his own life.

from childhood, how one's father, one's attendant, one's mother too speaks.[a] We have read the letters of 211 Cornelia, mother of the Gracchi ; they make it plain that her sons were nursed not less by their mother's speech than at her breast. It was my good fortune more than once to hear Laelia, the daughter of Gaius, speak, and it was apparent that her careful usage was coloured by her father's habit, and the same was true of her two daughters Muciae, with both of whom I have talked, and of her granddaughters the Liciniae, both of whom I have heard ; one, the wife of Scipio, I imagine that you too, Brutus, have sometimes heard speak."

" Yes," said Brutus, " and with great pleasure ; the more so because she was the daughter of Lucius Crassus."

"What," said I, "is your judgement of Crassus, 212 the son of this Licinia, who bore the name of Crassus by adoption, according to the will of [his grand-father, the orator] Crassus ? "

" He is reputed to have been a man of extraordinary ability," he replied, " and the other son, Scipio,[b] my colleague, seems to me an excellent speaker both in private conversation and in public discourse."

" Your estimate is quite right Brutus," I said, " and the reason is that his blood flows from the very fountain head of Wisdom herself—from his two grandfathers Scipio and Crassus, of whom I have already spoken, and from three great-grandfathers : Quintus Metellus,[c] the father of the four famous sons, Publius Scipio, who in private station freed the commonwealth from the domination of Tiberius

[c] On Q. Metellus, father of four famous sons, see 81 and note.

cavit, Q. Scaevola augure, qui peritissimus iuris
213 idemque percomis est habitus. Iam duorum aba-
vorum quam est illustre nomen, P. Scipionis, qui
bis consul fuit, qui est Corculum dictus, alterius
omnium sapientissimi, C. Laeli.

O generosam, inquit, stirpem et tamquam in
unam arborem plura genera, sic in istam domum
multorum insitam atque innatam[1] sapientiam!

LIX. Similiter igitur suspicor, ut conferamus parva
magnis, Curionis, etsi pupillus relictus est, patrio
fuisse instituto puro sermone assuefactam domum ;
et eo magis hoc iudico quod neminem, ex his
quidem qui aliquo in numero fuerunt, cognovi in
omni genere honestarum artium tam indoctum, tam
214 rudem. Nullum ille poetam noverat, nullum legerat
oratorem, nullam memoriam antiquitatis collegerat ;
non publicum ius, non privatum et civile cognoverat.
Quamquam hoc quidem fuit etiam in aliis et magnis
quidem oratoribus, quos parum his instructos artibus
vidimus, ut Sulpicium, ut Antonium. Sed ei tamen
unum illud habebant dicendi opus elaboratum ;
idque cum constaret ex quinque notissimis partibus,
nemo in aliqua parte earum omnino nihil poterat ;
in quacumque enim una plane clauderet, orator
esse non posset ; sed tamen alius in alia excellebat
215 magis. Reperiebat quid dici opus esset et quo
modo praeparari et quo loco locari, memoriaque ea

---

¹ innatam *Cuiaccius*, inluminatam *L.*

ᵃ The distinctions involved in these three divisions are
explained at the beginning of the Justinian *Digest* I. 1. 1, 2 :
ius publicum, ius privatum, of which the later is *collectum ex
praeceptis naturalibus aut gentium aut civilibus* (*ius civile*).
The orators' ignorance of the law and their frequent blunders
in consequence is the theme of satirical comment in *de Or.* 1.
197 and esp. 237 ff.

Gracchus, and Quintus Scaevola the augur, who was esteemed the most learned in the law and at the same time a man of most gracious bearing. As to his two 213 great-great-grandfathers, how distinguished is the name of Publius Scipio, who was twice consul and bore the familiar name of Corculum, and of that other, wisest of all, Gaius Laelius ! "

" Truly a noble stock ! " said Brutus, " and as upon a single tree one may see the fruits of many grafts, so upon that house was ingrafted the wisdom of many ancestors and became a part of it."

" Yes, and so in like manner, I fancy, to compare small with great, Curio though he was left an orphan became accustomed to that pure idiom which his father's rule had made the habit of his home. I incline to this opinion the more because out of all the orators I have known of any rank at all, I have never known one so completely untutored and un-skilled in any one of the liberal arts ; he knew no 214 poet, he had read no orator, he had acquired no knowledge of history, he had no acquaintance with public law, none with private and civil law.ᵃ To be sure this last deficiency applied to other orators as well, and some of them great, such as Sulpicius and Antonius, whom we have noted as inadequately trained in these arts ; but they at all events had this one quality—a thorough mastery of the art of speaking. Now this consists of five parts, as every one knows, and in no one of these parts can any one be wholly impotent ; for if in any single one he were clearly crippled he could not be an orator. And yet it is possible for one to show superior excellence in one part, another in another. Thus Antonius found readily 215 what needed to be said, how to preface and arrange it,

comprehendebat Antonius; excellebat autem actione.
Erant[que] ei quaedam ex his paria cum Crasso,
quaedam etiam superiora; at Crassi magis nitebat
oratio. Nec vero Sulpicio neque Cottae dicere
possumus neque cuiquam bono oratori rem ullam
ex illis quinque partibus plane atque omnino defuisse.

216 Itaque in Curione hoc verissime iudicari potest,
nulla re una magis oratorem commendari quam
verborum splendore et copia. Nam cum tardus
in cogitando tum in struendo dissipatus fuit. LX.
Reliqua duo sunt, agere et meminisse; in utroque
cachinnos irridentium commovebat. Motus erat
is quem et C. Iulius in perpetuum notavit, cum ex
eo in utramque partem toto corpore vacillante quae-
sivit quis loqueretur[1] e lintre, **et** Cn. Sicinius homo
impurus, sed admodum ridiculus, neque aliud in eo
217 oratoris simile quicquam. Is cum tribunus plebis
Curionem et Octavium consules produxisset Curioque
multa dixisset sedente Cn. Octavio collega, qui
devinctus erat fasciis et multis medicamentis propter
dolorem artuum delibutus, 'numquam,' inquit,
'Octavi, collegae tuo gratiam referes; qui nisi
se suo more iactavisset, hodie te istic muscae come-
dissent.' Memoria autem ita fuit nulla, ut aliquotiens, tria cum proposuisset, aut quartum adderet
aut tertium quaereret; qui in iudicio privato vel
maximo, cum ego pro Titinia Cottae peroravissem,
ille contra me pro Ser. Naevio diceret, subito totam

---

[1] loqueretur *vulg.*, *Quintil. 11. 3, 129*, loquetur *L.*

---

[a] Gaius Julius Caesar Strabo, the wit, characterized in
177, where see note.
[b] Note the colloquialisms of *hodie* (not essentially temporal,
but emphatic) and *istic*.
184

and all his plan he retained with a sure memory : but his excellence was in action. In some of these respects he was the equal of Crassus, in some superior ; but in Crassus the brilliant thing was his language. To neither Sulpicius nor to Cotta nor indeed to any good orator can we say that any one of these five parts was wholly and absolutely lacking.

" Now in the case of Curio we may conclude with 216 singular truth that an orator wins commendation by no one thing so much as by the excellence and wealth of his diction ; for in invention he was slow and in arrangement disorderly. There remain two points, action and memory, for both of which he evoked the laughter and ridicule of his audience. His action was of a kind which Gaius Julius [a] branded once for all, when as Curio was reeling and swaying his whole body from side to side, he asked: 'Who is the fellow there talking from a skiff ? ' And again Gnaeus Sicinius, a man of coarse but hilarious wit—the only oratorical quality that he possessed—made a jest to the same effect. When as tribune of the people he had 217 presented the consuls Curio and Octavius, and Curio had spoken at great length, while his colleague Octavius sat by swathed in bandages and reeking of medicinal salves for his gout, Sicinius said, turning to Octavius : ' You can never thank your colleague enough, Octavius ; for if he had not thrashed about in his way, the flies would surely have eaten you alive right here and now.' [b] As for memory, it was so completely lacking that sometimes when he had announced three points he would add a fourth or want a third. Again in a private suit of great importance, when I had finished my plea in behalf of Cotta's client Titinia, and he was speaking in rebuttal for Servius

causam oblitus est idque veneficiis et cantionibus
218 Titiniae factum esse dicebat. Magna haec im-
memoris ingeni signa ; sed nihil turpius quam quod
etiam in scriptis obliviscebatur quid paulo ante
posuisset, ut in eo libro, ubi se exeuntem e senatu
et cum Pansa nostro et cum Curione filio collo-
quentem facit, cum senatum Caesar consul habuisset,
omnisque ille sermo ductus ⟨est⟩ e percontatione
fili quid in senatu esset actum ; in quo multis verbis
cum inveheretur in Caesarem Curio disputatioque
esset inter eos, ut est consuetudo dialogorum, cum
sermo esset institutus senatu misso, quem senatum
Caesar consul habuisset, reprehendit eas res quas
idem Caesar anno post et deinceps reliquis annis
administravisset in Gallia.

219 LXI. Tum Brutus admirans : Tantamne fuisse
oblivionem, inquit, in scripto praesertim, ut ne
legens quidem umquam senserit quantum flagiti
commisisset ?

Quid autem, inquam, Brute, stultius quam, si ea
vituperare volebat quae vituperavit, non eo tempore instituere sermonem, cum illarum rerum iam
tempora praeterissent ? Sed ita totus errat ut in
eodem sermone dicat in senatum se Caesare consule
non accedere et id dicat ipso consule exiens e senatu.
Iam, qui hac parte animi, quae custos est ceterarum

ᵃ These words are bracketed by editors, but without good
reason. The exact indication of time and circumstance,
repeated in almost the same words just below, emphasizes the
grossness of the anachronism. Many such superfluous
repetitions are found in our treatise. *Cf.* 255 and note.

ᵇ The scene of this dialogue was placed in Caesar's
consulship 59 B.C., but in the anachronistic manner of
dialogue writing it included allusion to events of later date.
The treatise was a political attack and, to judge from the

Naevius, he suddenly forgot the whole case, and could only say in explanation that the potions and incantations of Titinia were the cause of it. That 218 sort of thing is evidence enough of a feeble memory. But worse than that, he would even forget in his writings what he had set down before ; as in that dialogue where he represents himself as walking away from a session of the senate which Caesar as consul had convoked,[a] and talking with my young friend Pansa and his own son Curio. The whole dialogue took its start from his son's asking what business the senate had transacted, in the course of which Curio inveighed at length against Caesar, and discussion arose between the interlocutors in the manner of dialogue. While the conversation began at the adjournment of a session of the senate which Caesar as consul had convoked, he proceeds nevertheless to censure the same Caesar for administrative acts in Gaul a year later and in the years ensuing."[b]

At this Brutus expressing his amazement said : 219 " Could his memory have been so bad that even in a written account he should not on re-reading have observed what a flagrant blunder he had made ? "

" Yes," I replied, " and what could be so stupid, when it was his purpose to censure just what he does censure, as not to place the scene of his dialogue at a time when the events in question were already past. But more than that, he fell into such complete confusion as to say in the same dialogue, that during Caesar's consulship he did not go near the senate, and yet says this on coming away from the senate precisely when Caesar was consul. If then a man's mind was

allusions to Curio's hostility, as reported by Suetonius, probably quite scurrilous. *Cf.* Suet. *Caes.* 50 and 51.

ingeni partium, tam debilis esset ut ne in scripto
quidem meminisset quid paulo ante posuisset, huic
minime mirum est ex tempore dicenti solitam
220 effluere mentem.   Itaque cum ei nec officium deesset
et flagraret studio dicendi, perpaucae ad eum causae
deferebantur.   Orator autem vivis eius aequalibus
proximus optimis numerabatur propter verborum
bonitatem, ut ante dixi, et expeditam ac profluen-
tem quodam modo celeritatem.   Itaque eius orationes aspiciendas tamen censeo.   Sunt illae quidem
languidiores, verum tamen possunt augere et quasi
alere id bonum quod in illo mediocriter fuisse con-
cedimus, quod habet tantam vim ut solum sine
aliis in Curione speciem oratoris alicuius effecerit.
Sed ad instituta redeamus.

221   LXII. In eodem igitur numero eiusdem aetatis C.
Carbo fuit illius eloquentissimi viri filius, non satis
acutus orator, sed tamen orator numeratus est ; erat
in verbis gravitas et facile dicebat et auctoritatem
naturalem quandam habebat oratio. Acutior Q.
Varius rebus inveniendis nec minus verbis expeditus.
Fortis vero actor et vehemens et verbis nec inops nec
abiectus et quem plane oratorem dicere auderes,
Cn. Pomponius lateribus pugnans, incitans animos,
222 acer acerbus criminosus.   Multum ab his aberat L.
Fufius, tamen ex accusatione M'. Aquili diligentiae
fructum ceperat.   Nam M. Drusum tuum magnum

ᵃ Quintus Varius, of Spanish birth and called Hybrida,
tribune in 91 B.C. and author of the vindictive law referred to
in 205 and 304, to which he himself fell a victim.
188

so feeble in that faculty, which is the custodian of
the rest of his intelligence, that even in a written work
he could not recall what he had set down just before,
there is small reason to wonder that his memory often
deserted him in extempore speech. In consequence, 220
though he enjoyed influential connexions and was
zealous in cultivating oratory, very few cases were
brought to him. Still as an orator his contemporaries
reckoned him as next in rank to the best, because of
the excellence of his diction, as I have said, and the
unembarrassed ease and fluency of his speech. Thus
in spite of his defects I consider his orations worth
looking at. They are to be sure somewhat spiritless,
but they may augment and in a sense feed that
particular excellence which we acknowledge he
possessed in moderate degree. Indeed this is so
important that by itself and without other merits it
gave to Curio the semblance of an orator in some
sort. But let me come back to my theme.

" To the same group of that time belonged Gaius 221
Carbo, son of the great orator of that name,—not a
speaker of much acumen, and yet he was accounted
an orator ; his diction was dignified and he spoke
readily and his whole style possessed a certain natural authority. More penetrating in invention was
Quintus Varius and with a diction not less ready.[a]
But for vigour and vehemence of action and with
a diction neither mean nor lacking in abundance
Gnaeus Pomponius stood out, a man whom you
would venture to call a real orator, fighting with lung-
power, rousing his auditors, sharp, sarcastic, skilful in
insinuating guilt. Far inferior to these was Lucius 222
Fufius, who yet in the accusation of Manius Aquilius
earned the reward of diligence. As for Marcus

avunculum, gravem oratorem ita dumtaxat cum de re
publica diceret, L. autem Lucullum etiam acutum,
patremque tuum, Brute, iuris quoque et publici et
privati sane peritum, M. Lucullum, M. Octavium Cn.
f., qui tantum auctoritate dicendoque valuit ut legem
Semproniam frumentariam populi frequentis suffragiis
abrogaverit, Cn. Octavium M. f., M. Catonem
patrem, Q. etiam Catulum filium abducamus ex acie,
id est a iudiciis, et in praesidiis rei publicae, cui facile
223 satis facere possint, collocemus. Eodem Q. Caepionem referrem, nisi nimis equestri ordini deditus a
senatu dissedisset.

Cn. Carbonem M. Marium et ex eodem genere
compluris minime dignos elegantis conventus auribus
aptissimos cognovi turbulentis contionibus. Quo in
genere, ut in his perturbem aetatum ordinem, nuper
L. Quinctius fuit ; aptior etiam Palicanus auribus
224 imperitorum. Et quoniam huius generis facta mentio
est, seditiosorum omnium post Gracchos L. Appuleius
Saturninus eloquentissimus visus est ; magis specie
tamen et motu atque ipso amictu capiebat homines
quam aut dicendi copia aut mediocritate prudentiae.
Longe autem post natos homines improbissimus
C. Servilius Glaucia, sed peracutus et callidus cum
primisque ridiculus. Is ex summis et fortunae et
vitae sordibus in praetura consul factus esset, si

Drusus, your great-uncle, an orator of weight, in public deliberations at all events ; Lucius Lucullus too, a man of acuteness ; and your father, Brutus, learned in both public and private law ; Marcus Lucullus also ; Marcus Octavius, son of Gnaeus, whose authority and words availed to abrogate by the votes of a full assembly the grain law of Gaius Gracchus ; Gnaeus Octavius son of Marcus ; Marcus Cato the father, and Quintus Catulus the younger— all these let us withdraw from the battle line, that is from court practice, and station them on the ramparts of the state, where they are qualified to render adequate defence. To this same station I would relegate 223 Quintus Caepio, had he not through excessive devotion to the equestrian order deserted the senate.

" Gnaeus Carbo, Marcus Marius, and several others of the same type I recognize, not as worthy of the ears of a select audience, but well fitted for the turbulence of popular assemblies. Of this type (to disturb in their enumeration the chronological order), Lucius Quinctius was a recent example ; Palicanus likewise, better suited to the taste of the ignorant. And since I have started on speakers of this type, of all 224 the radicals who succeeded the Gracchi, Lucius Appuleius Saturninus seemed to be the best speaker, though he took the fancy of the public rather by externals, such as his action or even his dress, than by any real faculty of expression or of sound sense, with which he was but meagrely endowed. The most impudent demagogue however in the memory of man was Gaius Servilius Glaucia, but very shrewd and clever, and a master at provoking a laugh. Rising from the lowest condition, whether of environment or of character, he would have been made consul while

rationem eius haberi licere iudicatum esset ; nam et
plebem tenebat et equestrem ordinem beneficio legis
devinxerat. Is praetor, eodem die quo Saturninus
tribunus plebis, Mario et Flacco consulibus publice est
interfectus ; homo simillimus Atheniensis Hyperboli,
cuius improbitatem veteres Atticorum comoediae
225 notaverunt.   Quos Sex. Titius consecutus, homo
loquax sane et satis acutus, sed tam solutus et mollis
in gestu ut saltatio quaedam nasceretur cui saltationi
Titius nomen esset. Ita cavendum est ne quid in
agendo dicendove facias, cuius imitatio rideatur.
LXIII. Sed ad paulo superiorem aetatem revecti
sumus ; nunc ad eam de qua aliquantum sumus locuti
revertamur.

226   Coniunctus igitur Sulpici aetati P. Antistius fuit,
rabula sane probabilis, qui multos cum iacuisset[1]
annos neque contemni solum sed inrideri etiam solitus
esset, in tribunatu primum contra C. Iuli illam consulatus petitionem extraordinariam veram causam
agens est probatus ; et eo magis quod eandem causam cum ageret eius collega ille ipse Sulpicius, hic
plura et acutiora dicebat. Itaque post tribunatum
primo multae ad eum causae, deinde omnes maxi-
227 mae quaecumque erant deferebantur. Rem videbat
acute, componebat diligenter, memoria valebat ; verbis non ille quidem ornatis utebatur sed tamen non

---

[1] iacuisset *Baehrens*, tacuisset *L*.

---

[a] The *senatus consultum ultimum* (Cic. *pro Rab. perd.* 20),
which gave the consuls dictatorial power, was directed at
these two men (100 B.C.).

still praetor if it had been held that his candidacy
could be considered ; for he had the people with him
and the allegiance of the equites through the benefits
of his law.   But as praetor he was put to death by
act of the state,[a] on the same day with the tribune of
the people Saturninus, in the consulship of Marius and
Flaccus.   He was a man very like Hyperbolus the
Athenian, whose shameless demagogy the old Attic
comedy branded.   Sextus Titius was a disciple of 225
these two, a voluble fellow and not lacking in acuteness, but in bearing so languishing and effeminate
that a kind of dance came into vogue which was
called ' the Titius.'   It shows what care must be
used to avoid anything in style of action or speaking
which can be made absurd by imitation.   But I have
reverted to a somewhat earlier time ; now let me
return to the period of which I have already said
something.

   " Associated with the time of Sulpicius was Publius 226
Antistius, a pettifogger not without merit, who
after many years of obscurity, during which he was
treated with contempt and even ridicule, won favour
finally in his tribuneship by carrying to success a just
indictment against the irregular candidacy of Gaius
Julius for the consulship.   This was the more note-
worthy because, while his colleague, the famous
Sulpicius, participated in the same case, Antistius
made a fuller and more penetrating argument.   In
consequence after his tribuneship many cases began
to be brought to him, and eventually all the most
important of whatever sort.   He found the point 227
at issue acutely, arranged his argument carefully
and possessed a sure memory.   His vocabulary was
not elaborate nor yet commonplace ; his style was

abiectis; expedita autem erat et perfacile currens
oratio; et erat eius quidam tamquam habitus non
inurbanus; actio paulum cum vitio vocis tum etiam
ineptiis claudicabat. Hic temporibus floruit eis,
quibus inter profectionem reditumque L. Sullae
sine iure fuit et sine ulla dignitate res publica; hoc
etiam magis probabatur, quod erat ab oratoribus
quaedam in foro solitudo. Sulpicius occiderat, Cotta
aberat et Curio, vivebat e reliquis patronis eius aetatis nemo praeter Carbonem et Pomponium, quorum
utrumque facile superabat.

228   LXIV. Inferioris autem aetatis erat proximus L.
Sisenna, doctus vir et studiis optimis deditus, bene
Latine loquens, gnarus rei publicae, non sine facetiis,
sed neque laboris multi nec satis versatus in causis;
interiectusque inter duas aetates Hortensi et Sulpici
nec maiorem consequi poterat et minori necesse erat
cedere. Huius omnis facultas ex historia ipsius
perspici potest, quae cum facile omnis vincat superiores, tum indicat tamen quantum absit a summo
quamque genus hoc scriptionis nondum sit satis
Latinis litteris illustratum. Nam Q.[1] Hortensi
admodum adulescentis ingenium ut Phidiae signum
simul aspectum et probatum est.

229   Is L. Crasso Q. Scaevola consulibus primum in foro
dixit et apud hos ipsos quidem consules, et cum eorum
qui adfuerunt, tum ipsorum consulum qui omnis
intellegentia anteibant, iudicio discessit probatus.
Undeviginti annos natus erat eo tempore, est autem

[1] Nam Q. *edd.*, Namque *L.*

---

[a] Sulpicius and Cotta, the pair of orators named next in
succession to Antonius and Crassus (183 and 201). Sulpicius
was put to death as a partisan of Marius in 88 B.C., Cotta
had been exiled by the *lex Varia* in 90.

unembarrassed and fluent and its whole tone was not without a certain urbanity ; his action both from defect of voice and especially from some tasteless mannerisms was rather awkward. His flourishing period fell between the departure and the return of Lucius Sulla, when the state was without law and commanded no respect. For this reason he won the more favour because the forum was in a sense deserted. Sulpicius had fallen, Cotta ª and Curio were absent from the city, and of remaining advocates no one was still living but Carbo and Pomponius, both of whom he surpassed easily.

" Of the younger generation his nearest rival was 228 Lucius Sisenna, a man of scholarly training and devoted to liberal studies, a user of pure Latin, versed in affairs of state, not without wit ; but he had no great industry nor adequate experience at the bar. Falling between the eras of Hortensius and Sulpicius, he did not succeed in overtaking the elder, and was obliged to yield before the younger. His ability can best be seen from his history, which while surpassing all its predecessors, yet reveals how far from perfection this type of writing is with us, and how inadequately as yet it has been cultivated in Latin letters. As for the genius of the young Quintus Hortensius, like a statue of Phidias, it required only to be seen to be approved.

" Hortensius began his public career in the con- 229 sulship of Lucius Crassus and Quintus Scaevola, and in the presence of these consuls as presiding officers he won the approval not only of all who were present, but of the consuls themselves, whose competence as judges far surpassed the rest of his audience. He was then only nineteen years of age. His death

L. Paullo C. Marcello consulibus mortuus ; **ex** quo
videmus eum in patronorum numero annos quattuor et
quadraginta fuisse.   Hoc de oratore paulo post plura
dicemus ; hoc autem loco voluimus ⟨eius⟩[1] aetatem in
disparem oratorum aetatem includere.   Quamquam
id quidem omnibus usu venire necesse fuit, quibus
paulo longior vita contigit, ut et cum multo maioribus
natu quam essent ipsi et cum aliquanto minoribus
compararentur.   Ut Accius isdem aedilibus ait se et
Pacuvium docuisse fabulam, cum ille octoginta, ipse
triginta annos natus esset, sic Hortensius non cum suis
aequalibus solum sed et mea cum aetate et cum tua,
230 Brute, et cum aliquanto superiore coniungitur, si
quidem et Crasso vivo dicere solebat et magis iam
etiam vigebat cum[2] Antonio ; et Philippo iam sene
pro Cn. Pompei bonis dicente, in illa causa adulescens
cum esset princeps fuit ; et in eorum quos in Sulpici
aetate posui numerum facile pervenerat ; et suos inter
aequalis M. Pisonem M. Crassum Cn. Lentulum P.
Lentulum Suram longe praestitit ; et me adulescen-
tem nactus octo annis minorem quam erat ipse multos
annos in studio eiusdem laudis exercuit ; et tecum
simul, sicut ego pro multis, sic ille pro Appio Claudio
dixit paulo ante mortem.
231   lxv. Vides igitur ut ad te oratorem, Brute,

---

[1] eius *add. Margraff.*
[2] Antonio et cum *L, transpos. Madvig.*

---

[a] A suit brought against the son, Pompey the triumvir,
for restitution of public property misappropriated by his
father (cos. 89 B.C.).

occurred in the consulship of Lucius Paullus and
Gaius Marcellus. We see thus that his career as an
advocate lasted for a period of forty-four years. Of
his character as an orator I shall say more presently.
Here it was my purpose only to insert his name and
time between the ranks of orators of different generations with whom he came in contact. It is inevitable
in the case of men who live a long life of activity that
they come into comparison with men much older
than themselves as well as with some much younger.
Thus, for example, Accius tells us that Pacuvius
and himself each produced a play under direction of the same aediles when the former was
eighty and he himself thirty. In like manner Hortensius was associated not only with his contemporaries, but also with my time and yours, Brutus, as 230
well as with a time somewhat earlier than his own.
For he had already begun to speak during the lifetime of Crassus, and with still greater success while
Antonius was yet alive. In the prosecution for the
property of Gnaeus Pompeius [a] he was, though a
mere youth, the principal speaker along with Philippus, then an old man ; into the ranks of those whom
I have placed in the period of Sulpicius he entered
with easy recognition ; amongst his own contemporaries, Marcus Piso, Marcus Crassus, Gnaeus
Lentulus, Publius Lentulus Sura, he held a place of
acknowledged supremacy ; he encountered me, in
youthful career, eight years younger than himself, and
we were rivals for the same prize for many years ;
finally shortly before his death, like my association
with him in behalf of so many others, he was associated with you, in behalf of Appius Claudius.

" You see that this has brought us all the way 231

pervenerimus tam multis inter nostrum tuumque
initium dicendi interpositis oratoribus ; ex quibus,
quoniam in hoc sermone nostro statui neminem
eorum qui viverent nominare, ne vos curiosius elice-
retis ex me quid de quoque iudicarem, eos qui
iam sunt mortui nominabo.

Tum Brutus : Non est, inquit, ista causa quam
dicis, quam ob rem de eis qui vivunt nihil velis
dicere.

Quaenam igitur, inquam, est ?

Vereri te, inquit, arbitror ne per nos hic sermo
tuus emanet et ei tibi suscenseant quos praeterieris.

Quid ? vos, inquam, tacere non poteritis ?

Nos quidem, inquit, facillime ; sed tamen te
arbitror malle ipsum tacere quam taciturnitatem
nostram experiri.

232   Tum ego : Vere tibi, inquam, Brute, dicam.   Non
me existimavi in hoc sermone usque ad hanc aetatem esse venturum ; sed ita traxit ordo aetatum
orationem ut iam ad minores etiam pervenerim.

Interpone igitur, inquit, si quos videtur ; deinde
redeamus ad te et ad Hortensium.

Immo vero, inquam, ad Hortensium ; de me alii
dicent, si qui volent.

Minime vero, inquit.   Nam etsi me facile omni tuo
sermone tenuisti, tamen is mihi longior videtur,
quod propero audire de te ; nec vero tam de virtutibus dicendi tuis, quae cum omnibus tum certe

down to you, Brutus, and yet how many orators inter-
vene between my beginnings and yours ! Of these
however, since it was my fixed purpose in this discussion to name none of those still living, lest you
should inquire too curiously about my judgement of
particular persons, I shall name only those who are
now dead."

" The reason you assign for not choosing to
speak of men now living is not in fact the real one,"
said Brutus.

" What then is ? " I asked.

" You are afraid, I suspect," he replied, " that
this discussion may leak out through us, and that
the feelings of those whom you fail to mention
will be hurt."

" What ? Can't you keep a secret ? "

" To be sure we can, and very well too ; still I
suspect you prefer to keep your own counsel rather
than to risk our silence."

" Well, I will tell you frankly that I never thought 232
in this talk to come down to our time. But the
sequence of period on period has carried me along
against my intention, so that I have come now even
to my own juniors."

" Very well, then," said Brutus, " introduce any that
you like at this point and then come back to yourself
and to Hortensius."

" To Hortensius, yes," I replied ; " about me
others will speak if they choose."

" Not at all," said he ; " for though everything
that you have said has been of the utmost interest
to me, yet it begins to seem a trifle long because of
my impatience to hear about you yourself. I don't
mean about the merits of your oratory, which of

199

mihi notissimae sunt, quam quod gradus tuos et quasi processus dicendi studeo cognoscere.

233 Geretur, inquam, tibi mos, quoniam me non ingeni praedicatorem esse vis sed laboris mei. Verum interponam, ut placet, alios et a M. Crasso, qui fuit aequalis Hortensi, exordiar.

LXVI. Is igitur mediocriter a doctrina instructus, angustius etiam a natura, labore et industria, et quod adhibebat ad obtinendas causas curam etiam et gratiam, in principibus patronis aliquot annos fuit. In huius oratione sermo Latinus erat, verba non abiecta, res compositae diligenter, nullus flos tamen neque lumen ullum, animi magna, vocis parva contentio, omnia fere ut similiter atque uno modo dicerentur. Nam huius aequalis et inimicus C. Fimbria non ita diu iactare se potuit; qui omnia magna voce dicens verborum sane bonorum cursu quodam incitato ita furebat tamen, ut mirarere tam alias res agere populum, ut esset insano inter

234 disertos locus. Cn. autem Lentulus multo maiorem opinionem dicendi actione faciebat quam quanta in eo facultas erat; qui cum esset nec peracutus, quamquam et ex facie et ex vultu videbatur, nec abundans verbis, etsi fallebat in eo ipso, sic intervallis exclamationibus, voce suavi et canora, †ad-

---

a Kroll recalls the saying of Lessing: " Seines Fleisses darf sich jeder rühmen."

course I know very well, as everyone else does, but
rather I am very eager to learn about your steps in
the development of it."

" I'll humour your wish," I said, " since you do not 233
demand that I be the herald of my own genius, but
only of my industry.[a]   However I will first introduce
some others if you don't mind, and begin with Marcus
Crassus, the contemporary of Hortensius.

" With only a moderate rhetorical training and
with even less natural endowment, yet by hard work
and application, and especially by careful use of
his personal influence in ensuring the success of his
pleas, he was for some years one of the leaders at
the bar.   His oratory was characterized by a pure
Latinity, a vocabulary not vulgar nor commonplace,
by careful arrangement of matter, but it was quite
devoid of any flower or lustre of ornament ; much
liveliness of thought, but little of voice and delivery,
so that nearly everything was said in one uniform
manner.   As for Gaius Fimbria, his contemporary and
enemy, he did not succeed for long in making himself conspicuous ; he shouted everything at the top
of his voice, and though his vocabulary was not bad
he raged along with such a torrent of words that you
wondered what the people could be thinking of to
give a madman place in the ranks of orators. Gnaeus 234
Lentulus too won a more favourable reputation for
eloquence by his delivery than his actual ability
warranted.   He was not in fact a man of much acuteness, though the expression of his countenance gave
him that appearance, nor was he resourceful in language, though in that too he gave an impression of
being so ; for by the effective use of pauses, ejacu-
lations, a voice sonorous and agreeable, he won such

mirando inridebat†[1] calebat in agendo, ut ea quae
deerant non desiderarentur. Ita, tamquam Curio
copia non nulla verborum, nullo alio bono, tenuit
235 oratorum locum, sic Lentulus ceterarum virtutum
dicendi mediocritatem actione occultavit, in qua
excellens fuit. Nec multo secus P. Lentulus, cuius
et excogitandi et loquendi tarditatem tegebat
formae dignitas, corporis motus plenus et artis et
venustatis, vocis et suavitas et magnitudo ; sic in
hoc nihil praeter actionem fuit, cetera etiam minora
quam in superiore.
236   LXVII. M. Piso quidquid habuit, habuit ex disciplina maximeque ex omnibus qui ante fuerunt
Graecis doctrinis eruditus fuit. Habuit a natura
genus quoddam acuminis, quod etiam arte lima-
verat, quod erat in reprehendendis verbis versutum
et sollers, sed saepe stomachosum, non numquam
frigidum, interdum etiam facetum. Is laborem
quasi cursum forensem diutius non tulit, quod et
corpore erat infirmo et hominum ineptias ac stultitias,
quae devorandae nobis sunt, non ferebat iracundius-
que respuebat sive morose, ut putabatur, sive ingenuo
liberoque fastidio. Is cum satis floruisset adulescens,
minor haberi est coeptus postea ; deinde ex virginum
iudicio magnam laudem est adeptus et ex eo tempore

---

[1] admirando inridebat *L*, ad mirandum illiciebat, ita
calebat *Madvig*, admirandum in modum calebat *Ellendt*.

---

[a] The text cannot be restored with certainty. The
translation corresponds essentially to Madvig's conjectures.
[b] A similar but less favourable judgement of M. Pupius
Piso, consul in 61 B.C., is given in *ad Att.* 1. 13, 2, where he
is called *cavillator illo genere moroso quod etiam sine
dicacitate ridetur.* Warburton cited this passage from the

favour by the warmth of his delivery [a] that the
qualities which he lacked were scarcely missed.
Thus as Curio by some wealth of diction and without any other good quality held the rank of orator,
so Lentulus by the excellence of his delivery cloaked 235
the mediocrity of his other gifts. In a manner not
very different Publius Lentulus covered up his slowness of thought and speech by dignity of bearing ;
his action was full of art and grace, and he possessed
a strong and pleasing voice ; he had in short nothing
but delivery ; all his other qualities were inferior to
the preceding Lentulus.

" Whatever excellence Marcus Piso possessed he 236
had as the result of training, and of all who had
gone before him none was more thoroughly versed
in Greek learning. He possessed a natural acumen
which he had sharpened by training ; it showed itself
in shrewd and adroit cavil about the strict use of
terms, but often it was ill-tempered, not infrequently
forced and frigid, yet sometimes witty.[b] The hard
labour of the forum, comparable to running a race,
he did not endure for long, partly because his
physical strength was not equal to it, and partly
because he could not put up with all the human
ineptitude and stupidity which we barristers have
to engorge. It roused his anger and he would
have no more of it, whether from a temper
naturally morose, as people believed, or from high-
minded scorn and disgust. After a youthful career
of success he began to be less regarded for a time ;
then from his success in the case of the Vestal

Brutus in characterization of Bentley (Monk, *Life of
Bentley*, ii. p. 411). It might be applied with equal appos-
iteness to that other Bentley, the late A. E. Housman.

quasi revocatus in cursum tenuit locum tam diu
quam ferre potuit laborem ; postea quantum de-
237 traxit ex studio tantum amisit ex gloria. P. Murena
mediocri ingenio, sed magno studio rerum veterum,
litterarum et studiosus et non imperitus, multae industriae et magni laboris fuit. C. Censorinus Graecis
litteris satis doctus, quod proposuerat explicans ex-
pedite, non invenustus actor, sed iners et inimicus
fori. L. Turius parvo ingenio sed multo labore, quoquo modo poterat, saepe dicebat ; itaque ei paucae
238 centuriae ad consulatum defuerunt. C. Macer auctoritate semper eguit, sed fuit patronus propemodum diligentissimus. Huius si vita, si mores, si vul-
tus denique non omnem commendationem ingeni
everteret, maius nomen in patronis fuisset. Non
erat abundans, non inops tamen ; non valde nitens,
non plane horrida oratio ; vox gestus et omnis actio
sine lepore ; at in inveniendis componendisque rebus mira accuratio, ut non facile in ullo diligentiorem
maioremque cognoverim, sed eam ut citius veteratoriam quam oratoriam diceres. Hic etsi etiam in
publicis causis probabatur, tamen in privatis illus-
triorem obtinebat locum.
239 LXVIII. C. deinde Piso statarius et sermonis
plenus orator, minime ille quidem tardus in ex-
cogitando, verum tamen vultu et simulatione multo
etiam acutior quam erat videbatur. Nam eius

---

^a The allusion is probably to 'the acquittal of the Vestal
Virgins' which is referred to in Cicero's third oration against
Catiline (4, 9) as a scandal or disaster lending portentous
significance to the year 63, the tenth anniversary of the
famous case. Nothing more is known of it. One might
surmise that the charge against them was unchastity (incest),
and that they had been acquitted against the evidence.

Virgins[a] he won great fame, and from that time, as if called back into the race, he held his position as long as he could bear the labour of it ; after that, what he relaxed in effort he lost in renown. Publius 237 Murena had but moderate ability ; he was a great student of history, devoted to letters and not unlearned in them, a man of varied and laborious activity. Gaius Censorinus had good Greek training ; he was adept at lucid presentation, his delivery was not without grace, but he was lazy and hated the forum. Lucius Turius, a man of small talent, but hard working, with such skill as he could command was a frequent speaker; as the result of his efforts he all but gained the consulship, failing by only a few votes. Gaius Macer all his life was deficient in 238 character and standing, but as a pleader he lacked little of being the most active. If his life, his character, even his very face, had not robbed his talent of everything to commend it, his name as a pleader would have been far greater. His language was not copious nor yet meagre, not brilliant nor again crude ; his voice, his gesture, his whole delivery were without charm ; but upon invention and arrangement of matter he bestowed an extraordinary care, such as I have scarcely seen surpassed in anyone ; you would call it however adroit routine rather than oratory. Though he won recognition in criminal cases, yet he held a more conspicuous place in civil suits.

" Then there was Gaius Piso, an orator of the 239 stationary or quiet type ; his manner of speaking was wholly conversational ; by no means slow in invention, yet by countenance and expression he gave the appearance of greater acumen than he possessed.

aequalem M'. Glabrionem bene institutum avi
Scaevolae diligentia socors ipsius natura neglegens-
que tardaverat. Etiam L. Torquatus elegans in
dicendo, in existimando admodum prudens, toto
genere perurbanus. Meus autem aequalis Cn. Pompeius vir ad omnia summa natus maiorem dicendi
gloriam habuisset, nisi eum maioris gloriae cupiditas ad bellicas laudes abstraxisset. Erat oratione
satis amplus, rem prudenter videbat ; actio vero
eius habebat et in voce magnum splendorem et in
240 motu summam dignitatem. Noster item aequalis
D. Silanus vitricus tuus studi ille quidem habuit non
multum sed acuminis et orationis satis. Q. Pompeius
A. f., qui Bithynicus dictus est, biennio quam nos
fortasse maior, summo studio dicendi multaque doctrina, incredibili labore atque industria ; quod scire
possum ; fuit enim mecum et cum M. Pisone cum
amicitia tum studiis exercitationibusque coniunctus.
Huius actio non satis commendabat orationem ; in
hac enim satis erat copiae, in illa autem leporis parum.
241 Erat eius aequalis P. Autronius voce peracuta atque
magna nec alia re ulla probabilis, et L. Octavius
Reatinus, qui cum multas iam causas diceret, adulescens est mortuus—is tamen ad dicendum veniebat
magis audacter quam parate ; et C. Staienus, qui
se ipse adoptaverat et de Staieno Aelium fecerat,

---

[a] Gnaeus Pompeius (Magnus), the triumvir, born 106 B.C.,
the year of Cicero's birth (*meus aequalis*).

[b] Implying that audacity and lack of careful preparation
were especially unbecoming in a young man, though they
might be condoned to age and experience.

As to his contemporary Manius Glabrio, his own
sloth and negligence retarded his career, though he
had received a careful training at the hands of his
grandfather Scaevola. Lucius Torquatus was a precise speaker, very sound in critical judgement, and
in all respects a man of perfect urbanity. Gnaeus
Pompeius my contemporary,[a] destined by nature to
pre-eminence, would have enjoyed greater glory for
eloquence had not ambition for still greater glory
drawn him off to the prizes of a military career.
His language had some elevation and he possessed
good judgement in discerning the question at issue ;
but chiefly a fine voice and great dignity of bearing
made his delivery impressive. Another contem- 240
porary, Decimus Silanus, your stepfather, Brutus,
lacked in application, but he possessed a good share
of intelligence and adequate oratorical skill. Quintus
Pompeius, son of Aulus, who was called Bithynicus,
perhaps two years my senior, was very ambitious
to speak well ; he was thoroughly trained, and in-
credibly hard-working. I have reason to know, because he was intimately associated with me and with
Marcus Piso as friend and companion in our rhetorical
studies and exercises. His delivery did not do
justice to his style ; the latter was not lacking in
fullness, the former was without charm. Publius 241
Autronius was another of about the same age, a
man with a loud shrill voice and nothing else to
commend him. Lucius Octavius of Reate died while
still a young man, though he had already spoken
in many cases ; but for all his youth he used to rely
on audacity rather than on preparation.[b] Then
too there was Gaius Staienus, who managed his own
adoption, and from a Staienus made himself an

fervido quodam et petulanti et furioso genere dicendi ; quod quia multis gratum erat et probabatur, ascendisset ad honores, nisi in facinore manifesto deprehensus poenas legibus et iudicio dedisset. LXIX. 242 Eodem tempore C. L. Caepasii fratres fuerunt, qui multa opera, ignoti homines et repentini, quaestores celeriter facti sunt, oppidano quodam et incondito genere dicendi. Addamus huc etiam, ne quem vocalem praeterisse videamur, C. Cosconium Calidianum, qui nullo acumine eam tamen verborum copiam, si quam habebat, praebebat populo cum multa concursatione magnoque clamore. Quod idem faciebat Q. Arrius, qui fuit M. Crassi quasi secundarum. Is omnibus exemplo debet esse quantum in hac urbe polleat multorum oboedire tempori 243 multorumque vel honori vel periculo servire. His enim rebus infimo loco natus et honores et pecuniam et gratiam consecutus etiam in patronorum, sine doctrina, sine ingenio, aliquem numerum pervenerat. Sed ut pugiles inexercitati, etiam si pugnos et plagas Olympiorum cupidi ferre possunt, solem tamen saepe ferre non possunt, sic ille cum omni iam fortuna prospere functus labores etiam magnos excepisset, illius iudicialis anni severitatem quasi solem non tulit.

244 Tum Atticus : Tu quidem de faece, inquit, hauris

ᵃ The provisions of the *lex Pompeia* of 52 B.C. restricted the plaintiff to two hours, the defendant to three hours. The unrestricted time and the enormous length of orations in the earlier republic are referred to by Tacitus, *Dialogus* (20 and 36). The Olympic games were celebrated in mid-summer. Pausanias (6. 42, 1) reports that the foot races were run before sunrise, the pentathlon and other socalled " heavy events " were held in the middle of the day. The summer heat of Olympia was proverbial.

Aelius. He cultivated an intense, fretful, all but crazy style of speaking, which however many liked, and it found such favour that he would have gone on to the higher honours if he had not been caught in open misdeeds and paid the penalty exacted by the laws and the courts. To the same time be- 242 longed the brothers Gaius and Lucius Caepasius, who through untiring effort, though newcomers and quite unknown, rose quickly to the rank of quaestor ; their style of speaking was provincial and without form. Not to be accused of passing over anyone with a tongue in his head let me add to them Gaius Cosconius Calidianus ; though without ideas, he proffered such wordy resourcefulness as he possessed to the people, who thronged to hear him and shouted their applause. Quintus Arrius, who played second-fiddle to Marcus Crassus, did much the same. He ought to be remembered as a lesson to every one of the significance in our city of placing oneself at the service of many, as occasion arises, and of making oneself useful to them, whether for their political ambition or for their defence at law. By such 243 devices Arrius, of humblest birth, attained to high office and wealth and favour, and though without training or ability came to be recognized in the ranks of pleaders. But like boxers of insufficient training and experience, even if in their eagerness for the Olympic crown they may be able to stand up against fists and blows, yet often cannot support the noonday sun, so in like manner Arrius, after having successfully withstood the shock of great exertions, could not survive the hardships of that year of court restrictions,[a] which was for him the noonday sun."

Here Atticus interrupted : " You're drawing from 244

idque iam dudum, sed tacebam ; hoc vero non putabam, te usque ad Staienos et Autronios esse venturum.

Non puto, inquam, existimare te ambitione me labi, quippe de mortuis ; sed ordinem sequens in memoriam notam et aequalem necessario incurro. Volo autem hoc perspici, omnibus conquisitis qui in multitudine dicere ausi sint, memoria quidem dignos perpaucos, verum qui omnino nomen habuerint, non ita multos fuisse. Sed ad sermonem institutum revertamur.

245 LXX. T. Torquatus T. f. et doctus vir ex Rhodia disciplina Molonis et a natura ad dicendum satis solutus atque expeditus, cui si vita suppeditavisset, sublato ambitu, consul factus esset, plus facultatis habuit ad dicendum quam voluntatis. Itaque studio huic non satis fecit, officio vero nec in suorum necessariorum causis nec in sententia senatoria defuit.

246 Etiam M. Pontidius municeps noster multas privatas causas actitavit, celeriter sane verba volvens nec hebes in causis, vel dicam plus etiam quam non hebes, sed effervescens in dicendo stomacho saepe iracundiaque vehementius ; ut non cum adversario solum sed etiam, quod mirabile esset, cum iudice ipso, cuius delenitor esse debet orator, iurgio saepe contenderet. M. Messalla minor natu quam nos,

---

[a] The *lex Pompeia de ambitu*, of 52 B.C., which imposed penalty of exile upon candidates convicted of bribery, intimidation, and other vicious forms of campaigning.

[b] That is, a native of Arpinum, Cicero's birth-place.

the dregs now, and have been for some time. However I have held my tongue ; but really I did not think that you would get down to men like Staienus and Autronius."

" I don't imagine you thought that any desire to ingratiate myself made me descend so far, at all events dealing with men no longer living ; but following the chronological sequence the names occurred to me inevitably of those who were my acquaintances and contemporaries. Besides it is my wish to make it clear, that when all have been brought together who have ventured to speak in public, very few deserve to be remembered, while the number of those who have won any name whatever has not been large. But let me return and go on as I had planned.

" Titus Torquatus, son of Titus, was thoroughly 245 trained in the school of Molo at Rhodes, and he possessed such fair natural endowment for ready and fluent speaking that, had he lived and profited by the law which forbade campaigning,[a] he would have made the consulship. But his ability to speak was greater than his ambition, and in consequence he never devoted enough attention to it. However he was never wanting in devotion to the cases of those dependent on him, nor unequal to expression of his opinion in the senate. Marcus Pontidius also, my 246 fellow-townsman,[b] was active in many private suits ; a rapid speaker and in the prosecution of cases not dull-witted, though to say ' not dull-witted ' scarcely describes him, since he would fairly boil over with vexation and spleen, and fall to wrangling not only with the opposing counsel, but, more remarkable, with the judge himself, whom it is the orator's business to conciliate. Marcus Messalla, my junior,

nullo modo inops, sed non nimis ornatus genere verborum ; prudens, acutus, minime incautus patronus, in causis cognoscendis componendisque diligens, magni laboris, multae operae multarumque causa-
247 rum.   Duo etiam Metelli, Celer et Nepos, nihil in causis versati, nec sine ingenio nec indocti, hoc erant populare dicendi genus assecuti.   Cn. autem Lentulus Marcellinus nec umquam indisertus et in consulatu pereloquens visus est, non tardus sententiis, non inops verbis, voce canora, facetus satis. C. Memmius L. f. perfectus litteris, sed Graecis, fastidiosus sane Latinarum, argutus orator verbisque dulcis sed fugiens non modo dicendi verum etiam cogitandi laborem, tantum sibi de facultate detraxit quantum imminuit industriae.

248   LXXI. Hoc loco Brutus : Quam vellem, inquit, de his etiam oratoribus qui hodie sunt tibi dicere liberet ; et, si de aliis minus, de duobus tamen quos a te scio laudari solere, Caesare et Marcello, audirem non minus libenter quam audivi de eis qui fuerunt.

Cur tandem ? inquam ;   an exspectas quid ego iudicem de istis qui tibi sunt aeque noti ac mihi ?

Mihi mehercule, inquit, Marcellus satis est notus,
249 Caesar autem parum ;   illum enim saepe audivi, hic, cum ego iudicare iam aliquid possem, afuit.

Quid igitur de illo iudicas, quem saepe audivisti ?

---

^a To this Memmius as patron Lucretius dedicated his great poem, not a happy choice, as one may conclude from this characterization as well as from other evidence (*cf. ad Fam.* 13. 1).

did not lack facility, but his diction possessed no great distinction; as pleader he showed judgement, shrewdness, and caution, diligence in mastering and arranging his case, great industry and devotion, and was engaged in many cases. The two Metelli, Celer 247 and Nepos, though not engaged in private suits, lacked neither talent nor training; they both cultivated the style of speaking which belongs to the popular assembly. Gnaeus Lentulus Marcellinus too was always thought of as a competent speaker, and in his consulship gave the impression of great eloquence; not slow in thought, nor unresourceful in language, he was possessed of a sonorous voice and considerable wit. Gaius Memmius,[a] son of Lucius, highly trained in letters, but only Greek, for he scorned Latin, was an orator of the subtle ingenious type with a pleasing diction, but averse to the labour not only of speaking, but even of thinking. His skill waned in proportion to his relaxation of effort."

At this point Brutus remarked : " How I wish that 248 you felt inclined to speak about the orators of to-day, and if not about others, at least about two whom I know you admire, Caesar and Marcellus. I should like to hear about them quite as much as I have enjoyed hearing about men no longer living."

" But why, pray ? " I replied. " Why should you expect me to pass judgement about men who are as well known to you as to me ? "

" True enough," he replied, " so far as Marcellus is concerned, but not so of Caesar. Marcellus I have 249 heard often; but from the time when I was old enough to form a judgement Caesar has been away from Rome."

" Well, what is your opinion about the one you have heard ? "

Quid censes, inquit, nisi id, quod habiturus es similem tui ?

Ne ego, inquam, si ita est, velim tibi eum placere quam maxime.

Atqui et ita est, inquit, et vehementer placet ; nec vero sine causa. Nam et didicit et omissis ceteris studiis unum id egit seseque cotidianis com-
250 mentationibus acerrime exercuit. Itaque et lectis utitur verbis et frequentibus ⟨sententiis⟩[1] et splendore vocis dignitate motus fit speciosum et illustre quod dicitur, omniaque sic suppetunt, ut ei nullam deesse virtutem oratoris putem ; maximeque laudandus est, qui hoc tempore ipso, quod[2] liceat in hoc communi nostro et quasi fatali malo, consoletur se cum conscientia optimae mentis tum etiam usurpatione et renovatione doctrinae. Vidi enim Mytilenis nuper virum atque, ut dixi, vidi plane virum. Itaque cum eum antea tui similem in dicendo viderim, tum vero nunc a doctissimo viro tibique, ut intellexi, amicissimo Cratippo instructum omni copia multo videbam similiorem.
251 Hic ego : Etsi, inquam, de optimi viri nobisque amicissimi laudibus libenter audio, tamen incurro in

[1] sententiis *add. Jahn.*
[2] quod *Peter,* cum L (*defendit Ellendt*).

---

[a] M. Claudius Marcellus, consul (with Servius Sulpicius) in 51 B.C., a leader of the senatorial opposition to Caesar, but distrustful of Pompey. He did not take active part in the Civil War, but withdrew to the autonomous city of Mytilene (in the province of Asia), where he was unmolested by Caesar. In spite of the urging of Cicero and other friends he was reluctant to seek pardon, but finally in May of the year 45 B.C. he began his return journey, but during a pause of a few days at Athens he was killed by one of his own retinue. This account of the life of Marcellus in exile

" What else can it be," he replied, " than that in him you are destined to see a counterpart of yourself?"

" In that case certainly I should wish him to please you as much as possible."

" But I really mean what I say," said Brutus, " and indeed his oratory does please me very much, and with good reason; for he has studied hard, he has devoted himself to this one goal to the exclusion of all else, and by unremitting practice he has kept himself at the top of form. The result shows in his use of 250 carefully chosen words and in wealth and variety of ideas. What he says too receives an external charm and brilliancy from a fine voice and dignified action. All this he commands so skilfully as to make me feel that he lacks no quality that an orator should have. I admire him too most of all because in this time, which has touched us all as with the hand of a malign fate, he finds such consolation as may be in the consciousness of his unswerving loyalty, and in resumption and enjoyment of scholarly pursuits. I saw him at Mytilene not long ago, and, as I have implied, I saw there a man indeed. As when before I had recognized his resemblance to you in style of speaking, so now after having enjoyed the instruction of the learned Cratippus (your good friend also, as I learned) he seemed to me more like you than ever."[a]

" It is pleasant," I replied, " to hear praise of so 251 good a man and so dear a friend, but it brings me

and of his character is influenced by the letter of Brutus to Cicero, to which reference is made at the beginning and at the end of our treatise (11 and 330). On the identity of this letter with the treatise of Brutus *de Virtute*, see Int. pp. 6 and 7.

memoriam communium miseriarum, quarum oblivionem quaerens hunc ipsum sermonem produxi
longius. Sed de Caesare cupio audire quid tandem
Atticus iudicet.

LXXII. Et ille : Praeclare, inquit, tibi constas, ut
de eis qui nunc sint nihil velis ipse dicere ; et hercule si sic ageres, ut de eis egisti qui iam mortui
sunt, neminem ut praetermitteres, ne tu in multos
Autronios et Staienos incurreres. Qua re sive hanc
turbam effugere voluisti sive veritus ⟨es⟩ ne quis se
aut praeteritum aut non satis laudatum queri posset,
de Caesare tamen potuisti dicere, praesertim cum
et tuum de illius ingenio notissimum iudicium esset
nec illius de tuo obscurum.

252   Sed tamen, Brute, inquit Atticus, de Caesare et
ipse ita iudico et de hoc huius generis acerrimo exis-
timatore saepissime audio, illum omnium fere oratorum Latine loqui elegantissime ; nec id solum
domestica consuetudine, ut dudum de Laeliorum
et Muciorum familiis audiebamus, sed quamquam
id quoque credo fuisse, tamen, ut esset perfecta illa
bene loquendi laus, multis litteris et eis quidem
reconditis et exquisitis summoque studio et dili-
253 gentia est consecutus ; quin etiam in maximis occupationibus ad te ipsum, inquit in me intuens, de
ratione Latine loquendi accuratissime scripsit primo-

ᵃ The treatise *de Analogia*, a Greek title, which is here
paraphrased for a Latin audience. The work was dedicated
to Cicero and the citation is apparently drawn from the
introductory dedication. *Cf.* the translator's discussion of

back to remembrance of our common misery, to forget which was one reason why I have spun out this discussion so long. But to come back to Caesar, I should like to hear what Atticus has to say of him."

" You make it very plain," said Brutus, " that you mean to be consistent in your purpose to say nothing of the living. Indeed if you were to treat of the living as you have done of the dead, and pass over no one, you would certainly encounter many an Autronius and Staienus. But whether it was your purpose to avoid reference to the present rabble of pleaders, or were afraid of complaints from one or another that he had been passed over or not treated with enough consideration, you could at all events have spoken about Caesar, inasmuch as your judgement about his genius is perfectly well known, and his concerning you is not obscure."

" Be that as it may, Brutus," interposed Atticus, 252 " my own judgement of Caesar—and I have more than once heard it confirmed by the competent judgement of our friend here—is, that of all our orators he is the purest user of the Latin tongue. While he has that distinction by family inheritance, as we heard a moment ago about the Laelii and Mucii, yet—though I accept that too as an important influence—he has sought to bring to perfection that merit of correct speech by diligent and enthusiastic studies of a recondite and esoteric kind. And more than 253 that, in the midst of the most absorbing activities he wrote and dedicated to you," Atticus continued, turning to me, " his careful treatise on the principles of correct Latinity,[a] and prefaced his treatment

the nature and date of this treatise in *Cl. Phil.* i. (1906), pp. 98-120.

CICERO

que in libro dixit[1] verborum dilectum originem esse
eloquentiae tribuitque,[1] mi Brute, huic nostro, qui
me de illo maluit quam se dicere, laudem singularem ; nam scripsit his verbis, cum hunc nomine
esset affatus : ac si, ut[2] cogitata praeclare eloqui possent, non nulli studio et usu elaboraverunt, cuius
te paene principem copiae atque inventorem bene
de nomine ac dignitate populi Romani meritum esse
existimare debemus, hunc facilem et cotidianum
novisse sermonem num[3] pro relicto est habendum ?

254   LXXIII. Tum Brutus : Amice hercule, inquit, et
magnifice te laudatum puto, quem non solum principem atque inventorem copiae dixerit, quae erat
magna laus, sed etiam bene meritum de populi
Romani nomine et dignitate. Quo enim uno
vincebamur a victa Graecia, id aut ereptum[4] illis est
255   aut certe nobis cum Graecis communicatum. Hanc
autem, inquit, gloriam testimoniumque Caesaris tuae
quidem supplicationi non, sed triumphis multorum
antepono.

Et recte quidem, inquam, Brute ; modo sit hoc
Caesaris iudici, non benevolentiae testimonium.

---

[1] dixit, tribuit *Eberhard*, dixerit, tribuerit *L*.
[2] ut *codd. det.*, *Lambinus*.
[3] num *Lallemand*, nunc *L*.
[4] aut ⟨per te⟩ ereptum *suspic. Piderit, ex Plut. Cic. 4*,
διὰ σοῦ.

---

[a] *Copia* (*copiosus*) is used to describe the fullness of
rhetorical language (and so as a synonym for eloquence) in
contrast to natural or dialectical speech (*eloqui* in contrast
to *loqui*). Thus in 138 the full development of Latin
eloquence in Crassus and Antonius is called *Latine dicendi
copia*. Macrobius (5. 1, 7) in defining four styles calls
the first *copiosum, in quo Cicero dominatur*. In the *Orator*
97 *copiosus* is an attribute and the most essential one of the
grand style. Some preceding discussion in Caesar's dedica-

with the statement that the choice of words was the foundation of eloquence. Upon our friend here, who prefers to have me rather than himself speak about Caesar, he bestowed praise of a unique kind; for after addressing him by name in his dedication, he uses these words : ' And if, to the task of giving brilliant and oratorical expression to their thought, some have devoted unremitting study and practice— wherein we must recognize that you, as almost the pioneer and inventor of eloquence,[a] have deserved well of the name and prestige of Rome—yet are we therefore to look upon a mastery of the easy and familiar speech of daily life as a thing that now may be neglected ? ' "

At this Brutus broke in : " Friendly surely and 254 splendid praise I consider it, to call you at once the pioneer and inventor of eloquence, and to add that you have deserved well of the name and prestige of Rome. For the one thing in which conquered Greece still remained our conqueror, we have now wrested from her, or at all events we now share with her. The glory of such testimony from Caesar I hold to be 255 greater, I would not say than the public thanksgiving proffered to you,[b] but than many a triumph."

" Quite right, Brutus," I replied, " if only this is Caesar's sincere judgement and not merely friendly

tion to Cicero may have made the phrase *principem copiae* less bald and abrupt than it now seems.

[b] The *supplicatio* decreed upon the discovery and suppression of the conspiracy of Catiline. It is alluded to in the third oration against Cat. (23). The whole passage following is an echo and development of words used by Caesar (doubtless in this same place) in praise of Cicero, *omnium triumphorum laurea maior*, cited by Pliny, *Nat. Hist.* 7. 117.

Plus enim certe attulit huic populo dignitatis,
quisquis est ille, si modo est aliquis, qui non illus-
travit modo sed etiam genuit in hac urbe dicendi
copiam, quam illi qui Ligurum castella expugna-
verunt, ex quibus multi sunt, ut scitis, triumphi.
256 Verum quidem si audire volumus, omissis illis divinis
consiliis, quibus saepe constituta est imperatorum
sapientia salus civitatis aut belli aut domi, multo
magnus orator praestat minutis imperatoribus. At
prodest plus imperator. Quis negat ? Sed tamen
—non metuo ne mihi acclametis ; est autem quod sen-
tias dicendi liber locus—malim mihi L. Crassi unam
pro M'. Curio dictionem quam castellanos triumphos
duo. At plus interfuit rei publicae castellum capi Li-
257 gurum quam bene defendi causam M'. Curi. Credo ;
sed Atheniensium quoque plus interfuit firma tecta
in domiciliis habere quam Minervae signum ex ebore
pulcherrimum ; tamen ego me Phidiam esse mallem
quam vel optimum fabrum tignarium. Qua re non
quantum quisque prosit, sed quanti quisque sit
ponderandum est ; praesertim cum pauci pingere
egregie possint aut fingere, operarii autem aut baiuli
258 deesse non possint. LXXIV. Sed perge, Pomponi, de
Caesare et redde quae restant.

---

^a Cicero has an obtrusive habit of repetition when he
wishes to urge a point important for his argument. Thus
he presents the compliment of Caesar first in the words of
Caesar himself in 253, repeats it in the mouth of Brutus in
254, and takes it up again here in his own comment.
Similarly in discussing the dogma of agreement between the
critic and the people concerning the quality of oratory the
principle is stated no less than five times (183-198). *Cf.* also
Suadai medulla in 59. Such examples may be an index

evidence of goodwill. For certainly the man—whoever he may be, and if in fact there be such an one—who was first to reveal and demonstrate to Rome the resources of eloquence [a] has contributed more to the prestige of our people than those who have stormed successfully some Ligurian fortresses, which as you know have yielded many a triumph. And in truth, if you will but give it hearing, 256 apart from examples of superhuman genius, in which the intelligence of military leaders has often been the salvation of the commonwealth in the field as well as at home, the great orator is far more significant than the mediocre military leader. But the military leader is of more practical value. I do not deny it. Still—and I'm not afraid of your protests, since here we are at liberty to say what we think—I should for myself choose rather the single speech of Lucius Crassus in defence of Manius Curius than two of those petty outpost triumphs. But, you urge, the capture of a Ligurian outpost was more important for the state than a successful defence of Manius Curius. Quite true ; but it was likewise more important for the 257 people of Athens to have tight roofs over their heads than to possess the famous ivory statue of Minerva ; yet I should have preferred to be a Phidias than to be a master-roofer. Thus in weighing a man's significance it is not how useful he is that should enter in, but what is his real worth. There are few competent painters or sculptors, but there is no danger of a shortage of porters and labourers. But go on, Pom- 258 ponius, with regard to Caesar and discharge the rest of your debt."

of rapid composition (or dictation), of which there are other evidences. *Cf.* 218 and note.

Solum quidem, inquit ille, et quasi fundamentum oratoris vides, locutionem emendatam et Latinam, cuius penes quos laus adhuc fuit, non fuit rationis aut scientiae, sed quasi bonae consuetudinis. Mitto C. Laelium Philum[1] Scipionem ; aetatis illius ista fuit laus tamquam innocentiae sic Latine loquendi—nec omnium tamen, nam illorum aequalis Caecilium et Pacuvium male locutos videmus—sed omnes tum fere, qui nec extra urbem hanc vixerant neque eos aliqua barbaries domestica infuscaverat, recte loquebantur. Sed hanc certe rem deteriorem vetustas fecit et Romae et in Graecia. Confluxerunt enim et Athenas et in hanc urbem multi inquinate loquentes ex diversis locis. Quo magis expurgandus est sermo et adhibenda tamquam obrussa ratio, quae mutari non potest, nec utendum pravissima consuetudinis regula. 259 T. Flamininum, qui cum Q. Metello consul fuit, pueri vidimus; existimabatur bene Latine, sed litteras nesciebat. Catulus erat ille quidem minime indoctus, ut a te paulo est ante dictum, sed tamen suavitas vocis et lenis appellatio litterarum bene loquendi famam confecerat. Cotta, qui se valde dilatandis litteris a similitudine Graecae [2] locutionis abstraxerat sonabatque contrarium Catulo subagreste quiddam planeque subrusticum, alia quidem quasi inculta et silvestri via ad eandem laudem pervenerat. Sisenna

[1] Philum *Heraeus*, Pilum *L.*
[2] Graecae *L*, rectae *Simon.*

---

[a] L. Furius Philus, the excellence of whose speech is referred to in 108. For Laelius and Scipio see 83 and 211.

[b] *Litteras nesciebat*, that is the science of grammar; *litterae* γράμματα, *litterarum scientia* γραμματική. Cotta, just below, is L. Aurelius Cotta, *praetorius* (137), not the great orator Gaius.

" The ground," he continued, " or so to speak the
foundation, on which oratory rests is, you see, a
faultless and pure Latin diction. Those who have
enjoyed this distinction hitherto have had it, not as the
result of study and theory, but as heirs of good usage.
I need not refer to Gaius Laelius, Philus,[a] or Scipio ;
pure Latinity, not less than uprightness of character,
was the mark of their time, though not quite universal,
since we note that their contemporaries Caecilius and
Pacuvius did not use a pure idiom ; still, practically
every one, unless his life was passed outside Rome, or
some crudeness of home environment had tainted his
speech, in those days spoke well and correctly. But
lapse of time has brought about some deterioration in
this respect both at Rome and in Greece. For as to
Athens, so to our city, there has been an influx of many
impure speakers coming from different places. It has
created a situation which calls for a purge of language
and the invoking of theory as an objective control or
touchstone, not subject to change like the easily
distorted rule of common usage. I recall in my boy- 259
hood seeing Titus Flamininus, who was consul with
Quintus Metellus. He was esteemed a user of pure
Latin, but he was quite ignorant of grammatical
theory.[b] Catulus, the elder, was by no means untrained, as you have observed, but it was rather the
natural charm of his voice and nice enunciation which
gave him the reputation of pure speech. Cotta from
his habit of using broad vowels was as far removed as
possible from resemblance to Greek enunciation, and,
in contrast to Catulus, his speech had a rural, downright
rustic sound, and yet he too by a woodland path and
over untilled fields, so to speak, attained to a similar
reputation for pure speech. Then there was Sisenna,

autem quasi emendator sermonis usitati cum esse
vellet, ne a C. Rusio quidem accusatore deterreri
potuit quo minus inusitatis verbis uteretur.
260 Quidnam istuc est ? inquit Brutus, aut quis est
iste C. Rusius ?

Et ille : Fuit accusator, inquit, vetus, quo accusante C. Hirtilium Sisenna defendens dixit quaedam
eius sputatilica esse crimina. LXXV. Tum C. Rusius :
Circumvenior, inquit, iudices, nisi subvenitis. Sisenna
quid dicat nescio ; metuo insidias. Sputatilica, quid
est hoc ? sputa quid sit scio, tilica nescio. Maximi
risus ; sed ille tamen familiaris meus recte loqui
261 putabat esse inusitate loqui. Caesar autem rationem
adhibens consuetudinem vitiosam et corruptam pura
et incorrupta consuetudine emendat. Itaque cum
ad hanc elegantiam verborum Latinorum—quae,
etiam si orator non sis et sis ingenuus civis Romanus,
tamen necessaria est—adiungit illa oratoria ornamenta dicendi, tum videtur tamquam tabulas bene
pictas collocare in bono lumine. Hanc cum habeat praecipuam laudem in communibus, non video
cui debeat cedere. Splendidam quandam minimeque veteratoriam rationem dicendi tenet, voce motu

---

ᵃ Sisenna's invention is cited as an example of perverse
theory, an analogical formation to match κατάπτυστα, " to
be spat upon," its 'strangeness heightened by a double
suffix—*ilis* and *-icus* (*cf. volatilis* and *volaticus*). No Latin
adjectives appear to have been made from *sputum* (*sputatus*),
just as English has no adjectives from " spit." " Spitable,"
" spitabilical," " spitabilicious " have been suggested as
English renderings, but they are more fantastic even than
sputatilica.

ᵇ Flamininus and Catulus (in 259) are examples of good
diction acquired naturally from environment and usage.
Cotta and Sisenna show perversions of a theory. Caesar in
contrast aimed to observe good usage, and, when corrupted,

who professed to be a reformer of current usage. Even the retort of Gaius Rusius, a professional prosecuting barrister, did not succeed in deterring him from using strange and unheard-of words."

" What do you refer to," said Brutus, " and who 260 was that Gaius Rusius ? "

" He was a veteran prosecutor," replied Atticus, " conducting a case against Gaius Hirtilius, whom Sisenna was defending. In the course of it Sisenna characterized certain accusations as "sputatilica""[a]; whereupon Rusius cried out : ' I am undone, judges, unless you come to my rescue. What Sisenna is saying I do not understand and I fear he has laid a trap for me. " Sputatilica ! " What is that ? " Sputa " I understand, but " tilica " I do not understand.' There was a great laugh ; and in fact that good friend of mine did believe that correct speech was unfamiliar speech. Caesar however by invoking 261 rational theory strives to correct distorted and corrupt usage by restoring usage pure and uncorrupted.[b] Thus by joining to this careful selection of Latin words—a selection incumbent on every true offspring of Roman blood whether orator or not—the characteristic embellishments of oratorical style, he produces an effect as of placing a well-painted picture in a good light. Having this peculiar merit of a choice vocabulary in addition to the qualities common to other orators, I do not see to whom he should give place. He is master of an eloquence which is brilliant and with no suggestion of routine, and which in respect of voice, gesture, and the speaker's whole

to restore it by principle (*rationem adhibens*). Suetonius in his life of Caesar, chh. 55 and 56, refers to this passage of the *Brutus* with some direct citations.

forma etiam magnificam et generosam[1] quodam
modo.

262   Tum Brutus : Orationes quidem eius mihi vehementer probantur. Compluris autem legi atque etiam
commentarios, quos idem[2] scripsit rerum suarum.

Valde quidem, inquam, probandos ; nudi enim
sunt, recti et venusti, omni ornatu orationis tamquam
veste detracta. Sed dum voluit alios habere parata,
unde sumerent qui vellent scribere historiam, ineptis
gratum fortasse fecit, qui illa volent calamistris
inurere, sanos quidem homines a scribendo deterruit ;
nihil est enim in historia pura et illustri brevitate
dulcius. Sed ad eos, si placet, qui vita excesserunt,
revertamur.

263   LXXVI. C. Sicinius igitur Q. Pompei illius, qui
censor fuit, ex filia nepos, quaestorius mortuus est ;
probabilis orator, iam vero etiam probatus, ex hac
inopi ad ornandum, sed ad inveniendum expedita
Hermagorae disciplina. Ea dat rationes certas et praecepta dicendi, quae si minorem habent apparatum—
sunt enim exilia—tamen habent ordinem et quasdam
errare in dicendo non patientis vias ; has ille tenens
et paratus ad causas veniens, verborum non egens,
ipsa illa comparatione disciplinaque dicendi iam in
264 patronorum numerum pervenerat. Erat etiam vir

---

[1] magnifica et generosa *L, corr. Corradus ex Sueton. Caes. 55.*
[2] quos idem *Stangl,* quosdam *L.*

---

a Hermagoras of Temnus in Aeolis, perhaps the most
influential rhetorical theorist after Aristotle. His activity
belongs to the middle of the second century B.C. His
writings dealt with argument and proof and did not embrace
style. Nothing from him has survived in direct citation,
but his system plays a great rôle in subsequent treatises

physique, possesses a certain noble and high-bred quality."

At this point Brutus broke in: " His orations 262 certainly seem to me very admirable; I have read a number of them, as well as the *Commentaries* which he wrote about his own deeds."

" Admirable indeed ! " I replied ; " they are like nude figures, straight and beautiful ; stripped of all ornament of style as if they had laid aside a garment. His aim was to furnish others with material for writing history, and perhaps he has succeeded in gratifying the inept, who may wish to apply their curling irons to his material ; but men of sound judgement he has deterred from writing, since in history there is nothing more pleasing than brevity clear and correct. But now let us come back if you will to those who are no longer living.

" Gaius Sicinius, son of the daughter of Quintus 263 Pompeius the censor, died while still only quaestor. He was an orator deserving of praise, nay even had won a recognized place. He was from the school of Hermagoras, which, though meagre in embellishment, is effective in invention.[a] It furnishes certain general principles and rules which, though they help little in giving fullness to treatment and are in fact barren, still have the virtue of order and of fixing lines which do not permit one to stray. Keeping close to them and coming to his cases always well prepared, not lacking either in verbal readiness, with only this equipment and schooling in oratory, he had already at the time of his death attained a recognized place in the ranks of pleaders. Contemporary with Sicinius 264

of rhetorical " invention." *Cf.* G. Thiele, *Hermagoras*, Strassburg, 1893.

doctus in primis C. Visellius Varro, consobrinus meus,
qui fuit cum Sicinio aetate coniunctus. Is, cum post
curulem aedilitatem iudex quaestionis esset, est mortuus ; in quo fateor vulgi iudicium a iudicio meo dis-
sensisse. Nam populo non erat satis vendibilis ;
praeceps quaedam et cum idcirco obscura quia
peracuta, tum rapida et celeritate caecata oratio ;
sed neque verbis aptiorem cito alium dixerim neque
sententiis crebriorem ; praeterea perfectus in litteris
iurisque civilis iam a patre Aculeone traditam tenuit
disciplinam.

265 Reliqui sunt, qui mortui sint, L. Torquatus, quem
tu non tam cito rhetorem dixisses, etsi non deerat
oratio, quam, ut Graeci dicunt, πολιτικόν ; erant in eo
plurimae litterae nec eae vulgares, sed interiores
quaedam et reconditae, divina memoria, summa
verborum et gravitas et elegantia, atque haec
omnia vitae decorabat gravitas et integritas. Me
quidem admodum delectabat etiam Triari in illa
aetate plena litteratae senectutis oratio. Quanta
severitas in vultu ! quantum pondus in verbis ! quam
nihil non consideratum exibat ex ore !

266 Tum Brutus Torquati et Triari mentione com-
motus—utrumque enim eorum admodum dilexerat :
Ne ego, inquit, ut omittam cetera quae sunt in-

---

a *Iudex quaestionis*, an officer appointed as vice-praetor
to preside over a body of *iudices* assigned to the investigation
and adjudication of criminal cases. *Cf.* scholia, *in Vat.*
(p. 323 Orelli), and Mommsen, *Abriss d. röm. Staatsrechts*,
p. 251.

b The contrast between ῥήτωρ, the professional orator or
pleader, and πολιτικός, the citizen who speaks as affairs of
state (πόλις) require his participation, is not infrequent in
Greek. Demosthenes in his private orations is ῥήτωρ, in

was a man of conspicuous learning, my cousin Gaius
Visellius Varro, who after holding the office of curule
aedile died while serving as foreman of a panel of
judges.[a] In his case I confess that the judgement of
the multitude was at variance with my own, for his
oratory found no ready sale with the public. His
manner of speaking was abrupt, closely reasoned,
and on that account obscure, and his language too
suffered in clearness from the rapidity of his speech.
Yet I could not easily name his superior in appropriateness of diction, nor in abundance and compactness of thought. His literary training besides was
thorough, and mastery of the civil law he possessed
as an inheritance from his father Aculeo.

" There remain still of those who are dead two men : 265
Lucius Torquatus, whom you would call not so much
a technically trained orator (though he did not lack the
ability to speak) as what the Greeks call *politicus*,[b]
a cultivated man and citizen. He had wide reading,
not merely in literature of the current kind, but in
more obscure and technical subjects, superhuman
memory, great dignity and precision of language, and
all this was adorned by the dignity and genuineness of
his life. I took pleasure too in the style of Triarius,
which in spite of his youth possessed the maturity of
age passed in the companionship of letters. What
earnestness of expression in his face, what weight in
his words, how nothing ill-considered proceeded from
his lips ! "

" Ah ! " said Brutus, stirred by the mention of 266
Torquatus and Triarius, both of whom had been very
dear to him, " there are I know a thousand other

his speeches against Macedonian encroachment he is
πολιτικός (*cf. ad Att.* 2. 1, 3).

numerabilia, de istis duobus cum cogito, doleo nihil tuam perpetuam auctoritatem de pace valuisse! nam nec istos excellentis viros nec multos alios praestantis civis res publica perdidisset.

Sileamus, inquam, Brute, de istis, ne augeamus dolorem ; nam et praeteritorum recordatio est acerba et acerbior exspectatio reliquorum. Itaque omittamus lugere et tantum quid quisque dicendo potuerit, quoniam id quaerimus, praedicemus.

267 LXXVII. Sunt etiam ex eis qui eodem bello occiderunt M. Bibulus, qui et scriptitavit accurate, cum praesertim non esset orator, et egit multa constanter. Appius Claudius socer tuus, collega et familiaris meus ; hic iam et satis studiosus et valde cum doctus tum etiam exercitatus orator et cum auguralis tum omnis publici iuris antiquitatisque nostrae bene peritus fuit. L. Domitius nulla ille quidem arte, sed Latine tamen et multa cum liber-
268 tate dicebat. Duo praeterea Lentuli consulares, quorum Publius, ille nostrarum iniuriarum ultor, auctor salutis, quicquid habuit, quantumcumque fuit, illud totum habuit e disciplina ; instrumenta naturae deerant ; sed tantus animi splendor et tanta magnitudo ut sibi omnia quae clarorum virorum essent non dubitaret asciscere eaque omni dignitate obtineret. L. autem Lentulus satis erat fortis orator, si modo orator, sed cogitandi non ferebat laborem ;

---

* M. Calpurnius Bibulus, throughout his career a consistent but futile opponent of Caesar. Both were consuls in 59 B.C. The words of Cicero have perhaps an intentional ambiguity ; *egit multa*, contrasting him as a speaker with his diligence as a writer, and also referring to his long activity in public life. It is possible that *scriptitavit* refers to the writing of speeches for others (*cf.* 169).

reasons, but thinking of those two men, how I grieve
that your persistent advocacy of peace was without
avail! For had it been otherwise their great gifts
and those of other leading men need not have been
lost to the state."

" Let us not speak of that, Brutus," I replied. " It
only adds to our sorrow ; for while to recall the past
is pain enough, dread of the future is a pain still
sharper. So let us put aside our laments, and let me
go on to set forth the capabilities of orators one by
one, which is the object of our inquiry.

" Among those who fell in the same war was Marcus 267
Bibulus, whose activity in writing, and writing carefully, is surprising, since he was no orator ; he spoke
also in support of many measures with stubborn
consistency.[a] Another was Appius Claudius, your
father-in-law, and my augural colleague and friend.
Unlike Bibulus he was a student of oratory, learned
in its theory and experienced in its practice. He
was besides thoroughly versed in augural and public
law, and well acquainted with our earlier history.
Lucius Domitius on the other hand was quite without
training, but his command of Latin was good and he
spoke with great freedom and boldness. Then there 268
were the two Lentuli, both ex-consuls ; of whom
Publius, the avenger of my wrongs and author of my
recall from banishment, had gained from study whatever skill he possessed ; natural equipment he lacked
altogether ; yet his mind was so brilliant, his spirit
so noble, that he aspired to all the honours which
belong by right to distinction, and held them with
becoming dignity. Lucius Lentulus was an orator of
considerable vigour, if you could call him an orator at
all ; but the labour of thinking out a case bored him.

vox canora, verba non horrida sane, ut[1] plena esset animi et terroris oratio; quaereres in iudiciis fortasse melius, in re publica quod erat esse iudicares satis.

269 Ne T. quidem Postumius contemnendus in dicendo; de re publica vero non minus vehemens orator quam bellator fuit, effrenatus et acer nimis, sed bene iuris publici leges atque instituta cognoverat.

Hoc loco Atticus: Putarem te, inquit, ambitiosum esse, si, ut dixisti, ei quos iam diu colligis viverent. Omnis enim commemoras, qui ausi aliquando sunt stantes loqui, ut mihi imprudens M. Servilium praeterisse videare.

270 LXXVIII. Non, inquam, ego istuc ignoro, Pomponi, multos fuisse qui verbum numquam in publico fecissent, cum melius aliquanto possent quam isti oratores quos colligo dicere; sed his commemorandis etiam illud assequor, ut intellegatis primum ex omni numero quam non multi ausi sint dicere, deinde ex eis ipsis quam pauci fuerint laude digni.

271 Itaque ne hos quidem equites Romanos, amicos nostros qui nuper mortui sunt,[2] P. Cominium Spoletinum, quo accusante defendi C. Cornelium, in quo et compositum dicendi genus et acre et expeditum

---

[1] *Locus ut videtur aut lacun. aut corrupt.*
[2] omittam *add. edd. rec.*

---

[a] L. Cornelius Lentulus, prosecutor in 61 B.C. of P. Clodius, the later enemy of Cicero; follower of Pompey, consul 49 B.C. The vehemence of his attacks upon the proposals conciliatory to Caesar are alluded to at the beginning of Caesar's *Civil War*. They confirm the characterization given here—*plena terroris oratio*. (*Bell. Civ.* 1. 2 *Marcellus perterritus conviciis (Lentuli) a sua sententia discessit.*)

[b] Following Atticus's ironical remark about passing over

He had a pleasing voice, and his diction was not too harsh; his whole style of speaking was intense, even threatening.[a] For practice in the courts you would perhaps demand something better; for matters of state you could consider his equipment adequate. Titus Postumius, finally, was a speaker not to be 269 despised. As a political orator certainly he spoke with the same energy that he showed as a soldier, unbridled and bitter, but with sound knowledge of constitutional law and precedents."

At this point Atticus interrupted: "If you had not explained your purpose, and if all those whom you have been enumerating were still living, I should suspect that by their mention you were trying to curry favour with them. You have been naming every man that ever dared to stand up in public and speak, so that I wonder whether it was not through inadvertence that you passed over Marcus Servilius."

"No, Pomponius," I replied; "I am not unaware 270 that there were many who never uttered a word in public who were better speakers than many of those whom I have enumerated. But in mentioning these it is my purpose to show you first of all how out of the whole possible number not many have ventured to speak, and in the second place how few of them have earned distinction. For this reason not even 271 two Roman knights, friends of mine who have died recently [s all I pass over][b]: Publius Cominius of Spoletum, against whose prosecution I defended Gaius Cornelius; his style was well ordered, penetrating and fluent; also Titus Accius of Pisaurum,

M. Servilius, Cicero proceeds to name two others, not repeating the verb (*praeteribo*) implied from the words of Atticus (*praeterisse*, just above).

fuit; T. Accium Pisaurensem, cuius accusationi respondi pro A. Cluentio, qui et accurate dicebat et satis copiose, eratque praeterea doctus Hermagorae praeceptis, quibus etsi ornamenta non satis opima dicendi, tamen, ut hastae velitibus amentatae, sic apta quaedam et parata singulis causarum generibus argumenta traduntur.

272 Studio autem neminem nec industria maiore cognovi—quamquam ne ingenio quidem qui praestiterit facile dixerim C. Pisoni genero meo. Nullum tempus illi umquam vacabat aut a forensi dictione aut a commentatione domestica aut a scribendo aut a cogitando; itaque tantos processus efficiebat ut evolare, non excurrere videretur; eratque verborum et dilectus elegans et apta et quasi rotunda constructio; cumque argumenta excogitabantur ab eo multa et firma ad probandum tum concinnae acutaeque sententiae; gestusque natura ita venustus ut ars etiam, quae non erat, et e disciplina motus quidam videretur accedere. Vereor ne amore videar plura quam fuerint in illo dicere, quod non ita est; alia enim de illo maiora dici possunt, nam nec continentia nec pietate nec ullo genere virtutis quemquam eiusdem aetatis cum illo conferendum puto.

273 LXXIX. Nec vero M. Caelium praetereundum arbitror, quaecumque eius in exitu vel fortuna vel mens fuit; qui quamdiu auctoritati meae paruit, talis

---

[a] C. Calpurnius Piso, first husband of Tullia, quaestor 58 B.C., died in that year.

[b] Young friend and protégé of Cicero, who defended him in the extant oration *pro Caelio* in 56 B.C. During Cicero's absence in Cilicia 51–50 Caelius went over to the party of Caesar and entered upon a demagogical career which resulted in a violent death in 48 B.C. In oratorical style he

in reply to whose prosecution I spoke in behalf of
Aulus Cluentius ; he was a painstaking speaker and
tolerably eloquent ; he was moreover trained in the
precepts of Hermagoras, which though they do not
supply the richer embellishments of oratory, yet
furnish outlines of argument ready made and appli-
cable to every type of case,—spears, as it were, ready
fitted with straps for the skirmisher to throw.

" For zeal and industry I have never known anyone—no, nor for talent either, who surpassed my
son-in-law Gaius Piso.[a] There was never a moment
when he was not occupied either with pleading in
the forum or with rehearsal at home, whether of
writing or of planning; his progress was so swift that
he seemed to fly rather than to run ; his words
were carefully chosen, his sentences compact and
periodic ; his argument was varied and convincing,
his ideas shrewd and neatly put ; his bodily movement and gesture had a natural grace, which gave
the impression of art and training, though that was
not the case. I'm afraid lest my affection may lead
me to credit him with more virtues than he really
possessed. But it is not so, for I could truthfully
name other and greater qualities in him than these ;
in fact for self-control, for devotion, or indeed for
any other virtue I do not think that anyone of his
time could be compared with him.

" Marcus Caelius again was a man whom I should
not pass over, whether chance or choice determined
the end of his political career.[b] So long as he had
regard for me and my counsel, in his capacity as
tribune, he held out with incomparable firmness

affected archaism and is probably to be reckoned among
the group of Atticists.

tribunus plebis fuit ut nemo contra civium perditorum
popularem turbulentamque dementiam a senatu et
a bonorum causa steterit constantius. † Quam[1] eius
actionem multum tamen et splendida et grandis et
eadem in primis faceta et perurbana commendabat
oratio. Graves eius contiones aliquot fuerunt, acres
accusationes tres eaeque omnes ex rei publicae contentione susceptae; defensiones, etsi illa erant in eo
meliora quae dixi, non contemnendae tamen sane-
que tolerabiles. Hic cum summa voluntate bonorum
aedilis curulis factus esset, nescio quo modo discessu
meo discessit a sese ceciditque, postea quam eos imitari coepit quos ipse perverterat.

274   Sed de M. Calidio dicamus aliquid, qui non fuit
orator unus e multis, potius inter multos prope singularis fuit, ita reconditas exquisitasque sententias
mollis et perlucens vestiebat oratio. Nihil tam tene-
rum quam illius comprehensio verborum, nihil tam
flexibile, nihil quod magis ipsius arbitrio fingeretur,
ut nullius oratoris aeque in potestate fuerit; quae
primum ita pura erat ut nihil liquidius, ita libere
fluebat ut nusquam adhaeresceret; nullum nisi loco
positum et tamquam in vermiculato emblemate, ut ait
Lucilius, structum verbum videres; nec vero ullum
aut durum aut insolens aut humile aut [in] longius
ductum; ac non propria verba rerum sed pleraque

[1] quam L, antiquam, mancam, miram alia tempt. edd.
An fort.</i> iniquam?</p>

[a] In a fragment cited by Quint. (11. 1, 51), curiously apt
for illustration of this passage, Caelius himself reveals that
his oratory was characterized habitually by traits (<i>voltus
molestus, vox immoderata, gestus iactans</i>) which may well have
been summed up by Cicero in the word <i>iniquam</i> (mss. <i>quam</i>).</p>
[b] Calidius, somewhat the senior of Caelius and Calvus, is
perhaps to be looked upon as the earliest of the new oratorical

on the side of the senate and the best men of the
state against the turbulence and madness of the
most reckless demagogues. [A delivery uneven and
unconciliatory] [a] was offset by a style brilliant and
impressive, conspicuous especially for its cleverness
and wit. He made some important public speeches
and three merciless prosecutions, all of which arose out
of political ambition and rivalry. His court speeches
in defence of himself and others, although inferior to
those which I have mentioned, were not negligible, indeed quite tolerable. He was made curule aedile with
the full support of conservative men, but to my sorrow
after my departure he fell away from his own past
standards, and imitating the example of men whom
he himself had misled, he brought about his own fall.

"But coming now to Marcus Calidius let me say 274
a word or two about him.[b] He was not just one
orator out of the many of his time, but he stood out
from the many as a figure unique, marked by a
flexible and translucent style which fitted his original
and penetrating thought like a garment. You cannot imagine anything smoother than the structure of
his sentences, anything more plastic at the bidding
of his will. In this he was without a peer. His language was like a clear flowing stream unimpeded by
any hindrance. You saw every word standing in its
proper place like a stone in a mosaic design (as Lucilius says),[c] and none was harsh, unusual, trivial or
far-fetched ; nor was he restricted to words in their
proper meanings, but he employed many meta-

school to which Calvus gave the name of Atticism. Like
Caelius he was an earlier friend and supporter of Cicero, but
went over to the side of Caesar.

[c] Lucilius v. 84 (Marx), cited in *Orator* 149.

translata, sic tamen ut ea non inruisse in alienum
locum sed immigrasse in suum diceres; nec vero
haec soluta nec diffluentia sed astricta numeris, non
aperte nec eodem modo semper sed varie dissimu-
275 lanterque conclusis. Erant autem et verborum et
sententiarum illa lumina quae vocant Graeci σχήματα,
quibus, tamquam insignibus in ornatu distinguebatur
omnis oratio. Qua de re agitur autem illud quod
multis locis in iuris consultorum includitur formulis,
276 id ubi esset videbat. LXXX. Accedebat ordo rerum
plenus   artis,   actio   liberalis   totumque   dicendi
placidum et sanum genus. Quod si est optimum
suaviter dicere, nihil est quod melius hoc quaerendum
putes. Sed cum a nobis paulo ante dictum sit tria
videri esse quae orator efficere deberet, ut doceret ut
delectaret ut moveret, duo summe tenuit, ut et rem
illustraret disserendo et animos eorum qui audirent
devinciret voluptate; aberat tertia illa laus, qua
permoveret atque incitaret animos, quam plurimum
pollere diximus; nec erat ulla vis atque contentio,
sive consilio, quod eos quorum altior oratio actioque
esset ardentior furere atque bacchari arbitraretur,
sive quod natura non esset ita factus, sive quod non
consuesset, sive quod non posset. Hoc unum illi, si
nihil utilitatis habebat, afuit, si opus erat, defuit.
277   Quin etiam memini, cum in accusatione sua Q.

---

a The *formula* was the praetor's prescript to the *iudex*
who was to conduct the trial. Though issued by the praetor,
it was doubtless often formulated by the plaintiff's attorney.
It contained exposition of the point at issue (*res de qua agitur*),
the claim of the plaintiff, and authorization to condemn or
absolve according to the law and the evidence. See Gaius **4.**
39 ff. and example *ibid.* 47.

phorically, yet so skilfully that they seemed not to
have usurped an alien place, but rather to have
found their own. Furthermore his words were not
left loose and disjointed, but were bound together
by rhythms, not obvious nor uniform but varied and
disguised. He made use too of those high lights of 275
word play and the manner of putting an idea, which
the Greeks call postures or figures, with which, like
decorative designs distributed here and there, all
his style was pointed. Moreover he saw clearly
' the point at issue,' that familiar phrase which is often
included in the formulae ᵃ of jurisconsults. Add to 276
this an arrangement of subject-matter guided by
rhetorical art, a delivery free and dignified, and
a general manner of speaking quiet and sincere. If
then charm represents the best oratory, you would
say that nothing better than a Calidius need be
sought. But since, as I have said already, there
are three things which the orator must effect, to
teach to please and to move, two of these he possessed in the highest degree, namely, perfect lucidity
of exposition and the ability to hold his audience by
the charm of his words. The third merit, which
consists in moving the listener and in arousing his
emotions,—the orator's chief source of power, as I
have said—he lacked, and he was in fact quite without force and intensity. This may have been due
to deliberate choice, as of one holding that a more
elevated style and a more vehement delivery were
frenzy and delirium, or to a natural indisposition to
that sort of thing, or to established habit, or to actual
inability. This one quality was lacking to him ; if
useless call it a lack, if essential, a defect.

" I recall a case in point : In his indictment and 277

Gallio crimini dedisset sibi eum venenum paravisse,
idque a se esse deprensum, seseque chirographa
testificationes indicia quaestiones manifestam rem
deferre diceret, deque eo crimine accurate et exquisite disputavisset, me in respondendo, cum essem
argumentatus quantum res ferebat, hoc ipsum etiam
posuisse pro argumento, quod ille, cum pestem
capitis sui, cum indicia mortis se comperisse manifesto et manu tenere diceret, tam solute egisset,

278 tam leniter, tam oscitanter. ' Tu istuc, M. Calidi,
nisi fingeres, sic ageres ? praesertim cum ista eloquentia alienorum hominum pericula defendere
acerrime soleas, tuum neglegeres ? Ubi dolor ?
ubi ardor animi, qui etiam ex infantium ingeniis
elicere voces et querelas solet ? Nulla perturbatio
animi nulla corporis, frons non[1] percussa non femur,
pedis, quod minimum est, nulla supplosio. Itaque
tantum afuit ut inflammares nostros animos, som-
num isto loco vix tenebamus.' Sic nos summi
oratoris vel sanitate vel vitio pro argumento ad
diluendum crimen usi sumus.

279 Tum Brutus : Atque dubitamus, inquit, utrum
ista sanitas fuerit an vitium ? Quis enim non
fateatur, cum ex omnibus oratoris laudibus longe

---

[1] frons non *L, transp.* Quint. 11. 3, 123.

prosecution of Quintus Gallius he charged that
Gallius had attempted to poison him, that he had
discovered the plot and had laid before the court
clear evidence of it in the form of writings in the
hand of Gallius, depositions, circumstantial evidence,
and confessions under torture. All this he set forth
with great pains and careful detail. I appeared for
the defence, and after presenting such arguments as
my client's case afforded, I used as an argument in
rebuttal this very point : that although he professed
to have learned of a threat against his own life, to
have obtained and to hold in hand proofs of a plot
laid for his death, yet he had presented his case with
perfect calmness, lackadaisically, and almost with
a yawn : ' Come now, Marcus Calidius, would you 278
present your case in that way if it were not all a
figment of your imagination ? And that eloquence
of yours, which you have always used so vigorously
for the defence of others, is it credible that you
should fail to invoke it for your own ? What trace of
anger, of that burning indignation, which stirs even
men quite incapable of eloquence to loud outbursts
of complaint against wrongs ? But no hint of agita-
tion in you, neither of mind nor of body ! Did you
smite your brow, slap your thigh, or at least stamp
your foot ? No. In fact, so far from touching my
feelings, I could scarcely refrain from going to sleep
then and there.' In such fashion I used this great
orator's manner of speaking, whether we call it wise
restraint or a defect of eloquence, as an argument
for breaking down his accusation."

At this Brutus said : " Can we hesitate whether 279
to call it restraint or a defect ? Why, every one
must acknowledge that of all the resources of an

ista sit maxima, inflammare animos audientium et quocumque res postulet modo flectere, qui hac virtute caruerit, id ei quod maximum fuerit defuisse ?

LXXXI. Sit sane ita, inquam ; sed redeamus ad eum qui iam unus restat, Hortensium, tum de nobismet ipsis, quoniam id etiam, Brute, postulas, pauca dicemus. Quamquam facienda mentio est, ut quidem mihi videtur, duorum adulescentium, qui si diutius vixissent magnam essent eloquentiae laudem consecuti.

280 C. Curionem te, inquit Brutus, et C. Licinium Calvum arbitror dicere.

Recte, inquam, arbitraris ; quorum quidem alter [quod verisimile dixisset][1] ita facile soluteque verbis volvebat satis interdum acutas, crebras quidem certe sententias, ut nihil posset ornatius esse, nihil expeditius. Atque hic parum a magistris institutus naturam habuit admirabilem ad dicendum ; industriam non sum expertus, studium certe fuit. Qui si me audire voluisset, ut coeperat, honores quam opes consequi maluisset.

Quidnam[2] est, inquit, istuc ? et quem ad modum distinguis ?

281 Hoc modo, inquam : cum honos sit praemium virtutis iudicio studioque civium delatum ad aliquem, qui eum sententiis, qui suffragiis adeptus est, is mihi et honestus et honoratus videtur. Qui autem occasione aliqua etiam invitis suis civibus nactus est imperium, ut ille cupiebat, hunc nomen

---

[1] *Secl. Lambinus.*   [2] quinam *F, fort. recte.*

[a] C. Scribonius Curio, son of the Curio characterized in 210 above, whose flight from Rome with the tribunes marked the beginning of the Civil War (Jan. 7, 49 B.C.).

orator far the greatest is his ability to inflame the minds of his hearers and to turn them in whatever direction the case demands. If the orator lacks that ability, he lacks the one thing most essential."

" Quite so," I replied. " But now let us come back to the one man who still remains, Hortensius. After that I will say a little about myself, since you, Brutus, demand it. And yet I ought to make mention I think of two young men who, had they lived longer, would have attained to great renown for eloquence."

" You refer to Gaius Curio and Gaius Licinius 280 Calvus I'm sure," said Brutus.

" Yes, you're quite right," I replied. " Of these the former [a] with free and facile diction gave well rounded form to thoughts which, if not always acute, were at all events abundant ; nothing more nicely elaborated or freer from constraint can be imagined. Never adequately trained by teachers, he made up for it by a remarkable natural gift for eloquence. I cannot speak of his industry, but his ardour certainly was great. Had he chosen to lend ear to me he would have sought honours rather than power."

" What do you mean by that, and how do you distinguish between them ? " said Brutus.

" It is like this," I replied. " Since honour is a 281 reward of merit proffered to one by the judgement and goodwill of his fellow citizens, I hold that the man who has obtained it by the verdict of their votes has the right to be esteemed at once worthy of honour and honoured. But when a man through some chance circumstance, or even against the will of his fellow citizens, has secured a position of power, as Curio strove to do, he has succeeded in obtaining the

243

honoris adeptum, non honorem puto. Quae si ille
audire voluisset, maxima cum gratia et gloria ad
summam amplitudinem pervenisset, ascendens gradi-
bus magistratuum, ut pater eius fecerat, ut reliqui
clariores viri. Quae quidem etiam cum P. Crasso
M. f., ⟨cum⟩ initio aetatis ad amicitiam se meam
contulisset, saepe egisse me arbitror, cum eum
vehementer hortarer ut eam laudis viam rectis-
simam esse duceret quam maiores eius ei tritam
282 reliquissent.   Erat enim cum institutus optime tum
etiam perfecte planeque eruditus, ineratque et
ingenium satis acre et orationis non inelegans
copia, praetereaque sine arrogantia gravis esse
videbatur et sine segnitia verecundus.   Sed hunc
quoque absorbuit aestus quidam insolitae adulescentibus gloriae, qui quia navarat miles operam
imperatori, imperatorem se statim esse cupiebat,
cui muneri mos maiorum aetatem certam, sortem
incertam reliquit.   Ita gravissimo suo casu, dum
Cyri et Alexandri similis esse voluit, qui suum
cursum transcurrerant, et L. Crassi et multorum
Crassorum inventus est dissimillimus.
283   LXXXII. Sed ad Calvum—is enim nobis erat pro-
positus—revertamur ; qui orator fuit cum litteris
eruditior quam Curio tum etiam accuratius quoddam dicendi et exquisitius afferebat genus ; quod
quamquam scienter eleganterque tractabat, nimium

ᵃ P. Licinius Crassus, son of the triumvir, served ably
under Caesar in Gaul, and as commander of cavalry perished
with his father in the disastrous expedition against the
Parthians (53 B.C.).   The harsh judgement of Cicero is not
explained by any evidence we possess.   It is a curious fact
that the charges of inexperience, unseemly ambition, and
consequent recklessness, which are here directed against the
son, are all exemplified in the conduct of the elder Crassus as

title of honour, but not I think the honour itself. Had he chosen to entertain considerations such as these, rising through the grades of public office as his father and other distinguished men had done before him, he would have attained to the highest dignity with unanimous favour and applause. Considerations such as these I can testify that I urged also more than once upon Publius Crassus,[a] son of Marcus, who at an early age sought the circle of my friendship, and I exhorted him with all my power to follow that straight path to renown which his ancestors had trodden and made smooth for him. For he 282 had enjoyed excellent upbringing and had received a thorough and complete training. His mind was good, if not brilliant, his language choice and abundant, and in addition he had dignity without arrogance, and modesty without sloth. But he too was swept away and engulfed by a tide of ambition unsuited to his years. Because as a subordinate he had served a commander, he became ambitious to be made forthwith a commander himself, a rank for which our usage has fixed a certain age, but uncertain assignment. But he fell ingloriously, and though aspiring to be like Cyrus or Alexander, whose careers had been so swift, he was discovered to be wholly unlike Lucius Crassus and many another of his family.

" But now let me come back to Calvus as I pro- 283 posed. He was an orator of much more thorough theoretical training than Curio, and presented a style of speaking more carefully elaborated and more original. Though he handled it with a scholar's

portrayed by Plutarch. The Lucius Crassus referred to at the end of 282 is the great orator (138, 143).

tamen inquirens in se atque ipse sese observans metuensque ne vitiosum colligeret, etiam verum sanguinem deperdebat. Itaque eius oratio nimia religione attenuata doctis et attente audientibus erat illustris, ⟨a⟩ multitudine autem et a foro, cui nata eloquentia est, devorabatur.

284 Tum Brutus : Atticum se, inquit, Calvus noster dici oratorem volebat ; inde erat ista exilitas quam ille de industria consequebatur.

Dicebat, inquam, ita, sed et ipse errabat et alios etiam errare cogebat. Nam si quis eos qui nec inepte dicunt nec odiose nec putide Attice putat dicere, is recte nisi Atticum probat neminem. Insulsitatem enim et insolentiam tamquam insaniam quandam orationis odit, sanitatem autem et integritatem quasi religionem et verecundiam oratoris probat. Haec omnium debet oratorum eadem 285 esse sententia. Sin autem ieiunitatem et siccitatem et inopiam, dum modo sit polita, dum urbana, dum elegans, in Attico genere ponit, hoc recte dumtaxat ; sed quia sunt in Atticis alia meliora, videat ne ignoret et gradus et dissimilitudines et vim et varietatem Atticorum. 'Atticos,' inquit, ' volo imitari.' Quos ?

ᵃ It may interest students of English diction to note that in these words (*metuensque ne vitiosum colligeret*) we have a forerunner of our much overworked " meticulous," which, however, in its present vogue has for the most part lost its proper meaning of " cautious " or " painstaking " through timidity or fear of error.

ᵇ It would appear from this passage that Calvus was the one who introduced to Rome the name Attic (Atticism) as designation of the new tendency in oratorical style, a revolt against the abundance and elaboration which characterized the traditional Roman manner represented by Hortensius and Cicero. Atticism, as the name indicates, must already

knowledge and discrimination, yet from excessive self-examination and fear of admitting error he lost true vitality.[a] His language thus through over-scrupulousness seemed attenuated, and while scholars and careful listeners recognized its quality, the multitude and the forum, for whom eloquence exists, missing its finer flavour gulped it down whole."

Here Brutus interposed : " Our good friend 284 Calvus liked to think of himself as Attic. That was the reason for that meagreness of style which he cultivated deliberately."

" Yes, I know," I replied ; " so he said ; but he was in error and caused others to err with him.[b] If one holds that those who do not rant, nor speak pedantically nor with affectation, are Attic, he will be quite right in admiring no one who is not Attic. Tasteless bombast and preciosity he will abominate as a form of madness ; sanity and wholesomeness of style he will look upon as a decent and almost religious obligation in an orator. This should be the common judgement of all orators. But if meagreness and dryness and 285 general poverty are put down as Attic, with of course the proviso that it must have finish and urbanity and precision, that is good so far as it goes. But because there are in the category of Attic other qualities better than these, one must beware not to overlook the gradations and dissimilarities, the force and variety of Attic orators. ' My aim is,' you say, ' to imitate Attic models.' Which, pray ? for they are

have existed as a movement or tendency in Greek schools, but its precise origins are lost in the meagre record of the Hellenistic period. It was a refinement of the older doctrine of correct Greek—Ἑλληνισμός, which in this movement came to be Ἀττικισμός. Caesar's grammatical theories were derived from Atticistic sources (258, above).

nec enim est unum genus. Nam quid est tam
dissimile quam Demosthenes et Lysias ? quam idem
et Hyperides ? quam horum omnium Aeschines ?
Quem igitur imitaris ? Si aliquem, ceteri ergo
Attice non dicebant ? si omnis, qui potes, cum sint
ipsi dissimillimi inter se ? In quo illud etiam quaero,
Phalereus ille Demetrius Atticene dixerit ? Mihi
quidem ex illius orationibus redolere ipsae Athenae
videntur. At est floridior, ut ita dicam, quam
Hyperides, quam Lysias ; natura quaedam aut
voluntas ita dicendi fuit.

286 LXXXIII. Et quidem duo fuerunt per idem tempus
dissimiles inter se, sed Attici tamen ; quorum Charisius multarum orationum, quas scribebat aliis, cum
cupere videretur imitari Lysiam ; Demochares
autem, qui fuit Demostheni sororis filius, et orationes scripsit aliquot et earum rerum historiam
quae erant Athenis ipsius aetate gestae non tam
historico quam oratorio genere perscripsit. Ac
Charisi vult Hegesias esse similis, isque se ita putat
Atticum, ut veros illos prae se paene agrestis putet.
287 At quid est tam fractum, tam minutum, tam in
ipsa, quam tamen consequitur, concinnitate puerile ?
' Atticorum similes esse volumus.' Optime. ' Sunt-
ne igitur hi Attici oratores ? ' Quis negare potest ? ' Hos imitamur.' Quo modo, qui sunt et inter
se dissimiles et aliorum ? ' Thucydidem,' inquit,
' imitamur.' Optime, si historiam scribere, non

ᵃ Hegesias of Magnesia ad Sipylum (in Lydia), orator,
historian and biographer. Strabo calls him the inaugurator of
the Asiatic style. For later Atticists he came to be regarded
as the type of all that was un-Attic, affected, and trivial.

not all of one type. Who, for example, are more
unlike than Demosthenes and Lysias ? Than either
of them and Hyperides, than all of these and Aeschines ? Whom then are you going to imitate ? If
one only, do you mean that all the others did not
speak pure Attic ? If all, how can you imitate
them when they are so unlike each other ? And here
I venture to put this question : did Demetrius of
Phaleron speak pure Attic ? To me at least his
orations exhale the very fragrance of Athens. But,
you say, he is more florid (if I may use the term) than
Hyperides or Lysias. That was, I presume, his
natural bent or perhaps his deliberate choice.

" Take another example : there were two orators 286
of the same time wholly unlike each other yet both
thoroughly Attic, Charisius and Demochares. Of
these the former was the author of many speeches
which he wrote for others, in which he appears to
have made Lysias his model ; the latter, Demochares,
nephew of Demosthenes, wrote some speeches and
was author of a history of Athens in his own time,
written in a style rather oratorical than historical.
(It was Charisius whom Hegesias [a] strove to be like,
and he regarded himself so thoroughly Attic that he
considered the native Attic writers almost uncouth
rustics in comparison with himself. But where will 287
you find anything so broken, so minced, anything
so puerile as that balance and antithesis which he
cultivated ?) ' Our aim is to be Attic.' Good. ' Are
these two then Attic orators ? ' Surely ; who can
deny it ? ' These are the men we imitate.' But
how, when they are so unlike one another and unlike
still others unnamed ? ' Thucydides,' you say, ' we
strive to imitate.' Very good, if you are thinking of

si causas dicere cogitatis. Thucydides enim rerum
gestarum pronuntiator sincerus et grandis etiam
fuit ; hoc forense concertatorium iudiciale non
tractavit genus. Orationes autem quas interposuit
—multae enim sunt—eas ego laudare soleo ; imitari neque possim si velim, nec velim fortasse si
possim. Ut si quis Falerno vino delectetur, sed
eo nec ita novo ut proximis consulibus natum velit,
nec rursus ita vetere ut Opimium aut Anicium consulem quaerat. ' Atqui hae notae sunt optimae.'
Credo ; sed nimia vetustas nec habet eam quam
quaerimus suavitatem nec est iam sane tolerabilis ;
288 num igitur qui hoc sentiat, si is potare velit, de dolio
sibi hauriendum putet ? Minime ; sed quandam
sequatur aetatem. Sic ego istis censuerim et novam
istam quasi de musto ac lacu fervidam orationem
fugiendam nec illam praeclaram Thucydidi nimis
veterem tamquam Anicianam notam persequendam.
Ipse enim Thucydides si posterius fuisset, multo
maturior fuisset et mitior.

289 LXXXIV. ' Demosthenem igitur imitemur.' O di
boni ; quid, quaeso, nos aliud agimus aut quid aliud
optamus ? At non assequimur ; isti enim videlicet
Attici nostri quod volunt assequuntur. Ne illud

---

^a Lucius Opimius, consul in 121 B.C., Lucius Anicius,
consul in 160 B.C. The vintage of Opimius is referred to by
Pliny (N.H. 14. 55).
^b The lively style of this whole passage (284-288) is a
notable example of monologistic dialogue, of the type
familiar in satire and moral discourse. It is commonly
called in modern criticism " the diatribe style," but with
doubtful appropriateness. The manner of anticipatory
statement of an opposing argument and of quick refutation
by one and the same speaker was highly developed in the

writing history, but not if you contemplate pleading cases. Thucydides was a herald of deeds, faithful and even grand, but our forensic speech with its wrangling, its atmosphere of the court-room, he never used. As for the speeches which he introduced (and they are numerous) I have always praised them ; but imitate them ?—I could not if I wished, nor should I wish to, I imagine, if I could. To illustrate : it is as if a man were fond of Falernian wine, but did not want it so new as last year's, nor again so old as to search out a cask from the vintages of Opimius or Anicius.[a] ' But those brands are acknowledged to be the best ! ' Yes I know, but too old a wine has not the mellowness which we want, and in fact it is scarcely longer fit to drink. If that then is one's feeling, need he go to the 288 other extreme and hold, if he wants a potable wine, that it must be drawn from the fresh vat ? Certainly not ; he would look for a wine of moderate age. In like manner I hold that those friends of yours do well to shun this new oratory still in a state of ferment, like must from the basin of the wine-press, and conversely that they ought not to strive for the manner of Thucydides,—splendid doubtless, but, like the vintage of Anicius, too old. Thucydides himself if he had lived at a somewhat later time would have been mellower and less harsh.[b]

" ' Should we then make Demosthenes our model ? ' 289 There, by heavens, you have it ! and what better I ask, do we seek, what better can we wish for ? But we do not it is true succeed in our effort ; these fellows however, our self-styled Atticists, quite obviously it would seem do succeed in what they have

oratory of the courts of law, and passed over naturally to the moral indictments of the satirist.

quidem intellegunt, non modo ita memoriae proditum esse sed ita necesse fuisse, cum Demosthenes
dicturus esset, ut concursus audiendi causa ex tota
Graecia fierent. At cum isti Attici dicunt, non
modo a corona, quod est ipsum miserabile, sed etiam
ab advocatis relinquuntur. Qua re si anguste et
exiliter dicere est Atticorum, sint sane Attici ;
sed in comitium veniant, ad stantem iudicem dicant ;
subsellia grandiorem et pleniorem vocem desiderant.
290 Volo hoc oratori contingat, ut cum auditum sit eum
esse dicturum, locus in subselliis occupetur, com-
pleatur tribunal, gratiosi scribae sint in dando et
cedendo loco, corona multiplex, iudex erectus ;
cum surgat is qui dicturus sit, significetur a corona
silentium, deinde crebrae assensiones, multae admirationes ; risus cum velit, cum velit fletus, ut
qui haec procul videat, etiam si quid agatur nesciat,
at placere tamen et in scaena esse Roscium intellegat.
Haec cui contingant, eum scito Attice dicere, ut
de Pericle audimus, ut de Hyperide, ut de Aeschine,
291 de ipso quidem Demosthene maxime. Sin autem
acutum prudens et idem sincerum et solidum et
exsiccatum genus orationis probant nec illo graviore
ornatu oratorio utuntur et hoc proprium esse Atticorum volunt, recte laudant. Est enim in arte tanta

---

^a " The benches " indicate a large and important trial such
as is described in the following section. In ordinary private
suits all the parties stood except, presumably, the *iudex*
himself.
^b The most famous actor of Cicero's time. His name had
become proverbial for perfection in any art (*de Orat.* 1. 130).

set themselves. They don't even see, not only that history records it, but it must have been so, that when Demosthenes was to speak all Greece flocked to hear him. But when these Atticists of ours speak they are deserted not only by the curious crowd, which is humiliating enough, but even by the friends and supporters of their client. So then if to speak in a pinched and meagre way is Attic, why let them enjoy their title of Atticists. But let them come to the place of assembly, let them speak before a praetor standing to give his opinion without a jury. The benches call for a louder and fuller voice.[a] This is 290 what I wish for my orator : when it is reported that he is going to speak let every place on the benches be taken, the judges' tribunal full, the clerks busy and obliging in assigning or giving up places, a listening crowd thronging about, the presiding judge erect and attentive ; when the speaker rises the whole throng will give a sign for silence, then expressions of assent, frequent applause ; laughter when he wills it, or if he wills, tears ; so that a mere passer-by observing from a distance, though quite ignorant of the case in question, will recognize that he is succeeding and that a Roscius [b] is on the stage. If this is what happens be assured that he is speaking like an Attic orator, that he is faring as we read of Pericles, of Hyperides, of Aeschines, of Demosthenes most of all. But if they 291 prefer rather a style of speaking that is acute and judicious, while at the same time pure, sound, and matter-of-fact, which does not make use of any bolder oratorical embellishment, and if moreover they will have it that this style is peculiarly and properly Attic, they are quite right in their approbation. For in an art so comprehensive and so varied there is a

tamque varia etiam huic minutae subtilitati locus.
Ita fiet ut non omnes, qui Attice, idem bene, sed
ut omnes, qui bene, idem etiam Attice dicant.   Sed
redeamus rursus ad Hortensium.

292   LXXXV. Sane quidem, inquit Brutus; quamquam
ista mihi tua fuit periucunda a proposita oratione
digressio.

Tum Atticus : Aliquotiens sum, inquit, conatus,
sed interpellare nolui.   Nunc quoniam iam ad
perorandum spectare videtur sermo tuus, dicam,
opinor, quod sentio.

Tu vero, inquam, Tite.

Tum ille : Ego, inquit, ironiam illam quam in
Socrate dicunt fuisse, qua ille in Platonis et Xenophontis et Aeschini libris utitur, facetam et elegantem puto.   Est enim et minime inepti hominis et
eiusdem etiam faceti, cum de sapientia disceptetur,
hanc sibi ipsum detrahere, eis tribuere illudentem,
qui eam sibi arrogant, ut apud Platonem Socrates
in caelum effert laudibus Protagoram Hippiam
Prodicum Gorgiam ceteros, se autem omnium
rerum inscium fingit et rudem.   Decet hoc nescio
quo modo illum, nec Epicuro, qui id reprehendit,
assentior.   Sed in historia, qua tu es usus in
omni sermone, cum qualis quisque orator fuisset
exponeres, vide quaeso, inquit, ne tam reprehen-
denda sit ironia quam in testimonio.

Quorsus, inquam, istuc ? non enim intellego.

293   Quia primum, inquit, ita laudavisti quosdam

---

a In the sections following (292-297) Atticus takes issue
with Cicero's praise of the more important early orators.
What Atticus says represents in fact Cicero's own judgement
of them viewed absolutely, rather than from the point of
view of historical development.

place even for such small refinements of workmanship. Our conclusion then will be, not that all who speak in an Attic style speak well, but that all who speak well deserve the title of Attic. But now let us come back to Hortensius."

"Very well," said Brutus, "though I have found 292 this digression from your proposed argument extremely interesting."

At this point Atticus : " Several times," he said, " I have tried to break in, but I did not like to interrupt you. Now, however, since your talk seems to look toward its conclusion, I will say with your consent what I think." *a*

"By all means, Titus."

"I grant," he continued, "that that irony, which they say was found in Socrates, and which he uses in the dialogues of Plato, Xenophon, and Aeschines, is a choice and clever way of speaking. It marks a man as free from conceit, and at the same time witty, when discussing wisdom, to deny it to himself and to attribute it playfully to those who make pretensions to it. Thus Socrates in the pages of Plato praises to the skies Protagoras, Hippias, Prodicus, Gorgias, and the rest, while representing himself as without knowledge of anything and a mere ignoramus. This somehow fits his character, and I cannot agree with Epicurus who censures it. But in an historical account, such as you have professed in all your discussion of the character of orators, consider pray whether such irony is not as censurable as it would be in the witness box."

"What are you driving at," I replied; "I don't think I understand you."

"Why, this ; first of all you have lavished praise 293

oratores ut imperitos posses in errorem inducere.
Equidem in quibusdam risum vix tenebam, cum
Attico Lysiae Catonem nostrum comparabas, magnum
mehercule hominem vel potius summum et singularem
virum! nemo dicet secus; sed oratorem? sed etiam
Lysiae similem, quo nihil potest esse pictius? Bella
ironia, si iocaremur; sin asseveramus, vide ne religio
nobis tam adhibenda sit quam si testimonium
294 diceremus. Ego enim Catonem tuum ut civem, ut
senatorem, ut imperatorem, ut virum denique cum
prudentia et diligentia tum omni virtute excellentem
probo; orationes autem eius ut illis temporibus
valde laudo; significant enim formam quandam
ingeni, sed admodum impolitam et plane rudem.
Origines vero cum omnibus oratoris laudibus refertas
diceres et Catonem cum Philisto et Thucydide com-
parares, Brutone te id censebas an mihi probaturum?
Quos enim ne e Graecis quidem quisquam imitari
potest, his tu comparas hominem Tusculanum
nondum suspicantem quale esset copiose et ornate
295 dicere. LXXXVI. Galbam laudas. Si ut illius aetatis principem, assentior—sic enim accepimus; sin
ut oratorem, cedo quaeso orationes—sunt enim—et
dic hunc, quem tu plus quam te amas, Brutum velle
te illo modo dicere. Probas Lepidi orationes.
Paulum hic tibi assentior, modo ita laudes ut anti-
quas; quod item de Africano, de Laelio, cuius tu

upon some orators in a manner to mislead those
unacquainted with them. In fact, sometimes I
could scarcely refrain from laughter, as when you
compared with the Athenian Lysias our good old
Cato—a great man, good heavens yes ! indeed one of
the greatest and unique ! no one could say otherwise.
But an orator ? and like Lysias, with all his incomparable finish ? Pleasant irony, if we are jesting ;
but if we are making a sober statement, consider that
we should be as scrupulous as if we were giving
testimony on oath. Your Cato, the citizen, the 294
senator, the commander, the man in short pre-eminent
in prudence, in conscientious discharge of duty, and
in every virtue, I admire. His speeches too for their
time I praise heartily ; they reveal some outlines of
genius for all their lack of finish and utter rudeness.
But when you characterized his *Origines* as crammed
with every stylistic virtue and compared Cato with
Philistus and Thucydides, did you fancy that you
could persuade Brutus of that, or me either ? With
men whom no Greek writers have been able to rival
you compare a man of Tusculum who had not yet
the faintest notion of what it means to speak with
oratorical fullness and elaboration. Again you 295
praise Galba ; if as the first speaker of his day I
agree—history tells us that ; but if as an orator,
produce his orations pray—they are available—and
tell me whether you would wish Brutus here, whom
you profess to love more than yourself, to speak
in that fashion. You express approbation of the
speeches of Lepidus. To that I can give some assent
if you praise them only as specimens of archaic eloquence. When in like manner you speak of Africanus
and of Laelius, than whose language you say nothing

oratione negas fieri quicquam posse dulcius, addis
etiam nescio quid augustius; nomine nos capis
summi viri vitaeque elegantissimae verissimis laudibus. Remove haec; ne ista dulcis oratio ita sit
296 abiecta ut eam aspicere nemo velit. Carbonem in
summis oratoribus habitum scio; sed cum in ceteris
rebus tum in dicendo semper, quo iam[1] nihil est melius,
id laudari, qualecumque est, solet. Dico idem de
Gracchis, etsi de eis ea sunt a te dicta quibus ego
assentior. Omitto ceteros; venio ad eos in quibus
iam perfectam putas esse eloquentiam, quos ego
audivi, sine controversia magnos oratores, Crassum
et Antonium. De horum laudibus tibi prorsus
assentior, sed tamen non isto modo : ut Polycliti
Doryphorum sibi Lysippus aiebat, sic tu suasionem
legis Serviliae tibi magistram fuisse. Haec ger-
mana ironia est. Cur ita sentiam non dicam, ne me
297 tibi assentari putes. Omitto igitur quae de his ipsis,
quae de Cotta, quae de Sulpicio, quae modo de
Caelio dixeris. Hi enim fuerunt certe oratores;
quanti autem et quales tu videris. Nam illud
minus curo quod congessisti operarios omnis, ut
mihi videantur mori voluisse non nulli, ut a te in
oratorum numerum referrentur.

LXXXVII. Haec cum ille dixisset : Longi sermonis initium pepulisti, inquam, Attice, remque

---

[1] quo iam *Jahn*, quoniam *L*.

---

[a] The meaning of the comparison must be that Lysippus
so far surpassed Polyclitus that, in professing to have taken
the Doryphorus of Polyclitus for his model, he cannot be
taken seriously. We are told in fact that Lysippus when
asked whom he followed replied, *naturam ipsam imitandam
esse, non artificem* (Pliny, *N.H.* 34. 61).

can be more charming, nay even more august, you trick us with the name of a great man and the genuine glory of the purest of lives. Put that aside, and you will find I fear that charm of language so slight a thing as scarcely to deserve notice. As for Carbo, I am well aware that he was accounted one of our greatest orators ; but as in other things so in oratory it is customary to praise whatever is not surpassed in its day, regardless of its true value. I could say the same of the Gracchi, though to some of the things you said about them I assent. Passing over others, I come to those two in whom you consider that perfect eloquence was finally realized, Antonius and Crassus. I myself heard them speak, and they were without question great orators. With your praise of them I am quite in agreement, and yet not quite as you put it ; you said that the speech of Crassus in support of the Servilian law was your teacher ; in the same manner I suppose as Lysippus used to say that the Doryphorus of Polyclitus was his model.[a] Now that is nothing but the veriest irony. Why I think so I shall not say lest you suspect me of flattery. I pass over therefore what you said of them, what you said of Cotta, of Sulpicius, and what you have just said of Caelius. These were at all events real orators ; how great and what their character, it is for you to say. As for all that throng of mere day-labourers whom you brought together, your judgements give me less concern ; you have been so hospitable that some now living would have gladly died, I fancy, for the sake of finding themselves placed in your category of orators."

When he had finished speaking, I replied : " You have started something that would keep us talking a long time, Atticus, and the subject you raise is

commovisti nova disputatione dignam, quam in aliud
298 tempus differamus. Volvendi enim sunt libri cum
aliorum tum in primis Catonis. Intelleges nihil illius
liniamentis nisi eorum pigmentorum, quae inventa
nondum erant, florem et colorem defuisse. Nam de
Crassi oratione sic existimo, ipsum fortasse melius
potuisse scribere, alium, ut arbitror, neminem. Nec
in hoc εἴρωνα me duxeris[1] esse, quod eam orationem
mihi magistram fuisse dixerim. Nam etsi tute[2]
melius existimare videris de ea, si quam nunc habemus, facultate, tamen adulescentes quid in Latinis
299 potius imitaremur non habebamus. Quod autem
plures a nobis nominati sunt, eo pertinuit, ut paulo
ante dixi, quod intellegi volui, in eo cuius omnes
cupidissimi essent, quam pauci digni nomine evade-
rent. Quare εἴρωνα me, ne si Africanus quidem fuit,
ut ait in historia sua C. Fannius, existimari velim.

Ut voles, inquit Atticus. Ego enim non alienum a
te putabam, quod et in Africano fuisset et in Socrate.
300 Tum Brutus : De isto postea ; sed tu, inquit me
intuens, orationes nobis veteres explicabis ?

Vero, inquam, Brute ; sed in Cumano aut in
Tusculano aliquando, si modo licebit, quoniam utroque
in loco vicini sumus. Sed iam ad id unde digressi
sumus revertamur.
301 LXXXVIII. Hortensius igitur cum admodum
adulescens orsus esset in foro dicere, celeriter ad
maiores causas adhiberi coeptus est. Quamquam

---

[1] yroniam eduxeris L, corr. Baehrens.
[2] tute Stangl, ut tu L.

---

* This concluding portion of the treatise (301 to the
epilogue 330) harks back to the opening words on the death
of Hortensius (see sections 1, 228, and 279), and interweaves
with the account of that orator Cicero's own career. It is

worthy of a fresh discussion ; but we must put it off to
another time. We should have to turn over many 298
books, especially of Cato as well as of others ; you
would see that his drawing was sharp and that it
lacked only some brightness and colours which had
not yet been discovered. As for that speech of
Crassus, I hold quite sincerely that he himself might
have written it better, but certainly no one else. Nor
should you think that I was using irony in calling it
my teacher. For though you appear to have a better
opinion of such skill as I now possess, yet in my youth
there did not exist a better Latin model for me to
follow. As for my naming so many names, my 299
purpose was, as I said before, to make it clear how few
worthy of mention had emerged in that which was
the ambition of all. I should not wish therefore to be
thought of as using irony, even if Africanus did, as
Gaius Fannius tells us in his history."

" As you will," replied Atticus. " For my part I did
not think alien to you something that was present in
Africanus and Socrates."

" About that, later," interrupted Brutus. " But 300
won't you now," he said turning to me, " go over
with us some of those early speeches ? "

" Very gladly, Brutus," I replied, " but some other
day, if opportunity offers, at my house in Cumae or
Tusculum, where we are neighbours. But now let me
come back to the point from which we disgressed.

" We were speaking of Hortensius [a] : At a very 301
early age he began to speak in the forum, and very
soon came to be employed in cases of greater importance. Though his beginnings fell in the period of

the earliest considerable piece of autobiography that has
come down to us from antiquity.

inciderat in Cottae et Sulpici aetatem, qui annis decem ⟨erant⟩ maiores, excellente tum Crasso et Antonio, dein Philippo, post Iulio, cum his ipsis dicendi gloria comparabatur. Primum memoria tanta quantam in nullo cognovisse me arbitror, ut quae secum commentatus esset, ea sine scripto verbis eisdem redderet quibus cogitavisset. Hoc adiumento ille tanto sic utebatur ut sua et commentata et scripta et nullo referente omnia adversariorum dicta memi-302 nisset. Ardebat autem cupiditate sic ut in nullo umquam flagrantius studium viderim. Nullum enim patiebatur esse diem quin aut in foro diceret aut meditaretur extra forum. Saepissime autem eodem die utrumque faciebat. Attuleratque minime vulgare genus dicendi; duas quidem res quas nemo alius : partitiones quibus de rebus dicturus esset et collectiones eorum quae[1] essent dicta contra quaeque 303 ipse dixisset. Erat in verborum splendore elegans, compositione aptus, facultate copiosus ; eaque erat cum summo ingenio tum exercitationibus maximis consecutus. Rem complectebatur memoriter, dividebat acute, nec praetermittebat fere quicquam quod esset in causa aut ad confirmandum aut ad refellendum. Vox canora et suavis, motus et gestus etiam plus artis habebat quam erat oratori satis. Hoc igitur florescente Crassus est mortuus, Cotta

[1] eorum quae *Jahn*, memorquae *F*, memor et quae *OGB*.

Cotta and Sulpicius, who were ten years older, when Crassus and Antonius, then Philippus, and afterwards Julius, were still at the height of their reputations, yet in renown as a speaker he was constantly compared with these veterans. First of all he possessed a memory of such accuracy as I can testify never to have known in anyone. What he had prepared in private he could reproduce without memorandum in the very words of his original thought. This great natural gift he used so well that he was able without the aid of prompting to recall not only his own words, whether merely thought out or written down, but also all that was said by the other side. He was fired too with such ambition that his 302 devotion to study surpassed anything that I have ever seen. He did not suffer a day to go by without either speaking in the forum or declaiming outside. Very often indeed he would do both on the same day. He brought to the forum a style which was far from commonplace, two things in fact in which he was unique : heads or divisions of what he meant to say, followed by summaries of what had been said on the other side, and of what he himself had said. In 303 choice of words he was brilliant and at the same time fastidious, felicitous in their combination, and resourceful in his command of them. He owed this skill partly to his own great talent and partly to his unremitting practice in rhetorical exercises. He always knew his case by heart and divided it sharply into its parts ; he seldom overlooked anything in the case pertinent to confirmation or refutation ; his voice was sonorous and agreeable ; his delivery and gesture even a little too studied for the orator. His genius had thus come to its first flowering when Crassus died,

CICERO

pulsus, iudicia intermissa bello, nos in forum
venimus.

304 LXXXIX. Erat Hortensius in bello primo anno
miles, altero tribunus militum, Sulpicius legatus;
aberat etiam M. Antonius; exercebatur una lege
iudicium Varia, ceteris propter bellum intermissis;
quoi[1] frequens aderam, quamquam pro se ipsi dicebant oratores non illi quidem principes, L. Memmius
et Q. Pompeius, sed oratores tamen, teste diserto
utique[2] Philippo, cuius in testimonio contentio et
305 vim accusatoris habebat et copiam. Reliqui qui
tum principes numerabantur in magistratibus erant
cotidieque fere a nobis in contionibus audiebantur.
Erat enim tribunus plebis tum C. Curio, quamquam is
quidem silebat ut erat semel a contione universa
relictus; Q. Metellus Celer non ille quidem orator,
sed tamen non infans; diserti autem Q. Varius C.
Carbo Cn. Pomponius, et hi quidem habitabant in
rostris; C. etiam Iulius aedilis curulis cotidie fere
accuratas contiones habebat.

Sed me cupidissimum audiendi primus dolor
percussit Cotta cum est expulsus. Reliquos frequenter audiens acerrimo studio tenebar cotidieque et scribens et legens et commentans oratoriis
tantum exercitationibus contentus non eram. Iam
consequente anno Q. Varius sua lege damnatus ex-

---

[1] quoi *Martha*, qui *L*, cui *vulg.*
[2] utique *Jahn*, uterque *L*.

---

[a] *In bello*, the Social War, 91-88 B.C. The *lex Varia*,
introduced by the tribune of the plebs Q. Varius (221
above) in 91, was a partisan measure directed against the
senatorial leaders as authors of the war: *quorum dolo malo
socii ad arma ire coacti essent* (Val. Max. 8. 6, 4). Its execu-
tion was long remembered as a reign of terror and bloodshed.

264

Cotta was exiled, the courts suffered the interruption of war, and I entered the forum.

" In the first year of the war [a] Hortensius served in 304 the ranks, in the second as military tribune, Sulpicius as an adjutant ; absent from Rome also was Marcus Antonius. The only court still active was taken up by cases under a single law, the Varian ; all others because of the war were suspended. At its hearings I was present constantly, and though the accused speaking in their own defence were not orators of the first rank—men like Lucius Memmius and Quintus Pompeius, still they were orators ; and there was one at least really eloquent, Philippus, witness against the accused, whose vehemence in testimony had all the force and eloquence of a prosecutor. The remaining 305 speakers of the time who were accounted the leaders held public office, and almost every day I heard them speak in the popular assemblies. Gaius Curio was then tribune of the people, but he too no longer spoke after having once been deserted by the whole assembly ; Quintus Metellus, also, no real orator, yet not without some capacity for public speech. But speakers of real ability were Quintus Varius, Gaius Carbo, Gnaeus Pomponius, who all but lived on the rostra. Gaius Julius [b] too as a curule aedile delivered carefully prepared harangues almost daily.

" The first blow to my eagerness to hear fell with the banishment of Cotta. I continued however to listen to those who were left, and though I wrote and read and declaimed daily with unflagging interest, yet I was not satisfied to confine myself only to rhetorical exercises. In the year following Quintus Varius went

[b] C. Julius Caesar Strabo, aedile 90 B.C. See above 177 and note.

306 cesserat; ego autem iuris civilis studio multum
operae dabam Q. Scaevolae Q. f., qui quamquam
nemini se ad docendum dabat, tamen consulentibus respondendo studiosos audiendi docebat. Atque huic anno proximus Sulla consule et Pompeio
fuit. Tum P. Sulpici in tribunatu cotidie contio-
nantis totum genus dicendi penitus cognovimus;
eodemque tempore, cum princeps Academiae Philo
cum Atheniensium optimatibus Mithridatico bello
domo profugisset Romamque venisset, totum ei me
tradidi admirabili quodam ad philosophiam studio
concitatus, in quo hoc etiam commorabar attentius,
etsi rerum ipsarum varietas et magnitudo summa
me delectatione retinebat, sed tamen sublata iam
307 esse in perpetuum ratio iudiciorum videbatur. Occiderat Sulpicius illo anno tresque proximo trium
aetatum oratores erant crudelissime interfecti, Q.
Catulus M. Antonius C. Iulius. Eodem anno etiam
Moloni Rhodio Romae dedimus operam et actori
summo causarum et magistro.

xc. Haec etsi videntur esse a proposita ratione[1]
diversa, tamen idcirco a me proferuntur ut nostrum
cursum perspicere, quoniam voluisti, Brute, possis—
nam Attico haec nota sunt—et videre quem ad
modum simus in spatio Q. Hortensium ipsius vesti-
giis persecuti.

308 Triennium fere fuit urbs sine armis, sed oratorum
aut interitu aut discessu aut fuga—nam aberant
etiam adulescentes M. Crassus et Lentuli duo—

---

[1] a proposita ratione *vulg.*, a proposito ratione *L, Reis*, a
proposita oratione *Ascensius, edd. rec. plerique.*

---

[a] Gn. Pompeius, consul 89 B.C., father of the triumvir.
[b] On the probable error in time of this statement see 312
and note.

into exile, a victim of his own law. I meantime, for 306
the study of civil law, attached myself to Quintus
Scaevola, the son of Quintus, who though he took no
pupils, yet by the legal opinions given to his clients
taught those who wished to hear him. The year
following this was the consulship of Sulla and Pompeius.[a] Publius Sulpicius was tribune at that time
and addressed the people almost daily, so that I came
to know his style thoroughly. At this time Philo,
then head of the Academy, along with a group of
loyal Athenians, had fled from Athens because of the
Mithridatic war and had come to Rome. Filled with
enthusiasm for the study of philosophy I gave myself
up wholly to his instruction. In so doing I tarried
with him the more faithfully, for though the variety
and sublimity of his subject delighted and held me,
yet it appeared as if the whole institution of courts
of justice had vanished for ever. In that year Sulpi- 307
cius had fallen, and in the year following three orators
representing three different periods met a cruel
death, Quintus Catulus, Marcus Antonius, Gaius
Julius. At this time too I devoted myself to study
at Rome with Molo of Rhodes, famous as a pleader
and teacher.[b]

" Though all this may seem alien to my proposed
programme, yet I have set it forth that you might see
the course of my development, as was your wish,
Brutus (for Atticus is familiar with it all), and note
how closely my career followed the very footprints of
Hortensius.

" For a space of about three years the city was free 308
from the threat of arms ; but because whether of the
death or absence or exile of orators (for even younger
men like Marcus Crassus and the two Lentuli were

primas in causis agebat Hortensius, magis magisque
cotidie probabatur Antistius, Piso saepe dicebat,
minus saepe Pomponius, raro Carbo, semel aut
iterum Philippus. At vero ego hoc tempore omni
noctes et dies in omnium doctrinarum meditatione
309 versabar. Eram cum Stoico Diodoto, qui cum
habitavisset apud ⟨me⟩ mecumque vixisset, nuper
est domi meae mortuus. A quo cum in aliis rebus
tum studiosissime in dialectica exercebar, quae
quasi contracta et astricta eloquentia putanda est ;
sine qua etiam tu, Brute, iudicavisti te illam iustam
eloquentiam, quam dialecticam esse dilatatam putant, consequi non posse. Huic ego doctori et eius
artibus variis atque multis ita eram tamen deditus
ut ab exercitationibus oratoriis nullus dies vacuus
310 esset. Commentabar declamitans—sic enim nunc
loquuntur—saepe cum M. Pisone et cum Q. Pompeio aut cum aliquo cotidie, idque faciebam multum etiam Latine, sed Graece saepius, vel quod
Graeca oratio plura ornamenta suppeditans consuetudinem similiter Latine dicendi afferebat, vel
quod a Graecis summis doctoribus, nisi Graece dicerem, neque corrigi possem neque doceri.

311 Tumultus interim recuperanda re publica et
crudelis interitus oratorum trium Scaevolae Carbonis Antisti, reditus Cottae Curionis Crassi Lentulo-
rum Pompei, leges et iudicia constituta, recuperata
res publica ; ex numero autem oratorum Pomponius

ᵃ " Zeno, on being asked wherein dialectic differed from
rhetoric, clenched his hand and then threw it open. ' In
this,' he replied, indicating that the clenched hand was the
compactness and brevity of dialectic, the open hand and
spread of the fingers the breadth and expansiveness of
rhetoric." (Sextus Emp. *adv. Math.* 2. 7.)

away from Rome) Hortensius held the first place
in pleadings, Antistius enjoyed a reputation daily
increasing, Piso spoke often, less often Pomponius,
Carbo rarely, Philippus only once or twice. During
all this time I spent my days and nights in study of
every kind. I worked with Diodotus the Stoic, who 309
made his residence in my house, and after a life of
long intimacy died there only a short time ago. From
him, apart from other subjects, I received thorough
training in dialectic, which may be looked upon as
a contracted or compressed eloquence. Without it
you too, Brutus, have held that eloquence properly so
called (which your philosophers tell us is an expanded
dialectic) *a* is impossible. But though I devoted
myself to his teaching and to the wide range of
subjects at his command, yet I allowed no day to
pass without some rhetorical exercises. I prepared 310
and delivered declamations (the term now in vogue),
most often with Marcus Piso and Quintus Pompeius,
or indeed with anyone, daily. This exercise I
practised much in Latin, but more often in Greek,
partly because Greek, offering more opportunity for
stylistic embellishment, accustomed me to a similar
habit in using Latin, but partly too because the fore-
most teachers, knowing only Greek, could not, unless
I used Greek, correct my faults nor convey their
instruction.

" Meantime, in the process of restoring orderly 311
government, violence broke out again, and there
followed the cruel death of three orators, Scaevola,
Carbo, and Antistius ; the return of Cotta, Curio,
the Lentuli, and Pompeius followed ; measures
were enacted for the constitution of the courts, and
stable government was at length restored. From

Censorinus Murena sublati. Tum primum nos ad causas et privatas et publicas adire coepimus, non ut in foro disceremus, quod plerique fecerunt, sed ut, quantum nos efficere potuissemus, docti in
312 forum veniremus. Eodem tempore Moloni dedimus operam ; dictatore enim Sulla legatus ad senatum de Rhodiorum praemiis venerat. Itaque prima causa publica pro Sex. Roscio dicta tantum commendationis habuit ut non ulla esset quae non digna nostro patrocinio videretur. Deinceps inde multae, quas nos diligenter elaboratas et tamquam elucubratas afferebamus.

313   xci. Nunc quoniam totum me non naevo aliquo aut crepundiis, sed corpore omni videris velle cognoscere, complectar non nulla etiam quae fortasse videantur minus necessaria. Erat eo tempore in nobis summa gracilitas et infirmitas corporis, procerum et tenue collum, qui habitus et quae figura non procul abesse putatur a vitae periculo, si accedit labor et laterum magna contentio. Eoque magis hoc eos quibus eram carus commovebat, quod omnia sine remissione sine varietate, vi summa vocis et
314 totius corporis contentione dicebam. Itaque cum me et amici et medici hortarentur ut causas agere desisterem, quodvis potius periculum mihi adeundum quam a sperata dicendi gloria discedendum putavi.

---

[a] Reference to study with Molo at Rome was made above (307) and is here repeated as if for the first time. Editors bracket the words in 307, but it is more likely that the repetition is Cicero's, due to an error of memory in placing Molo's visit to Rome in 87 B.C. It was then corrected (in 312) to the true time, 81 B.C. The statement in 307 of Molo's presence in Rome, though erroneous, fits the context perfectly ; in 312, while correct, it is an awkward intercalation, suggesting later insertion.

the ranks of orators, however, Pomponius, Censorinus, and Murena had been taken. It was not until this time that I first began to undertake cases both civil and criminal, for it was my ambition, not (as most do) to learn my trade in the forum, but so far as possible to enter the forum already trained. At this time too 312 I devoted myself to study with Molo ; for it chanced that he came to Rome in the dictatorship of Sulla as member of a commission to the senate with regard to the reimbursement of Rhodes.[a] Thus my first criminal case, spoken in behalf of Sextus Roscius, won such favourable comment that I was esteemed not incompetent to handle any litigation whatsoever. There followed then in quick succession many other cases which I brought into court, carefully worked out, and, as the saying is, smelling somewhat of the midnight oil.

" Since it appears to be your wish to know me 313 through and through, not just by a birthmark or a rattle,[b] but by my whole body, I venture to include some particulars which may seem superfluous. I was in those days very slender and far from robust, my neck long and thin, that type of physique which is commonly thought of as incurring risk of life itself if subjected to the strain of hard work and heavy demands upon the voice and lungs. It gave the greater anxiety to those who were solicitous for my welfare, that it was my habit to speak without variety of modulation and with voice and whole body at high tension. My friends and my physicians urged me 314 to desist from pleadings altogether ; but I resolved to run any risk rather than abandon my ambition for

[b] Typical marks of identification or recognition (ἀναγνω-ρίσματα) which resolve the plot in so many ancient plays.

Sed cum censerem remissione et moderatione vocis
et commutato genere dicendi me et periculum
vitare posse et temperatius dicere, ut consuetudinem dicendi mutarem, ea causa mihi in Asiam
proficiscendi fuit. Itaque cum essem biennium
versatus in causis et iam in foro celebratum meum
nomen esset, Roma sum profectus.

315 Cum venissem Athenas, sex mensis cum Antiocho
veteris Academiae nobilissimo et prudentissimo
philosopho fui studiumque philosophiae numquam
intermissum a primaque adulescentia cultum et semper auctum hoc rursus summo auctore et doctore
renovavi. Eodem tamen tempore Athenis apud
Demetrium Syrum veterem et non ignobilem dicendi
magistrum studiose exerceri solebam. Post a me
Asia tota peragrata est[1] cum summis quidem oratoribus, quibuscum exercebar ipsis libentibus;
quorum erat princeps Menippus Stratonicensis meo
iudicio tota Asia illis temporibus disertissimus; et,
si nihil habere molestiarum nec ineptiarum Atticorum est, hic orator in illis numerari recte potest.

316 Assiduissime autem mecum fuit Dionysius Magnes;
erat etiam Aeschylus Cnidius, Adramyttenus Xenocles. Hi tum in Asia rhetorum principes numera-

---

[1] *Lacunam suspicit Kroll*, ⟨fuique⟩ *cum Kayser*.

---

[a] The symmetry of the sentence is broken to resume and
emphasize the true reason (*ea causa*) for his leaving Rome.
It was apparently believed that Cicero left from fear of Sulla,
whose freedman and agent Chrysogonus he had attacked in
his defence of Sext. Roscius (Plutarch, *Cicero* 3).

[b] If the text is not corrupt Cicero says that he was attended
in his travels by the most distinguished orators of Asia.
Even allowing for some extravagance this does not seem
likely. Kroll is perhaps right in suspecting a lacuna.
quidem after *summis* is without clear significance as the

oratorical renown. However, having come to the conclusion that with relaxation and better control of my voice, as well as with modification of my general style of speaking, I should at once avoid risk to my health and acquire a more tempered style,—to effect this change in habit of speaking was the reason for my departure for Asia Minor.[a] Thus I had been active in practice for two years, and my name was already well known in the forum, at the time when I left Rome.

Arriving at Athens I spent six months with An- 315 tiochus, the wise and famous philosopher of the Old Academy, and with him as my guide and teacher I took up again the study of philosophy, which from my early youth I had pursued, and had made some progress in, and had never wholly let drop. But at the same time at Athens I continued zealously with rhetorical exercises under the direction of Demetrius the Syrian, an experienced teacher of eloquence not without some reputation. Afterwards I travelled through all of Asia Minor and was with the most distinguished orators of the region,[b] who were generous in giving me opportunity to practise declamatory exercises with them. The chief of these was Menippus of Stratonicea, in my judgement the most eloquent man of all Asia in that time ; and certainly, if to speak without affectation and without offence to good taste is Attic, he was an orator who could justly be placed in that category. But the one 316 most constantly with me was Dionysius of Magnesia. There was also Aeschylus of Cnidus and Xenocles of Adramyttium. These men were at that time accounted

text stands. The translation corresponds to the suggestion of Kayser.

bantur. Quibus non contentus Rhodum veni meque
ad eundem quem Romae audiveram Molonem ap-
plicavi, cum actorem in veris causis scriptoremque
praestantem tum in notandis animadvertendisque
vitiis et instituendo docendoque prudentissimum.
Is dedit operam, si modo id consequi potuit, ut
nimis redundantis nos et supra fluentis iuvenili
quadam dicendi impunitate et licentia reprimeret
et quasi extra ripas diffluentis coerceret. Ita recepi
me biennio post non modo exercitatior sed prope
mutatus. Nam et contentio nimia vocis resederat[1]
et quasi deferverat oratio lateribusque vires et
corpori mediocris habitus accesserat.

317 xcii. Duo tum excellebant oratores qui me imitandi cupiditate incitarent, Cotta et Hortensius;
quorum alter remissus et lenis et propriis verbis
comprehendens solute et facile sententiam, alter ornatus, acer et non talis qualem tu eum, Brute, iam
deflorescentem cognovisti, sed verborum et actionis
genere commotior. Itaque cum Hortensio mihi
magis arbitrabar rem esse, quod et dicendi ardore
eram propior et aetate coniunctior. Etenim videram
in isdem causis, ut pro M. Canuleio, pro Cn. Dolabella consulari, cum Cotta princeps adhibitus esset,
priores tamen agere partis Hortensium. Acrem
enim oratorem, incensum et agentem et canorum,
concursus hominum forique strepitus desiderat.

318 Unum igitur annum, cum redissemus ex Asia, causas

---

[1] resederat *Lambinus*, reciderat *L.*

the principal teachers of oratory in Asia. However, not content with them, I went to Rhodes and attached myself to Molo, whom I had already heard at Rome. He was distinguished, not merely as a practical advocate and composer of speeches for others, but was particularly skilful in criticizing and correcting faults, and wise in his whole system of teaching. He made it his task to repress if possible the redundance and excess of my style, which was marked by a youthful impetuousness and lack of restraint, and to check it so to speak from over-flowing its banks. Thus I came back after two years' absence not only better trained, but almost trans-formed. My voice was no longer over-strained, my language had lost its froth, my lungs had gained strength and my body had put on weight.

" At that time two orators stood out above the 317 rest to invite my emulation, Cotta and Hortensius. The one was relaxed and quiet, constructing his sentences smoothly and easily, without the language of metaphor ; the other was ornate, vivid, not at all like the man as you knew him, Brutus, in his decline, but altogether livelier in diction and delivery. Com-paring the two I saw that Hortensius was the man I had to do with ; that in warmth of style I was more like him, and nearer in point of age. I had noted too in cases where both were retained, as for Marcus Canuleius or for Gnaeus Dolabella, the ex-consul, that though Cotta was employed as the chief advo-cate, yet Hortensius played the leading rôle. And with good reason too, since a great throng of people and the din of the forum call for an orator of anima-tion, of fire and action and full voice. Thus, during 318 the first year after my return from Asia, I pleaded

nobilis egimus, cum quaesturam nos, consulatum
Cotta, aedilitatem peteret Hortensius. Interim me
quaestorem Siciliensis excepit annus, Cotta ex consulatu est profectus in Galliam, princeps et erat
et habebatur Hortensius. Cum autem anno post
ex Sicilia me recepissem, iam videbatur illud in me,
quicquid esset, esse perfectum et habere maturitatem quandam suam. Nimis multa videor de me,
ipse praesertim ; sed omni huic sermoni propositum
est non ut ingenium et eloquentiam meam perspicias,
unde longe absum, sed ut laborem et industriam.
319 Cum igitur essem in plurimis causis et in principibus
patronis quinquennium fere versatus, tum in patrocinio Siciliensi maximum in certamen veni designatus aedilis cum designato consule Hortensio.

XCIII. Sed quoniam omnis hic sermo noster non
solum enumerationem oratorum verum etiam praecepta quaedam desiderat, quid tamquam notandum et animadvertendum sit in Hortensio breviter
320 licet dicere. Nam is post consulatum—credo quod
videret ex consularibus neminem esse secum com-
parandum, neglegeret autem eos qui consules non
fuissent—summum illud suum studium remisit
quo a puero fuerat incensus, atque in omnium rerum
abundantia voluit beatius, ut ipse putabat, remissius
certe vivere. Primus et secundus annus et tertius
tantum quasi de picturae veteris colore detraxerat,
quantum non quivis unus ex populo, sed existimator
doctus et intellegens posset cognoscere. Longius

some conspicuous cases, when I was candidate for the
quaestorship, Cotta for the consulship, and Hortensius
for the office of aedile. Thereupon my year in Sicily
as quaestor followed ; Cotta after his consulship
went to Gaul ; Hortensius remained as the leading
advocate and was so regarded. On my return from
Sicily a year later it was apparent that whatever
talent I possessed had reached full development and
a certain maturity. I fear that too much is being
said of me, especially since I am saying it ; but the
purpose of all this part of my talk is not to parade my
talent or my eloquence, which is far from my intention,
but only to let you see how hard I worked and how industrious I was. After some five years of practice taken 319
up with many cases and in association with the leading
pleaders of the day, finally as aedile elect I crossed
swords with Hortensius, consul elect, in defence of
the province of Sicily—a duel of real magnitude.

  " But since all this discussion of ours aims not
merely to enumerate orators, but to teach some
lessons as well, let me point out briefly what in
Hortensius I venture to think was open to criticism
or censure. After his consulship, seeing, I fancy, that 320
no one else of consular rank was his rival, and making
no account of those who had not held that office, he
relaxed that ardour which had burned in him from
his youth. He made up his mind, now that he had
attained affluence, to get more enjoyment out of
life, as he professed, or at all events to take life
more easily. One year, a second, and even a third,
lived in this fashion, took away something (like
the slow fading of the colours in an old picture), not
so much as an ordinary observer, but only a trained
and intelligent critic, would perceive. But as this

autem procedens, ut in ceteris eloquentiae partibus,
tum maxime in celeritate et continuatione verborum
adhaerescens, sui dissimilior videbatur fieri cotidie.

321 Nos autem non desistebamus cum omni genere
exercitationis tum maxime stilo nostrum illud
quod erat augere, quantumcunque erat. Atque
ut multa omittam in hoc spatio et in his post
aedilitatem annis, praetor et[1] primus et incredibili
populari voluntate sum factus. Nam cum propter
assiduitatem in causis et industriam tum propter
exquisitius et minime vulgare orationis genus animos hominum ad me dicendi novitate converteram.

322 Nihil de me dicam, dicam de ceteris ; quorum nemo
erat qui videretur exquisitius quam vulgus hominum
studuisse litteris, quibus fons perfectae eloquentiae
continetur, nemo qui philosophiam complexus esset
matrem omnium bene factorum beneque dicto-
rum, nemo qui ius civile didicisset rem ad privatas
causas et ad oratoris prudentiam maxime neces-
sariam, nemo qui memoriam rerum Romanarum
teneret, ex qua, si quando opus esset, ab inferis
locupletissimos testis excitaret, nemo qui breviter
arguteque illuso adversario laxaret iudicum animos
atque a severitate paulisper ad hilaritatem risum-
que traduceret, nemo qui dilatare posset atque a
propria ac definita disputatione hominis ac temporis
ad communem quaestionem universi generis oratio-

---

[1] praetor et *Lambinus*, et praetor *L.*

process went on, affecting his eloquence as a whole, and especially arresting the swift and smooth flow of his language, his decline from his former self began to be apparent daily.

" I, on the other hand, did not cease from efforts 321 to increase such gifts as I had by every type of exercise, and particularly by writing. To pass over much in this period and in the years which followed my aedileship, I was made praetor, and because of great popular favour towards me I stood first among the candidates chosen. For not only my constant activity and industry as a pleader, but also my style of speaking, more thoroughly considered than the conventional manner of the forum, had by its novelty drawn the attention of men to me. I say nothing 322 of myself ; I shall speak rather of others. Of them there was not one who gave the impression of having read more deeply than the average man, and reading is the well-spring of perfect eloquence ; no one whose studies had embraced philosophy, the mother of excellence in deeds and in words ; no one who had mastered thoroughly the civil law, a subject absolutely essential to equip the orator with the knowledge and practical judgement requisite for the conduct of private suits ; no one who knew thoroughly Roman history, from which as occasion demanded he could summon as from the dead most unimpeachable witnesses ; no one who with brief and pointed jest at his opponent's expense was able to relax the attention of the court and pass for a moment from the seriousness of the business in hand to provoke a smile or open laughter ; no one who understood how to amplify his case, and, from a question restricted to a particular person and time, transfer it to universals ;

nem traducere, nemo qui delectandi gratia digredi
parumper a causa, nemo qui ad iracundiam magno
opere iudicem, nemo qui ad fletum posset adducere,
nemo qui animum eius, quod unum est oratoris maxime proprium, quocumque res postularet, impellere.

323 xciv. Itaque cum iam paene evanuisset Hortensius et ego anno meo, sexto autem post illum
consulem consul factus essem, revocare se ad industriam coepit, ne cum pares honore essemus, aliqua
re superiores videremur.[1] Sic duodecim post meum
consulatum annos in maximis causis, cum ego mihi
illum, sibi me ille anteferret, coniunctissime versati
sumus, consulatusque meus, qui illum primo leviter
perstrinxerat, idem nos rerum mearum gestarum,
324 quas ille admirabatur, laude coniunxerat.   Maxime
vero perspecta est utriusque nostrum exercitatio,
paulo ante quam perterritum armis hoc studium,
Brute, nostrum conticuit subito et obmutuit, cum
lege Pompeia ternis horis ad dicendum datis ad
causas simillimas inter se vel potius easdem novi
veniebamus cotidie ; quibus quidem causis tu
etiam, Brute, praesto fuisti complurisque et nobiscum et solus egisti ; ut qui non satis diu vixerit
Hortensius tamen hunc cursum confecerit : annis
ante decem[2] causas agere coepit quam tu es natus ;
idem quarto ⟨et⟩ sexagesimo anno, perpaucis ante

[1] superiores videremur *L*, superior esse viderer *Jahn,
edd. rec.*

[2] decem *L*, sedecim *Nipperdey.*

---

[a] The ideal orator outlined is of course Cicero himself.
The equipment which he desiderates is essentially a summary
of the treatise *de Oratore.*   An interesting analogue (without
any suggestion of dependence) is Dryden's enumeration of
the qualities that shall equip a greater poet than had yet
arisen (*Works*, vol. 13, p. 28).

no one who knew how to enliven it with brief digression ; no one who could inspire in the judge a feeling of angry indignation, or move him to tears, or in short (and this is the one supreme characteristic of the orator) sway his feelings in whatever direction the situation demanded.[a]

" Thus when Hortensius had all but vanished from 323 the forum, and I at the earliest legal age, six years after him, was made consul, he began to resume his activity, as if fearing lest, now that I was his equal in career, I should appear to boast some point of superiority to him. Thus, for twelve years following my consulship, we were associated in the conduct of the most important suits in perfect harmony, with deference on the part of each to the other's special skill. My consulship, which at first had in some measure wounded his vanity, proved in the end a bond, because of the praise he bestowed on it in admiration of what I had accomplished. Our mutual 324 activity was made manifest most conspicuously only a short time before this our common study, Brutus, shrinking before the threat of arms, suddenly fell silent and remains dumb. The provisions of the Pompeian[b] law granted only three hours each to speakers for the defence, yet we appeared daily in cases of great similarity, or almost identical, with novelty of treatment in each. In some of these cases you also, Brutus, had a hand, whether jointly with us or alone. Thus, though Hortensius's life was not so long as it should have been, he nevertheless completed a career which began ten years before you were born,[c] and in his sixty-fourth year, only a few days before his

[b] On the Pompeian law of 52 B.C., see 243 and note.
[c] Birth of Brutus, 85 B.C. See Münzer in *P.-W.* 10, p. 974.

mortem diebus, una tecum socerum tuum defendit
Appium. Dicendi autem genus quod fuerit in
utroque, orationes utriusque etiam posteris nostris
indicabunt.

325 xcv. Sed si quaerimus cur adulescens magis
floruerit dicendo quam senior Hortensius, causas
reperiemus verissimas duas. Primum, quod genus
erat orationis Asiaticum adulescentiae magis concessum quam senectuti. Genera autem Asiaticae
dictionis duo sunt, unum sententiosum et argutum,
sententiis non tam gravibus et severis quam con-
cinnis et venustis, qualis in historia Timaeus, in dicendo autem pueris nobis Hierocles Alabandeus, magis
etiam Menecles frater eius fuit, quorum utriusque
orationes sunt in primis ut Asiatico in genere laudabiles.
Aliud autem genus est non tam sententiis frequen-
tatum quam verbis volucre atque incitatum, quale est
nunc Asia tota, nec flumine solum orationis, sed
etiam exornato et faceto[1] genere verborum, in quo
fuit Aeschylus Cnidius et meus aequalis Milesius
Aeschines. In his erat admirabilis orationis cursus,
326 ornata sententiarum concinnitas non erat. Haec autem, ut dixi, genera dicendi aptiora sunt adulescentibus, in senibus gravitatem non habent. Itaque
Hortensius utroque genere florens clamores faciebat
adulescens; habebat enim et Meneclium illud studium
crebrarum venustarumque sententiarum, in quibus,

---

[1] faceto *L*, facto *Ruhnken probabiliter.*

---

[a] It would appear that the term Asiatic applied to oratory
was current and used without reproach. The superior wealth
and importance of the cities of Asia Minor in the period
after Alexander gave a significance to forensic oratory and
an opportunity for its exercise which was lacking to Greece
proper. The earliest teachers of oratory at Rome were from

death, participated with you in the defence of your father-in-law Appius. As for the style of oratory which marked us both, our speeches will permit posterity to judge.

" If we raise the question, why in his youth 325 Hortensius enjoyed a more brilliant reputation than in his age, we shall find two good reasons : first, because his oratorical style was the Asiatic, a manner condoned in youth, but less suited to age.[a] Of the Asiatic style there are two types, the one sententious and studied, less characterized by weight of thought than by the charm of balance and symmetry. Such was Timaeus the historian ; in oratory Hierocles of Alabanda in my boyhood, and even more so his brother Menecles, both of whose speeches are masterpieces in this Asiatic style. The other type is not so notable for wealth of sententious phrase, as for swiftness and impetuosity—a general trait of Asia at the present time—combining with this rapid flow of speech a choice of words refined and ornate. This is the manner of which Aeschylus of Cnidus and my contemporary Aeschines of Miletus were representatives. Their oratory had a rush and movement which provoked admiration, but it lacked elaborate symmetry of phrase and sentence. Both 326 of these styles, as I have said, are better suited to youth ; in older men they lack weight and dignity. Thus Hortensius, skilled in both manners, won great applause as a young man, for he made a cult of those gracefully pointed phrases in the manner of Menecles and used them often ; but as

Asiatic schools (see above, 104), and Roman oratory down to and including Cicero was essentially Asiatic. The term is applied by Plutarch to the oratory of Mark Antony.

ut in illo Graeco, sic in hoc erant quaedam magis
venustae dulcesque sententiae quam aut necessariae
aut interdum utiles ; et erat oratio cum incitata et
vibrans tum etiam accurata et polita. Non proba-
bantur haec senibus—saepe videbam cum irridentem
tum etiam irascentem et stomachantem Philippum—
sed mirabantur adulescentes, multitudo movebatur.

327 Erat excellens iudicio vulgi et facile primas tenebat
adulescens ; etsi enim genus illud dicendi auctoritatis
habebat parum, tamen aptum esse aetati videbatur.
Et certe, quod et ingeni quaedam forma elucebat [et]
exercitatione perfecta, verborumque erat ⟨arte⟩
astricta comprehensio,[1] summam hominum admirationem excitabat. Sed cum iam honores et illa senior
auctoritas gravius quiddam requireret, remanebat
idem nec decebat idem ; quodque exercitationem
studiumque dimiserat, quod in eo fuerat acerrimum,
concinnitas illa crebritasque sententiarum pristina
manebat, sed ea vestitu illo orationis quo con-
suerat ornata non erat. Hoc tibi ille, Brute, minus
fortasse placuit quam placuisset, si illum flagrantem
studio et florentem facultate audire potuisses.

328 XCVI. Tum Brutus : Ego vero, inquit, et ista
quae dicis video qualia sint et Hortensium mag-

---

[1] *locus confusus, partim corruptus, sic traditur* : quod
et ingeni quaedam forma lucebat et exercitatione perfecta
verborum eratque astricta comprehensio *L*, elucebat *Lambinus, et secl. Schütz,* arte *inserui.*

---

[a] The text of this sentence is confused as given by the
MSS., but it would seem that Cicero means to say that the

with the Greek, so with him, they were often merely
graceful and of pleasant sound, not necessary nor
always useful ; and again his language could be
swift and vibrant without loss of careful finish. This
sort of thing was not looked upon with favour by
older men,—how often have I seen Philippus listening to him with a derisive smile, sometimes even with
anger and impatience !—but all the younger generation was filled with admiration, and the people
were carried away by it. In the judgement of the 327
public the young Hortensius was pre-eminent and
easily held the first place ; for though his type of
eloquence lacked weight and authority, still it
seemed suited to his youth, and at any rate, because
some beauty of natural endowment perfected by
assiduous practice shone forth in him, and because
his words were put compactly into artistic periods,[a]
he provoked great and universal admiration. But
when official honours and the authority demanded
of age called for something more substantial, he
remained the same when the same style no longer
became him. When for some time he had relaxed
that practice and application which had formerly
been unremitting, though his earlier habit of neatly
balanced phrase and thought remained, it was now
no longer dressed out with the same richness of
language as formerly. For this reason perhaps,
Brutus, he pleased you less than he would have
if you had heard him while still burning with his
earlier fire and at the height of his power."

  " Yes," replied Brutus, " I recognize very well 328
the qualifications you make, and still I have always

ingenium of Hortensius was brought to perfection by *exercitatio* and *ars.* On *arte astricta comprehensio, cf.* 140.

num oratorem semper putavi maximeque probavi
pro Messalla dicentem, cum tu afuisti.

Sic ferunt, inquam, idque declarat totidem quot
dixit, ut aiunt, scripta verbis oratio.   Ergo ille
a Crasso consule et Scaevola usque ad Paullum
et Marcellum consules floruit, nos in eodem cursu
fuimus a Sulla dictatore ad eosdem fere consules.
Sic Q. Hortensi vox exstincta fato suo est, nostra
publico.

329   Melius, quaeso, ominare, inquit Brutus.

Sit sane ut vis, inquam, et id non tam mea causa
quam tua ; sed fortunatus illius exitus, qui ea non
vidit cum fierent quae providit futura.   Saepe enim
inter nos impendentis casus deflevimus, cum belli
civilis causas in privatorum cupiditatibus inclusas,
pacis spem a publico consilio esse exclusam vide-
remus.   Sed illum videtur felicitas ipsius qua semper
est usus ab eis miseriis quae consecutae sunt morte
vindicavisse.

330   Nos autem, Brute, quoniam post Hortensi
clarissimi oratoris mortem orbae eloquentiae quasi
tutores relicti sumus, domi teneamus eam saeptam
liberali custodia et hos ignotos atque impudentis
procos repudiemus tueamurque ut adultam virginem
caste et ab amatorum impetu quantum possumus
prohibeamus.   Equidem etsi doleo me in vitam paulo
serius tamquam in viam ingressum, prius quam

---

* That is from 95 to 50 B.C.   The dictatorship of Sulla,
81 B.C.

thought Hortensius a great orator, and I admired him particularly speaking in defence of Messalla while you were away."

" That seems to be the general verdict," I answered, " and the written speech, reproduced I am told exactly as spoken, confirms your judgement. His career thus was one of success from the consulship of Crassus and Scaevola down to Paulus and Marcellus[a] ; mine was parallel to his from the dictatorship of Sulla down to about the same time. Thus the voice of Hortensius was silenced only by his own death, mine by the death of the republic."

" Words of better omen, pray ! " said Brutus.   329

" Be it as you will," I replied, " and if so, it is not so much for me as for you.   But his end was fortunate in that he did not live to see and experience that future which he foresaw.   Many a time we lamented together the disasters impending, seeing the threat of civil war present in the ambitions of individuals in self-interest, and the hope of peaceful adjustment absent from public policy.   But that felicity, peculiarly his own, which attended him all his life interposed, it would seem, to shield him by a timely death from the calamities which have followed.

" As for us, Brutus, since with the death of Hor- 330 tensius we are left to be the guardians of orphaned eloquence, let us keep her within our own walls, protected by a custody worthy of her liberal lineage. Let us repel the pretensions of these upstart and impudent suitors, and guard her purity, like that of a virgin grown to womanhood, and, so far as we can, shield her from the advances of rash admirers. I have indeed reason to grieve that I entered on the road of life so late that the night, which has fallen

confectum iter sit, in hanc rei publicae noctem
incidisse, tamen ea consolatione sustentor quam tu
mihi, Brute, adhibuisti tuis suavissimis litteris, quibus me forti animo esse oportere censebas, quod ea
gessissem quae de me etiam me tacente ipsa lo-
querentur, mortuo viverent[que][1]; quae, si recte
esset, salute rei publicae, sin secus, interitu ipso testimonium meorum de re publica consiliorum darent.

331 xcvii. Sed in te intuens, Brute, doleo, cuius in
adulescentiam per medias laudes quasi quadrigis
vehentem transversa incurrit misera fortuna rei
publicae. Hic me dolor tangit,[2] haec cura sollicitat
et hunc mecum socium eiusdem et amoris et iudici.
Tibi favemus, te tua frui virtute cupimus, tibi optamus
eam rem publicam in qua duorum generum amplis-
simorum renovare memoriam atque augere possis.
Tuum enim forum, tuum erat illud curriculum, tu
illuc veneras unus, qui non linguam modo acuisses
exercitatione dicendi sed et ipsam eloquentiam
locupletavisses graviorum artium instrumento et
isdem artibus decus omne virtutis cum summa elo-
332 quentiae laude iunxisses. Ex te duplex nos afficit
sollicitudo, quod et ipse re publica careas et illa te.

---

[1] mortuo viverentque *L*, que *seclusi.*
[2] tangit *L*, angit *Corradus, Lambinus.*

---

[a] This is the letter referred to at the beginning (11 and 12)
which, as we have already noted, was probably the epistolary
treatise *de Virtute.* From it the words following are presumably an extract in general import. Allusion to the title
may be contained in the words below, *te tua frui virtute*

upon the commonwealth, has overtaken me before
my journey was ended ; yet I am sustained by the
consolations which your affectionate letter afforded
me.[a] In it you said that I ought to be of good
courage, reflecting that I had accomplished things
which, without words of mine, will speak for me,
and after my death will still live ; that the preservation of the state, if it survive, even its downfall, if
it should not, will bear witness to the wisdom of the
measures I undertook in its behalf.

But I grieve more deeply when I look on you, 331
Brutus, whose youthful career, faring in triumph
amidst the general applause, has been thwarted by
the onset of a malign fortune. This is the grief which
touches me most closely, this the care which disquiets
me, and not me only, but my friend here who shares
my love and esteem for you. Upon you our affection
rests, for you we share the ardent wish that you
may reap the reward of your virtue, for you we
crave such a constitution of public affairs as shall
make it possible for you to maintain the fame of two
great houses and add to them a new lustre. Yours
was the forum, yours was that arena, you were conspicuous in bringing thither, not only a tongue
sharpened by training to eloquence, but eloquence
itself, enriched and equipped with arts of graver import, and through such studies you had joined to your
renown for eloquence all that grace which belongs
to the study of virtue. On your account a two-fold 332
concern touches us, that you are bereft of the republic, and the republic of you. And yet, though

cupimus, where tua, strongly stressed by position, may
contrast Brutus's own virtus with the virtus which he had
commended to Cicero.

Tu tamen, etsi cursum ingeni tui, Brute, premit haec
importuna clades civitatis, contine te in tuis peren-
nibus studiis et effice id quod iam prope modum vel
plane potius effeceras, ut te eripias ex ea quam ego
congessi in hunc sermonem turba patronorum. Nec
enim decet te ornatum uberrimis artibus, quas cum
domo haurire non posses arcessivisti ex urbe ea
quae domus est semper habita doctrinae, numerari
in vulgo patronorum. Nam quid te exercuit Pammenes vir longe eloquentissimus Graeciae? quid illa
vetus Academia atque eius heres Aristus hospes et
familiaris meus, si quidem similes maioris partis
333 oratorum futuri sumus? Nonne cernimus vix singulis aetatibus binos oratores laudabilis constitisse?
Galba fuit inter tot aequalis unus excellens, cui,
quem ad modum accepimus, et Cato cedebat senior
et qui temporibus illis aetate inferiores fuerunt,
Lepidus postea, deinde Carbo; nam Gracchi in
contionibus multo faciliore et liberiore genere
dicendi, quorum tamen ipsorum ad aetatem laus
eloquentiae perfecta nondum fuit; Antonius Crassus,
post Cotta Sulpicius, Hortensius—nihil dico amplius; tantum dico, si mihi accidisset ut numerarer

the cruel rout of civic life has checked the free
course of your genius, hold yourself to those studies
which you have never relaxed, and see to it (as you
had almost, or rather quite, accomplished already)
that you set yourself apart from the throng of
pleaders which I have crowded into this discussion.
For having furnished your mind so richly with those
studies, which, not finding at home, you went to
seek in that city which has always been recognized
as the home of learning, it would ill become you to be
content with a place in the common run of pleaders.
To what purpose the training of Pammenes the
most eloquent teacher of Greece ? To what purpose
the instruction of the famous Old Academy, and of the
heir to its doctrines, my friend and guest Aristus,
if after all we are to turn out no better than the
major part of orators ? Do we not see that in each 333
period scarcely so many as two orators have maintained a place of distinction ? Galba among so
many contemporaries was the one pre-eminent,
before whom, we are told, Cato of the older generation gave way, and all of that time who were his
juniors. After him Lepidus, then Carbo. I need
not remind you of the Gracchi, characterized in
their popular harangues by a much freer and more
flexible style of speaking, though even down to
their time the art of eloquence still fell short of
highest distinction ; Antonius and Crassus, afterwards
Cotta and Sulpicius, Hortensius—I will say nothing
further, but add only, that if it had been my lot
to be reckoned merely as one amongst the multitude of pleaders . . . [*I should have preferred to re-
nounce the oratorical career altogether rather than undergo*

in multis . . . si operosa est concursatio magis opportunorum[1] . . .

[1] *Flavio Biondo in subscr. B*: " non erat amplius in exemplari, a quo abscissae sunt chartae duae ; quamquam ut mihi videtur nedum chartae. sed pauca admodum deficiunt." *V. degli Ardizzi in subscr. O*: "non inveni plura in perveteri codice, fortunae quidem iniquitas id totum si tamen quiddam erat recidit." *Cf. etiam Martha in ed. 1892 (1907) p. xxx, n. 3.*

---

[a] There seems to be no certain way of fitting the final words of the manuscript into the thought, which proceeds along clearly enough as far as *in multis*. The argument is manifestly a continuation of the exhortation above *ut te*

the labour and stress of competition with more fortunate rivals.[a]]

eripias . . . ex turba patronorum, and the phrase *ut numerarer in multis* may have contained the idea of preferring renunciation to mediocrity, which is suggested in the italicized words above. How much is lost cannot of course be determined, but scarcely enough to fill out the *duae chartae* of which Flavio Biondo speaks; the words preserved point to the imminent conclusion of the epilogue. Some additional phrases furnishing a conclusion to the setting must have followed. In section 24 the interlocutors take their seats —*sedentes si videtur agamus*, and these words may suggest a simple ending like that of *de Or.* 3. 230 : *sed iam surgamus, nosque curemus et aliquando ab hac contentione disputationis animos nostros curaque laxemus.*

ORATOR

INTRODUCTION

THE *Orator* was written in the latter part of the year
46 B.C. It is thus the latest of Cicero's rhetorical
works, and rounds out the discussion of questions
raised in the earlier works with a brilliant defence
of his own career as an orator. In the form of a
letter addressed to Marcus Junius Brutus, it osten-
sibly, and perhaps actually, answers a request of
Brutus for a picture of the perfect orator. It was
traditional to discuss the training of an orator
under five heads : invention (*inventio*), arrangement
(*collocatio*), diction and style (*elocutio*), delivery (*actio*),
memory (*memoria*). These five points are all touched
on in the *Orator*, but with varying emphasis. There
is a bare allusion to *memoria* ; *inventio, collocatio* and
actio are dismissed with a few paragraphs, and three-
quarters of the treatise is devoted to *elocutio*.

The reason for the lack of proportion in the treatment of the different topics lies in the controversial
nature of the book. It is not a complete and impartial
account of the perfect orator, but a defence of his
own oratorical practice against the criticism of the
" Attici." This was a name adopted by a group of
orators of whom Calvus and Brutus were the most
prominent. They had a definite and precise programme which called for a plain and lucid style
with a minimum of rhetorical ornament, a studied

297

neglect of rhythm, and an infrequent use of emotional appeal. Their style was the severe style of the logician ; their object to instruct rather than to move. They took as models the Attic writers of the fifth and early fourth centuries—Thucydides, Lysias, Xenophon. Their name was a synonym for purism, and indicated their belief that the spread of the Greek language into Asia in the wake of Alexander's armies had been the cause of corruption of taste and degeneracy of style.

Such a group inevitably crossed swords with Cicero, who was by nature and training an exuberant rhetorician rather than a cool logician. In the *Brutus*, written earlier in the year, he had criticized the position of the " Attici." This had drawn a reply from Brutus, and the debate is continued in the *Orator*. Cicero was denounced by the Attici for exuberance and verbosity, for the use of rhythmical cadences which in their opinion softened and weakened his style, and for the frigidity of his wit. To all of these charges there is a reply in the *Orator*, though in the practised manner of the advocate, the defence takes the form at times of an attack on the opponent. To the Atticist claim to possess the only true style he opposes Demosthenes, the master of all styles. He devotes the most extensive section of the work to the subject of rhythm, showing its antiquity among the Greeks and giving a theoretical account of its use which, though confused by maladroit combinations of Greek sources, is the best ancient account of the theory and practise of prose rhythm. Uneven as the treatise is, it contains many sound critical judgements, and is a worthy valedictory from the man who created artistic Latin prose.

INTRODUCTION

The principal manuscripts of the *Orator* fall into two classes, the *Integri* and the *Mutili*. The oldest representative of the latter group is the Codex Abrincensis (A), a ninth-century manuscript formerly in the monastery of Mont-St.-Michel and now in the library at Avranches. From it, as Heerdegen has shown, the thirty-seven other manuscripts of this group are derived. It contains portions of the *De Oratore* and of the *Orator* ; the latter begins at section 91 with the words *aliquan]toque robustius* and runs to *trochaeum quo* (sic) *enim* in section 191. There is then another lacuna extending to section 231, where the manuscript begins with *sem]perque versetur*, and continues to the end of the work.

The manuscripts containing the whole of the *Orator* (*Integri*) are derived from a codex found in 1421 by Gherardo Landriani, bishop of Lodi, near Milan, and called from the place of its discovery Codex Laudensis (L). It contained the *De Inventione*, the *Ad Herennium*, the *De Oratore*, the *Brutus* and the *Orator*. The appearance of a manuscript containing the *Brutus*, unknown up to this time, and the complete text of the *Orator* and *De Oratore*, aroused great excitement in humanistic circles, and copies were eagerly sought. L disappeared a few years later. For determining the readings of L the following manuscripts are of use ; all are either direct copies of L or of a copy of it made by Cosimo of Cremona: Florentinus Magliabecchianus I, 1, 14 (F), copied from L in 1422 or 1423. It contains the *Orator* and *Brutus*. The text is not divided into paragraphs, and in this it probably represents the

text of L more accurately than do the next two manuscripts.

Cosimo's copy is the source of Ottobonianus 2057 (O), a codex written in 1422. It contains the *De Oratore*, the *Brutus*, and the *De Optimo Genere Oratorum*. It was corrected by comparison with L, and such corrections are marked in the manuscript by *vet.*, and are designated in the apparatus by the symbol O^v. Emendations by later hands in this manuscript are designated by O².

Vaticanus Palatinus 1469 (P), likewise a copy of Cosimo's codex, contains the *De Oratore* and the *Orator*. O and P are paragraphed at the same points; this they derived from Cosimo's copy. P was corrected as was O by reference to L.

Mutinensis α Q 8, 25 (M) written in 1425, contains the *Brutus*, the *Elogia Marii et Fabii* and the *Orator*. It is a copy of P, corrected by reference to Cosimo's exemplar.[a]

The two traditions (A and L) differ considerably, and neither deserves to be followed exclusively. The Editor must choose between two readings on the basis of probability. Even where A and L agree the text is in many places obviously corrupt. The hand of the emender has been busy from the days of the humanists. I cite occasionally the emendations of Codex Laurentianus 50, 1 (ρ), Codex Vaticanus 1709 man. 3 (β), Codex Laurentianus 50, 18

---

[a] Professor Durham of Cornell University announced in 1913 that a manuscript in his possession bears a subscription showing that it was a copy of the Codex of Lamola. As Lamola is known to have made a copy of an old Codex (probably L), this manuscript affords an interesting comparison with the other derivatives of L.

man. 2 (λ), Codex Laurentianus 50, 31 (π), **Codex Einsidlensis** 307 (ε), Codex Vitebergensis, now Halensis Yg 24 (f), and of the early printed editions (vulg.).

The following stemma, taken essentially from the edition of P. Reis, Leipzig 1932, shows the relation of the principal manuscripts :

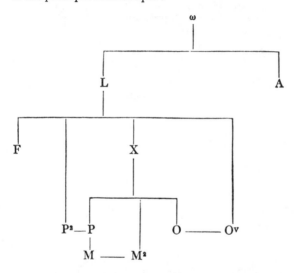

For this edition I have collated AFOPM from photographs. For the readings of the other manuscripts I have depended on the testimony of other editors—Heerdegen, Sandys, Reis.

INTRODUCTION

A codex Abrincensis 238.
F codex Florentinus Magliabecchianus I 1, 14.
P codex Vaticanus Palatinus 1469.
O codex Ottobonianus 2057.
M codex Mutinensis α Q 8, 25.
L consensus of FOP, or where they do not agree, the reading that may fairly be assumed to have been in the codex Laudensis.
β codicis Vaticani 1709 man. 3.
ε codex Einsidlensis 307.
λ codicis Laurentiani 50, 18 man. 2.
π codex Laurentianus 50, 31.
ρ codex Laurentianus 50, 1.
f codex Vitebergensis, nunc Halensis Y g 24.
   vulg. = early printed editions.

BIBLIOGRAPHY [a]

TEXTS AND EDITIONS

Ferdinand Heerdegen, *M. Tulli Ciceronis ad M. Brutum Orator*, Leipzig, 1884.

> Heerdegen's classification of the manuscripts is the basis of all recent study of the text.

Thomas Stangl, *M. Tulli Ciceronis Orator ad M. Brutum*, Leipzig, 1885.

Augustus Samuel Wilkins, *M. Tulli Ciceronis Rhetorica*. Tomus II. *Brutus, Orator, De Optimo Genere Oratorum, Partitiones Oratoriae, Topica*. Oxford, no date, Introduction dated 1903. Photostatic reproduction 1935.

M. Tulli Ciceronis Scripta quae manserunt omnia. Orator ed. Peter Reis. Leipzig, 1932, 1962–1963.

> Reis gives a full and accurate critical apparatus.

O. Jahn and W. Kroll, *Brutus* ; *Orator*, Ed. 6, B. Kytzler, Berlin, 1962.

Opere Retoriche. Vol. 1 ed. and trans. by G. Norcio, Turin, 1970 (*de Oratore, Brutus, Orator*).

O. Seel, *Orator*, Heidelberg, 1952.

---

[a] Sandys' edition (1885) gives a full bibliography. The scope of this series hardly permits covering the intervening fifty years on a similar scale. I have therefore listed only the titles which I have found most useful.

303

BIBLIOGRAPHY

Karl Wilhelm Piderit, *Ciceros Orator ad M. Brutum*, second edition revised by Halm, Leipzig, 1876.

John Edwin Sandys, *M. Tulli Ciceronis ad M. Brutum Orator*. Cambridge, 1885.

   The best edition in English and in some ways the best in any language. The translator has profited by many of the versions in this edition. It contains a full bibliography.

Wilhelm Kroll, *M. Tulli Ciceronis Orator*, Berlin, 1913.

   An excellent commentary. The parallels from Greek sources are particularly enlightening.

ARTICLES

Remigio Sabbadini, " La composizione dell' ' Orator ' Ciceroniano." *Rivista di filologia*, xliv. (1916), pp. 1-22.

   The best analysis of Cicero's method in composing the Orator.

Sebastian Schlittenbauer. " Die Tendenz von Ciceros Orator." *Jahrbücher für Philologie*, Supplementband xxviii. (1903), pp. 181-248.

Peter Reis, " Studia Tulliana ad Oratorem pertinentia." *Dissertationes Argentoratenses Selectae*, xii., pp. 1-101.

   A full discussion of the text tradition.

Thomas Stangl, " Cicerofund Charles L. Durhams." *Berliner philologische Wochenschrift* (1913), pp. 829-832 and 860-864.

Johannes Stroux, " Zum Texte von Ciceros Orator. Kritische Beiträge." *Jahresbericht des Philologischen Vereins zu Berlin*, xxxix. (1913), pp. 251-270.

BIBLIOGRAPHY

Johannes Stroux, " Handschriftliche Studien zu Cicero de Oratore. Die Rekonstruktion des Handschrifts von Lodi," Leipzig, 1921.

G. L. Hendrickson, " The Peripatetic Mean of Style and the Three Stylistic Characters." *American Journal of Philology*, xxv. (1904), pp. 125-126.

G. L. Hendrickson, " The Origin and Meaning of the Ancient Characters of Style." *American Journal of Philology*, xxvi. (1905), pp. 249-290.

G. L. Hendrickson, " Cicero de Optimo Genere Oratorum." *American Journal of Philology*, xlvii. (1926), pp. 109-123.

G. L. Hendrickson, " Cicero's Correspondence with Brutus and Calvus on Oratorical Style." *American Journal of Philology*, xlvii. (1926), pp. 234-258.

OTHER TRANSLATIONS

E. Jones, *Cicero's Brutus or History of Famous Orators ; also his Orator, or Accomplished Speaker, now first translated into English.* London, 1776 (reprinted 1808 with a few changes, as vol. ii. of *Cicero on Oratory and Orators*). London, J. and J. Richardson, etc.

This is a paraphrase rather than a translation, but it is done in a vigorous style.

Charles Duke Yonge, in Bohn's Classical Library, vol. iv. of *Cicero's Orations.* London, 1856. Inaccurate.

Henri Bornecque, *Cicero, L'Orateur : Texte et Traduction.* In Collection Guillaume Budé. Paris, 1921.

M. TULLI CICERONIS

ORATOR

1 I. Utrum difficilius aut maius esset negare tibi saepius idem roganti an efficere id quod rogares diu
multumque, Brute, dubitavi. Nam et negare ei
quem unice diligerem cuique me carissimum esse
sentirem, praesertim et iusta petenti et praeclara
cupienti, durum admodum mihi videbatur; et suscipere tantam rem, quantam non modo facultate
consequi difficile esset sed etiam cogitatione com-
plecti, vix arbitrabar esse eius qui vereretur repre-
2 hensionem doctorum atque prudentium. Quid enim
est maius quam, cum tanta sit inter oratores bonos
dissimilitudo, iudicare quae sit optima species et
quasi figura dicendi? Quod quoniam me saepius
rogas, aggrediar non tam perficiendi spe quam ex-
periendi voluntate. Malo enim, cum studio tuo sim
obsecutus, desiderari a te prudentiam meam quam,
si id non fecerim, benevolentiam.

3 Quaeris igitur idque iam saepius, quod eloquentiae
genus probem maxime et quale mihi videatur illud,
quo nihil addi possit, quod ego summum et perfectis-

MARCUS TULLIUS CICERO

ORATOR

For a long time I debated earnestly with myself, 1
Brutus, as to which course would be more difficult or
more serious—to deny your oft repeated request, or
to do what you ask. For it seemed hard indeed to refuse one whom I whole-heartedly love, and who I know
returns my affection, especially since his request
is reasonable and his curiosity honourable ; and to
undertake a task so great as to be difficult to attain
in practice or even to grasp with the imagination
seemed hardly the act of a man who respects the
opinions of the learned and judicious. For what 2
greater task can there be than to decide what is the
finest ideal and type of oratory, when good orators
exhibit such variety ? But in view of your repeated
requests, I shall approach the task, not so much in
hope of success as from a willingness to try. I
prefer, in fact, that you should find me deficient in
judgement in yielding to your desire, rather than
lacking in kindness should I refuse.

You ask me, then, and have done so repeatedly, 3
what style of oratory I most approve, and what
seems to be the nature of that style, deficient in no
respect, which I think consummate and perfect. On

simum iudicem. In quo vereor ne, si id quod vis
effecero eumque oratorem quem quaeris expressero,
tardem studia multorum, qui desperatione debilitati
experiri id nolent quod se assequi posse diffidant.
4 Sed par est est omnis omnia experiri, qui res magnas
et magno opere expetendas concupiverunt. Quodsi
quem aut natura sua aut illa praestantis ingeni vis
forte deficiet aut minus instructus erit magnarum
artium disciplinis, teneat tamen eum cursum quem
poterit. Prima enim sequentem honestum est in
secundis tertiisque consistere. Nam[1] in poetis non
Homero soli locus est, ut de Graecis loquar, aut
Archilocho aut Sophocli aut Pindaro, sed horum vel
5 secundis vel etiam infra secundos. Nec vero Aristotelem in philosophia deterruit a scribendo amplitudo
Platonis, nec ipse Aristoteles admirabili quadam
scientia et copia ceterorum studia restinxit. 11. Nec
solum ab optimis studiis excellentes viri deterriti
non sunt, sed ne opifices quidem se ab[2] artibus suis
removerunt, qui aut Ialysi quem Rhodi vidimus non
potuerunt aut Coae Veneris pulchritudinem imitari,
nec simulacro Iovis Olympii aut doryphori statua[3]
deterriti reliqui minus experti sunt quid efficere aut
quo progredi possent. Quorum tanta multitudo fuit,
tanta in suo cuiusque genere laus, ut cum summa
6 miraremur, inferiora tamen probaremus. In orato-

---

[1] nam λ, an L.   [2] ab P²M, om. alii.
          [3] statua βπ, statuae L.

---

[a] The picture of the Rhodian hero Ialysus was the masterpiece of Protogenes ; the Coan Aphrodite was by Apelles.
The statue of Zeus at Olympia by Phidias was regarded as

this question I am afraid that if I do what you wish and portray that ideal orator, I may discourage the studies of many who in the weakness of despair will refuse to try what they have no hope of being able to attain. But it is fair that men should leave 4 nothing untried if they have aspired to great and ambitious undertakings. In case anyone happens to lack physical endowment or outstanding intellectual ability, or is insufficiently trained in cultural studies, let him at least maintain the best course he can. For it is no disgrace for one who is striving for the first place to stop at second or third. Among poets, for example, there is room, not only for Homer, to cite instances from Greek literature, or Archilochus or Sophocles or Pindar, but also for those of a second or even lower rank. And in philosophy, 5 I am sure, the magnificence of Plato did not deter Aristotle from writing, nor did Aristotle with all his marvellous breadth of knowledge put an end to the studies of others. Moreover, not only were outstanding men not deterred from undertaking liberal pursuits, but even craftsmen did not give up their arts because they were unable to equal the beauty of the picture of Ialysus which we saw at Rhodes, or of the Coan Venus; nor did the statue of Jupiter at Olympia or the Doryphorus[a] deter the other sculptors from trying to see what they could accomplish or what progress they could make. There were so many of them and such was the merit of each in his own class, that while we admire the best we can nevertheless approve the less excellent. Among orators, certainly among Greek 6

one of the wonders of the ancient world. The Doryphorus of Polyclitus was the most famous of his athletic figures.

ribus vero, Graecis quidem, admirabile est quantum
inter omnis unus excellat. Ac tamen, cum esset Demosthenes, multi oratores magni et clari fuerunt et
antea fuerant nec postea defecerunt. Quare non est
cur eorum qui se studio eloquentiae dediderunt spes
infringatur[1] aut languescat industria. Nam neque
illud ipsum quod est optimum desperandum est et
in praestantibus[2] rebus magna sunt ea quae sunt
optimis proxima.

7 Atque ego in summo oratore fingendo talem in-
formabo qualis fortasse nemo fuit. Non enim quaero
quis fuerit, sed quid sit illud quo nihil esse possit
praestantius, quod in perpetuitate dicendi non saepe
atque haud scio an nunquam[3] in aliqua autem parte
eluceat aliquando, idem apud alios densius, apud alios
8 fortasse rarius. Sed ego sic statuo, nihil esse in ullo
genere tam pulchrum, quo non pulchrius id sit unde
illud ut ex ore aliquo quasi imago exprimatur. Quod
neque oculis neque auribus neque ullo sensu percipi
potest, cogitatione tamen[4] et mente complectimur.
Itaque et Phidiae simulacris, quibus nihil in illo
genere perfectius videmus, et eis picturis quas nomi-
9 navi cogitare tamen possumus pulchriora. Nec vero
ille artifex cum faceret Iovis formam aut Minervae,
contemplabatur aliquem e quo similitudinem duceret,
sed ipsius in mente insidebat species pulchritudinis
eximia quaedam, quam intuens in eaque defixus
ad illius similitudinem artem et manum dirigebat.

---

[1] infringatur βε, infringat *L*.
[2] praestantibus λ, praesentibus *L*.
[3] numquam ε[1], unquam *L*ε[2].
[4] tamen *Reis :* tantum *L*.

---

[a] Referring to the Athena Parthenos of Phidias.

orators, it is amazing how one man has pre-eminence over all. Yet during the lifetime of Demosthenes many orators attained great distinction ; the same was true of the preceding period, and there was no dearth of great orators in later times. Therefore there is no reason why those who have devoted themselves to the study of oratory should abandon hope or lessen their activity. For we must not despair of attaining the best, and in a noble undertaking that which is nearest to the best is great.

Consequently in delineating the perfect orator I 7 shall be portraying such a one as perhaps has never existed. Indeed I am not inquiring who was the perfect orator, but what is that unsurpassable ideal which seldom if ever appears throughout a whole speech but does shine forth at some times and in some places, more frequently in some speakers, more rarely perhaps in others. But I am firmly of the opinion 8 that nothing of any kind is so beautiful as not to be excelled in beauty by that of which it is a copy, as a mask is a copy of a face. This ideal cannot be perceived by the eye or ear, nor by any of the senses, but we can nevertheless grasp it by the mind and the imagination. For example, in the case of the statues of Phidias, the most perfect of their kind that we have ever seen, and in the case of the paintings I have mentioned, we can, in spite of their beauty, imagine something more beautiful. Surely 9 that great sculptor, while making the image of Jupiter or Minerva,[a] did not look at any person whom he was using as a model, but in his own mind there dwelt a surpassing vision of beauty ; at this he gazed and all intent on this he guided his artist's hand to produce the likeness of the god. Accordingly,

III. Ut igitur in formis et figuris est aliquid perfectum et excellens, cuius ad cogitatam speciem
imitando referuntur ea quae sub oculos ipsa[1] non
cadunt, sic perfectae eloquentiae speciem animo vide-
10 mus, effigiem auribus quaerimus.   Has rerum formas
appellat ἰδέας ille non intellegendi solum sed etiam
dicendi gravissimus auctor et magister Plato, easque
gigni negat et ait semper esse ac ratione et intellegentia contineri ; cetera nasci, occidere, fluere,
labi, nec diutius esse uno et eodem statu.   Quicquid
est igitur de quo ratione et via disputetur, id est
ad ultimam sui generis formam speciemque redi-
gendum.

11   Ac video hanc primam ingressionem meam, non
ex oratoriis[2] disputationibus ductam sed e media
philosophia repetitam et ea quidem cum antiqua
tum subobscura,[3] aut reprehensionis aliquid aut
certe admirationis habituram.   Nam aut mirabuntur
quid haec pertineant ad ea quae quaerimus—quibus
satis faciet res ipsa cognita, ut non sine causa alte
repetita videatur—aut reprehendent quod inusitatas
12 vias indagemus, tritas relinquamus.   Ego autem
et me saepe nova videri dicere intellego, cum per-
vetera dicam sed inaudita plerisque, et fateor me
oratorem, si modo sim aut etiam quicumque sim, non
ex rhetorum officinis, sed ex Academiae spatiis
exstitisse.   Illa enim sunt curricula multiplicium
variorumque sermonum, in quibus Platonis primum

---

[1] *fortasse* re ipsa.   *Cf.* § 18.
[2] oratoriis β, oratoris *L*.
[3] ea . . . antiqua . . . subobscura *Bake*, eam . . . antiquam . . . subobscuram *L*.

as there is something perfect and surpassing in the
case of sculpture and painting—an intellectual ideal
by reference to which the artist represents those
objects which do not themselves appear to the
eye,[a] so with our minds we conceive the ideal of
perfect eloquence, but with our ears we catch only
the copy. These patterns of things are called ἰδέαι 10
or ideas by Plato,[b] that eminent master and teacher
both of style and of thought ; these, he says, do not
" become " ; they exist for ever, and depend on
intellect and reason ; other things come into being
and cease to be, they are in flux and do not remain
long in the same state. Whatever, then, is to be
discussed rationally and methodically, must be
reduced to the ultimate form and type of its class.

I know that this introduction of mine, which does 11
not derive from the discussions on the subject of
oratory, but from the heart of philosophy, and an
ancient and rather obscure philosophy at that, will
arouse criticism, or at least cause astonishment. For
readers either will wonder how this can be relevant to
our investigation—these will be satisfied when the
facts are all laid before them so that it will seem
reasonable to go so far back—or will criticize us for
leaving the well-trodden paths and hunting for new
ones.   However, I am aware that I often seem to 12
be making original remarks when what I am saying
is very old but generally unknown ; and I confess
that whatever ability I possess as an orator comes,
not from the workshops of the rhetoricians, but from
the spacious grounds of the Academy. There indeed
is the field for manifold and varied debate, which was

---

[a] *e.g.*, gods or mythological personages who are wholly
imaginary.   [b] *Symposium* 211 A.

sunt impressa vestigia. Sed et huius et aliorum philosophorum disputationibus et exagitatus maxime orator est et adiutus—omnis enim ubertas et quasi silva dicendi ducta ab illis est—nec satis tamen instructus[1] ad forensis causas, quas, ut illi ipsi di-

13 cere solebant, agrestioribus Musis reliquerunt. Sic eloquentia haec forensis spreta a philosophis et repudiata multis quidem illa adiumentis magnisque caruit, sed tamen ornata verbis atque sententiis iactationem habuit in populo nec paucorum iudicium reprehensionemque pertimuit : ita et doctis eloquentia popularis et disertis elegans doctrina defuit.

14 IV. Positum sit igitur in primis quod post magis intellegetur, sine philosophia non posse effici quem quaerimus eloquentem, non ut in ea tamen omnia sint, sed ut sic adiuvet ut palaestra histrionem ; parva enim magnis saepe rectissime conferuntur. Nam nec latius atque copiosius de magnis variisque rebus sine philosophia potest quisquam dicere—

15 si quidem etiam in Phaedro Platonis hoc Periclem praestitisse ceteris dicit[2] oratoribus Socrates, quod is Anaxagorae physici fuerit auditor. A quo censet eum cum alia praeclara quaedam et magnifica didicisse tum[3] uberem et fecundum fuisse gnarumque, quod est eloquentiae maximum, quibus orationis modis quaeque animorum partes pellerentur. Quod idem de Demosthene existimari potest cuius

---

[1] instructus *Reis*, instructa *L*.
[2] dicit ρ, dicat *L*.
[3] didicisse tum *Schütz*, didicisset *L*.

---

[a] Plato, *Phaedrus* 269 E.   Cicero gives a free adaptation rather than a translation.

first trodden by the feet of Plato. By his discussions and those of other philosophers the orator has been severely criticized but has also received assistance—for all richness of style, and what may be called the raw material of oratory is derived from them—but he has not received from the philosophers sufficient training for pleading in the courts of law. They left this to the ruder Muses, as they were wont to say themselves. Consequently the eloquence of the 13 courts, scorned and rejected by the philosophers, lost much valuable assistance ; nevertheless with a veneer of verbiage and maxims it vaunted itself before the populace, and did not fear the unfavourable criticism of the few. As a result the learned lacked an eloquence which appealed to the people, and the fluent speakers lacked the refinement of sound learning.

Let us assume, then, at the beginning what will 14 become clearer hereafter, that philosophy is essential for the education of our ideal orator ; not that philosophy is everything, but that it helps the orator as physical training helps the actor (for it is frequently illuminating to compare great things with small). For no one can discuss great and varied subjects in a copious and eloquent style without philosophy—as, for example, in Plato's *Phaedrus* Socrates says 15 that Pericles surpassed other orators because he was a pupil of Anaxagoras, the natural philosopher.[a] From him Socrates thinks that Pericles learned much that was splendid and sublime, and acquired copiousness and fertility, and—most important to eloquence—knowledge of the kind of speech which arouses each set of feelings. The same may be held true of Demosthenes, from whose *Epistles* one

315

ex epistulis intellegi licet quam frequens fuerit
16 Platonis auditor ; nec vero sine philosophorum disciplina genus et speciem cuiusque rei cernere neque
eam definiendo explicare nec tribuere in partis
possumus nec iudicare quae vera quae falsa sint
neque cernere consequentia, repugnantia videre,
ambigua distinguere. Quid dicam de natura rerum,
cuius cognitio magnam oratori[1] suppeditat copiam ?
An credas[2] de vita, de officiis, de virtute, de moribus sine multa earum ipsarum rerum disciplina aut
17 dici aut intellegi posse ? v. Ad has tot tantasque
res adhibenda sunt ornamenta innumerabilia ; quae
sola tum quidem tradebantur ab eis qui dicendi
numerabantur magistri ; quo fit ut veram illam et
absolutam eloquentiam nemo consequatur, quod
alia intellegendi alia dicendi disciplina est et ab
aliis rerum ab aliis verborum doctrina quaeritur.
18 Itaque M. Antonius, cui vel primas eloquentiae
patrum nostrorum tribuebat aetas, vir natura peracutus et prudens, in eo libro quem unum reliquit
disertos ait se vidisse multos, eloquentem omnino
neminem. Insidebat videlicet in eius mente species
eloquentiae quam cernebat animo, re ipsa non videbat. Vir autem acerrimo ingenio—sic enim fuit—
multa et in se et in aliis desiderans neminem plane
19 qui recte appellari eloquens posset videbat. Quodsi
ille nec se nec L. Crassum eloquentem putavit,

---

[1] oratori *Ernesti*, orationis *L.*
[2] an credas *addidi*, an credamus *Kroll.*

---

[a] The *Epistles* of Demosthenes are now considered
spurious.
[b] He is still referring to the split between rhetoricians and
philosophers beginning with Plato.
[c] Antonius (143–87 b.c.) shared with his contemporary,

may learn how diligent a pupil he was of Plato.[a]
Surely without philosophical training we cannot dis- 16
tinguish the genus and species of anything, nor
define it nor divide it into subordinate parts, nor
separate truth from falsehood, nor recognize "con-
sequents," distinguish "contradictories" or analyse
"ambiguities." What am I to say about the study of
natural philosophy, which affords the orator a wealth
of material ? Again, would you think one could speak
or think about life or duty or virtue or morals without thorough training in these very subjects ? To 17
express these many important ideas one must use
innumerable stylistic ornaments ; which at that
time [b] comprised the sole instruction given by those
accounted teachers of rhetoric. As a consequence
no one attains to that true and perfect eloquence,
because there is one course of training in thought,
and another in expression ; from one group of
teachers we seek instruction in facts, from others
instruction in language. This is the reason why 18
Marcus Antonius,[c] who was regarded by our fathers'
generation as easily the first in eloquence, and was a
man naturally keen and intelligent, says in his sole
published work that he had seen many good speakers,
but none who were eloquent. Obviously there was
in his mind an ideal of eloquence which he appre-
hended by the intellect but had never actually seen.
Being a man of subtle intellect—this description is
certainly true—he found much to seek both in himself
and in others, and saw no one at all who could
rightly be called eloquent. But if he did not consider 19
himself or Lucius Crassus eloquent, he certainly had

Crassus, the honours in oratory at Rome. They are the
principal speakers in Cicero's dialogue *De Oratore*.

habuit profecto comprehensam animo quandam
formam eloquentiae, cui quoniam nihil deerat, eos
quibus aliquid aut plura deerant in eam formam
non poterat includere. Investigemus hunc igitur,
Brute, si possumus, quem nunquam vidit Antonius
aut qui omnino nullus unquam fuit. Quem si
imitari atque exprimere non possumus, quod idem
ille vix deo concessum esse dicebat, at qualis esse
debeat poterimus fortasse dicere.

20 Tria sunt omnino genera dicendi, quibus in singulis
quidam floruerunt, peraeque autem, id quod volumus,
perpauci in omnibus. Nam et grandiloqui, ut ita
dicam, fuerunt cum ampla et sententiarum gravitate
et maiestate verborum, vehementes, varii, copiosi,
graves, ad permovendos et convertendos animos
instructi et parati—quod ipsum alii aspera, tristi,
horrida oratione neque perfecta atque conclusa consecuti sunt,[1] alii levi[2] et structa[3] et terminata—
et contra tenues acuti, omnia docentes et dilucidiora,
non ampliora facientes, subtili quadam et pressa
oratione et[4] limata ; vi. in eodemque genere alii
callidi, sed impoliti et consulto[5] rudium similes et
imperitorum, alii in eadem ieiunitate concinniores,

21 idem faceti, florentes etiam et leviter ornati. Est
autem quidam interiectus inter hos[6] medius et quasi
temperatus[7] nec acumine posteriorum nec fulmine
utens superiorum, vicinus amborum, in neutro excellens, utriusque particeps vel utriusque, si verum
quaerimus, potius expers, isque uno tenore, ut aiunt,
in dicendo fluit nihil afferens praeter facultatem et

---

[1] consecuti sunt *addidit Kayser*.   [2] levi $\pi\epsilon M$, leni *L*.
[3] structa *Ernesti*, instructa *L*.   [4] *addidit Lambinus*.
[5] consulto $\beta\lambda$, inconsulto *L*.   [6] hos *Nonius, omisit L*.
[7] temperatus *Nonius*, temperandus *L*.

a mental picture of eloquence, and as this was deficient in no respect, he could not identify with it
those who were deficient in one or more points.   Let
us search, then, Brutus, if we can, for this man whom
Antonius never saw, or who has never existed at all.
If we cannot present an exact copy—he said this was
scarcely within the power of a god—yet we may be
able to say what he ought to be like.

There are in all three oratorical styles, in each of 20
which certain men have been successful, but very
few have attained our ideal of being equally successful in all. The orators of the grandiloquent style,
if I may use an old word, showed splendid power of
thought and majesty of diction ; they were forceful,
versatile, copious and grave, trained and equipped to
arouse and sway the emotions ; some attained their
effect by a rough, severe, harsh style, without regular construction or rounded periods ; others used a
smooth, ordered sentence-structure with a periodic
cadence. At the other extreme were the orators who
were plain, to the point, explaining everything and
making every point clear rather than impressive,
using a refined, concise style stripped of ornament.
Within this class some were adroit but unpolished
and intentionally resembled untrained and unskilful
speakers ; others had the same dryness of style, but
were neater, elegant, even brilliant and to a slight
degree ornate. Between these two there is a mean 21
and I may say tempered style, which uses neither the
intellectual appeal of the latter class nor the fiery
force of the former; akin to both, excelling in neither,
sharing in both, or, to tell the truth, sharing in neither,
this style keeps the proverbial " even tenor of its way,"
bringing nothing except ease and uniformity, or at

aequalitatem aut addit aliquos ut in corona toros
omnemque orationem ornamentis modicis verborum
22 sententiarumque distinguit. Horum singulorum generum quicumque vim in singulis[1] consecuti sunt,
magnum in oratoribus nomen habuerunt. Sed quaerendum est satisne id quod volumus effecerint.
VII. Videmus enim fuisse quosdam qui idem ornate
ac graviter, idem versute et subtiliter dicerent. Atque utinam in Latinis talis oratoris simulacrum
reperire possemus. Esset egregium non quaerere
23 externa, domesticis esse contentos. Sed ego idem,
qui in illo sermone nostro qui est expositus in
Bruto multum tribuerim Latinis, vel ut hortarer
alios vel quod amarem meos, recordor longe omnibus unum anteferre Demosthenem, quem velim[2]
accommodare ad eam quam sentiam eloquentiam,
non ad eam quam in aliquo ipse cognoverim. Hoc
nec gravior exstitit quisquam nec callidior nec tem-
peratior. Itaque nobis monendi sunt ei quorum
sermo imperitus increbruit, qui aut dici se desiderant
Atticos aut ipsi Attice volunt dicere, ut mirentur
hunc maxime, quo ne[3] Athenas quidem ipsas magis
credo fuisse Atticas. Quid enim sit Atticum discant
eloquentiamque ipsius viribus, non imbecillitate sua
24 metiantur. Nunc enim tantum quisque laudat
quantum se posse sperat imitari. Sed tamen eos
studio optimo, iudicio minus firmo praeditos docere
quae sit propria laus Atticorum non alienum puto.

---

[1] in singulis πf, singulis L, singulis aetatibus *Heerdegen*.
[2] quem velim *Muther*, que vim *FO*, quem vim *P*.
[3] ne βλ, *om. L*.

most adding a few posies[a] as in a garland, and diversifying the whole speech with simple ornaments of thought and diction. Those who have 22 gained power in one or another of these three styles have had a great name as orators, but it is open to question whether they have attained the result which we desire. We see, to be sure, that there have been some whose speech was ornate and weighty, and also shrewd and plain. Would that we could find an example of such an orator among the Romans ! It would be fine not to seek our models among foreigners, but to be content with our own. But I recall that in that dialogue which I published 23 under the title of *Brutus*, though I paid high tribute to Romans, both to encourage others and because I loved my own people, still I placed Demosthenes far above all others,[b] as one whom I might consent to identify with that ideal eloquence, not with that which I had myself found in anyone. No one has ever excelled him either in the powerful, the adroit or the tempered style. For this reason we must advise those whose misguided views have been spread abroad, who desire to be called " Atticists " or insist that they speak in the Attic style,—we must advise them to admire that man above all who, I am sure, was as Attic as Athens itself. Let them learn what is Attic, and measure eloquence by his strength, not by their own weakness. At the present time one praises only what 24 one hopes to be able to imitate. However, as these are men of high ambition but poor judgement, I think it not out of place to explain to them the true glory of Atticism.

[a] The *tori*, " posies," seem to have been small bouquets set into a garland of leaves.　　　　　　[b] *Brutus* 35.

VIII. Semper oratorum eloquentiae moderatrix fuit
auditorum prudentia. Omnes enim qui probari
volunt voluntatem eorum qui audiunt intuentur ad
eamque et ad eorum arbitrium et nutum totos se
25 fingunt et accommodant. Itaque Caria et Phrygia
et Mysia, quod minime politae minimeque elegantes
sunt, asciverunt aptum suis auribus opimum[1] quoddam et tanquam adipale dictionis genus quod eorum
vicini non ita lato interiecto mari Rhodii nunquam
probaverunt, Graecia autem multo minus, Atheni-
enses vero funditus repudiaverunt. Quorum semper
fuit prudens sincerumque iudicium, nihil ut possent
nisi incorruptum audire et elegans. Eorum religioni
cum serviret orator, nullum verbum insolens, nullum
26 odiosum ponere audebat. Itaque hic, quem praestitisse diximus ceteris, in illa pro Ctesiphonte oratione
longe optima summissius a primo, deinde dum de
legibus disputat pressius, post sensim incendens iudices, ut vidit ardentis, in reliquis exultavit audacius. Ac tamen in hoc ipso diligenter examinante
verborum omnium pondera reprehendit Aeschines
quaedam et exagitat illudensque dura, odiosa, in-
tolerabilia esse dicit, quin etiam quaerit ab ipso,
cum quidem eum beluam appellet, utrum illa verba
an portenta sint, ut Aeschini ne Demosthenes
27 quidem videatur Attice dicere. Facile est enim
verbum aliquod ardens, ut ita dicam, notare idque
restinctis iam animorum incendiis irridere. Itaque
se purgans iocatur Demosthenes: negat in eo[2]
positas esse fortunas Graeciae, hocine an illo verbo

[1] opimum F^2, optimum F^1OP.   [2] eo $\pi\lambda$, eos L.

---

[a] Generally known as the oration *On the Crown.*
[b] Aeschines, *In Ctes.* 166 ff.

The eloquence of orators has always been controlled by the good sense of the audience, since all who desire to win approval have regard to the goodwill of their auditors, and shape and adapt themselves completely according to this and to their opinion and approval. Accordingly, Caria, Phrygia and Mysia, where there 25 is the least refinement and taste, have adopted a rich and unctuous diction which appeals to their ears. But their neighbours, the Rhodians, though separated only by a narrow strait, never approved this style, Greece showed it even less favour, and the Athenians utterly repudiated it, holding with sound and discerning judgement that they could listen to nothing that was not pure and well chosen. The orator who complied with their scruples dared not use a word that was unusual or offensive. As an illustra- 26 tion, Demosthenes, who, I said, excels all others, in his masterpiece, the famous oration *In Defence of Ctesiphon*,[a] began calmly, then in his discussion of the laws he continued without adornment ; after that he gradually aroused the jury, and when he saw them on fire, throughout the rest of the oration he boldly overleaped all bounds ; yet, careful as he was to weigh every word, Aeschines criticizes and attacks some points, and in mockery calls his language harsh, offensive and intolerable,[b] even asking him, while denouncing him as a brute, whether these are words or monstrosities. Aeschines, then, thought that not even Demosthenes was " Attic." It is easy, indeed, 27 to criticize some flaming word, if I may use this expression, and to laugh at it when the passion of the moment has cooled. That is why Demosthenes in excusing himself jestingly says that the fortunes of Greece did not depend on his using this word or

usus sit,[1] huc an illuc manum porrexerit. Quonam igitur modo audiretur Mysus aut Phryx Athenis, cum etiam Demosthenes exagitetur ut putidus ? Cum vero inclinata ululantique voce more Asiatico canere coepisset, quis eum ferret aut potius quis non iuberet auferri ?

28 IX. Ad Atticorum igitur auris[2] teretes et religiosas qui se accommodant, ei sunt existimandi Attice dicere. Quorum genera plura sunt ; hi unum modo quale sit suspicantur. Putant enim qui horride inculteque dicat, modo id eleganter enucleateque faciat, eum solum Attice dicere. Errant, quod solum ; 29 quod Attice, non falluntur. Istorum enim iudicio, si solum illud est Atticum, ne Pericles quidem dixit Attice, cui primae sine controversia deferebantur. Qui si tenui genere uteretur, nunquam ab Aristophane poeta fulgere, tonare, permiscere Graeciam dictus esset. Dicat igitur Attice venustissimus ille scriptor ac politissimus Lysias—quis enim id possit negare ?—dum intellegamus hoc esse Atticum in Lysia, non quod tenuis sit atque inornatus, sed quod nihil[3] habeat insolens aut ineptum. Ornate vero et graviter et copiose dicere aut Atticorum sit aut ne 30 sit Aeschines neve Demosthenes Atticus. Ecce autem aliqui se Thucydidios esse profitentur, novum quoddam imperitorum et inauditum genus. Nam

[1] hocine an illo verbo usus sit *addidit Sauppe ex Aug. Cresc. 2. 1, 2 et Ambr. Luc. 2. 42.*
[2] aures πβλ, aut res *L.*
[3] nihil βλ, nonnihil *L.*

---

[a] Dem. *De Cor.* 232.
[b] The self-styled " Attici " whom Cicero is criticizing.
[c] *Acharnians* 530-531.

that, or extending his hand in this direction or in that.[a] What reception would a Mysian or Phrygian have had at Athens, when even Demosthenes was censured as affected ? If he had ever begun to sing in the Asiatic manner, in a whining voice with violent modulations, who would have put up with him ? Rather I might say, who would not have cried " Put him out " ?

Those speakers, then, who conform to the refined 28 and scrupulous Attic taste, must be considered to speak in Attic style. There are many kinds of Atticists : but these of our day [b] apprehend the nature of one kind only. They think that the only one who attains the Attic norm is he who speaks in rough and unpolished style, provided only that he is precise and discriminating in thought. Their mistake is in assuming him to be the only one ; they are quite right in calling him Attic. If this 29 is the only Attic style, then, according to their principles, even Pericles did not speak in the Attic manner, yet every one granted his pre-eminence. If he had used the plain style, Aristophanes [c] would never have said that he " lightened, and thundered, and embroiled all Greece." Let us agree, then, that the Attic manner of speech belonged to Lysias, that most charming and exquisite writer (who could deny it ?), provided that we understand that the Attic quality in Lysias is not that he is plain and unadorned, but that he has nothing strange or wanting in taste. On the other hand, we must concede that ornate, vehement and eloquent language is found in the Attic orators, or else deny that Aeschines and Demosthenes are Attic. And here come some who take the title 30 " Thucydideans,"—a new and unheard-of group of

qui Lysiam secuntur, causidicum quendam secuntur,
non illum quidem amplum atque grandem, subtilem
et elegantem tamen et qui[1] in forensibus causis
possit praeclare consistere. Thucydides autem res
gestas et bella narrat et proelia, graviter sane et
probe, sed nihil ab eo transferri potest ad forensem
usum et publicum. Ipsae illae contiones ita multas
habent obscuras abditasque sententias vix ut intel-
legantur; quod est in oratione civili vitium vel
31 maximum. Quae est autem in hominibus tanta
perversitas, ut inventis frugibus glande vescantur?
An victus hominum Atheniensium beneficio excoli
potuit, oratio non potuit? Quis porro unquam
Graecorum rhetorum a Thucydide quicquam duxit?
At laudatus est ab omnibus. Fateor; sed ita ut
rerum explicator prudens, severus, gravis, non ut
in iudiciis versaret causas, sed ut in historiis bella
32 narraret. Itaque nunquam est numeratus orator,
nec vero, si historiam non scripsisset, nomen eius
exstaret, cum praesertim fuisset honoratus et nobilis.
Huius tamen nemo neque verborum neque sententiarum gravitatem imitatur, sed cum mutila quaedam
et hiantia locuti sunt, quae vel sine magistro facere
potuerunt, germanos se putant esse Thucydidas.
Nactus sum etiam qui Xenophontis similem esse se
cuperet, cuius sermo est ille quidem melle dulcior,
sed a forensi strepitu remotissimus.
33 Referamus igitur nos ad eum quem volumus

[1] et qui β, nec qui L.

[a] The allusion is to the legend that the human race lived
on acorns until Triptolemus, the favourite of Demeter, sowed
grain in Attica.
[b] *i.e.* teacher of oratory.

ignoramuses. Those who follow Lysias at least follow a pleader of sorts, not indeed grand and stately, but for all that refined and precise, and able to hold his own famously in the law-court. Thucydides, on the other hand, gives us history, wars and battles— fine and dignified, I grant, but nothing in him can be applied to the court or to public life. Those famous speeches contain so many dark and obscure sentences as to be scarcely intelligible, which is a prime fault in a public oration. Are men so perverse as to live on 31 acorns after grain has been discovered? Are we, then, to suppose that the diet of men could be improved by the assistance of the Athenians,[a] but that their oratory could not? Furthermore, what Greek rhetorician [b] ever took any examples from Thucydides? Every one praises him, I grant, but as an intelligent, serious and dignified commentator on events,—one to describe wars in history, not to handle cases in law-courts. Consequently he has 32 never been classed as an orator, nor, to tell the truth, would his name be known unless he had written his history, although he was of noble birth and had been honoured with public office.[c] No one, however, succeeds in imitating his dignity of thought and diction, but when they have spoken a few choppy, disconnected phrases, which they could have formed well enough without a teacher, each one thinks himself a regular Thucydides. I have even seen a man who wished to resemble Xenophon, whose style is indeed sweeter than honey, but far removed from the wrangling of the forum.

Let us return, then, to our task of delineating that 33

[c] Thucydides was elected a general in the Peloponnesian War.

incohandum et ea quidem[1] eloquentia informandum
quam in nullo cognovit Antonius. x. Magnum opus
omnino et arduum, Brute, conamur ; sed nihil
difficile amanti puto. Amo autem et semper amavi
ingenium, studia, mores tuos. Incendor[2] porro
cotidie magis non desiderio solum quo quidem
conficior, congressus nostros, consuetudinem victus,
doctissimos sermones requirens tuos, sed etiam
admirabili fama virtutum incredibilium, quae specie
34 dispares prudentia[3] coniunguntur. Quid enim tam
distans quam a severitate comitas ? Quis tamen
unquam te aut sanctior est habitus aut dulcior ?
Quid tam difficile quam in plurimorum controversiis
diiudicandis ab omnibus diligi ? Consequeris tamen,
ut eos ipsos quos contra statuas aequos placatosque
dimittas. Itaque efficis ut, cum gratiae causa nihil
facias, omnia tamen sint grata quae facis. Ergo omnibus ex[4] terris una Gallia communi non ardet incendio,
in qua frueris ipse tua virtute,[5] cum in Italiae luce[6]
cognosceris versarisque in optimorum civium vel
flore vel robore. Iam quantum illud est quod in
maximis occupationibus nunquam intermittis studia
doctrinae, semper aut ipse scribis aliquid aut me
35 vocas ad scribendum. Itaque hoc sum aggressus
statim Catone absoluto, quem ipsum nunquam

[1] ea quidem *Kayser :* eadem *L.*
[2] incendor πλ, incendiosior *L.*
[3] prudentia πβλ, prudentiae *L.*
[4] ex *addidit Halm.*
[5] tua virtute *Sandys :* te *L.*
[6] luce βλ, lucem *L.*

---

[a] He refers to the civil war between Caesar and the
Pompeian party. Brutus had been appointed governor of
Cisalpine Gaul in 46 B.C.

ideal orator and moulding him in that eloquence which
Antonius had discovered in no one. This is doubtless
a great and arduous task, Brutus, but nothing, I think,
is hard for a lover. And I do love and always have
loved your talents, your interests and your character.
As time goes on my heart grows warmer day by day,
not only with a consuming desire to be with you, to talk
to you, to listen to your learned discourse, but also
because of your wonderful reputation for amazing
virtues, which, though apparently incompatible, are
harmonized by your wisdom. For example, is there 34
any difference so great as that between kindliness
and severity ? Yet, who was ever considered more
upright or more genial than you ? What is so hard as
to please everybody in settling a multitude of disputes ? You are able, however, to send away even
the unsuccessful litigants with friendly and contented
feelings. The result is that, though you do nothing
to gain favour, everything you do is favourably
received. Consequently Gaul is the only country in
the world which is not ablaze in the general conflagra-
tion.[a] There you reap the reward of your merit,
gaining fame in the full light of Italy, and associating
with the best of citizens [b] both in the flower of youth
and in the strength of manhood. Most important of
all—even in your busiest days you never neglect the
pursuit of learning, but are always either writing
something yourself or arousing me to write. I began 35
this work, then, as soon as I had finished *Cato*,[c] which

[b] Cicero emphasizes the fact that the inhabitants of
Brutus's province (Cisalpine Gaul, *i.e.* North Italy) have the
high dignity of Roman citizenship.

[c] The work in praise of Cato, the opponent of Caesar,
who committed suicide at Utica.

attigissem tempora timens inimica virtuti, nisi tibi
hortanti et illius memoriam mihi caram excitanti
non parere nefas esse duxissem. Sed testificor me
a te rogatum et recusantem[1] haec scribere esse au-
sum. Volo enim mihi tecum commune esse crimen,
ut, si sustinere tantam quaestionem non potuero,
iniusti oneris impositi tua culpa sit, mea recepti :
in quo tamen iudici nostri errorem laus tibi dati
muneris compensabit.

36   XI. Sed in omni re difficillimum est formam, qui[2]
χαρακτὴρ Graece dicitur, exponere optimi, quod
aliud aliis videtur optimum. Ennio delector, ait
quispiam, quod non discedit a communi more verborum. Pacuio, inquit alius ; omnes apud hunc
ornati elaboratique sunt versus, multa apud alterum
neglegentius. Fac alium Accio ; varia enim sunt
iudicia ut in Graecis nec facilis explicatio, quae forma
maxime excellat. In picturis alios[3] horrida inculta[4]
opaca, contra alios[5] nitida laeta collustrata delectant.[6]
Quid est quo praescriptum[7] aliquod aut formulam
exprimas, cum in suo quodque genere praestat et
genera plura sint ? Hac ego religione non sum ab
hoc conatu repulsus, existimavique in omnibus rebus

[1] recusantem λ, recusandum L.
[2] qui *Tulich :* quod L.
[3] alios ε²f², alius L.
[4] abdita et *ante* opaca *seclusit Madvig.*
[5] alios ε², alius L.
[6] delectant πε, delectat L.
[7] praescriptum β, perscriptum L.

• Cicero, afraid that his encomium of Cato will be un-
favourably received by Caesar, is trying to shift the blame
to Brutus. Cicero was, however, mistaken ; Caesar was not
offended.

I would never have undertaken through fear of this
age so unfriendly to virtue, had I not considered it
base not to yield when you urged so strongly and
kindled the memory of one so dear to me.[a] I call you
to witness that it was because you asked me that I
dared, albeit reluctantly, to write this book. For I
wish that you should share the reproach with me, so
that if I cannot defend myself against so weighty a
charge, you may take the blame for imposing an
excessive task on me, as I take the blame for accepting
it. However, any error in my judgement will be
counterbalanced by the glory of dedicating the work
to you.

It is always difficult to describe the " form " or 36
" pattern " of the " best " (for which the Greek
word is χαρακτήρ [b]) because different people have
different notions of what is best. " I like Ennius,"
says one, " because his diction does not depart from
common usage." " I like Pacuvius," says another,
" for all his lines are embellished and carefully
elaborated ; in Ennius there is much careless work."
Suppose that another likes Accius. There is a
difference of opinion, as there is in the case of
Greek authors, and it is not easy to explain which
type is the most excellent. In the case of painting, some like pictures rough, rude and sombre,
others on the contrary prefer them bright, cheerful
and brilliantly coloured. How can you draw up a
rule or formula, when each is supreme in its own
class, and there are many classes ? This misgiving,
however, did not deter me from my undertaking ;
I held that in all things there is a certain " best,"

[b] *i.e.* " distinctive mark " or " character," " stamp on a
coin."

esse aliquid optimum, etiam si lateret, idque ab eo posse qui eius rei gnarus esset iudicari.

37 Sed quoniam plura sunt orationum genera eaque diversa neque in unam formam cadunt omnia, laudationum et descriptionum[1] et historiarum et talium suasionum, qualem Isocrates fecit Panegyricum multique alii qui sunt nominati sophistae, reliquarumque rerum formam quae absunt a forensi contentione, eiusque totius generis quod Graece ἐπιδεικτικὸν nominatur, quia[2] quasi ad inspiciendum delectationis causa comparatum est, non complectar hoc tempore ; non quo neglegenda sit ; est enim illa quasi nutrix eius oratoris quem informare volumus et de quo molimur aliquid exquisitius dicere. XII. Ab hac et verborum copia alitur et eorum constructio et numerus liberiore quadam fruitur licentia.

38 Datur etiam venia concinnitati sententiarum et argutiis, certique et circumscripti verborum ambitus conceduntur, de industriaque non ex insidiis sed aperte ac palam elaboratur, ut verba verbis quasi demensa et paria respondeant, ut crebro conferantur pugnantia comparenturque contraria et ut[3] pariter extrema terminentur eundemque referant in cadendo sonum ; quae in veritate causarum et rarius multo facimus et certe occultius. In Panathenaico autem

---

[1] et descriptionum *Stroux :* scriptionum *L.*
[2] quia *vulg.*, qua *L,* quod *λf.*
[3] et ut *f,* et aut *L,* aut *Heerdegen.*

---

[a] The deliberative (address to legislative bodies), the forensic (address to judicial bodies), the epideictic (including all other speeches, eulogies, patriotic addresses, etc.).
[b] Aristotle, *Rhet.* 1. 3, 2, says that the audience at such an oration act as spectators rather than as judges.

even if it is not apparent, and that this can be recognized by one who is expert in that subject.

There are several[a] kinds of speeches differing one 37 from the other, and impossible to reduce to one type; so I shall not include at this time that class to which the Greeks give the name *epideictic* because they were produced as show-pieces, as it were, for the pleasure they will give,[b] a class comprising eulogies, descriptions,[c] histories,[d] and exhortations like the *Panegyric*[e] of Isocrates, and similar orations by many of the Sophists, as they are called, and all other speeches unconnected with battles of public life. Not that their style is negligible; for it may be called the nurse of that orator whom we wish to delineate and about whom we design to speak more particularly. This style increases one's vocabulary and allows the use of a somewhat greater freedom in rhythm and sentence structure. It likewise indulges in a neatness 38 and symmetry of sentences, and is allowed to use well defined and rounded periods; the ornamentation is done of set purpose, with no attempt at concealment, but openly and avowedly, so that words correspond to words as if measured off in equal phrases, frequently things inconsistent are placed side by side, and things contrasted are paired[f]; clauses are made to end in the same way and with similar sound. But in actual legal practice we do this less frequently and certainly less obviously. In the *Panathenaicus* Isocrates con-

[a] *e.g.* the *Euboicus* of Dio of Prusa.

[b] History was regularly regarded in antiquity as a branch of rhetoric, much to the disadvantage of history.

[e] In the form of an exhortation to the Greeks to unite against Persia, but largely devoted to the praise of Athens.

[f] Cicero's roundabout way of translating the Greek " antithesis."

Isocrates ea studiose consectatum fatetur; non enim ad iudiciorum certamen sed ad[1] voluptatem aurium
39 scripserat. Haec tractasse Thrasymachum Calchedonium primum et Leontinum ferunt Gorgiam, Theodorum inde Byzantium multosque alios quos λογοδαιδάλους appellat in Phaedro Socrates. Quorum satis arguta multa sed ut modo primumque nascentia minuta et versiculorum similia quaedam nimiumque[2] depicta. Quo magis sunt Herodotus Thucydidesque mirabiles; quorum aetas cum in eorum tempora quos nominavi incidisset, longissime tamen ipsi a talibus deliciis vel potius ineptiis afuerunt. Alter enim sine ullis salebris quasi sedatus amnis fluit, alter incitatior fertur et de bellicis rebus canit etiam quodam modo bellicum. Primisque ab his, ut ait Theophrastus, historia commota est ut auderet uberius quam superiores et ornatius dicere.
40 XIII. Horum aetati successit Isocrates, qui praeter ceteros eiusdem generis laudatur semper a nobis, nonnunquam, Brute, leniter et erudite repugnante te; sed cedas[3] mihi fortasse, si quid in eo laudem cognoveris. Nam cum concisus ei Thrasymachus minutis numeris videretur et Gorgias, qui tamen primi traduntur arte quadam verba vinxisse,[4] Theodorus[5] autem praefractior nec satis, ut ita dicam, rotundus, primus instituit dilatare verbis et mollioribus numeris

---

[1] ad λ, *omisit L.*   [2] nimiumque *F*, minimeque *OP.*
[3] cedas *Ernesti :* credas *L.*
[4] vinxisse *codex Gudianus 38,* iunxisse *L.*
[5] Theodorus *Ernesti :* Thucydides *L,* Theodectes *Nonius.*

---

[a] Isocrates, *Panathenaicus* 1. 2.
[b] Plato, *Phaedrus* 266 E.
[c] This is true of Herodotus, but Thucydides was certainly

fesses that he strove eagerly for these effects,[a] for he had written, not for a trial in court, but to entertain the audience. Thrasymachus of Calchedon and Gorgias 39 of Leontini are said to have been the first to practise this and, after them, Theodorus of Byzantium and many others called "cunning artificers of speech" by Socrates in the *Phaedrus.*[b] They show many clever phrases but these are like a new and immature product, choppy, resembling verselets, and sometimes over-ornamented. Therefore Herodotus and Thucydides are the more admirable because, though contemporary with those whom I have just mentioned, they are far removed from such tricks, or I might better say, from such folly.[c] Herodotus flows along like a peaceful stream without any rough water; Thucydides moves with greater vigour, and in his description of war, sounds, as it were, the trumpet of war. These were the first, as Theophrastus says, to rouse history to speak in a fuller and more ornate style than their predecessors had used. In the next generation came Isocrates, 40 who is always praised by me more than the others of this group, not without an occasional quiet and scholarly objection from you, Brutus; but you may, perhaps, grant my point if I tell you what I praise in him. For inasmuch as Thrasymachus and Gorgias—the first according to tradition to attempt an artificial arrangement of words—seemed to him to be cut up into short rhythmical phrases, and Theodorus on the other hand seemed too rugged and not "round" enough, as one may say, Isocrates was the first to undertake to expand his phrases,

influenced by the Gorgianic style, as other ancient critics were aware.

explere sententias. In quo cum doceret eos qui
partim in dicendo partim in scribendo principes exstiterunt, domus eius officina habita eloquentiae est.

41 Itaque ut ego, cum a nostro Catone laudabar, vel
reprehendi me a ceteris facile patiebar, sic Isocrates
videtur prae[1] testimonio Platonis aliorum iudicia
debere contemnere. Est enim, ut scis, quasi in extrema pagina Phaedri his ipsis verbis loquens Socrates:
" adulescens etiam nunc, o Phaedre, Isocrates, est,
sed quid de illo augurer libet dicere." " Quid
tandem?" inquit ille. " Maiore mihi ingenio videtur esse quam ut cum orationibus Lysiae com-
paretur, praeterea ad virtutem maior indoles ; ut
minime mirum futurum sit, si, cum aetate proces-
serit, aut in hoc orationum genere cui nunc studet
tantum, quantum pueris, reliquis praestet omnibus
qui unquam orationes attigerunt aut, si contentus
his non fuerit, divino aliquo animi motu maiora
concupiscat ; inest enim natura philosophia[2] in
42 huius viri mente quaedam." Haec de adulescente
Socrates auguratur, at ea de seniore scribit Plato
et scribit aequalis et quidem exagitator omnium
rhetorum hunc miratur unum. Me autem qui
Isocratem non diligunt una cum Socrate et cum
Platone errare patiantur. Dulce igitur orationis
genus et solutum et fluens,[3] sententiis argutum,
verbis sonans est in illo epidictico genere, quod
diximus proprium sophistarum, pompae quam pugnae
aptius, gymnasiis et palaestrae dicatum, spretum et

---

[1] prae *addidit Heerdegen.*
[2] philosophia *vulg.:* philosophiae *L.*
[3] fluens *Orelli:* effluens *L.*

---

[a] Plato, *Phaedrus* 279 A.

and round out the sentences with softer rhythms. Through his teaching of this to his pupils, who attained eminence, some as speakers and some as writers, his home came to be regarded as the laboratory of eloquence. Consequently, just as when 41 Cato praised me I could easily endure even to be censured by all others, so Isocrates should, I think, make light of the criticisms of others in comparison with the judgement of Plato. For as you know, on almost the last page of the *Phaedrus* ᵃ Socrates is represented as speaking these words : " Isocrates is a young man now, my dear Phaedrus, but I should like to tell you my prophecy about him." " What is it ? " said he. " He seems to me to possess too great talent to be judged by the standard of Lysias's speeches, and, furthermore, he has a greater capacity for achievement. It would not at all surprise me if, as he grows older, he will excel all who have ever engaged in oratory in this style which he now affects, as much as a man surpasses a boy ; or if he is not content with this, by some divine impulse he will aspire to greater things ; for nature has implanted a real philosophy in the man's mind." Socrates 42 made this prophecy about the youth, but Plato wrote it when Isocrates was in middle life, and writing as a contemporary, and as a critic too of all rhetoricians, he admires him only. As for me, those who dislike Isocrates must let me err with Socrates and Plato. The epideictic oration, then, has a sweet, fluent and copious style, with bright conceits and sounding phrases. It is the proper field for sophists, as we said, and is fitter for the parade than for the battle ; set apart for the gymnasium and the palaestra, it is spurned and rejected in the forum. But

pulsum foro. Sed quod educata huius nutrimentis eloquentia[1] ipsa se postea colorat et roborat, non alienum fuit de oratoris quasi incunabulis dicere. Verum haec ludorum atque pompae ; nos autem iam in aciem dimicationemque veniamus.

43 XIV. Quoniam tria videnda sunt oratori : quid dicat et quo quidque loco et quo modo, dicendum omnino est quid sit optimum in singulis, sed aliquanto secus atque in tradenda arte dici solet. Nulla praecepta ponemus—neque enim id suscepimus—sed excellentis eloquentiae speciem et formam adumbrabimus ; nec quibus rebus ea paretur 44 exponemus, sed qualis nobis esse videatur. Ac duo breviter prima ; sunt enim non tam insignia ad maximam laudem quam necessaria et tamen cum multis paene communia. Nam et invenire et iudicare quid dicas magna illa quidem sunt et tanquam animi instar in corpore, sed propria magis prudentiae quam eloquentiae ; qua tamen in causa est vacua prudentia ? Noverit igitur hic quidem orator quem summum esse volumus argumentorum 45 et rationum locos. Nam quoniam, quicquid est quod in controversia aut in contentione versetur, in eo aut sitne aut quid sit aut quale sit quaeritur : sitne, signis ; quid sit, definitionibus ; quale sit, recti pravique partibus—quibus ut uti possit orator, non ille volgaris sed hic excellens, a propriis per-

---

[1] est *post* eloquentia *omisit Serv. ad Aen. 1. 176, expunxit Poggius in* π.

---

[a] To use the technical rhetorical terms, (1) *inventio*, discussed in §§ 44-49 ; (2) *dispositio* (50) ; (3) *actio* (55-60) and *elocutio* (61-236).
[b] Literally, Is it ? What is it ? Of what sort is it ?

because eloquence receives nourishment from this until it later takes on colour and strength by itself, it was not amiss to speak of what we may call the cradle of the orator. So much for the school and the parade ; let us now enter the thick of the fray.

The orator must consider three things, what to 43 say,[a] in what order, and in what manner and style to say it. It will therefore be our task to explain what is best in each division, but in a way somewhat different from that which is usually followed in a text-book. We shall lay down no rules—that was not our undertaking—but we shall outline the form and likeness of surpassing eloquence : nor shall we explain how this is to be produced, but how it looks to us. The first two topics I shall treat briefly, for 44 they are not specially marked out for the highest praise, but are rather fundamental, and apart from that are shared in common with many other pursuits. For to discover and decide what to say is important, to be sure, and is to eloquence what the mind is to the body ; but it is a matter of ordinary intelligence rather than of eloquence. For that matter is there any cause in which intelligence is superfluous ? Our perfect orator, then, should be acquainted with the topics of reasoning and argument. For in 45 all matters under controversy and debate the questions which are asked are : (1) Was it done ? (2) What was done ? (3) What was the nature of the act ?[b] The question, Was it done ? is answered by evidence ; the question, What was done ? by definition ; the question, What was the nature of the act ? by the principles of right and wrong. To be able to use these the orator—not an ordinary one, but this outstanding orator—always removes the

sonis et temporibus semper, si potest, avocat controversiam. Latius enim de genere quam de parte
disceptare licet, ut quod in universo sit probatum
46 id in parte sit probari necesse—haec igitur quaestio
a propriis personis et temporibus ad universi generis
orationem traducta appellatur θέσις. In hac Aristoteles adulescentis non ad philosophorum morem
tenuiter disserendi, sed ad copiam rhetorum, in
utramque partem ut ornatius et uberius dici posset,[1]
exercuit idemque locos—sic enim appellat—quasi
argumentorum notas tradidit unde omnis in utram-
47 que partem traheretur oratio. xv. Faciet[2] igitur
hic noster—non enim declamatorem aliquem de
ludo aut rabulam de foro, sed doctissimum et per-
fectissimum quaerimus—ut, quoniam loci certi
traduntur, percurrat omnis, utatur aptis, generatim
dicat, ex quo emanant[3] etiam qui communes[4] appellantur loci. Nec vero utetur imprudenter hac
copia, sed omnia expendet et seliget. Non enim
semper nec in omnibus causis ex isdem . . .[5] argu-
48 mentorum momenta sunt. Iudicium igitur adhibebit
nec inveniet solum quid dicat sed etiam expendet.
Nihil enim est feracius ingeniis, eis praesertim quae
disciplinis exculta sunt. Sed ut segetes fecundae
et uberes non solum fruges verum herbas etiam
effundunt inimicissimas frugibus, sic interdum ex
illis locis aut levia quaedam aut causis aliena aut

[1] posset *Lambinus :* possit *L.*
[2] faciet *Gulielmius apud Gruterum :* facile *L.*
[3] emanant *vulg.*, emanent *L.*
[4] communes *vulg. :* communis *FO*, quominus *P.*
[5] locis eadem *suppl. Madvig.*

discussion, if he can, from particular times and persons, because the discussion can be made broader about a class than about an individual, so that whatever is proved about the class must necessarily be true of the individual. Such an inquiry, removed 46 from particular times and persons to a discussion of a general topic, is called θέσις or "thesis." Aristotle trained young men in this, not for the philosophical manner of subtle discussion, but for the fluent style of the rhetorician, so that they might be able to uphold either side of the question in copious and elegant language. He also taught the "Topics"— that was his name for them—a kind of sign or indication of the arguments from which a whole speech can be formed on either side of the question. Therefore our orator—it is not a mere declaimer in 47 a school that we seek, or a ranter in the forum, but a scholarly and finished speaker—our orator, finding certain definite "topics" enumerated, will run rapidly over them all, select those which fit the subject, and then speak in general terms. This is the source of the commonplaces, as they are called.[a] But he will not use this stock unintelligently, but weigh everything and select. For the decisive arguments are not always to be found [in the same categories]. Therefore he will exercise judgement, and 48 will not only discover something to say, but will estimate its value. Nothing is more fruitful than the human mind, particularly one which has had the discipline of education. But just as fruitful and fertile fields produce not only crops but harmful weeds, so sometimes from these categories arguments are derived which are inconsequential, im-

---

[a] *i.e.* general arguments.

49 non utilia gignuntur. Quorum nisi[1] ab oratoris
iudicio dilectus magnus adhibebitur, quonam modo
ille in bonis haerebit et habitabit suis aut[2] molliet
dura aut occultabit quae dilui non poterunt atque
omnino opprimet, si licebit, aut abducet animos
aut aliud afferet quod oppositum probabilius sit
quam illud quod obstabit ?

50 Iam vero ea quae invenerit qua diligentia col-
locabit. Quoniam id secundum erat de tribus.
Vestibula nimirum honesta aditusque ad causam
faciet illustris ; cumque animos prima aggressione
occupaverit, confirmabit sua[3] infirmabit eludetque[4]
contraria, de firmissimis alia prima ponet alia postrema inculcabitque leviora.

Atque in primis duabus dicendi partibus qualis es-
51 set summatim breviterque descripsimus. XVI. Sed,
ut ante dictum est, in his partibus, etsi graves
atque magnae sunt, minus et artis est et laboris.
Cum autem et quid et quo loco dicat invenerit, illud
est longe maximum, videre quonam modo. Scitum
est enim quod Carneades noster dicere solebat,
Clitomachum eadem[5] dicere, Charmadam autem

---

[1] nisi *addidit Stangl.*
[2] aut λ, ut *L.*
[3] confirmabit sua *addidit Halm.*
[4] eludetque *Bake :* excludetque *L.*
[5] eadem πβ, ea *L.*

---

[a] *Cf.* a similar comparison in Pindar, *Ol.* 6. 1 : χρυσέας
ὑποστάσαντες εὐτυχεῖ προθύρῳ θαλάμου κίονας, ὡς ὅτε θαητὸν
μέγαρον πάξομεν· ἀρχομένου δ᾽ ἔργου πρόσωπον χρὴ θέμεν
τηλαυγές.
[b] Carneades (214/3–129/8 B.C.), head of the New Academy
at Athens. He is referred to as " our " because both Cicero
and Brutus adhered to this school of philosophy. Carneades

material or useless. And unless the orator's judge- 49
ment exercises a rigid selection among these, how
can he linger and dwell on his strong points, or
make the difficulties seem slight, or conceal what
cannot be explained away, and even suppress it
entirely, if feasible, or distract the attention of
the audience, or bring up some other point which
if brought forward can be established more easily
than the one which he feels will stand in his way ?

The results of his invention he will set in order 50
with great care. (Arrangement, it will be remembered, was the second of the three points to
discuss.) The orator will certainly make fair
" porches " [a] and gorgeous approaches to his oration.
And when he has gained attention by the introduction, he will establish his own case, refute and
parry the opponent's argument, choosing the
strongest points for the opening and closing, and
inserting the weaker points in between.

So far we have sketched briefly and summarily the
qualifications of our orator in relation to the first
two parts of oratory. These divisions are weighty 51
and important, but, as has been said before, they
require less art and labour. When, however, the
speaker has discovered what to say and how to
arrange his subject-matter, then comes the all-
important question of the manner of presentation.
It was a shrewd remark that our Carneades [b] used
to make, that Clitomachus repeated the substance
of his teaching, but Charmadas reproduced the

was famous for eloquence as well as philosophy. Clitomachus and Charmadas were two pupils of Carneades ;
Clitomachus, a foreigner, grasped the philosophical teachings
of his master, but failed to attain his eminence in oratory.

eodem etiam modo dicere. Quodsi in philosophia
tantum interest quem ad modum dicas, ubi res
spectatur, non verba penduntur, quid tandem in
causis existimandum est, quibus totis moderatur
52 oratio ? Quod quidem ego, Brute, ex tuis litteris
sentiebam non te id sciscitari,[1] qualem ego in inveniendo et in collocando summum esse oratorem
vellem, sed id mihi quaerere videbare, quod genus
ipsius orationis optimum iudicarem : rem difficilem,
di immortales, atque omnium difficillimam. Nam
cum est oratio mollis et tenera et ita flexibilis, ut
sequatur quocumque torqueas, tum et naturae
variae et voluntates multum inter se distantia effece-
53 runt genera dicendi. Flumen aliis verborum volubili-
tasque cordi est, qui ponunt in orationis celeritate
eloquentiam ; distincta alios et interpuncta intervalla,
morae respirationesque delectant. Quid potest esse
tam diversum ? Tamen est in utroque aliquid excellens. Elaborant alii in[2] lenitate et aequabilitate et
puro quasi quodam et candido genere dicendi ; ecce
aliqui duritatem et severitatem quandam in verbis
et orationis quasi maestitiam secuntur ; quodque
paulo ante divisimus, ut alii graves, alii tenues, alii
temperati vellent videri, quot orationum genera
esse diximus totidem oratorum reperiuntur.
54 XVII. Et quoniam coepi iam cumulatius hoc munus
augere quam a te postulatum est—tibi enim tantum de orationis genere quaerenti respondi etiam
breviter de inveniendo et collocando—ne nunc quidem solum de orationis modo dicam sed etiam de

---

[1] sciscitari $\pi\beta f$, scitari L.
[2] in $M\pi$, omiserunt FOP.

style also. If style, then, makes so much difference
in philosophy, where the attention is concentrated
on the meaning, and words as such are not weighed,
what must we think of the importance of style in
suits at law which are wholly swayed by oratorical
skill? On this point I judged from your letter, 52
Brutus, that you did not seek my opinion of oratorical perfection in invention and disposition, but
I thought you wished to know what I considered
the best oratorical style. A hard task, I swear;
indeed the hardest of all. For not only is language
soft, pliant and so flexible that it follows wherever
you turn it, but also the varieties in ability and taste
have produced styles widely different. Fluency and 53
volubility please those who make eloquence depend
on swiftness of speech; others like clearly marked
pauses, and breathing spells. Could two things be
more different? Yet there is something good in
each. Some spend their labour on smoothness and
uniformity, and on what we may call a pure and
clear style; others affect a harshness and severity of
language and an almost gloomy style. And so,
according to our previous division of orators into
three classes,[a] those who aim to be impressive, or
plain, or moderate, there are found to be as many
kinds of orators as we said there were styles of
oratory.

Since I have begun to carry out my task somewhat 54
more fully than you requested—you asked only about
the use of language, but I included a brief treatment
of invention and arrangement in my answer—so
now I shall speak not merely about the method of
expression, but also about the manner of delivery.

* Cf. §§ 20, 21.

actionis. Ita praetermissa pars nulla erit, quandoquidem de memoria nihil est hoc loco dicendum
quae communis est multarum artium.

55 Quo modo autem dicatur id est in duobus : in
agendo et in eloquendo. Est enim actio quasi
corporis quaedam eloquentia, cum constet e voce
atque motu. Vocis mutationes totidem sunt quot
animorum, qui maxime voce commoventur. Itaque
ille perfectus quem iam dudum nostra indicat oratio,
utcumque se affectum videri et animum audientis
moveri volet, ita certum vocis admovebit sonum.
De quo plura dicerem, si hoc praecipiendi tempus
esset aut si tu hoc quaereres. Dicerem etiam de
gestu, cum quo iunctus est voltus. Quibus omnibus dici vix potest quantum intersit quem ad modum
56 utatur orator. Nam et infantes actionis dignitate
eloquentiae saepe fructum tulerunt et diserti de-
formitate agendi multi infantes putati sunt, ut iam
non sine causa Demosthenes tribuerit et primas et
secundas et tertias actioni. Si enim eloquentia
nulla sine hac, haec autem sine eloquentia tanta
est, certe plurimum in dicendo potest. Volet igitur
ille qui eloquentiae principatum petet et contenta
voce atrociter dicere et summissa leniter et inclinata
57 videri gravis et inflexa miserabilis. Mira est enim
quaedam natura vocis cuius quidem e tribus omnino

---

^a There were normally five chapters in a treatise on
rhetoric : invention, arrangement, expression, memory,
delivery.

^b This saying of Demosthenes is reported by several
ancient authors, *e.g.* Philodemus, περὶ ῥητορικῆς 1. 196, 3
(Sudhaus): Δημοσθένης καὶ πρῶτον καὶ δεύτερον καὶ τρίτον

Consequently no essential topic will be omitted,[a] for there is no need of discussing memory in this connexion; it is common to many arts.

Manner of speech falls into two sections, delivery 55 and use of language. For delivery is a sort of language of the body, since it consists of movement or gesture as well as of voice or speech. There are as many variations in the tones of the voice as there are in feelings, which are especially aroused by the voice. Accordingly the perfect orator, whom we have been delineating for some time, will use certain tones according as he wishes to seem himself to be moved and to sway the minds of his audience. I should be more explicit on this point if this were the occasion for instruction, or if you desired it. I might also speak about gestures, which include facial expression. The way in which the orator uses these makes a difference which can scarcely be described. For many poor 56 speakers have often reaped the rewards of eloquence because of a dignified delivery, and many eloquent men have been considered poor speakers because of an awkward delivery. Demosthenes was right, therefore, in considering delivery to be the first, second and third in importance.[b] If, then, there can be no eloquence without this, and this without eloquence is so important, certainly its rôle in oratory is very large. Therefore the one who seeks supremacy in eloquence will strive to speak intensely with a vehement tone, and gently with lowered voice, and to show dignity in a deep voice, and wretchedness by a plaintive tone. For the voice possesses 57 a marvellous quality, so that from merely three

εἶναι τὴν ὑπόκρισιν ἐν τῇ ῥητορικῇ. *Cf.* also Pseudo-Plutarch, *Vita X Orat.* 845 в, and Cicero, *Brutus* 142.

sonis, inflexo, acuto, gravi, tanta sit et tam suavis varietas perfecta in cantibus.   xvııı. Est autem etiam in dicendo quidam cantus obscurior, non hic e Phrygia et Caria rhetorum epilogus paene canticum, sed ille quem significat Demosthenes et Aeschines, cum alter alteri obicit vocis inflexiones.[1] (Dicit plura etiam Demosthenes illumque saepe prae-

58 dicat[2] voce dulci et clara fuisse.)   In quo illud etiam notandum mihi videtur ad studium persequendae suavitatis in vocibus : ipsa enim natura, quasi modularetur hominum orationem, in omni verbo posuit acutam vocem nec una plus nec a postrema syllaba citra tertiam ; quo magis naturam ducem

59 ad aurium voluptatem sequatur industria.   Ac vocis bonitas quidem optanda est ; non est enim in nobis sed tractatio atque usus in nobis.   Ergo ille princeps variabit et mutabit : omnis sonorum tum intendens tum remittens persequetur gradus. Idemque motu sic utetur, nihil ut supersit : in gestu status erectus et celsus ; rarus incessus nec ita longus ; excursio moderata eaque rara ; nulla mollitia cervicum, nullae argutiae digitorum, non ad numerum articulus cadens ; trunco magis toto se ipse moderans et virili laterum flexione, brachi

---

[1] inflexiones *Nonius :* flexiones *L.*
[2] praedicat *Stroux :* dicat *L.*

---

[a] Epilogue was the technical term for the concluding appeal to the emotions of the audience. Longinus (*Rhet. Graeci* 1. 197, 4. Sp.) says that in such appeals the tone is between speech and song.
[b] The lyrical and recitative passages of a Roman comedy.
[c] Demosthenes (*De Corona* 259, 291) accuses Aeschines of shouting, howling and bellowing.   Aeschines in turn (*In*

registers, high, low and intermediate, it produces such a rich and pleasing variety in song. There is, moreover, even in speech, a sort of singing—I do not mean this " epilogue " [a] practised by Phrygian and Carian rhetoricians which is almost like a *canticum* [b] in a play—but the thing which Demosthenes [c] and Aeschines mean when they accuse each other of vocal modulations. (Demosthenes goes still farther and says that Aeschines had a clear and pleasant voice.) Here I ought to emphasize a point which 58 is of importance in attaining an agreeable voice : nature herself, as if to modulate human speech, has placed an accent, and only one, on every word, and never farther from the end of the word than the third syllable. Therefore let art follow the leadership of nature in pleasing the ear. Certainly 59 natural excellence of voice is to be desired ; this is not in our power, but the use and management of the voice is in our power. The superior orator will therefore vary and modulate his voice ; now raising and now lowering it, he will run through the whole scale of tones. He will also use gestures in such a way as to avoid excess : he will maintain an erect and lofty carriage, with but little pacing to and fro, and never for a long distance. As for darting forward, he will keep it under control and employ it but seldom. There should be no effeminate bending of the neck, no twiddling of the fingers, no marking the rhythm with the finger-joint. He will control himself by the pose of his whole frame, and the vigorous and manly attitude of the body, extending the arm in moments

Ctesiphontem 209, 210) comments on the pitch of Demosthenes' voice—ὁ τόνος τῆς φωνῆς. It is this last phrase which Cicero translates by *vocis inflexiones.*

proiectione in contentionibus, contractione in re-
60 missis. Voltus vero qui secundum vocem plurimum
potest quantam affert tum dignitatem tum venustatem. In quo cum effeceris ne quid ineptum sit
aut voltuosum, tum oculorum est quaedam magna
moderatio. Nam ut imago est animi voltus sic
indices oculi ; quorum et hilaritatis et vicissim
tristitiae modum res ipsae de quibus agetur tem-
perabunt.

61 XIX. Sed iam illius perfecti oratoris et summae eloquentiae species exprimenda est. Quem hoc uno excellere, id est oratione, cetera in eo latere indicat
nomen ipsum. Non enim inventor aut compositor
aut actor qui[1] haec complexus est omnia, sed et
Graece ab eloquendo ῥήτωρ et Latine eloquens
dictus est. Ceterarum enim rerum quae sunt in
oratore partem aliquam sibi quisque vindicat,
dicendi autem, id est eloquendi, maxima vis soli
huic conceditur.

62 Quanquam enim et philosophi quidam[2] ornate
locuti sunt—si quidem et Theophrastus divinitate
loquendi nomen invenit et Aristoteles Isocratem
ipsum lacessivit et Xenophontis voce Musas quasi
locutas ferunt et longe omnium quicumque scripserunt aut locuti sunt exstitit et gravitate et suavitate[3] princeps Plato—tamen horum oratio neque

[1] qui *addidit Madvig.*
[2] quidam πε, quidem *L.*
[3] et suavitate *addidit Sauppe,* et suavitate et gravitate
codd. quidam dett.

---

[a] That is, the Latin word for eloquence (*eloquentia*) is
obviously derived from *eloquor,* " speak."
[b] That is, the orator is not named from any of the minor
functions of the orator which have just been discussed :

of passion, and dropping it in calmer moods. Further- 60
more, what dignity and charm are contributed by the
countenance, which has a rôle second only to the voice.
After ensuring that the expression shall not be silly or
grimacing, the next point is the careful control of the
eyes. For as the face is the image of the soul, so are
the eyes its interpreters, in respect of which the subjects under discussion will provide the proper limits
for the expression of joy or grief.

We must now turn to the task of portraying the 61
perfect orator and the highest eloquence. The very
word " eloquent " shows that he excels because of
this one quality, that is, in the use of language,
and that the other qualities are overshadowed by
this.[a] For the all-inclusive word is not " discoverer,"
or " arranger," or " actor," [b] but in Greek he is
called ῥήτωρ [c] from the word " to speak," and in Latin
he is said to be " eloquent." For everyone claims
for himself some part of the other qualities that go
to make up an orator, but the supreme power in
speaking, that is eloquence, is granted to him alone.

Certain philosophers, to be sure, had an ornate 62
style,—for example Theophrastus received his name
from his divinely beautiful language,[d] and Aristotle
challenged even Isocrates, and the Muses were said
to speak with the voice of Xenophon, and Plato was,
in dignity and grace, easily the first of all writers or
speakers—yet their style lacks the vigour and sting

inventio, invention or discovery of arguments, *dispositio*,
disposition or arrangement, *actio*, action or delivery.
  [c] Connected with the verb ἐρῶ, " speak."
  [d] His name, originally Tyrtamus, was changed by
Aristotle (Diog. Laert. 5. 38). Theophrastus is compounded
from θεός, " god," and φράζω, " speak."

nervos neque aculeos oratorios ac forensis habet.
63 Locuntur cum doctis quorum sedare animos malunt
quam incitare ; sic de[1] rebus placatis ac minime
turbulentis docendi causa non capiendi locuntur, ut
in eo ipso quod delectationem aliquam dicendo
aucupentur plus nonnullis quam necesse sit facere
videantur. Ergo ab hoc genere non difficile est hanc
64 eloquentiam de qua nunc agitur secernere. Mollis
est enim oratio philosophorum et umbratilis nec
sententiis nec verbis instructa popularibus[2] nec
vincta[3] numeris sed soluta liberius ; nihil iratum
habet, nihil invidum, nihil atrox, nihil miserabile,[4]
nihil astutum ; casta verecunda virgo incorrupta
quodam modo. Itaque sermo potius quam oratio
dicitur. Quanquam enim omnis locutio oratio est,
tamen unius oratoris[5] locutio hoc proprio signata
nomine est.
65 Sophistarum de quibus supra dixi magis dis-
tinguenda similitudo videtur, qui omnis eosdem
volunt flores quos adhibet orator in causis persequi.
Sed hoc differunt quod, cum sit eis propositum
non perturbare animos sed placare potius, nec tam
persuadere quam delectare, et apertius id faciunt
quam nos et crebrius, concinnas magis sententias
exquirunt quam probabilis, a re saepe discedunt,
intexunt fabulas, verba altius transferunt eaque ita
disponunt ut pictores varietatem colorum, paria
paribus referunt, adversa contrariis, saepissimeque

---

1 sic de πf, fide L ; si de *Stroux*, et de *Heerdegen*.
2 popularibus $\pi\beta f$, popularis L.
3 vincta $\pi\epsilon$, iuncta L.
4 miserabile ϵ^2, mirabile L.
5 oratoris ρ, orationis L.

necessary for oratorical efforts in public life. They **63**
converse with scholars, whose minds they prefer to
soothe rather than arouse ; they converse in this
way about unexciting and non-controversial subjects,
for the purpose of instructing rather than captivating ;
and some think they exceed due bounds in aiming to
give some little pleasure by their style.[a] It is therefore easy to distinguish the eloquence which we are
treating in this work from the style of the philosophers. The latter is gentle and academic ; it has no **64**
equipment of words or phrases that catch the popular
fancy ; it is not arranged in rhythmical periods, but
is loose in structure ; there is no anger in it, no
hatred, no ferocity, no pathos, no shrewdness ; it
might be called a chaste, pure and modest virgin.
Consequently it is called conversation rather than
oratory. While all speaking is oratory, yet it is the
speech of the orator alone which is marked by this
special name.

More care must be taken to distinguish the **65**
oratorical style from the similar style of the Sophists
mentioned above,[b] who desire to use all the ornaments which the orator uses in forensic practice. But
there is this difference, that, whereas their object is
not to arouse the audience but to soothe it, not so
much to persuade as to delight, they do it more
openly than we and more frequently ; they are on
the look-out for ideas that are neatly put rather than
reasonable ; they frequently wander from the subject, they introduce mythology, they use far-fetched
metaphors and arrange them as painters do colour
combinations ; they make their clauses balanced

---

[a] The Stoics deprecated any attention to elegance of style.
[b] § 37.

66 similiter extrema definiunt. xx. Huic generi historia
finitima est. In qua et narratur ornate et regio saepe
aut pugna describitur ; interponuntur etiam contiones
et hortationes. Sed in his tracta quaedam et fluens
expetitur, non haec contorta et acris oratio. Ab his
non multo secus quam a poetis haec eloquentia
quam quaerimus sevocanda est. Nam etiam poetae
quaestionem attulerunt, quidnam esset illud quo
ipsi differrent ab oratoribus : numero maxime vide-
bantur antea et versu, nunc apud oratores iam ipse
67 numerus increbruit. Quicquid est enim, quod sub
aurium mensuram aliquam cadit, etiamsi abest a
versu—nam id quidem orationis est vitium—numerus
vocatur, qui Graece ῥυθμὸς dicitur. Itaque video visum
esse nonnullis Platonis et Democriti locutionem,
etsi absit a versu, tamen, quod incitatius feratur et
clarissimis verborum luminibus utatur, potius poema
putandum quam comicorum poetarum, apud quos,
nisi quod versiculi sunt, nihil est aliud cotidiani dissimile sermonis. Nec tamen id est poetae maximum,
etsi est eo laudabilior quod virtutes oratoris perse-
68 quitur, cum versu sit astrictior. Ego autem, etiamsi
quorundam grandis et ornata vox est poetarum,
tamen in ea cum licentiam statuo maiorem esse
quam in nobis faciendorum iungendorumque verborum, tum etiam nonnullorum voluntate[1] vocibus
magis quam rebus inserviunt.[2] Nec vero, si quid
est unum inter eos simile—id autem est iudicium
electioque verborum—propterea ceterarum rerum

---

[1] voluntate λ, voluntati L, voluptati ρ.
[2] inserviunt ρ, inserviant L.

[a] He refers to the Gorgianic figures ; see Volkmann,
Rhetorik der Griechen und Römer, pp. 465-488.

and of equal length, frequently ending with similar sounds.[a] History is nearly related to this style. It 66 involves a narrative in an ornate style, with here and there a description of a country or a battle. It has also occasional harangues and speeches of exhortation. But the aim is a smooth and flowing style, not the terse and vigorous language of the orator. The eloquence which we are seeking must be distinguished from this no less than from the poetic style. For the poets have given rise to the inquiry as to the difference between them and the orators. It once seemed to be a matter of rhythm and verse, but now rhythm has become common in oratory. For everything which can be measured 67 by the ear, even if it does not make a complete verse —that is certainly a fault in prose—is called rhythm, in Greek ῥυθμός. For that reason some, I know, have held that the language of Plato and Democritus, which, though not in verse, has a vigorous movement and uses striking stylistic ornaments, has more right to be considered poetry than has comedy, which differs from ordinary conversation only by being in some sort of verse. However, this is not the chief mark of a poet, although he deserves more credit for seeking the virtues of the orator, limited as he is by the form of the verse. As for my own opinion, although some 68 poets use grand and figurative language, I recognize that they have a greater freedom in the formation and arrangement of words than we orators have, and also that, with the approval of some critics, they pay more attention to sound than to sense. And indeed if they have one point in common—this is discernment in selection of subject matter and choice of words—we cannot for that reason pass over their

dissimilitudo intellegi non potest. Sed id nec dubium est et, si quid habet quaestionis, hoc tamen ipsum ad id quod propositum est non est necessarium. Seiunctus igitur orator a philosophorum eloquentia, a sophistarum, ab historicorum, a poetarum, explicandus est nobis qualis futurus sit.

69 XXI. Erit igitur eloquens—hunc enim auctore Antonio quaerimus—is qui in foro causisque civilibus ita dicet, ut probet, ut delectet, ut flectat. Probare necessitatis est, delectare suavitatis, flectere victoriae ; nam id unum ex omnibus ad obtinendas causas potest plurimum. Sed quot officia oratoris tot sunt genera dicendi : subtile in probando, modicum in delectando, vehemens in flectendo ; in quo uno vis

70 omnis oratoris est. Magni igitur iudici, summae etiam facultatis esse debebit moderator ille et quasi temperator huius tripertitae varietatis. Nam et iudicabit quid cuique opus sit et poterit quocumque modo postulabit causa dicere. Sed est eloquentiae sicut reliquarum rerum fundamentum sapientia. Ut enim in vita sic in oratione nihil est difficilius quam quid deceat videre. Πρέπον appellant hoc Graeci, nos dicamus sane decorum. De quo praeclare et multa praecipiuntur et res est cognitione dignissima. Huius ignoratione non modo in vita sed saepissime et in

71 poematis et in oratione peccatur. Est autem quid deceat oratori videndum non in sententiis solum sed etiam in verbis. Non enim omnis fortuna non omnis honos non omnis auctoritas non omnis aetas

dissimilarity in other things. But there is no doubt a difference between poetry and oratory, and if there is any dispute about it, the investigation is not necessary for our present purpose. Distinguishing the orator, then, in point of style from the philosopher, the sophist, the historian and the poet, we must set forth what he is to be.

The man of eloquence whom we seek, following the 69 suggestion of Antonius, will be one who is able to speak in court or in deliberative bodies so as to prove, to please and to sway or persuade. To prove is the first necessity, to please is charm, to sway is victory ; for it is the one thing of all that avails most in winning verdicts. For these three functions of the orator there are three styles, the plain style for proof, the middle style for pleasure, the vigorous style for persuasion ; and in this last is summed up the entire virtue of the orator. Now the man who controls 70 and combines these three varied styles needs rare judgement and great endowment ; for he will decide what is needed at any point, and will be able to speak in any way which the case requires. For after all the foundation of eloquence, as of everything else, is wisdom. In an oration, as in life, nothing is harder than to determine what is appropriate. The Greeks call it πρέπον ; let us call it *decorum* or " propriety." Much brilliant work has been done in laying down rules about this ; the subject is in fact worth mastering. From ignorance of this mistakes are made not only in life but very frequently in writing, both in poetry and in prose. Moreover the orator must 71 have an eye to propriety not only in thought but in language. For the same style and the same thoughts must not be used in portraying every condition in life,

357

nec vero locus aut tempus aut auditor omnis eodem
aut verborum genere tractandus est aut sententiarum, semperque in omni parte orationis ut vitae
quid deceat est considerandum; quod et in re de qua
agitur positum est et in personis et eorum qui dicunt
72 et eorum qui audiunt. Itaque hunc locum longe et late
patentem philosophi solent in officiis tractare—non
cum de recto ipso disputant, nam id quidem unum
est—grammatici in poetis, eloquentes in omni et
genere et parte causarum. Quam enim indecorum est
de stillicidiis, cum apud unum iudicem dicas, amplissimis verbis et locis uti communibus, de maiestate
populi Romani summisse et subtiliter. xxII. Hi[1]
genere toto, at persona alii peccant aut sua aut
iudicum aut etiam adversariorum nec re solum sed
saepe verbo. Etsi sine re nulla vis verbi est, tamen
eadem res saepe aut probatur aut reicitur alio atque
73 alio elata verbo. In omnibusque rebus videndum est
quatenus. Etsi enim suus cuique modus est, tamen
magis offendit nimium quam parum. In quo Apelles
pictores quoque eos peccare dicebat qui non sentirent
quid esset satis. Magnus est[2] locus hic, Brute, quod
te non fugit, et magnum volumen aliud desiderat;
sed ad id quod agitur illud satis. Cum hoc decere—
quod semper usurpamus in omnibus dictis et factis,
minimis et maximis—cum hoc, inquam, decere dica-

---

[1] hi *Heerdegen :* hic *L.*
[2] est λ, esset *L.*

---

[a] The legal technicalities about water dripping from a roof
on adjoining property.

or every rank, position or age, and in fact a similar
distinction must be made in respect of place, time and
audience. The universal rule, in oratory as in life, is
to consider propriety. This depends on the subject
under discussion, and on the character of both the
speaker and the audience. The philosophers are 72
accustomed to consider this extensive subject under
the head of duties—not when they discuss absolute
perfection, for that is one and unchanging ; the
literary critics consider it in connexion with poetry ;
orators in dealing with every kind of speech, and in
every part thereof. How inappropriate it would be
to employ general topics and the grand style when
discussing cases of stillicide *a* before a single referee,
or to use mean and meagre language when referring
to the majesty of the Roman people. This would be
wrong in every respect ; but others err in regard to
character—either their own or that of the jury, or of
their opponents ; and not merely in the statement of
facts, but often in the use of words. Although a word
has no force apart from the thing, yet the same thing is
often either approved or rejected according as it is
expressed in one way or another. Moreover, in all 73
cases the question must be, " How far ? " For although the limits of propriety differ for each subject,
yet in general too much is more offensive than too
little. Apelles said that those painters also make this
error, who do not know when they have done enough.
This is an important topic, Brutus, as you well know,
and requires another large volume ; but for our
present discussion the following will be enough :
Since we say " This is appropriate "—a word we use
in connexion with everything we do or say, great or
small,—since, I repeat, we say " This is appropriate "

mus,[1] illud non decere, et id usquequaque quantum
sit appareat, in alioque ponatur aliudque totum sit,
74 utrum decere an oportere dicas—oportere enim
perfectionem declarat offici quo et semper utendum
est et omnibus, decere quasi aptum esse consenta-
neumque tempori et personae ; quod cum in factis
saepissime tum in dictis valet, in voltu denique et
gestu et incessu contraque item dedecere—quod si
poeta fugit ut maximum vitium qui peccat etiam,
cum probam orationem affingit improbo stultove
sapientis ; si denique pictor ille vidit, cum im-
molanda Iphigenia tristis Calchas esset, tristior[2]
Ulixes, maereret Menelaus, obvolvendum caput
Agamemnonis esse, quoniam summum illum luctum
penicillo non posset imitari ; si denique histrio quid
deceat quaerit : quid faciendum oratori putemus ?
Sed cum hoc tantum sit, quid in causis earumque
quasi membris faciat orator viderit : illud quidem
perspicuum est, non modo partis orationis sed etiam
causas totas alias alia forma dicendi esse tractandas.
75 XXIII. Sequitur ut cuiusque generis nota quaeratur
et formula, magnum opus et arduum, ut saepe iam
diximus ; sed ingredientibus considerandum fuit quid
ageremus, nunc quidem iam quocumque feremur
danda nimirum vela sunt. Ac primum informandus
est ille nobis quem solum quidam vocant Atticum.
76 Summissus est et humilis, consuetudinem imitans,

---

[1] dicamus *Ernesti*, dicimus *L*.
[2] tristior *Sauppe e Quint. 2. 13, 13*, maestior *L*.

---

[a] Timanthes of Cythnos, fl. *circa* 400 B.C.
[b] The translation alters the structure of this rambling and
incoherent sentence without, I hope, doing violence to the
thought.

and " That is not appropriate," and it appears how
important propriety is everywhere (and that it
depends upon something else and is wholly another
question whether you should say " appropriate " or
" right " ;—for by " right " we indicate the perfect 74
line of duty which every one must follow everywhere,
but " propriety " is what is fitting and agreeable to an
occasion or person ; it is important often in actions as
well as in words, in the expression of the face, in
gesture and in gait, and impropriety has the opposite
effect) ; the poet avoids impropriety as the greatest
fault which he can commit ; he errs also if he puts the
speech of a good man in the mouth of a villain, or that
of a wise man in the mouth of a fool ; so also the
painter [a] in portraying the sacrifice of Iphigenia, after
representing Calchas as sad, Ulysses as still more so,
Menelaus as in grief, felt that Agamemnon's head
must be veiled, because the supreme sorrow could not
be portrayed by his brush ; even the actor seeks for
propriety ; what, then, think you, should the orator
do ? [b] Since this is so important, let the orator
consider what to do in the speech and its different
divisions : it is certainly obvious that totally different
styles must be used, not only in the different parts of
the speech, but also that whole speeches must be now
in one style, now in another.

It follows that we must seek the type and pattern 75
of each kind—a great and arduous task, as we have
often said ; but we should have considered what to do
when we were embarking ; now we must certainly
spread our sails to the wind, no matter where it may
carry us. First, then, we must delineate the one
whom some deem to be the only true " Attic "
orator. He is restrained and plain, he follows the 76

ab indisertis re plus quam opinione differens. Itaque
eum qui audiunt, quamvis ipsi infantes sint, tamen
illo modo confidunt se posse dicere. Nam orationis
subtilitas imitabilis illa quidem videtur esse existi-
manti, sed nihil est experienti minus. Etsi enim
non plurimi sanguinis est, habeat tamen sucum aliquem oportet, ut, etiamsi illis maximis viribus careat,
77 sit, ut ita dicam, integra valetudine. Primum igitur
eum tanquam e vinculis numerorum eximamus.
Sunt enim quidam, ut scis, oratori numeri de quibus
mox agemus observandi ratione quadam, sed alio
in genere orationis, in hoc omnino relinquendi.
Solutum quiddam sit nec vagum tamen, ut ingredi
libere non ut licenter videatur errare. Verba etiam
verbis quasi coagmentare[a] neglegat. Habet enim
ille tanquam hiatus et concursus[1] vocalium molle
quiddam et quod indicet non ingratam neglegentiam
de re hominis magis quam de verbis laborantis.
78 Sed erit videndum de reliquis, cum haec duo ei
liberiora fuerint, circuitus conglutinatioque verborum. Illa enim ipsa contracta et minuta non negle-
genter tractanda sunt sed quaedam etiam negle-
gentia est diligens. Nam ut mulieres pulchriores[2]
esse dicuntur nonnullae inornatae quas id ipsum
deceat, sic haec subtilis oratio etiam incompta delectat ; fit enim quiddam in utroque, quo sit venus-
tius sed non ut appareat. Tum removebitur
omnis insignis ornatus quasi margaritarum, ne cala-

---

[1] et concursus *Quint. et Iul. Vict.:* concursu *L.*
[2] pulchriores *addidit Stroux.*

---

[a] For this figurative use of *coagmentare* cf. *Brutus* 68.

ordinary usage, really differing more than is sup-
posed from those who are not eloquent at all. Consequently the audience, even if they are no speakers
themselves, are sure they can speak in that fashion.
For that plainness of style seems easy to imitate at
first thought, but when attempted nothing is more
difficult. For although it is not full-blooded, it
should nevertheless have some of the sap of life, so
that, though it lack great strength, it may still be, so
to speak, in sound health. First, then, let us release 77
him from, let us say, the bonds of rhythm. Yes, the
orator uses certain rhythms, as you know, and these
we shall discuss shortly ; they have to be employed
with a definite plan, but in a different style of speech ;
in this style they are to be wholly eschewed. It
should be loose but not rambling ; so that it may seem
to move freely but not to wander without restraint.
He should also avoid, so to speak, cementing *a* his
words together too smoothly, for the hiatus and clash
of vowels have something agreeable about it and show
a not unpleasant carelessness on the part of a man who
is paying more attention to thought than to words.
But his very freedom from periodic structure and 78
cementing his words together will make it necessary
for him to look to the other requisites. For the short
and concise clauses must not be handled carelessly, but
there is such a thing even as a careful negligence.
Just as some women are said to be handsomer when
unadorned—this very lack of ornament becomes
them—so this plain style gives pleasure even when
unembellished : there is something in both cases
which lends greater charm, but without showing itself.
Also all noticeable ornament, pearls as it were, will be
excluded ; not even curling-irons will be used ; all 79

79 mistri quidem adhibebuntur. Fucati vero medicamenta candoris et ruboris omnia repellentur : elegantia modo et munditia remanebit. Sermo purus erit et Latinus, dilucide planeque dicetur, quid deceat circumspicietur. xxiv. Unum aberit quod quartum numerat Theophrastus in orationis laudibus : ornatum illud suave et affluens. Acutae crebraeque sententiae ponentur et nescio unde ex abdito erutae, idque[1] in hoc oratore dominabitur. Verecundus erit usus oratoriae quasi supellectilis.

80 Supellex est enim quodam modo nostra quae est in ornamentis alia rerum alia verborum. Ornatus autem verborum[2] duplex, unus simplicium alter collocatorum : simplex probatur in propriis usitatisque verbis quod aut optime sonat aut rem maxime explanat ; in alienis aut translatum et tractum[3] aliunde ut mutuo aut factum ab ipso et novum[4] aut priscum et inusitatum[5] ; sed etiam inusitata[5] ac

81 prisca sunt in propriis, nisi quod raro utimur. Collocata autem verba habent ornatum, si aliquid concinnitatis efficiunt, quod verbis mutatis non maneat manente sententia ; nam sententiarum ornamenta quae permanent, etiamsi verba mutaveris, sunt illa quidem permulta, sed quae emineant pauciora. Ergo ille tenuis orator, modo sit elegans, nec in faciendis verbis erit audax et in transferendis verecundus et parcus[6] in priscis in[7] reliquisque ornamentis et verborum et sententiarum demissior ;

---

[1] idque *Moser :* atque *L.*
[2] verborum β, *omisit L.*
[3] et tractum *Stroux :* aut factum *L.*
[4] et novum *Schütz :* aut novum *L.*
[5] inusitatum . . . inusitata ρ. usitatum . . . usitata *L.*
[6] et *post* parcus *seclusit Rivius.*
[7] in *addidit Reid.*

cosmetics, artificial white and red, will be rejected; only elegance and neatness will remain. The language will be pure Latin, plain and clear; propriety will always be the chief aim. Only one quality will be lacking, which Theophrastus mentions fourth among the qualities of style—the charm and richness of figurative ornament. He will employ an abundance of apposite maxims dug out from every conceivable hiding place; this will be the dominant feature in this orator. He will be modest in his use of what may be called the orator's stock-in-trade. For we do have 80 after a fashion a stock-in-trade, in the stylistic embellishments, partly in thought and partly in words. The embellishment given by words is twofold, from single words and from words as they are connected together. In the case of " proper " and ordinary words, that individual word wins approval which has the best sound, or best expresses the idea; in the case of variations from the common idiom we approve the metaphor, or a borrowing from some source, or a new formation or the archaic and obsolete (yet even obsolete and archaic words are to be classed as " proper " except that we rarely use them). Words 81 when connected together embellish a style if they produce a certain symmetry which disappears when the words are changed, though the thought remains the same; for the figures of thought which remain even if the words are changed are, to be sure, numerous, but relatively few are noticeable. Consequently the orator of the plain style, provided he is elegant and finished, will not be bold in coining words, and in metaphor will be modest, sparing in the use of archaisms, and somewhat subdued in using the other embellishments of language and of thought. Meta-

tralatione fortasse crebrior qua frequentissime sermo omnis utitur non modo urbanorum sed etiam
rusticorum, si quidem est eorum gemmare vitis,
sitire[1] agros, laetas esse segetes, luxuriosa frumenta.
82 Nihil horum parum audacter sed aut simile est illi
unde transferas, aut si res suum nullum habet nomen, docendi causa sumptum non ludendi videtur.
Hoc ornamento liberius paulo quam ceteris utetur
hic summissus nec tam licenter tamen, quam si
genere dicendi uteretur amplissimo. xxv. Itaque
illud indecorum, quod quale sit ex decoro debet intellegi, hic quoque apparet, cum verbum aliquod
altius transfertur idque in oratione humili ponitur
83 quod idem in alia deceret. Illam autem concinni-
tatem, quae verborum collocationem illuminat eis
luminibus quae Graeci quasi aliquos gestus orationis
σχήματα appellant, quod idem verbum ab eis etiam
in sententiarum ornamenta transfertur, adhibet
quidem hic subtilis, quem nisi quod solum ceteroqui[2]
recte quidam vocant Atticum, sed paulo parcius.
Nam sic[3] ut in epularum apparatu a[4] magnificentia
recedens non se parcum solum sed etiam elegantem
84 videri volet, et[5] eliget quibus utatur. Sunt enim
pleraque apta[6] huius ipsius oratoris de quo loquor
parsimoniae. Nam illa de quibus ante dixi huic
acuto fugienda sunt : paria paribus relata et similiter conclusa eodemque pacto cadentia et immu-

---

[1] sitire $F^2\epsilon f$, *Nonius*, scire L^1, lascivire P^2O^2.
[2] ceteroqui *Heerdegen :* ceteroque L, ceteroquin ρ.
[3] sic βλ, si L.
[4] a βλ, *omisit L.*
[5] et *addidit Bake.*
[6] apta *Lambinus :* aptae L.

---

* The buds are compared with jewels.

phor he may possibly employ more frequently because
it is of the commonest occurrence in the language of
townsman and rustic alike. The rustics, for example,
say that the vines are " bejewelled," *a* the fields
"thirsty," the crops "happy," the grain "luxuriant."
Any of these metaphors is bold enough, but there 82
is a similarity to the source from which the word
is borrowed, or if a thing has no proper term
the borrowing seems to be done in order to make
the meaning clear, and not for entertainment. The
restrained speaker may use this figure a little more
freely than others, but not so boldly as if he were
speaking in the grandest style. Consequently
impropriety—the nature of which should be plain from
what has been said about propriety—appears here
too, when a metaphor is far-fetched, and one is used
in the plain style which would be appropriate in
another. This unaffected orator whom certain 83
people call " Attic," and rightly so, except that he is
not the only " Attic "—this orator will also use the
symmetry that enlivens a group of words with the
embellishments that the Greeks call σχήματα, figures
as it were, of speech. (They apply the same word
also to figures of thought.) He will, however, be
somewhat sparing in using these. For as in the
appointments of a banquet he will avoid extravagant
display, and desire to appear thrifty, but also in good
taste, and will choose what he is going to use. There 84
are, as a matter of fact, a good many ornaments
suited to the frugality of this very orator I am
describing. For this shrewd orator must avoid all
the figures that I described above, such as clauses
of equal length, with similar endings, or identical
cadences, and the studied charm produced by the

tatione litterae quaesitae[1] venustates,[2] ne elaborata
concinnitas et quoddam aucupium delectationis
85 manifesto deprehensum appareat. Itemque si quae
verborum iterationes contentionem aliquam et
clamorem requirent, erunt ab hac summissione orationis alienae. Ceteris promiscue poterit uti, continuationem verborum modo relaxet et dividat
utaturque verbis quam usitatissimis, tralationibus
quam mollissimis. Etiam illa sententiarum lumina
assumat quae non erunt vehementer illustria.
Non faciet rem publicam loquentem nec ab inferis
mortuos excitabit nec acervatim multa frequentans
una complexione devinciet. Valentiorum haec laterum sunt nec ab hoc quem informamus aut exspectanda aut postulanda ; erit enim ut voce sic etiam
86 oratione suppressior. Sed pleraque ex illis convenient etiam huic tenuitati, quanquam isdem ornamentis utetur horridius ; talem enim inducimus.
Accedit actio non tragica nec scaenae sed modica
iactatione corporis, voltu tamen multa conficiens ;
non hoc quo dicuntur os ducere, sed illo quo significant ingenue quo sensu quidque pronuntient.
87 xxvi. Huic generi orationis aspergentur etiam
sales, qui in dicendo nimium quantum valent.
Quorum duo genera sunt, unum facetiarum alterum
dicacitatis. Utetur utroque; sed altero in narrando
aliquid venuste, altero in iaciendo mittendoque

---

[1] quasi *ante* quaesitae *seclusit Lambinus.*
[2] venustates F^2OP, venustatis F^1.

---

[a] *Cf. De Oratore* 2. 256, quoting from Cato, *nobiliorem,*
mobiliorem.

change of a letter,[a] lest the elaborate symmetry and a certain grasping after a pleasant effect be too obvious. Likewise if repetition of words requires **85** some emphasis and a raising of the voice, it will be foreign to this plain style of oratory. Other figures of speech he will be able to use freely, provided only he breaks up and divides the periodic structure and uses the commonest words and the mildest of metaphors. He may also brighten his style with such figures of thought as will not be exceedingly glaring. He will not represent the State as speaking [b] or call the dead from the lower world,[c] nor will he crowd a long series of iterations into a single period. This requires stronger lungs, and is not to be expected of him whom we are describing or demanded from him. For he will be rather subdued in voice as in style. But many of these figures of thought will be appro- **86** priate to this plain style, although he will use them somewhat harshly : such is the man we are portraying. His delivery is not that of tragedy nor of the stage ; he will employ only slight movements of the body, but will trust a great deal to his expression. This must not be what people call pulling a wry face, but must reveal in a well-bred manner the feeling with which each thought is uttered.

A speech of this kind should also be sprinkled with **87** the salt of pleasantry, which plays a rare great part in speaking. There are two kinds, humour and wit. He will use both ; the former in a graceful and charming narrative, the latter in hurling the shafts of

---

[b] *e.g. In Cat. 1* 18 (patria) tecum, Catilina, sic agit et quodam modo tacita loquitur.
[c] *e.g. Pro Caelio* 33 : Cicero calls Appius Claudius Caecus from the dead to witness the shame of his descendants.

ridiculo, cuius genera plura sunt ; sed nunc aliud
88 agimus. Illud admonemus tamen ridiculo sic usurum
oratorem, ut nec nimis frequenti ne scurrile sit, nec
subobsceno ne mimicum, nec petulanti ne impro-
bum, nec in calamitatem ne inhumanum, nec in
facinus ne odi locum risus occupet, neque aut sua
persona aut iudicum aut tempore alienum. Haec
89 enim ad illud indecorum referuntur. Vitabit etiam
quaesita nec ex tempore ficta sed domo allata quae
plerumque sunt frigida. Parcet et amicitiis et
dignitatibus, vitabit insanabilis contumelias, tantummodo adversarios figet nec eos tamen semper nec
omnis nec omni modo. Quibus exceptis sic utetur
sale et facetiis, ut ego ex istis novis Atticis talem
cognoverim neminem, cum id certe sit vel maxime
90 Atticum. Hanc ego iudico formam summissi oratoris sed magni tamen et germani Attici ; quoniam
quicquid est salsum aut salubre in oratione id proprium Atticorum est. E quibus tamen non omnes
faceti : Lysias satis et Hyperides, Demades praeter
ceteros fertur, Demosthenes minus habetur ; quo
quidem mihi nihil videtur urbanius sed non tam
dicax fuit quam facetus ; est autem illud acrioris
ingeni, hoc maioris artis.
91 Uberius est aliud aliquantoque[1] robustius quam
hoc humile de quo dictum est, summissius autem

---

[1] toque *hinc incipit A.*

---

[a] Cicero had discussed this at length in *De Oratore 2.*
253-289.
[b] The discussion of the plain style is extended by Cicero
out of all proportion to the space allotted to the middle and
370

ridicule. Of this latter there are several kinds,[a] but now we are discussing another subject. We here merely suggest that the orator should use ridicule with a care not to let it be too frequent lest it become buffoonery ; nor ridicule of a smutty nature, lest it be that of low farce ; nor pert, lest it be impudent ; nor aimed at misfortune, lest it be brutal, nor at crime, lest laughter take the place of loathing ; nor should the wit be inappropriate to his own character, to that of the jury, or to the occasion ; for all these points come under the head of impropriety. He will also avoid far-fetched jests, and those not made up at the moment but brought from home ; for these are generally frigid. He will spare friends and dignitaries, will avoid rankling insult ; he will merely prod his opponents, nor will he do it constantly, nor to all of them nor in every manner. With these exceptions he will use wit and humour in a way in which none of these modern " Attics " do, so far as I know, though this is certainly an outstanding mark of Attic style. For my part, I judge this to be the pattern of the plain orator—plain but great and truly Attic ; since whatever is witty and wholesome in speech is peculiar to the Athenian orators. Not all of them, however, are humorous. Lysias is adequate and so is Hyperides ; Demades is said to have excelled them all, Demosthenes is considered inferior. Yet it seems to me that none is cleverer than he ; still he is not witty so much as humorous ; the former requires a bolder talent, the latter a greater art.[b]

The second style is fuller and somewhat more robust than the simple style just described, but

grand styles, because this was the chief point of debate between him and the Atticists. See Introduction, p. 297.

quam illud de quo iam dicetur amplissimum. Hoc
in genere nervorum vel minimum, suavitatis autem
est vel plurimum. Est enim plenius quam hoc
enucleatum, quam autem illud ornatum copiosum-
92 que summissius. xxvii. Huic omnia dicendi ornamenta conveniunt plurimumque est in hac orationis[1]
forma suavitatis. In qua multi floruerunt apud
Graecos, sed Phalereus Demetrius meo iudicio
praestitit ceteris; cuius oratio cum sedate placideque
liquitur[2] tum illustrant eam quasi stellae quaedam
tralata verba atque mutata. Tralata dico, ut saepe
iam, quae per similitudinem ab alia re aut suavitatis
aut inopiae causa transferuntur; mutata, in quibus
pro verbo proprio subicitur aliud quod idem signi-
93 ficet sumptum ex re aliqua consequenti. Quod
quanquam transferendo fit, tamen alio modo transtulit cum dixit Ennius

arce et urbe orba sum[3]

alio modo,[4]

horridam Africam terribili tremere tumultu.[5]

Hanc ὑπαλλαγὴν rhetores, quia quasi summutantur
verba pro verbis, μετωνυμίαν grammatici vocant, quod

---

[1] orationis *L*, ornamenti *A*.
[2] liquitur *A*, loquitur *L*, labitur *Purgold*.
[3] arce et urbe orba sum *Lambinus e Tusc. 3. 44:* arcent
urbem orbam *A*, arcem et urbem orbas *L*.
[4] si pro patria arcem dixisset, et *post* modo *seclusit
Goeller. If he had said citadel for fatherland, and . . .*
[5] cum dicit pro Afris immutate Africam *post* tumultu
seclusit Halm. When he uses Africa for Africans.

---

[a] Literally " changed."
[b] Ennius, *Andromache*, Frag. 88 V.[2]. *Remains of Old
Latin*, L.C.L., i. p. 250.
[c] Ennius, *Annales* Frag. 310 V.[2]. Ennius wrote: "Africa

plainer than the grandest style which we shall
presently discuss. In this style there is perhaps a
minimum of vigour, and a maximum of charm. For
it is richer than the unadorned style, but plainer
than the ornate and opulent style. All the ornaments 92
are appropriate to this type of oration, and it possesses
charm to a high degree. There have been many conspicuous examples of this style in Greece, but in my
judgement Demetrius of Phalerum led them all.
His oratory not only proceeds in calm and peaceful
flow, but is lighted up by what might be called the
stars of " transferred " words (or metaphor) and
borrowed words. By " transferred " I now mean,
as often before, words transferred by resemblance
from another thing in order to produce a pleasing
effect, or because of lack of a " proper " word ; by
" borrowed "[a] I mean the cases in which there is substituted for a " proper " word another with the same
meaning drawn from some other suitable sphere.
It is, to be sure, a " transfer " when Ennius says   93

I am bereft of citadel and town,[b]

but a " transfer " of quite a different kind from that
which he uses when he says

Dread Africa trembled with terrible tumult.[c]

The latter is called ὑπαλλαγή or " hypallage " by
the rhetoricians, because as it were words are
exchanged[d] for words ; the grammarians call it
μετωνυμία or " metonymy " because nouns[e] are

terribili tremit horrida terra tumultu," *Remains*, i. p. 114.
Cf. Cic. *De Oratore* 3. 167.
[d] Latin *summutantur* = Greek ὑπαλλάττονται.
[e] Aeolic ὤνυμα is the basis of μετωνυμία for the word
metonymy.

373

94 nomina transferuntur. Aristoteles autem tralationi
et haec ipsa subiungit et abusionem quam κατάχρησιν
vocant, ut cum minutum dicimus animum pro parvo;
et abutimur verbis propinquis, si opus est vel quod
delectat vel quod decet.[1] Iam cum fluxerunt con-
tinuae plures tralationes, alia plane fit oratio ; itaque genus hoc Graeci appellant ἀλληγορίαν: nomine
recte, genere melius ille qui ista omnia tralationes
vocat. Haec frequentat Phalereus maxime suntque
dulcissima, et quanquam tralatio est apud eum multa
95 tamen immutationes nusquam crebriores. In idem
genus orationis—loquor enim de illa modica ac
temperata—verborum cadunt lumina omnia, multa
etiam sententiarum ; latae eruditaeque disputationes ab eodem explicabuntur et loci communes
sine contentione dicentur. Quid multa ? E philosophorum scholis tales fere evadunt ; et nisi coram
erit comparatus ille fortior, per se hic quem dico
96 probabitur. Est enim quoddam etiam insigne et
florens orationis genus pictum et expolitum[2] in
quo omnes verborum, omnes sententiarum illigantur
lepores. Hoc totum e sophistarum fontibus de-
fluxit in forum, sed spretum a subtilibus, repulsum
a gravibus in ea de qua loquor mediocritate consedit.
97 XXVIII. Tertius est ille amplus, copiosus, gravis,

---

[1] decet *A*, licet *L*.
[2] pictum et expolitum genus *AL*, *transposuit* **Reis**.

---

[a] Cicero intends *alia oratio* to be a literal translation of
ἀλληγορία.
[b] Demetrius of Phalerum, whom Cicero regards as the
outstanding orator in this style, was a Peripatetic.

transferred. Aristotle, however, classifies them 94
all under metaphor and includes also the misuse of
terms, which they call κατάχρησις or " catachresis,"
for example, when we say a " minute " mind instead
of " small " ; and we misuse related words on occasion
either because this gives pleasure or because it is
appopriate. When there is a continuous stream of
metaphors, a wholly different style of speech is produced ; consequently the Greeks call it ἀλληγορία or
" allegory."[a] They are right as to the name, but
from the point of view of classification Aristotle
does better in calling them all metaphors. The
Phalerian uses these very frequently, and they are
attractive to a degree ; and although he has many
metaphors, yet the cases of metonymy are more
numerous than in any other orator. To the same 95
oratorical style—I am discussing the mean and
tempered style—belong all figures of language,
and many of thought. This speaker will likewise
develop his arguments with breadth and erudition,
and use commonplaces without undue emphasis.
But why speak at length ? It is commonly the
philosophic schools which produce such orators[b] :
and unless he be brought face to face with the more
robust speaker, the orator whom I am describing
will find approval on his own merits. It is, as a mat- 96
ter of fact, a brilliant and florid, highly coloured and
polished style in which all the charms of language
and thought are intertwined. The sophists are the
source from which all this has flowed into the
forum, but scorned by the simple and rejected by the
grand, it found a resting-place in this middle
class of which I am speaking.

The orator of the third style is magnificent, opulent, 97

ornatus, in quo profecto vis maxima est. Hic est
enim cuius ornatum dicendi et copiam admiratae
gentes eloquentiam in civitatibus plurimum valere
passae sunt, sed hanc eloquentiam quae cursu magno
sonituque ferretur, quam suspicerent omnes, quam
admirarentur, quam se assequi posse diffiderent.
Huius eloquentiae est tractare animos, huius omni
modo permovere. Haec modo perfringit, modo
irrepit in sensus; inserit novas opiniones, evellit
98 insitas. Sed multum interest inter hoc dicendi genus
et superiora. Qui in illo subtili et acuto elaboravit,
ut callide arguteque diceret nec quicquam altius
cogitavit,[1] hoc uno perfecto magnus orator est si non
maximus; minimeque in lubrico versabitur et, si
semel constiterit, nunquam cadet. Medius ille autem
quem modicum et temperatum voco, si modo suum
illud satis instruxerit, non extimescet ancipitis dicendi
incertosque casus; etiamsi quando minus succedet,
ut saepe fit, magnum tamen periculum non adibit;
99 alte enim cadere non potest. At vero hic noster quem
principem ponimus, gravis, acer, ardens, si ad hoc
unum est natus aut in hoc solo se exercuit aut huic
generi studuit uni nec suam copiam cum illis duobus
generibus temperavit, maxime est contemnendus.
Ille enim summissus, quod acute et veteratorie dicit,
sapiens iam, medius suavis, hic autem copiosissimus,
si nihil est aliud, vix satis sanus videri solet. Qui
enim nihil potest tranquille, nihil leniter, nihil partite,
definite, distincte, facete dicere, praesertim cum

---

[1] cogitavit *Heerdegen:* cogitaret *L.* nec . . . cogitaret
omisit A.

376

stately and ornate; he undoubtedly has the greatest
power. This is the man whose brilliance and fluency
have caused admiring nations to let eloquence attain
the highest power in the state; I mean the kind
of eloquence which rushes along with the roar of
a mighty stream, which all look up to and admire,
and which they despair of attaining. This eloquence
has power to sway men's minds and move them in
every possible way. Now it storms the feelings, now
it creeps in; it implants new ideas and uproots the
old. But there is a great difference between this and 98
the other styles. One who has studied the plain and
pointed style so as to be able to speak adroitly and
neatly, and has not conceived of anything higher, if he
has attained perfection in this style, is a great orator,
if not the greatest. He is far from standing on
slippery ground, and, when once he gets a foothold,
he will never fall. The orator of the middle style,
whom I call moderate and tempered, once he has
drawn up his forces, will not dread the doubtful and
uncertain pitfalls of speaking. Even if not completely successful, as often happens, he will not run a
great risk; he has not far to fall. But this orator of 99
ours whom we consider the chief,—grand, impetuous
and fiery, if he has natural ability for this alone, or
trains himself solely in this, or devotes his energies
to this only, and does not temper his abundance with
the other two styles, he is much to be despised. For
the plain orator is esteemed wise because he speaks
clearly and adroitly; the one who employs the middle
style is charming; but the copious speaker, if he has
nothing else, seems to be scarcely sane. For a man
who can say nothing calmly and mildly, who pays
no attention to arrangement, precision, clarity or

377

causae partim totae sint eo modo partim aliqua ex
parte tractandae, si is non praeparatis auribus inflammare rem coepit, furere apud sanos et quasi inter
sobrios bacchari vinulentus videtur.

100 Tenemus igitur, Brute, quem quaerimus, sed
animo non manu[1] ; nam manu si prehendissem, ne
ipse quidem sua tanta eloquentia mihi persuasisset
ut se dimitterem. xxix. Sed inventus profecto
est ille eloquens quem nunquam vidit Antonius.
Quis est igitur is ? Complectar brevi disseram
pluribus. Is est enim eloquens qui et humilia subtiliter et alta[2] graviter et mediocria temperate potest
101 dicere. Nemo is, inquies, unquam fuit. Ne fuerit.[3]
Ego enim quid desiderem, non quid viderim disputo,
redeoque ad illam Platonis de qua dixeram rei formam
et speciem, quam etsi non cernimus tamen animo
tenere possumus. Non enim eloquentem quaero
neque quicquam mortale et caducum, sed illud
ipsum, cuius qui sit compos, sit eloquens ; quod
nihil est aliud nisi eloquentia ipsa quam nullis nisi
mentis oculis videre possumus. Is erit igitur eloquens,
ut idem illud iteremus, qui poterit parva summisse,
modica temperate, magna graviter dicere.

---

[1] non manu ; nam manu *Klotz :* nam manu *A*, non
manu *L*.
[2] alta *A*, magna *L*.
[3] ne fuerit *L*, ne . . . fueris (. . . dūtu *in marg.*) *A*, nedum
tu videris. ne fuerit *Heerdegen e codd. dett.*

pleasantry—especially when some cases have to be handled entirely in this latter style, and others largely so,—if without first preparing the ears of his audience he begins trying to work them up to a fiery passion, he seems to be a raving madman among the sane, like a drunken reveller in the midst of sober men.

We have him now, Brutus, the man whom we 100 are seeking, but in imagination, not in actual possession. If I had once laid my hands on him, not even he with his mighty eloquence would have persuaded me to let him go. But we have certainly discovered that eloquent orator whom Antonius never saw. Who is he, then? I will describe him briefly, and then expand the description at greater length. He in fact is eloquent who can discuss commonplace matters simply, lofty subjects impressively, and topics ranging between in a tempered style. You will say, " There never was such a man." I grant it; for I am arguing 101 for my ideal, not what I have actually seen, and I return to that Platonic Idea of which I had spoken; though we do not see it, still it is possible to grasp it with the mind. For it is not an eloquent *person* whom I seek, nor anything subject to death and decay, but that absolute quality, the possession of which makes a man eloquent. And this is nothing but abstract eloquence, which we can behold only with the mind's eye. He, then, will be an eloquent speaker—to repeat my former definition—who can discuss trivial matters in a plain style, matters of moderate significance in the tempered style, and weighty affairs in the grand manner.

102 Tota mihi causa pro Caecina de verbis interdicti fuit : res involutas definiendo explicavimus, ius civile laudavimus, verba ambigua distinximus. Fuit ornandus in Manilia lege Pompeius : temperata oratione ornandi copiam persecuti sumus. Ius omne retinendae maiestatis Rabiri causa continebatur : ergo in ea[1] omni genere amplificationis exarsimus.

103 At haec interdum temperanda et varianda sunt. Quod igitur in Accusationis septem libris non reperitur genus, quod in Habiti, quod in Corneli, quod in plurimis nostris defensionibus ? Quae[2] exempla selegissem, nisi vel nota esse arbitrarer vel ipsos[3] posse eligere qui quaererent. Nulla est enim ullo in genere laus oratoris, cuius in nostris orationibus non sit aliqua si non perfectio at conatus tamen

104 atque adumbratio. Non assequimur ; at quid sequi[4]

---

[1] ea *Heerdegen :* eo *A*, omisit *L*.
[2] quae *L*, quaeq. *A*, *fortasse* quae quidem *Heerdegen*.
[3] ipsos *Beier :* opes *A*, omisit *L*.
[4] at quid sequi *Heerdegen :* at quid siqui *A*, at quid si qui *F*, at quid (*P²*, qui *P¹*) si quid *P*, atqui si quid *O*.

---

[a] Aulus Caecina claimed title to property occupied by Sextus Aebutius. When Caecina tried to take possession Aebutius prevented him by force. Therefore Caecina obtained an order (*interdictum*) from the praetor in the following terms : *unde tu, Sex. Aebuti, A. Caecinam vi hominibus coactis armatis deiecisti, restituas* (Sextus Aebutius, restore Aulus Caecina to the place whence you violently expelled him by collecting and arming men). This interdict properly applied only in case a person had been driven from property which he was occupying. As Caecina had never had possession, Cicero had a bad case, and spent most of his argument trying to prove that *unde* (" whence ") in the interdict meant *a quo loco* (" from the neighbourhood

My speech *For Caecina*[a] was concerned wholly 102
with the words of the interdict : we explained
involved matters by the process of definition, we
praised the civil law, we drew distinctions between
ambiguous terms.   In the *Manilian Law*[b] the task was
to glorify Pompeius ; in the tempered and moderate
style we drew on the full resources of rhetorical
ornament.   The whole principle of maintaining the
dignity of the republic was at stake in the speech
In Defence of Rabirius,[c] therefore in this we blazed
forth with every kind of rhetorical amplification.
But these styles need to be modified at times and 103
varied.   Every style is used in the seven speeches of
Accusation,[d] in the speeches *In Defence of Habitus*,[e] *In
Defence of Cornelius*,[f] and for many of our clients.   I
should have quoted examples from these speeches
if I did not think they were well known or that
those who might be interested could find them.
There is no kind of oratorical merit which is not
found in our orations, if not in perfection, at least
attempted and adumbrated.   I have not reached 104

of ") as well as *e quo loco* (" out from ").   It is an example
of the plain style.
  [b] Delivered in 66 B.C. in support of a bill to appoint
Pompey to an extraordinary command of Roman armies
operating against Mithridates.
  [c] The speech for Rabirius is largely lost.   Rabirius was
prosecuted by Caesar in 63 B.C. for a political murder committed in 100 B.C.   The case was in essence an attack on the
authority of the Senate, hence Cicero's remark about the
majesty of the state.
  [d] Cicero can refer to the speeches against Verres as the
Accusation because it was the only time he was ever engaged
on the side of the prosecution.
  [e] Generally known as the *Pro Cluentio*.
  [f] This speech is lost.

deceat videmus. Nec enim nunc de nobis sed de re
dicimus. In quo tantum abest ut nostra miremur,
et usque eo difficiles ac morosi sumus[1] ut nobis non
satis faciat ipse Demosthenes. Qui quanquam unus
eminet inter omnis in omni genere dicendi, tamen
non semper implet auris meas ; ita sunt avidae et
capaces et saepe aliquid immensum infinitumque
105 desiderant. xxx. Sed tamen, quoniam et hunc tu
oratorem cum eius studiosissimo Pammene, cum
esses Athenis, totum diligentissime cognovisti nec
eum dimittis e manibus et tamen nostra etiam lectitas,
vides profecto illum multa perficere, nos multa
conari, illum posse, nos velle quocumque modo causa
postulet dicere. Sed ille magnus ; nam et successit
ipse magnis et maximos oratores habuit aequalis.
Nos magnum[2] fecissemus, si quidem potuissemus
quo contendimus pervenire in ea urbe in qua, ut ait
106 Antonius, auditus eloquens nemo erat. Atqui si
Antonio Crassus eloquens visus non est aut sibi
ipse, nunquam Cotta visus esset, nunquam Sulpicius,
nunquam Hortensius ; nihil enim ample Cotta, nihil
leniter Sulpicius, non multa graviter Hortensius ;
superiores magis ad omne genus apti, Crassum dico
et Antonium.[a]

Ieiunas igitur huius multiplicis et aequabiliter in
omnia genera fusae orationis auris civitatis accepimus
easque nos primi, quicumque eramus et quantulum-

---

[1] et . . . sumus *A*, ut . . . simus *L*.
[2] magnum *L*, minus magnum *A*, non minus magnum *γ*.

---

[a] Three representatives of the generation between Antonius
and Cicero. Cotta represents the plain style, Sulpicius the
grand, and Hortensius the middle.

the goal but I see what the proper goal is. I am not now discussing myself, but oratory. And in oratory I am so far from admiring my own work, and am so fastidious and hard to please that I am not content even with Demosthenes. Although he stands pre-eminent among all in every style of oratory, still he does not always satisfy my ears, so greedy and insatiate are they and so often yearn for something vast and boundless. However, since 105 you yourself studied this orator thoroughly and with the utmost diligence with his devoted admirer Pammenes during your stay at Athens, and have him constantly in your hands, and yet also find time to read my speeches over and over, you are aware, no doubt, that we merely attempt many things in which he attained perfection, and that he has the power, but we have only the desire to speak in whatever way the case demands. He is a great orator ; for he not only followed a succession of great orators, but also had orators of highest attainments as his contemporaries. It would have been a great achievement if in fact we had been able to attain the goal for which we are striving in that city where, according to Antonius, no eloquent speaker had ever been heard. But if Antonius did not consider Crassus 106 or himself eloquent, he would never have approved of Cotta, never of Sulpicius, never of Hortensius[a]; for Cotta had no grandeur, Sulpicius no mildness, and Hortensius was seldom impressive ; the elders —I mean Crassus and Antonius—were better fitted for every style.

The ears of the city, therefore, we found hungry for this varied type of oratory, displayed equally in all styles, and we were the first, however poor we may

cumque dicebamus, ad huius generis audiendi in-
107 credibilia studia convertimus.   Quantis illa clamoribus adulescentuli diximus de supplicio parricidarum,
quae nequaquam satis defervisse post aliquanto
sentire coepimus : "quid enim tam commune quam
spiritus vivis, terra mortuis, mare fluctuantibus,[1] litus
eiectis ?   Ita vivunt, dum possunt, ut ducere animam
de caelo non queant ; ita moriuntur ut eorum ossa
terra non tangat[2]; ita iactantur fluctibus ut nunquam alluantur ; ita postremo eiciuntur ut ne ad
saxa quidem mortui conquiescant" et quae secuntur ;
sunt enim omnia sicut adulescentis non tam re et
maturitate quam spe et exspectatione laudati.   Ab
hac indole iam illa matura : "uxor generi, noverca
108 fili, filiae paelex."   Nec vero hic erat unus ardor
in nobis ut hoc modo omnia diceremus.   Ipsa enim
illa[3] iuvenilis redundantia multa habet attenuata,
quaedam etiam paulo hilariora, ut[4] pro Habito, pro
Cornelio compluresque aliae.   Nemo enim orator tam
multa ne in Graeco quidem otio scripsit quam multa
sunt nostra, eaque hanc ipsam habent quam probo
109 varietatem.   xxxi. An ego Homero, Ennio, reliquis
poetis et maxime tragicis concederem ut ne omni-

---

[1] fluctuantibus *codd. orat. Rosc.*, eluctantibus *A*, fluctibus *L*.

[2] terra non tangat *L*, terram non tangant *A*.

[3] pro Roscio *seclusit Bake*.

[4] ut *Lambinus :* et *A*, at *L*.

---

[a] *Pro Roscio Amerino* 72.   Cicero repeats some of this
passage in *Verr.* 2. 96.

[b] The passage deals with the punishment of parricides ;
after being beaten with rods, the criminal was sewn in a
sack with a dog, a cock, a viper and a monkey, and thrown
into the sea.

have been and however little we may have accomplished, to turn them to an amazing interest in this style of oratory. What mighty applause greeted the 107 following passage from a speech of my youth [a] on the punishment of parricides, which somewhat later I came to feel was not sufficiently mellowed. " What indeed is so common as breath to living creatures, earth to the dead, the sea to those tossed on the waves, the shore to shipwrecked mariners ? Such is their life [b] while they are let live that they cannot breathe the free air of heaven ; they so die that the earth does not touch their bones ; they are so tossed on the billows that they are never washed clean by them ; so at last they are cast forth on the shore that, though dead, not even on the rocks can they rest in peace," etc. All these are the words of a young man who was applauded not so much for maturity of achievement as for promise of success. From this same natural faculty, now more matured, came the following [c] : " A wife to her son-in-law, a stepmother to her son, to her daughter a rival in love." Not that we always had the same passion 108 to make us say everything in this fashion. For that period of youthful exuberance produced many subdued passages, and some in a rather more genial vein, for example the speeches *In Defence of Habitus*, *In Defence of Cornelius*, and many others. For in fact no orator has written so much as we have, not even in the peaceful life enjoyed by the Greeks ; and these speeches of ours show precisely the variety of which I approve. Am I to yield to Homer, Ennius and all 109 the other poets, and more especially the tragic poets,

---

[c] From *Pro Cluentio* (§ 199), delivered fourteen years after the oration *Pro Roscio*.

bus locis eadem contentione uterentur crebroque
mutarent, nonnunquam etiam ad cotidianum genus
sermonis accederent, ipse nunquam ab illa acerrima
contentione discederem ? Sed quid poetas divino
ingenio profero ? Histriones eos vidimus[1] quibus
nihil posset in suo genere esse praestantius, qui non
solum in dissimillimis personis satis faciebant, cum
tamen in suis versarentur, sed et comoedum in
tragoediis et tragoedum in comoediis admodum pla-
110 cere vidimus : ego non elaborem ? Cum dico me, te,
Brute, dico ; nam in me quidem iam pridem effec-
tum est quod futurum fuit ; tu autem eodem modo
omnis causas ages ? Aut aliquod causarum genus
repudiabis ? Aut in isdem causis perpetuum et
eundem spiritum sine ulla commutatione obtinebis ?
Demosthenes quidem cuius nuper inter imagines tuas
ac tuorum, quod eum credo amares, cum ad te in
Tusculanum venissem, imaginem ex aere vidi, nil
Lysiae subtilitate cedit, nil argutiis et acumine
Hyperidi, nil levitate[2] Aeschini et splendore ver-
111 borum. Multae sunt eius totae orationes subtiles ut
contra Leptinem, multae totae graves ut quaedam
Philippicae, multae variae ut contra Aeschinem falsae
legationis, ut contra eundem pro causa Ctesiphontis.

[1] vidimus λγM[2], videmus AL.
[2] levitate AF, lenitate OP.

---

[a] The reference is probably to two actors whom Cicero
greatly admired, the comedian Roscius who was also
successful in tragedy (*De Orat.* 3. 102) and the tragedian
Aesopus, though there is no evidence except this passage
that he ever appeared in comedy. It was the wellnigh
universal custom in antiquity for actors to limit themselves
to either tragedy or comedy : see Plato, *Rep.* 395 A: οὐδέ τοι

the privilege of not employing in all passages alike
the same impassioned style but of changing their
tone frequently, even of passing over at times to the
language of everyday life, while I myself am never
to depart from that most vehement and impassioned
manner ? But why do I cite poets of divine genius ?
We have seen actors whose superiors in their own
class cannot be found, who not only gained approval
in utterly different parts while confining themselves
to their own proper spheres of tragedy and comedy,
but we have also seen a comedian *a* highly successful
in tragedy and a tragedian *a* in comedy. Should I 110
not take equal pains ? When I say " I," I mean
" you," Brutus ; for in my case what was to be has
been wrought out long ago ; but will *you* plead all
cases in the same manner ? Or will you refuse to take
a certain class of cases ? Or in the same cases will
you always keep to the same high pitch without
variation ? Take Demosthenes, for example, whose
statue in bronze I lately saw among those of yourself
and your kinsmen when I visited you at your Tusculan
villa, placed there, I am sure, because you admire
him ; he yields nothing to Lysias in simplicity,
nothing to Hyperides in refinement of expression
and subtlety, nothing to Aeschines in smoothness
and brilliance of language. Many of his speeches 111
are simple throughout—the one *Against Leptines* is
an example ; many are impassioned throughout,
as certain of the *Philippics* ; many are varied—the
one against Aeschines regarding *Malfeasance in the
Embassy,* and the one against Aeschines *In Defence*

ὑποκριταὶ κωμῳδοῖς τε καὶ τραγῳδοῖς οἱ αὐτοί. *Cf.* also
O'Connor, J. B., *Chapters in the History of Actors and Acting in Ancient Greece,* pp. 39-44.

Iam illud medium quotiens volt arripit et a gravissimo
discedens eo potissimum delabitur.   Clamores tamen
tum movet et tum in dicendo plurimum efficit cum
112 gravitatis locis utitur.   Sed   ab hoc   parumper
abeamus, quandoquidem de genere non de homine
quaerimus ; rei potius, id est eloquentiae, vim et
naturam explicemus.   Illud tamen quod iam ante
diximus meminerimus, nihil nos praecipiendi causa
esse dicturos atque ita potius acturos ut existimatores
videamur loqui, non magistri.   In quo tamen longius
saepe progredimur, quod videmus non te haec solum
esse lecturum, qui ea multo quam nos qui quasi docere
videmur[1] habeas notiora, sed hunc librum etiamsi
minus nostra commendatione tuo tamen nomine
divolgari necesse est.
113   XXXII. Esse igitur perfecte eloquentis puto non eam
tantum facultatem habere quae sit eius propria, fuse
lateque dicendi, sed etiam vicinam eius ac finitimam
dialecticorum scientiam assumere.   Quanquam aliud
videtur oratio esse aliud disputatio nec idem loqui
esse quod dicere ac tamen utrumque in disserendo
est ; disputandi ratio et loquendi dialecticorum sit,
oratorum autem dicendi et ornandi.   Zeno quidem
ille a quo disciplina Stoicorum est manu demonstrare
solebat quid inter has artis interesset ; nam cum
compresserat digitos pugnumque fecerat, dialecticam
aiebat eiusmodi esse ; cum autem deduxerat et
manum dilataverat, palmae illius similem eloquentiam
114 esse dicebat.   Atque etiam ante hunc Aristoteles
principio artis rhetoricae dicit illam artem quasi ex

---

[1] videmur *A*, videamur *L*.

---

[a] Commonly known as the *Oration on the Crown*.

of Ctesiphon.[a] The middle style he adopts whenever
he will, and after an elevated passage he glides
generally into this style. However, he gets the
applause and makes his speech count for most when
he uses the topics of the impassioned style. But let 112
us drop him for the time being, since we are discussing
a class and not an individual. Let us rather return to
our subject and discuss the essence and nature of
eloquence itself. However, let us remember what
we said before, that we shall not speak to instruct,
and shall conduct ourselves so as to seem critics rather
than teachers. Though in this we often go farther
because we know that you will not be the only reader
of these words ; you know those principles much
better than I do who seem to be giving instruction ;
but this book must of necessity obtain a wide circulation, more through your name than from any
worth of mine.

The man of perfect eloquence should, then, in 113
my opinion possess not only the faculty of fluent
and copious speech which is his proper province, but
should also acquire that neighbouring borderland
science of logic ; although a speech is one thing and
a debate another, and disputing is not the same as
speaking, and yet both are concerned with discourse—debate and dispute are the function of the
logicians; the orator's function is to speak ornately.
Zeno, the founder of the Stoic school, used to give
an object lesson of the difference between the two
arts ; clenching his fist he said logic was like that ;
relaxing and extending his hand, he said eloquence
was like the open palm. Still earlier Aristotle in 114
the opening chapter of his *Art of Rhetoric* [b] said

[b] Arist. *Rhet.* 1. 1: ἡ ῥητορική ἐστιν ἀντίστροφος τῇ διαλεκτικῇ.

altera parte respondere dialecticae, ut hoc videlicet differant inter se quod haec ratio dicendi latior sit, illa loquendi contractior. Volo igitur huic summo omnem quae ad dicendum trahi possit loquendi rationem esse notam. Quae quidem res, quod te his artibus eruditum minime fallit, duplicem habuit docendi viam. Nam et ipse Aristoteles tradidit praecepta plurima disserendi et postea qui dialec-
115 tici dicuntur spinosiora multa pepererunt. Ego eum censeo qui eloquentiae laude ducatur non esse earum rerum omnino rudem sed vel illa antiqua vel hac Chrysippi disciplina institutum. Noverit primum vim, naturam, genera verborum et simplicium et copulatorum; deinde quot modis quidque dicatur; qua ratione verum falsumne sit iudicetur; quid efficiatur e quoque, quid cuique consequens sit quidque[1] contrarium; cumque ambigue multa dicantur, quo modo quidque eorum dividi explanarique oporteat. Haec tenenda sunt oratori—saepe enim occurrunt—sed quia sua sponte squalidiora sunt, adhibendus erit in his explicandis quidam orationis nitor.

116 XXXIII. Et quoniam in omnibus quae ratione docentur et via primum constituendum est quid quidque sit—nisi enim inter eos qui disceptant convenit quid sit illud quod[2] ambigitur, nec recte disseri unquam nec[3] ad exitum perveniri potest—explicanda est saepe verbis mens nostra de quaque re atque involuta rei notitia definiendo aperienda

---

[1] quidque γ, quidve A, quodque L.
[2] quod A, de quo L.
[3] umquam nec A, nec unquam L.

---

[a] The latter half of this statement is not in Aristotle.

that rhetoric is the counterpart of logic, the difference obviously being that rhetoric was broader and
logic narrower.[a]   I therefore expect this perfect
orator of ours to be familiar with all the theory
of disputation which can be applied to speaking ;
this subject, as you well know from your training
along this line, has been taught in two different
ways.   Aristotle himself taught many principles of
argumentation, and the later dialecticians, as they
are called, produced many thorny speculations. For 115
my part I advise one who is attracted by the glory
of eloquence not to be entirely unacquainted with
these latter authors, but to be thoroughly trained
either in the older logic of Aristotle, or the newer
of Chrysippus. He should know first the force,
nature and classes of words, both singly and in the
sentence ; then the different modes of predication ;
the method of distinguishing truth from falsity ;
the proper deduction to be drawn from each, *i.e.*
what is consequent and what is contrary; and since
many ambiguous statements are made, he should
know how these can be solved and explained. These
are the things the orator must get,—for they are
continually coming up—but because in themselves
they are somewhat unattractive, a certain grace of
style will have to be used in presenting them.

Furthermore, since in all subjects that are taught 116
by systematic principles, we must first of all determine what each thing is—for unless the disputants
are agreed as to what is the subject under debate
there can be no proper discussion, nor can they
arrive at any result—we must frequently give a
verbal explanation of our ideas about each thing,
and must make plain by definition the obscure con-

est, siquidem est definitio oratio, quae quid sit id de
quo agitur ostendit quam brevissime. Tum, ut scis,
explicato genere cuiusque rei videndum est quae sint
eius generis sive formae sive partes, ut in eas tribuatur
117 omnis oratio. Erit igitur haec facultas in eo quem
volumus esse eloquentem, ut definire rem possit nec
id faciat tam presse et anguste quam in illis eruditis-
simis disputationibus fieri solet, sed cum explanatius
tum etiam uberius et ad commune iudicium popu-
laremque intellegentiam accommodatius. Idemque
etiam, cum res postulabit, genus universum in species certas, ut nulla neque praetermittatur neque
redundet, partietur ac dividet. Quando autem id
faciat aut quo modo,[1] nihil ad hoc tempus, quoniam,
ut supra dixi, iudicem esse me, non doctorem volo.

118 Nec vero a dialecticis modo sit instructus sed
habeat omnis philosophiae notos ac tractatos locos.
Nihil enim de religione, nihil de morte,[2] nihil de
pietate, nihil de caritate patriae, nihil de bonis rebus
aut malis, nihil de virtutibus aut vitiis, nihil de officio,[3]
nihil de dolore, nihil de voluptate, nihil de perturba-
tionibus animi et erroribus, quae saepe cadunt in
causas et ieiunius aguntur, nihil, inquam,[4] sine ea
scientia quam dixi graviter, ample, copiose dici et
119 explicari potest. XXXIV. De materia loquor orationis
etiam nunc, non de ipso genere dicendi. Volo enim
prius habeat orator rem de qua dicat dignam auribus
eruditis, quam cogitet quibus verbis quidque dicat
aut quo modo.[5] Quem etiam, quo grandior sit et

---

[1] id faciat aut quo modo *A*, aut (et *P*) quo modo id facias *L*.
[2] morte *L*, more *A*.   [3] officio *L*, officiis *A*.
[4] inquam *L*, umquam *A*.
[5] aut quo modo *omisit A*.

cept of a subject, since definition is a statement
giving the subject of discussion in the briefest
possible form. Then, as you know, after explaining
the genus of each thing we must consider what are
the species or subdivisions of the genus in question,
so that the whole speech may be divided between
them. The man whom we wish to be eloquent 117
will, then, possess the ability to define the subject,
and will not do it so briefly and compactly as is the
custom in the learned discussions of philosophers,
but with greater clarity and at the same time with
greater fullness, and in a way better adapted to the
ordinary judgement and popular intelligence. He
will likewise, when the subject demands this, divide
a genus into definite species, so that no species may
be left out or be superfluous. But when or how he
may do this is immaterial at present, since, as I said
above, I wish to be a critic, not a teacher.

He should not confine his study to logic, however, 118
but have a theoretical acquaintance with all the
topics of philosophy and practical training in de-
bating them. For philosophy is essential to a full,
copious and impressive discussion and exposition of
the subjects which so often come up in speeches and
are usually treated meagrely, whether they concern
religion, death, piety, patriotism, good and evil,
virtues and vices, duty, pain, pleasure, or mental dis-
turbances and errors. I am speaking now of the 119
raw material of the speech, not about its literary
style. For it is desirable that the orator should have
a subject worthy of a cultivated audience before
he considers the language or style of expression.
It is also desirable that he should not be ignorant
of natural philosophy either, which will impart

quodam modo excelsior, ut de Pericle dixi supra,[a]
ne physicorum quidem esse ignarum volo. Omnia
profecto, cum se a caelestibus rebus referet ad
humanas, excelsius magnificentiusque et dicet et
sentiet.

120 Cumque illa divina cognoverit, nolo ignoret ne
haec quidem humana. Ius civile teneat quo egent
causae forenses cotidie. Quid est enim turpius
quam legitimarum et civilium controversiarum
patrocinia suscipere, cum sis legum et civilis iuris
ignarus ? Cognoscat etiam rerum gestarum et
memoriae veteris ordinem, maxime scilicet nostrae
civitatis sed etiam imperiosorum populorum et regum
illustrium. Quem laborem nobis Attici nostri levavit
labor[b] qui conservatis notatisque temporibus, nihil
cum illustre praetermitteret, annorum septingen-
torum memoriam uno libro colligavit. Nescire
autem quid ante quam natus sis acciderit, id est
semper esse puerum. Quid enim est aetas hominis,
nisi ea memoria rerum veterum cum superiorum
aetate contexitur ? Commemoratio autem antiquitatis exemplorumque prolatio summa cum delectatione et auctoritatem orationi affert et fidem.

121 Sic igitur instructus veniet ad causas quarum
habebit genera primum ipsa cognita. Erit enim ei
perspectum nihil ambigi posse in quo non aut res
controversiam faciat aut verba : res aut de vero aut
de recto aut de nomine, verba aut de ambiguo aut
de contrario.[c] Nam si quando aliud in sententia

---

[a] § 15.
[b] The *Liber Annalis* of Titus Pomponius Atticus, dedicated to Cicero.　　　　　　　　　　　　[c] *Cf.* § 45.

grandeur and loftiness, as I said above[a] about Pericles. When he turns from a consideration of the heavens to human affairs, all his words and thoughts will assuredly be loftier and more magnificent.

Nor, while he is acquainted with the divine order 120 of nature, would I have him ignorant of human affairs. He should understand the civil law, which is needed daily in practice in the courts of law. What is more disgraceful than to attempt to plead in legal and civil disputes when ignorant of the statutes and the civil law ? He should also be acquainted with the history of the events of past ages, particularly, of course, of our state, but also of imperial nations and famous kings ; here our task has been lightened by the labour of our friend Atticus, who has comprised in one book[b] the record of seven hundred years, keeping the chronology definite and omitting no important event. To be ignorant of what occurred before you were born is to remain always a child. For what is the worth of human life, unless it is woven into the life of our ancestors by the records of history ? Moreover, the mention of antiquity and the citation of examples give the speech authority and credibility as well as affording the highest pleasure to the audience.

Thus equipped, then, he will come to the pleading 121 of causes : and first he must be acquainted with the different kinds of causes. For he will clearly recognize that there can be no dispute in which the controversy does not arise either about fact or about words : in the case of fact the dispute is about the truth of the charge, its justification or its definition[c] ; in the case of words whether they are ambiguous, or contradictory. For if there is ever a case in which

videtur esse aliud in verbis, genus est quoddam ambigui quod ex praeterito verbo fieri solet; in quo, quod est ambiguorum proprium, res duas significari
122 videmus. XXXV. Cum tam pauca sint genera causarum, etiam argumentorum praecepta pauca sunt. Traditi sunt e quibus ea ducantur duplices loci : uni e rebus ipsis, alteri assumpti.

Tractatio igitur rerum efficit admirabilem[1] orationem ; nam ipsae quidem res in perfacili cognitione versantur. Quid enim iam sequitur, quod quidem artis sit, nisi ordiri orationem, in quo aut concilietur auditor aut erigatur aut paret se ad discendum ; rem breviter exponere et probabiliter et aperte, ut quid agatur intellegi possit ; sua confirmare, adversaria evertere, eaque efficere non perturbate sed singulis argumentationibus ita concludendis, ut efficiatur quod sit consequens eis quae sumentur ad quamque rem confirmandam ; post omnia perorationem inflammantem restinguentemve concludere ? Has partis quem ad modum tractet singulas difficile dictu est hoc loco ; nec enim semper tractantur uno modo.
123 Quoniam autem non quem doceam quaero sed quem probem, probabo primum eum qui quid deceat viderit. Haec enim sapientia maxime adhibenda eloquenti est, ut sit temporum personarumque moderator. Nam nec semper nec apud omnis nec contra omnis

---

[1] admirabilem *A*, admirabiliorem *L*.

---

[a] This parenthetical sentence is added because the current rhetorical theory recognized three classes, which Cicero here reduces to two by subsuming *discrepantia scripti et voluntatis* under *ambiguum*. In *Topica* 96 he returns to the threefold division.

one thing is meant and another expressed, this is
a kind of ambiguity which usually arises from the
omission of a word ; in this case we see that there
are two meanings, and that is the characteristic of
ambiguity.[a] As there are so few kinds of causes, 122
the rules for arguments are likewise few. There
are, according to the usual theory, two sources from
which they may be drawn ; one, inherent in the case
itself, the other external to it.[b]

It is the treatment of the subject matter, then,
that makes the speech admirable ; the facts themselves are easy enough to acquire. For what remains
that is subject to the rules of art, except to begin the
speech in such a manner as to win the favour of the
audience or to arouse them or to put them in a recep-
tive mood ; to set forth the facts briefly, clearly and
reasonably, so that the subject under dispute may
be understood ; to prove one's own case and demolish
the adversary's, and to do this not confusedly, but
with arguments so conclusive as to prove what is the
natural consequence of the principles laid down to
prove each point ; finally to pronounce a peroration
either to inflame or to quench the passion of the
audience ? It is difficult to prescribe here how each
of these parts is to be handled ; as a matter of fact
they are not always handled in the same way. But 123
since I am not seeking a pupil to teach, but an orator
to approve, I shall begin by approving of one who
can observe what is fitting. This, indeed, is the form
of wisdom that the orator must especially employ
—to adapt himself to occasions and persons. In my
opinion one must not speak in the same style at all

[b] *e.g.*, arguments from probability belong to the first
class, documentary evidence to the latter.

nec pro omnibus nec cum[1] omnibus[2] eodem modo
dicendum arbitror. xxxvi. Is erit ergo eloquens,
qui ad id quodcumque decebit poterit accommodare
orationem. Quod cum statuerit, tum ut quicque
erit dicendum ita dicet : nec satura ieiune nec
grandia minute nec item contra, sed erit rebus ipsis
124 par et aequalis oratio ; principia verecunda, nondum elatis incensa verbis sed acuta sententiis vel ad
offensionem adversarii vel ad commendationem sui ;
narrationes credibiles nec historico sed prope coti-
diano sermone explicatae dilucide ; dein si tenues
causae, tum etiam argumentandi tenue filum et in
docendo et in refellendo idque ita tenebitur, ut
quanta ad rem tanta ad orationem fiat accessio ;
125 cum vero causa ea inciderit in qua vis eloquentiae
possit expromi, tum se latius fundet orator, tum reget
et flectet animos et sic afficiet ut volet, id est ut
causae natura et ratio temporis postulabit.

Sed erit duplex eius omnis ornatus ille admirabilis
propter quem ascendit in tantum honorem eloquentia.
Nam cum omnis pars orationis esse debet laudabilis,
sic ut verbum nullum nisi aut grave aut elegans
excidat, tum sunt maxime luminosae et quasi actuosae
partes duae : quarum alteram in universi generis
quaestione pono quam, ut supra dixi, Graeci appellant
θέσιν, alteram in augendis amplificandisque rebus

---

[1] cum *addidit Friedrich.*
[2] nec pro omnibus nec omnibus *omisit A.*

---

[a] § 46.

times, nor before all people, nor against all opponents, nor in defence of all clients, nor in partnership with all advocates. He, therefore, will be eloquent who can adapt his speech to fit all conceivable circumstances. Once this is determined, he will speak each part as it should be spoken ; a rich subject will not be treated meagrely, nor a grand subject in a paltry way, nor *vice versa,* but the speech will be proper and adequate to the subject. The beginning 124 will be modest, not yet warmed by elevated language, but distinguished by ideas designed either to rebuff the opponent or to recommend the speaker himself. The narrative will be credible, clearly expressed, not in the style of history but almost in the tone of everyday conversation. Thereafter if the case is slight, the thread of the argument will be slight, both in proof and in refutation, but will be so controlled that as the subject rises in importance the style will become more elevated. However, when a case presents itself 125 in which the full force of eloquence can be expended, then the orator will display his powers more fully ; then he will rule and sway men's minds, and move them as he will, that is as the nature of the cause and the exigency of the occasion demand.

He will also have completely at his command those two marvellous forms of ornament because of which eloquence climbs to such honour. Every part of the speech, to be sure, should be praiseworthy—no word should fall from the orator's lips that is not impressive or precise—but two parts are especially brilliant and effective ; the first is the discussion of a general principle, which as I have said above [a] the Greeks call θέσις or " proposition," the other consists in exalting and amplifying a theme ; their

126 quae ab isdem αὔξησις est nominata. Quae etsi
aequaliter toto corpore orationis fusa esse debet,
tamen in communibus locis maxime excellet; qui
communes sunt[1] appellati eo quod videntur multarum
idem esse causarum, sed proprii singularum esse
debebunt. At[2] vero illa pars orationis quae est de
genere universo totas causas saepe continet. Quicquid est enim illud in quo quasi certamen est con-
troversiae, quod Graece κρινόμενον dicitur, id ita dici
placet ut traducatur ad perpetuam quaestionem atque
uti de[3] universo genere dicatur, nisi cum de vero
127 ambigitur, quod quaeri coniectura solet. Dicetur
autem non Peripateticorum more—est enim illorum
exercitatio elegans iam inde ab Aristotele constituta
—sed aliquanto nervosius et ita de re communia
dicentur, ut et pro reis multa leniter dicantur et in
adversarios aspere. Augendis vero rebus et contra
abiciendis nihil est quod non perficere possit oratio;
quod et inter media argumenta faciendum est, quo-
tienscumque dabitur vel amplificandi vel minuendi
locus, et paene infinite in perorando.
128 XXXVII. Duae res sunt enim quae bene tractatae[4] ab
oratore admirabilem eloquentiam faciant. Quorum
alterum est quod Graeci ἠθικὸν vocant, ad naturas
et ad mores et ad omnem vitae consuetudinem ac-

---

[1] sunt γ, *omiserunt AL.*   [2] at γεf, ac *AL.*
[3] uti de *Stangl,* ut inde *A,* ut de *L.*
[4] Duae res sunt . . . tractatae *A,* duo sunt . . . trac-
tata *L.*

---

[a] *i.e.* anything in the speech which tends to reveal the
character of the speaker.

term for this is αὔξησις or "amplification." Though 126
the latter should be spread equally throughout the
whole of the speech, yet it will be especially note-
worthy in the "commonplaces," so called because they
seem to be the same in many causes. They should,
however, be appropriate to each particular cause.
And in fact that part of the speech which deals with a
general principle often includes the whole case. For
whatever that part may be called that deals with the
central point of the controversy, which the Greeks
call κρινόμενον or the issue, ought to be treated in
such a way as to transfer the subject to the realm
of universals and bring about a discussion of a
general principle. The only exception to this is when
the trial is concerned only with a question of fact,
which is customarily investigated by means of conjecture. The orator will treat these topics, not in 127
the fashion of the Peripatetics—to them belongs a
graceful method of philosophical discussion which as
a matter of fact goes back to Aristotle—but with
somewhat greater vigour; and general remarks
about the subject will be adapted in such a way as
to say much quietly in favour of the defendant, and
harshly against the opponents. There is no limit to
the power of an oration to exalt a subject or render
it contemptible. This must be done in the midst
of arguments, whenever an opening is offered to
amplify or disparage; and there is almost unlimited
opportunity for it in the peroration.

There are, for instance, two topics which if well 128
handled by the orator arouse admiration for his
eloquence. One, which the Greeks call ἠθικόν or
"expressive of character,"[a] is related to men's nature
and character, their habits and all the intercourse

401

commodatum; alterum quod idem παθητικὸν nominant, quo perturbantur animi et concitantur, in quo uno regnat oratio. Illud superius come, iucundum, ad benevolentiam conciliandam paratum, hoc vehemens, incensum, incitatum, quo causae eripiuntur; quod cum rapide fertur, sustineri nullo pacto potest.
129 Quo genere nos mediocres aut multo etiam minus, sed magno semper usi impetu saepe adversarios de statu omni deiecimus. Nobis pro familiari reo summus orator non respondit Hortensius; a nobis homo audacissimus Catilina in senatu accusatus obmutuit; nobis privata in causa magna et gravi cum coepisset Curio pater respondere, subito assedit, cum sibi
130 venenis ereptam memoriam diceret. Quid ego de miserationibus loquar? quibus eo sum usus pluribus quod, etiam si plures dicebamus, perorationem mihi tamen omnes relinquebant; in quo ut viderer excellere non ingenio sed dolore assequebar. Quae qualiacumque in me sunt—me enim ipsum paenitet[1] quanta sint—sed apparent in orationibus, etsi carent libri spiritu illo, propter quem maiora eadem illa cum aguntur quam cum leguntur
131 videri solent. xxxviii. Nec vero miseratione solum mens iudicum permovenda est—qua nos ita dolenter uti solemus ut puerum infantem in manibus perorantes tenuerimus, ut alia in causa excitato reo nobili, sublato etiam filio parvo plangore et lamenta-

---

[1] paenitet *A*, non paenitet *L*.

---

[a] Verres.
[b] Cicero in the *Brutus* 217 says that Curio's memory was always poor.
[c] Probably Lucius Flaccus.

of life ; the other, which they call παθητικόν or " relating to the emotions," arouses and excites the emotions : in this part alone oratory reigns supreme. The former is courteous and agreeable, adapted to win goodwill ; the latter is violent, hot and impassioned, and by this cases are wrested from our opponents ; when it rushes along in full career it is quite irresistible. My ability is mediocre or even 129 less than that, but I have always used a vigorous style, and by this kind of oratory I have often dislodged opponents. Hortensius, a consummate orator, made no reply in defence of his friend[a] whom I brought to trial ; the brazen Catiline was arraigned by me in the senate and was struck dumb ; the elder Curio began his reply to me in a private case of grave importance, and suddenly sat down, alleging that magical potions had robbed him of his memory.[b] Why should I mention appeals to pity ? 130 More of these are to be found in my orations, because even though there were several speakers on our side, they always let me make the closing speech. I owe my reputation for excellence on such occasions, not to any natural gift, but to a genuine sympathy. Whatever qualifications I possess—for I myself am sorry that they are not greater —can be seen in my orations, although books lack that breath of life which usually makes such passages seem more impressive when spoken than when read. Nor is the appeal for sympathy the only 131 way of arousing the emotions of the jury—though we are wont to use it so piteously that we have even held a babe in our arms during the peroration, and in another plea for a noble defendant[c] we told him to stand up, and raising his small son we

403

tione compleremus forum—sed est faciendum etiam,
ut irascatur iudex mitigetur, invideat faveat, con-
temnat admiretur, oderit diligat, cupiat taedeat,[1]
speret metuat, laetetur doleat ; qua in varietate
duriorum Accusatio suppeditabit exempla, mitio-
132 rum defensiones meae. Nullo enim modo animus
audientis aut incitari aut leniri potest, qui modus
a me non temptatus sit—dicerem perfectum, si ita
iudicarem, nec in veritate crimen arrogantiae pertimescerem[2] ; sed, ut supra dixi, nulla me ingeni
sed magna vis animi inflammat, ut me ipse non
teneam ; nec unquam is qui audiret incenderetur,
nisi ardens ad eum perveniret oratio. Uterer
exemplis domesticis, nisi ea legisses, uterer alienis
vel Latinis, si ulla reperirem, vel Graecis, si deceret.
Sed Crassi perpauca sunt nec ea iudiciorum, nihil
Antoni, nihil Cottae, nihil Sulpici ; dicebat melius
133 quam scripsit Hortensius. Verum haec vis, quam
quaerimus, quanta sit suspicemur,[3] quoniam exemplum non habemus, aut si exempla sequimur, a
Demosthene sumamus et quidem perpetuae dictionis ex eo loco unde in Ctesiphontis iudicio de
suis factis, consiliis, meritis in rem publicam aggressus est dicere. Ea profecto oratio in eam
formam, quae est insita in mentibus nostris, includi
sic potest ut maior eloquentia non requiratur.

---

[1] taedeat *A*, satietate officiatur *L*.
[2] pertimescerem *A*, *Augustinus, In Iohannis Evan.
Tract. 124. 58, 3 :* extimescerem *L*.
[3] suspicemur *L*, suspicamur *A*.

---

[a] Of Verres.   [b] § 130.
[c] Cicero dislikes to quote Greek at length in a treatise
intended for the general Roman public.

filled the forum with wailing and lamentation—but the juror must be made to be angry or appeased to feel ill will or to be well disposed, he must be made to feel scorn or admiration, hatred or love, desire or loathing, hope or fear, joy or sorrow. The sterner of these various emotions may be exemplified from the *Accusation,*[a] the milder from my speeches for the defence. For there is no way in which the 132 mind of the auditor may be aroused or soothed that I have not tried—I should say brought to perfection, if I really thought so, and if it were true I should not fear to be called conceited. But, as I said before,[b] it is no great intellectual gift, but a vigorous spirit which inflames me to such an extent that I am beside myself; and I am sure that the audience would never be set on fire unless the words that reached him were fiery. I should cite examples from my own speeches if you had not read them : I should cite the speeches of others,—in Latin if I could find any, in Greek if it were fitting to do so.[c] But there are only a few of Crassus's speeches, and they are not forensic ; nothing is extant of Antonius, of Cotta or of Sulpicius. Hortensius used to speak better than his written speeches would indicate. But let 133 us be content to surmise the importance of this vigour which we desire, since we have no examples ; or if we must have examples, let us cite Demosthenes, in particular the continuous passage in the oration *In Defence of Ctesiphon* beginning with his discussion of his acts, his counsel and his services to the state.[d] This speech certainly conforms so closely to the ideal which is in our minds that no greater eloquence need be sought.

[d] *De Cor.* 294 ff.

134 xxxix. Sed iam forma ipsa restat et χαρακτὴρ ille qui dicitur. Qui qualis debeat esse ex eis ipsis[1] quae supra dicta sunt intellegi potest. Nam et singulorum verborum et collocatorum lumina attigimus. Quibus sic abundabit, ut verbum ex ore nullum nisi aut elegans aut grave exeat, ex omnique genere frequentissimae tralationes erunt, quod eae propter similitudinem transferunt animos et referunt ac movent huc et illuc, qui motus cogitationis celeriter agitatus per se ipse delectat. Et reliqua ex collocatione verborum quae sumuntur quasi lumina magnum afferunt ornatum orationi. Sunt enim similia illis quae in amplo ornatu scaenae aut fori appellantur insignia, non quia sola ornent sed quod

135 excellant. Eadem ratio est horum quae sunt orationis lumina et quodam modo insignia : cum aut duplicantur iteranturque verba aut leviter[2] commutata ponuntur, aut ab eodem verbo ducitur saepius oratio aut in idem conicitur[3] aut utrumque, aut adiungitur idem iteratum aut idem ad extremum refertur, aut continenter unum verbum non in eadem

---

[1] iis ipsis *Lambinus*, his *A*, ipsis *L*.
[2] leviter *Gessner (ad Quint. 9. 1, 18)*, breviter *AL et Quint.*
[3] conicitur *A*, coicitur *L*.

---

[a] § 80.
[b] I take *duplicantur* and *iterantur* to refer to one and the same figure, called by the Auctor *Ad Herennium* (4. 38) *conduplicatio*; *e.g.*: Nunc etiam audes in horum conspectum venire, *proditor patriae, proditor*, inquam, *patriae*, venire audes in horum conspectum ?
[c] *e.g.* Cic. *Pro Sulla* 47: Noli id omnino putare a me esse *amissum* si quid tibi est *remissum* atque *concessum*. *Cf.* also *Orator* 27, *ferret . . . auferri.*
[d] Cic. *In Cat. I* 1: *Nihilne* te nocturnum praesidium Palati, *nihil* urbes vigiliae, *nihil* timor populi, *nihil* con-

There now remains the actual type and χαρακτήρ 134
or " character " as it is called ; its ideal form can be
recognized from what has been said above.[a] There
we touched on the ornaments of style both in the use
of single words and in their combinations. These will
be so plentiful that no word will fall from the orator's
lips that is not well chosen or impressive ; there will
be metaphors of all sorts in great abundance, because
these figures by virtue of the comparison involved
transport the mind and bring it back, and move it
hither and thither ; and this rapid stimulation of
thought in itself produces pleasure. The other ornaments derived from combinations of words lend great
brilliance to an oration. They are like those objects
which in the embellishment of a stage or of a forum
are called " ornaments," not because they are the
only ornament, but because they stand out from the
others. It is the same way with the embellishments 135
and, as it were, the ornaments, of style ; words are
redoubled and repeated,[b] or repeated with a slight
change,[c] or several successive phrases begin with the
same words[d] or end with the same,[e] or have both
figures,[f] or the same word is repeated at the beginning
of a clause[g] or at the end,[h] or a word is used immedi-

cursus bonorum omnium, *nihil* hic munitissimus habendi
senatus locus, *nihil* horum ora voltusque moverunt ?

[e] Cic. *Phil. II* 55 : Doletis tres exercitus populi Romani
interfectos ; interfecit *Antonius*. Desideratis clarissimos
cives ; eos quoque nobis eripuit *Antonius*. Auctoritas
huius ordinis afflicta est ; afflixit *Antonius*.

[f] Cic. *De Lege Agraria* 2. 22 : *Quis* legem tulit ? *Rullus* ;
quis maiorem partem populi suffragiis prohibuit ? *Rullus*.

[g] Cic. *Pro Milone* 91 : *excitate, excitate* ipsum, si potestis
a mortuis.

[h] Horace, *Carm.* 4. 1, 2 : parce, *precor, precor.*

sententia ponitur, aut cum similiter vel cadunt
verba vel desinunt, aut cum sunt[1] contrariis relata
contraria, aut cum gradatim sursum versus reditur,
aut cum demptis coniunctionibus dissolute plura
dicuntur, aut cum aliquid praetereuntes cur id
faciamus ostendimus, aut cum corrigimus nosmet
ipsos quasi reprehendentes, aut si est aliqua ex-
clamatio vel admirationis vel questionis, aut cum
eiusdem nominis casus saepius commutantur.

136 Sed sententiarum ornamenta maiora sunt; quibus
quia frequentissime Demosthenes utitur, sunt qui
putent idcirco eius eloquentiam maxime esse lauda-
bilem. Et vero nullus fere ab eo locus sine quadam
conformatione sententiae dicitur; nec quicquam
est aliud dicere nisi aut[2] omnis aut certe plerasque
aliqua specie illuminare sententias : quas cum tu
optime, Brute, teneas, quid attinet nominibus uti aut
137 exemplis ? Tantum modo notetur locus. XL. Sic
igitur dicet ille quem expetimus, ut verset saepe

---

[1] cum sunt *A*, multis modis (*om*. cum sunt) *L et Quint.*
[2] aut *βf*, quam aut *L*, omisit *A et Quint.*

---

[a] Cic. *Pro Roscio Amer.* 5 : his de *causis* ego huic *causae*
patronus exstiti.

[b] Auct. *Ad Heren.* 4. 28 : Hominem laudas *egentem
virtutis, abundantem felicitatis.*

[c] Cic. *Pro Quint.* 75: cogitent ita se graves esse, ut si
veritatem volent *retinere*, gravitatem possint *obtinere.*

[d] Cic. *Pro Cluent.* 15 : vicit *pudorem libido, timorem
audacia, rationem amentia.*

[e] Quint. 9. 3, 56 : Africano *virtutem industria, virtus
gloriam, gloria aemulos* comparavit. This term is not
exactly rendered by English *climax,* as it implies the use of
pairs of words, each pair repeating a word from the former.

[f] Auct. *Ad Heren.* 4. 41: Gere morem parenti, pare
cognatis, obsequere amicis, obtempera legibus.

ately in a different sense,[a] or words are used with
similar case endings [b] or other similar terminations [c] ;
or contrasting ideas are put in juxtaposition (antithesis [d]), or the sentence rises and falls in steps
(climax [e]) ; or many clauses are strung together
loosely without conjunctions [f] ; or sometimes we
omit something and give our reason for so doing [g] :
or we correct ourselves with a quasi-reproof [h] ; or
make some exclamation of surprise or complaint [i] ;
or use the same word repeatedly in different cases.[j]

The figures of thought, however, are of greater 136
importance ; it is the frequent use of these by
Demosthenes which makes some regard his eloquence
as particularly admirable. As a matter of fact scarcely
any topic is treated by him without some configura-
tion of thought. The whole essence of oratory is to
embellish in some fashion all, or, at any rate, most of
the ideas. As you understand these embellishments
perfectly, Brutus, why name them or cite examples ?
Let us be content merely to point out the subject. 137
The orator, then, whom we are trying to discover,
will make frequent use of the following figures [k] : he

[g] Cic. *In Cat. I* 14 : quod ego praetermitto et facile patior
sileri, ne in hac civitate tanti facinoris immanitas aut exstitisse aut non vindicata esse videatur.

[h] Cic. *Pro Caelio* 32 : quod quidem facerem vehementius,
nisi intercederent mihi inimicitiae cum istius mulieris viro—
fratre volui dicere : semper hic erro.

[i] Cic. *In Cat. I* 2 : O tempora ! O mores !

[j] Cic. *Pro Murena* 12 : a passage too long to quote here ;
Asia is used seven times, in four cases.

[k] Cicero proceeds to describe thirty-nine figures : the
technical terms of Latin rhetoric, the Greek words of which
they are translations for the most part, and references to discussions in Latin treatises on rhetoric are given in the notes.
Examples are generally too long to quote here.

multis modis eadem et una in re[1] haereat in ea-
demque commoretur sententia ; saepe etiam ut
extenuet aliquid,[2] saepe ut irrideat[3] ; ut declinet
a proposito deflectatque sententiam ; ut proponat
quid dicturus sit ; ut, cum transegerit iam aliquid,
definiat ; ut se ipse revocet ; ut quod dixit iteret ;
ut argumentum ratione concludat ; ut interrogando
urgeat ; ut rursus quasi[4] ad interrogata sibi ipse[4]
respondeat ; ut contra ac dicat accipi et sentiri
velit ; ut addubitet ecquid potius aut quo modo
dicat ; ut dividat in partis ; ut aliquid relinquat
ac[5] neglegat ; ut ante praemuniat ; ut in eo ipso,
in quo reprehendatur, culpam in adversarium con-
138 ferat ; ut saepe cum eis qui audiunt, nonnunquam
etiam cum adversario quasi deliberet ; ut hominum

---

[1] eadem et una in re *vulg.*, eadem et in una re *Quint.:*
eadem ut unam in rem *L*, eandem et unam rem et *A.*
[2] saepe . . . aliquid *omiserunt A, et tres codices Quint.*
[3] irrideat *L et Quint.*, redeat *A.*
[4] quasi *et* sibi ipse *omisit A.*
[5] ac *L*, ut *A.*

---

[a] *Commoratio,* ἐπιμονή : *Ad Heren.* 4. 58.
[b] *Extenuatio* or *deminutio,* μείωσις : *Ad Heren.* 4. 50.
[c] *Illusio,* διασυρμός, χλευασμός : Cic. *De Orat.* 3. 202.
[d] *Digressio,* παρέκβασις : Quintilian (9. 2, 56) cites an
example : Tum C. Varenus, is qui a familia Anchariana
occisus est : (hoc, quaeso, iudices, diligenter attendite).
[e] *Propositio,* προέκθεσις, and *enumeratio,* ἀνακεφαλαίωσις :
Cic. *De Orat.* 3. 203.   Cic. *De Imp. Cn. Pomp.* 20 : Quoniam
de genere belli dixi, nunc de magnitudine pauca dicam.
The combination of the two figures was also called *transitio.*
[f] *Reditus ad propositum,* ἄφοδος : Quint. 9. 3, 87 ; Cic.
De Orat. 3. 90 : Sed iam si placet, ad instituta redeamus.
[g] This seems to be the same as the first under figures of
style, above, p. 407.
[h] *Conclusio,* συμπέρασμα : *Ad Heren.* 4. 41.
[i] *Rogatio,* ἐρώτησις : Cic. *De Orat.* 3. 203.

will treat the same subject in many ways, sticking to
the same idea and lingering over the same thought[a]:
he will often speak slightingly of something[b] or
ridicule it[c]: he will turn from the subject and divert
the thought[d]; he will announce what he is about to
discuss[e] and sum up when concluding a topic[e]; he
will bring himself back to the subject[f]; he will repeat
what he has said[g]; he will use a syllogism[h]; he will
urge his point by asking questions[i] and will reply to
himself as if to questions[j]; he will say something, but
desire to have it understood in the opposite sense[k];
he will express doubt whether or how to mention
some point[l]; he will divide the subject into parts[m];
will omit or disregard some topic[n]; he will prepare
the way for what is to come[o]; he will transfer to his
opponent the blame for the very act with which he
is charged[p]; he will seem to consult the audience, 138
and sometimes even with the opponent[q]; he will

[j] *Subiectio*, ὑποφορά : *Ad Heren*. 4. 33.
[k] *Dissimulatio*, εἰρωνεία : Cic. *De Orat*. 3. 203.
[l] *Dubitatio*, διαπόρησις : *Ad Heren*. 4. 40.
[m] *Divisio*, μερισμός : *Ad Heren*. 4. 52.
[n] *Occultatio, praeteritio*, παράλειψις : *Ad Heren*. 4. 37.
Cic. *In Cat. I* 14 : Praetermitto ruinas fortunarum tuarum.
[o] *Praemunitio*, προπαρασκευή : the term here paraphrased
by Cicero is used by the rhetoricians with different meanings :
Quintilian (9. 2, 17) says, qualis Ciceronis contra Q.
Caecilium quod ad accusandum descendat qui semper de-
fenderit ; *i.e.* excuse or self-defence. Julius Rufinianus
(p. 46 Halm) cites as example : Cicero pro Milone ante
praemunit licere hominem occidere, et tum subicit occisum
P. Clodium iure. I have adopted the latter sense in the
translation.
[p] *Traiectio in alium*, μετάστασις : Cic. *De Orat*. 3. 204.
Cf. Cic. *In Cat. II* 3 : non est ista mea culpa sed temporum.
[q] *Communicatio*, ἀνακοίνωσις : Jul. Ruf. 41. 8. *Cf.* Cic.
In Caec. Div. 37-39.

sermones moresque describat; ut muta quaedam
loquentia inducat; ut ab eo quod agitur avertat
animos; ut saepe in hilaritatem risumve convertat;
ut ante occupet quod videat opponi; ut comparet
similitudines; ut utatur[1] exemplis; ut aliud alii
tribuens dispertiat; ut interpellatorem coerceat;
ut aliquid reticere se dicat; ut denuntiet quid
caveant; ut liberius quid audeat; ut irascatur
etiam, ut obiurget aliquando; ut deprecetur, ut
supplicet, ut medeatur; ut a proposito declinet aliquantum; ut optet, ut exsecretur; ut fiat eis apud
139 quos dicet familiaris. Atque alias etiam dicendi
quasi virtutes sequetur: brevitatem, si res petet;
saepe etiam rem dicendo subiciet oculis; saepe

---

[1] ut utatur *cod. Quint.*, *A*, utatur *AL*.

---

[a] *Descriptio* or *notatio*, ἠθοποιΐα, διατύπωσις: Cic.
Topica 83; *Ad Heren.* 4. 63.
[b] *Conformatio*, *prosopopoeia*, προσωποποιΐα: Cic. *De
Orat.* 3. 205; *Ad Heren.* 4. 66.
[c] *Aversio*, ἀποστροφή: Quint. 9. 2, 38.
[d] *Ad hilaritatem impulsio*, χαριεντισμός: Cic. *De Orat.*
3. 205.
[e] *Anteoccupatio*, προκατάληψις: Cic. *De Orat.* 3. 205.
[f] *Similitudo*, παραβολή: *Ad Heren.* 4. 59.
[g] *Exemplum*, παράδειγμα: Cic. *De Orat.* 3. 205.
[h] *Distributio*, διαίρεσις: Cic. *De Orat.* 3. 203; *Ad
Heren.* 4. 47. This differs from *divisio*, § 137, which means
outlining the topics of the speech. Here the reference is to
such instances as Cic. *Pro Milone* 20, where the general
idea that the community is in sorrow is broken up into six
parts: luget senatus, maeret equester ordo, tota civitas con-
fecta senio est, squalent municipia, afflictantur coloniae, agri
denique ipsi . . . desiderant.
[i] *Interpellantis coercitio*: Quint. 9. 2, 2.
[j] *Reticentia*, παρασιώπησις, παράλειψις: Aquila 24. 8.

portray the talk and ways of men *a*; he will make
mute objects speak *b*; he will divert the attention of
the audience from the point at issue *c*; he will
frequently provoke merriment and laughter *d*; he
will reply to some point which he sees is likely to be
brought up *e*; he will use similes *f* and examples *g*;
he will divide a sentence, giving part to a description of one person, part to another *h*; he will put
down interrupters *i*; he will claim to be suppres-
sing something *j*; he will warn the audience to
be on their guard *k*; he will take the liberty to
speak somewhat boldly *l*; he will even fly into a
passion *m* and protest violently *n*; he will plead
and entreat and soothe the audience *o*; he will
digress briefly *p*; he will pray *q* and curse *r*; he will
put himself on terms of intimacy with his audience.*s*
Moreover he will aim at other desirable virtues, so to 139
speak, of style: brevity, if the case demands *t*; often
also by his statement of the case he will make the
scene live before our eyes *u*; he will often exaggerate

It differs from *praeteritio* in that here the remark is actually
left unsaid.

k *Comminatio*, ἀπειλή or κατάπληξις : Jul. Ruf. 43. 13 (as
emended by Halm).

l *Licentia*, παρρησία : *Ad Heren.* 4. 48.

m *Iracundia*, ἀγανάκτησις : Cic. *De Orat.* 3. 205.

n *Obiurgatio*, ἐπιτίμησις : Jul. Ruf. 61. 19.

o *Deprecatio*, προπαραίτησις, *obsecratio*, δέησις, *purgatio*,
ἐπιθεράπευσις : Cic. *De Orat.* 3. 205.

p *Declinatio* : defined by Cic. *De Orat.* 3. 205, as not
superior illa digressio.

q *Optatio*, εὐχή : Cic. *De Orat.* 3. 205.

r *Exsecratio*, ἀρά : Cic. *De Orat.* 3. 205.

s *Conciliatio*, εὐνοίας παρασκευή : Cic. *De Orat.* 3. 205.

t *Brevitas*, συντομία : *Ad Heren.* 4. 68.

u *Imaginatio*, ἐνάργεια : Anon. *De schem. dianoeas*, Halm,
Rhet. Lat. Min. 71. 1.

supra feret quam fieri possit ; significatio saepe
erit maior quam oratio ; saepe hilaritas, saepe vitae
naturarumque imitatio. Hoc in genere—nam quasi
silvam vides—omnis eluceat oportet eloquentiae
magnitudo.

140 XLI. Sed haec nisi collocata et quasi structa et nexa
verbis ad eam laudem quam volumus aspirare non
possunt. De quo cum mihi deinceps viderem esse
dicendum, etsi movebant iam me illa quae supra
dixeram, tamen eis quae secuntur perturbabar
magis. Occurrebat enim posse reperiri non in-
vidos solum quibus referta sunt omnia, sed fautores
etiam laudum mearum, qui non censerent eius viri
esse, de cuius meritis tanta senatus iudicia fecisset
comprobante populo Romano quanta de nullo, de
artificio dicendi litteris tam multa mandare. Quibus
si nihil aliud responderem nisi me M. Bruto negare
roganti noluisse, iusta esset excusatio, cum et
amicissimo et praestantissimo viro et recta et honesta
141 petenti satis facere voluissem. Sed si profitear[1]—
quod utinam possem !—me studiosis dicendi praecepta et quasi vias quae ad eloquentiam ferrent
traditurum, quis tandem id iustus rerum existimator
reprehenderet ? Nam quis unquam dubitabit quin
in re publica nostra primas eloquentia tenuerit
semper urbanis pacatisque rebus, secundas iuris

---

[1] profitear *L :* profiteatur *A,* profiterer *Ernesti.*

---

[a] *Superlatio,* ὑπερβολή : *Ad Heren.* 4. 44.
[b] *Significatio,* ἔμφασις : *Ad Heren.* 4. 67.
[c] A repetition of χαριεντισμός : see above, p. 412, note *d.*
[d] Apparently a repetition of *descriptio,* above, p. 412, note *a.*
[e] §§ 36 and 75.

a statement above what could actually occur [a] ; his language will often have a significance deeper than his actual words [b] ; there will be passages in a lighter vein, [c] and a portrayal of life and manners. [d] In the employment of resources like these—you see what a mass of material is available—all the brilliance of style should be employed.

But these figures can win the praise at which we 140 aim only by being properly arranged, and, as it were, bound together into a neat structure of words. When I consider that I must next speak about this matter, I am disturbed, partly by the considerations noted above, [e] but more so by the following. For the thought occurred to me that there might be found, not only envious men—and the world is full of them—but even admirers of my success, who will think that it ill becomes one whose achievements have been praised more highly than those of any other man by the senate with the full approval of the Roman people to write so much about the technique [f] of oratory. If I had no answer to make to these except that I am unwilling to refuse the request of Marcus Brutus, this would be a sufficient excuse ; I should be granting the just and honourable request of a very dear friend and a most distinguished man. But if I were to profess that I 141 would instruct students of oratory, and explain to them the roads which lead to eloquence—I only wish I could !—what reasonable critic would find fault with me ? Will anyone ever doubt that in peaceful civil life eloquence has always held the chief place in our state, and jurisprudence has been of secondary

[f] *Cf. De Orat.* 1. 146 : sic esse non eloquentiam ex artificio, sed artificium ex eloquentia natum.

scientia ? Cum in altera gratiae, gloriae, praesidi plurimum esset, in altera persecutionum cautionumque praeceptio ; quae quidem ipsa auxilium ab eloquentia saepe peteret, ea vero repugnante 142 vix suas regiones finisque defenderet. Cur igitur ius civile docere semper pulchrum fuit hominumque clarissimorum discipulis floruerunt domus; ad dicendum si quis acuat aut adiuvet in eo iuventutem, vituperetur ? Nam si vitiosum est dicere ornate, pellatur omnino e civitate eloquentia ; sin ea non modo eos ornat penes quos est, sed etiam universam rem publicam, cur aut discere turpe est quod scire honestum est aut quod nosse pulcherrimum est id non gloriosum est docere ?

143   XLII. " At alterum factitatum est, alterum novum." Fateor ; sed utriusque rei causa est. Alteros enim respondentis audire sat erat, ut ei qui docerent nullum sibi ad eam rem tempus ipsi seponerent, sed eodem tempore et discentibus satis facerent[1] et consulentibus ; alteri cum domesticum tempus in cognoscendis componendisque causis, forense in agendis, relicum in sese ipsis reficiendis omne consumerent, quem habebant instituendi aut docendi locum ? Atque haud scio an plerique nostrorum oratorum ingenio[2] plus valuerint quam doctrina ; itaque illi dicere melius quam praecipere, nos contra fortasse possumus.[3]

---

[1] et discentibus id est studiosis ut satis faceret *A*.
[2] ingenio *L*, contra atque nos ingenio *A*.
[3] possumus melius docere *f, Jahn*.

importance ? The reason is that the former brings with it a large measure of popularity, glory and power ; the latter brings instruction in prosecution of suits and in securing bonds and warranties. Jurisprudence does indeed often ask aid from eloquence, and when opposed by eloquence can scarcely defend its own province and territory. Why, then, has it 142 always been honourable to teach civil law, and why have the houses of distinguished jurisconsults been thronged with pupils, while a man would be severely criticized if he trained young men for oratory or helped them in this ? If it is wrong to speak ornately, let us expel eloquence entirely from the state ; but if it adorns not only its possessor but the whole community, why is it shameful to learn what it is honourable to know ? Why is it not glorious to teach that which it is most excellent to know ?

"But the one is customary," you will say ; " the 143 other is a new thing." I grant the truth of the objection, but there is a reason for both facts. For all that the student of law needed was to listen to the jurisconsult as he rendered his opinions, so that the teachers set aside no time for teaching as such, but were able to satisfy both students and clients at the same time. In the case of the orators, their hours at home were spent in studying and preparing cases, their time in the forum was devoted to pleading, all the rest of their day was given to recruiting their strength ; hence what time had they left for training or teaching ? Moreover, I am inclined to think that most Roman orators had more talent than training ; consequently they were better able to speak than to lay down precepts ; but with us perhaps just the contrary is true.

144　　" At dignitatem docere[1] non habet." Certe, si
quasi in ludo ; sed si monendo, si cohortando, si
percontando, si communicando, si interdum etiam una
legendo audiendo, nescio cur non docendo[2] etiam aliquid aliquando si[3] possis meliores facere, cur nolis.
An quibus verbis sacrorum alienatio fiat docere honestum est,[4] quibus ipsa sacra retineri defendique
possint non honestum est ?

145　　" At ius profitentur etiam qui nesciunt ; eloquentiam autem illi ipsi qui consecuti sunt tamen ea
se valere dissimulant." Propterea quod prudentia
hominibus grata est, lingua suspecta. Num igitur
aut latere eloquentia potest aut id quod dissimulat
effugit aut est periculum ne quis putet in magna arte
et gloriosa turpe esse docere alios id quod ipsi fuerit

146 honestissimum discere ? Ac fortasse ceteri tectiores ;
ego semper me didicisse prae me tuli. Quid enim ?
Possem, cum et afuissem domo adulescens et horum
studiorum causa maria transissem et doctissimis
hominibus referta domus esset et aliquae fortasse
inessent in sermone nostro doctrinarum notae cumque
vulgo scripta nostra legerentur, dissimulare me didicisse ? Quid erat cur[5] ruberem[6] nisi quod parum
fortasse profeceram ?

XLIII. Quod cum ita sit, tamen ea quae supra dicta

[1] docere *A*, melius docere *L*.
[2] docendo *πf*, dicendo *AL*.
[3] si *P⁵γ*, om. *AL*.
[4] est *A*, est, ut est *L*.
[5] erat cur *omisit A*.
[6] ruberem *Kroll :* probarem *AL*.

---

a *Sacrorum alienatio* was the act of renouncing one's
obligations to observe the *sacra gentilicia* when one was
adopted into another family. As these *sacra* were a part

"But," you will say, "there is no distinction in teach- 144
ing." Of course not, if you teach like a schoolmaster;
but if by advice, by exhortation, by inquiry, by sharing
your knowledge, if at times even by reading aloud to
them or listening to their reading, if you could really
improve men by some teaching of this sort, I cannot
understand why you should decline to do so. Surely
it is honourable to teach the formula for surrendering
one's rights; is it not equally honourable to teach the
means of retaining and defending these rights? [a]

"But," you will say, "even men who are ignorant of 145
the law profess themselves jurisconsults, whereas the
very men who have attained eloquence nevertheless
pretend that they have no ability in it." The reason
is that practical knowledge is pleasing to men, but a
clever tongue suspect. For all that, can eloquence be
hidden, or does what it tries to conceal really escape
notice, or is there any danger that anyone will think
in connexion with this great and glorious art that it is
a disgrace to teach others what it was highly honourable for himself to learn? Others may perhaps be 146
more cautious; I have always been perfectly frank in
acknowledging that I have been a student. How could
I conceal the fact, when I left home as a youth and
crossed the seas to engage in these studies; when my
house was filled with learned men, my conversation
bore some marks perhaps of learning, and my books
were in general circulation? Why should I blush,
except, perhaps, because I had not made enough
progress?

This may be true; still there was more distinction

of one's rights as a Roman citizen, the phrase *sacra defendere*
means defend a citizen from a charge which would involve
forfeiture of these rights. *Cf. Legg. 2. 47.*

sunt plus in disputando quam ea de quibus dicendum
147 est dignitatis habuerunt. De verbis enim com-
ponendis et de syllabis propemodum dinumerandis
et demetiendis loquemur. Quae etiamsi sunt, sicuti
mihi videntur, necessaria tamen fiunt magnificentius
quam docentur. Est id omnino verum, at[1] proprie
in hoc dicitur. Nam omnium magnarum artium
sicut arborum altitudo nos delectat, radices stirpes-
que non item ; sed esse illa sine his non potest.
Me autem sive pervolgatissimus ille versus, qui
vetat[2]

> artem pudere proloqui quam factites,

dissimulare non sinit quin delecter, sive tuum studium
hoc a me volumen expressit, tamen eis quos aliquid
148 reprehensuros suspicabar respondendum fuit. Quodsi
ea quae dixi non ita essent, quis tamen se tam durum
agrestemque praeberet, qui hanc mihi non daret
veniam, ut cum meae forenses artes et actiones
publicae concidissent, non me aut desidiae, quod
facere non possum, aut maestitiae, cui resisto, potius
quam litteris dederem ? Quae quidem me antea in
iudicia atque in curiam deducebant, nunc oblectant
domi ; nec vero talibus modo rebus qualis hic liber
continet, sed multo etiam gravioribus et maioribus ;
quae si erunt perfectae, profecto forensibus nostris
rebus etiam domesticae[3] litterae respondebunt. Sed
ad institutam disputationem revertamur.

[1] at *Schenkl :* ut *A*, sed *L*.
[2] vetat *A*, vel ad *FO*[1], vel *O*[2]*P*.
[3] forensibus nostris rebus etiam domesticae *L*, maximis
rebus forensibus nostris et externis inclusae et domesticae *A*.

[a] Ribbeck[3], *Com. frag.* p. 137, *v.* 30.
[b] He refers to the series of philosophical works which
occupied the next two years.

in discussing the previous topics than those which are to follow. I am going to speak about the 147 collocation of words and almost about the counting and measuring of syllables. Even if these rules are necessary, as I think, still there is more glory in using them than in teaching them. That is true in general, and particularly true of this case. For it is true of all important arts as of trees, that their lofty height pleases us, but their roots and stems do not to the same degree ; yet the latter are essential to the former. As for me, however, whether it is that well-known verse forbidding to

> Blush to own the art you practise [a]

that will not allow me to conceal my delight, or it is your desire which has extorted this volume from me, nevertheless I have felt obliged to make reply to those who I suspected would find something to criticize. But even if the facts were not as I have 148 stated them, who would be hard or unfeeling enough to refuse me the favour of devoting myself to letters, now that my forensic practice and my public career have fallen in ruins, rather than to idleness, which is impossible for me, or to grief, against which I put up a bold front ? Literature was once my companion in the court and senate house ; now it is my joy at home ; nor am I busied merely with such matters as form the subject of this book, but with even greater and weightier themes.[b] If these are brought to completion, I am sure my forensic efforts will find a proper counterpart even in the literary labours of my seclusion. But we must now return to the discussion which we have begun.[c]

[c] In § 140.

149 XLIV. Collocabuntur igitur verba, aut ut inter se
quam aptissime cohaereant extrema cum primis
eaque sint quam suavissimis vocibus, aut ut forma
ipsa concinnitasque verborum conficiat orbem suum,
aut ut comprehensio numerose et apte cadat. Atque
illud primum videamus quale sit—quod vel maxime
desiderat diligentiam—ut fiat quasi structura quaedam nec tamen fiat operose ; nam esset cum infinitus
tum puerilis labor ; quod apud Lucilium scite
exagitat in Albucio Scaevola :

> quam lepide λέξεις compostae ut tesserulae omnes
> arte pavimento atque emblemate vermiculato !

150 Nolo haec tam minuta constructio appareat ; sed
tamen stilus exercitatus efficiet facile formulam[1]
componendi. Nam ut in legendo oculus sic animus
in dicendo prospiciet quid sequatur, ne extremorum
verborum cum insequentibus primis concursus aut
hiulcas voces efficiat aut asperas. Quamvis enim sua-
ves gravesve sententiae tamen, si inconditis[2] verbis
efferuntur, offendent auris, quarum est iudicium
superbissimum. Quod quidem Latina lingua sic
observat, nemo ut tam rusticus sit quin[3] vocalis

---

[1] formulam *A*, hanc viam *L*, formam ac viam *Reid.*
[2] inconditis *L*, incondite positis *A.*
[3] quin *AL*, qui *vulg.*

The arrangement of words in the sentence has 149
three ends in view : (1) that final syllables may fit the
following initial syllables as neatly as possible, and
that the words may have the most agreeable sounds ;
(2) that the very form and symmetry of the words
may produce their own rounded period ; (3) that the
period may have an appropriate rhythmical cadence.
Let us consider the nature of the first ; it requires
great care to see that there is a joining or structure,
as it were, and yet that it is not carried out with too
great exactness ; the labour would then be endless
and silly. That is the point in the style of Albucius
which Lucilius makes Scaevola satirize wittily in
these lines :

How charmingly he *fait ses phrases*, set in order like the lines
Of mosaic in a pavement, and his inlaid work he twines.[a]

I would not have the structure obtrude itself in such 150
trivialities ; but a practised pen will nevertheless
easily find the method of composition. For as the
eye looks ahead in reading, so in speaking the mind
will foresee what is to follow, so that the juxtaposition of final syllables with initial may not cause
harsh or " gaping "[b] sounds. For however agreeable or important thoughts may be, still if they are
expressed in words which are ill arranged, they will
offend the ear, which is very fastidious in its judgement. The Latin language, indeed, is so careful
on this point that no one is so illiterate as to be un-

[a] Lucilius 84-85 (Marx); *Remains of Old Latin*, iii. p. 28.
Tr. by Wilkins, on *De Oratore* 3. 171.
[b] The technical term for the clash of two vowels is *hiatus*,
" gaping."

151 nolit coniungere. In quo quidam Theopompum
etiam reprehendunt, quod eas litteras tanto opere
fugerit, etsi idem magister eius Isocrates [1]; at non
Thucydides, ne ille quidem haud [2] paulo maior scriptor
Plato nec solum in eis sermonibus qui διάλογοι dicuntur, ubi etiam de industria id faciendum fuit, sed in
populari oratione, qua mos est Athenis laudari in
contione eos qui sint in proeliis interfecti; quae sic
probata est, ut eam quotannis, ut scis, illo die recitari
necesse sit. In ea est crebra ista vocum concursio,
quam magna ex parte ut vitiosam fugit Demosthenes.

152 XLV. Sed Graeci viderint; nobis ne si cupiamus
quidem distrahere voces conceditur. Indicant orationes illae ipsae horridulae Catonis, indicant omnes [3]
poetae praeter eos qui, ut versum facerent, saepe
hiabant, ut Naevius:

> vos, qui accolitis Histrum fluvium atque algidam

et ibidem:

> quam nunquam vobis Grai atque barbari . . .

[1] Isocrates fecerat *A*, al. fecerat *in marg.* *O*[2].
[2] haud *βf*[3], aut *L*, *omisit A*.
[3] illae . . . omnes *omisit A*.

---

a The question of the pronunciation of Latin words in a
sentence is still debated. It would seem from this passage
that in prose as in poetry the combination of final vowel
plus an initial vowel was not pronounced as two vowels.
Cicero is not using exact, scientific language, and it is
therefore impossible to prove from his words whether the
final vowel was entirely suppressed (*elision*) or blended with
the following vowel (*synaloepha*). The latter method was
probably used by the Romans. I follow Heerdegen's
interpretation of *coniungere voces* in his edition of the *Orator,*

willing to run vowels together.[a]   In this connexion 151
some go so far as to criticize Theopompus for too
careful avoidance of such vowels, although the same is
true of his master Isocrates.[b]   But Thucydides did
not avoid such hiatus, nor did that much greater
author, Plato, either in his dialogues, where it was
to be introduced intentionally,[c] or in that public
oration which it is customary to deliver at Athens in
an assembly in honour of those fallen in battle ;
which was so popular that it had to be read aloud
every year, as you know, on that day.[d]   In this
there is frequent clash of vowels, which Demosthenes generally avoided as vicious.

But let the Greeks see to their own practice ; we 152
are not allowed to make a pause between vowels,
even if we should wish to do so.   This is shown by
those famous though slightly uncouth speeches of
Cato ; it is shown by all the poets save those who
for metrical reasons often permitted hiatus ; Naevius,
for example.

     vos qu*i* *a*ccolitis Histrum fluvium atque algidam,[e]
and
     quam numquam vobis Gra*i* *a*tque barbari[e] . . .

---

p. xxxiv : unam vocalem post alteram ita deinceps pro-
nuntiare, ut integer suus cuique sonus sit.

  [b] Isocrates and his pupils, among whom Theopompus the
historian was one of the most eminent, scrupulously avoided
the juxtaposition of final and initial vowel.

  [c] Avoidance of hiatus was an artificiality which would be
unnatural in the colloquial style of dialogue.

  [d] He refers to the funeral oration embedded in the
Menexenus of Plato.

  [e] Naevius 61, 62 R.³.   *Remains*, ii. pp. 122, 150.
                        Ye who dwell
By Ister's water and the region chill
Which ne'er to you have foreigners and Greeks . . .

at Ennius semel[1] : " Scipio invicte " et quidem nos :

hoc motu radiantis etesiae in vada ponti.

153 Hoc idem nostri saepius non tulissent, quod Graeci laudare etiam solent. Sed quid ego vocalis ? Sine vocalibus saepe levitatis[2] causa contrahebant, ut ita dicerent : multi' modis, in vas'[3] argenteis, palm' et[4] crinibus, tecti' fractis. Quid vero licentius quam quod hominum etiam nomina contrahebant, quo essent aptiora ? Nam ut duellum bellum et duis[5] bis, sic Duellium[6] eum qui Poenos classe devicit Bellium nominaverunt, cum superiores appellati essent semper Duelli. Quin etiam verba saepe contrahuntur non usus causa sed aurium. Quo modo enim vester Axilla Ala factus est nisi fuga litterae vastioris ? Quam litteram etiam e maxillis et taxillis et vexillo et pauxillo consuetudo elegans Latini sermonis 154 evellit. Libenter etiam copulando verba iungebant, ut sodes pro si audes, sis pro si vis. Iam in uno

[1] semel *L*, saepe *A*.
[2] levitatis *Kroll* : brevitatis *AL*.
[3] in vas' *Heerdegen* : vivas *L*, etuas *A*.
[4] palmet *A*, palma et *L*, palmi' *Ribbeck*.
[5] duis ρ[2], dus *A*, divis *FP*, duus *O*[1], buus *O*[2].
[6] duellum *A*, divillium *FP*[2], divellium *P*[1], duulium *O*[1], duellium *O*[2], Duillium *f*[2], *Heerdegen*.

[a] Vahlen[2], p. 213 frag. 3, *Remains*, i. p. 396. Scipio invincible.
[b] . . . So move Etesian winds that fall
Upon the waters of the gleaming sea.

From Cicero's translation of the *Phaenomena* of Aratus. The line in the original suggested the elision (151) :

τῆμος καὶ κελάδοντες ᾿Ετησίαι εὐρέι πόντῳ.

[c] Such shortenings as *etesiae in* are common in Greek hexameter verse.

But Ennius uses it only once; Scipi*o* invicte *a*;
another example can be cited from my own verse :

> hoc motu radiantis etesi*ae* in vada ponti.*b*

Our poets would not have permitted this very often, **153**
but the Greeks are accustomed even to praise it.*c*
But why confine the discussion to vowels ? Con-
sonants were frequently omitted in contractions,
for greater smoothness, as, for example *multi' modis*
(for *multis modis*), *in vas' argenteis* (for *in vasis argenteis*), *palm' et crinibus* (for *palmis et crinibus*), *tecti'
fractis* (for *tectis fractis*). What greater freedom
could be taken with language than to shorten men's
names to make them more compact. Thus, as *duellum* becomes *bellum*, and *duis*, *bis*, so they called
that Duellius who defeated the Carthaginians at
sea, Bellius, though all his ancestors had been called
Duellii. Moreover words are often contracted, not
for convenience, but merely for the sake of sound.
How was the name of your ancestor changed from
Axilla *d* to Ala except from a desire to avoid a harsh-
sounding letter ? The same letter is removed by
refined Latin speech from *maxillae, taxilli, vexillum*
and *pauxillum.e* They were also very ready to **154**
combine words by blending, *e.g. sodes* for *si audes*, and
sis for *si vis*. You may even find three words in

d Brutus's mother Servilia was descended from C. Servilius
Ahala. This is the normal spelling of the name which may
have been pronounced Ala in Cicero's time. Ala, " wing," is
from **aksla*, and axilla is a diminutive from the same
stem, but they are not related to Ahala. This etymology
was, however, not Cicero's own : the Fasti Consulares
Capitolini has the name Axilla as trib. mil. for 418 B.C.

e Giving malae, tali, velum and paulum. The forms with
" x " are really diminutives and not originals of the short
forms.

capsis tria verba sunt. Ain pro aisne, nequire pro
non quire, malle pro magis velle, nolle pro non velle,
dein etiam saepe et exin pro deinde et pro exinde
dicimus. Quid, illud non olet unde sit, quod dicitur
cum illis, cum autem nobis non dicitur, sed nobiscum ?
Quia si ita diceretur, obscenius concurrerent litterae,
ut etiam modo, nisi autem interposuissem, con-
currissent. Ex eo est mecum et tecum, non cum te
et cum me, ut esset simile illis vobiscum atque
nobiscum.

155   XLVI. Atque etiam a quibusdam sero iam emen-
datur antiquitas, qui haec reprehendunt. Nam pro
deum atque hominum fidem deorum aiunt. Ita
credo hoc illi nesciebant : an dabat hanc licentiam
consuetudo ? Itaque idem poeta qui inusitatius
contraxerat :

patris mei meum factum pudet

pro meorum factorum et

texitur, exitium examen rapit

pro exitiorum, non dicit liberum, ut plerique lo-

---

    [a] For *cape si vis*. This is probably wrong. *Capsis* is a
subjunctive on an s-aorist stem. Vollmer, however (*Glotta*, i.
1909, p. 116) believes it is from a syncopated imperative
cap + si vis.

    [b] *nequire* is formed not from *non quire* but from another
negative form *ne + quire*. *Nolle* shows a similar phenomenon.

    [c] *cum nobis* would have been pronounced by assimilation
as *cunnobis*, giving the word *cunno* with unpleasant con-
notation.

    [d] This paragraph relates to the controversy between the

one,—*capsis.*[a] We say *ain* for *aisne, nequire* foɪ *non quire,*[b] *malle* for *magis velle, nolle* for *non velle*, and *dein* and *exin* frequently for *deinde* and *exinde*. Is it not perfectly plain why we say *cum illis*, but use *nobiscum* rather than *cum nobis*? If the latter were used the letters would coalesce and produce an obscene meaning, as they would have done in this sentence unless I had placed *autem* between *cum* and *nobis.*[c] From that come *mecum* and *tecum*, used rather than *cum me* and *cum te*, so as to resemble *vobiscum* and *nobiscum.*

But certain people are beginning late in the day to emend the speech of our fathers, and they criticize this irregularity.[d] Instead of *deum* in the phrase *pro deum atque hominum fidem* they use the form *deorum.* I suppose our fathers did not know about that; or is it not true that usage sanctioned this licence? So the same poet who used the exceptional contraction in the line [e]

patris mei meum factum pudet

instead of saying *meorum factorum*, and again in [f]

texitur, exitium examen rapit

instead of *exitiorum*, does not say *liberum* as many of

155

" Anomalists," who took usage as the guide to correctness of speech, and the " Analogists," who endeavoured to formulate rules and remove the irregularities from the language. The particular point here discussed is the survival of the old form *-um* for the genitive plural of the second declension.

[e] Ennius, *Alexander* 59 V.[2], *Remains*, i. p. 240.

I am ashamed before my father of what I have done.

[f] *Ibid.* 66 V.[2], *Remains*, i. p. 242.

(A fleet) is built; it carries a swarm of deaths.

quimur, cum cupidos liberum aut in liberum loco dicimus, sed ut isti volunt :

> neque tu meum[1] unquam in gremium extollas liberorum
> ex te genus

et idem :

> namque Aesculapi liberorum.

At ille alter in Chryse non solum :

> cives, antiqui amici maiorum meum

quod erat usitatum, sed durius etiam :

> consilium socii, augurium atque extum interpretes;

idemque pergit :

> postquam prodigium horriferum, portentum[2] pavos[3];

quae non sane sunt in omnibus neutris[4] usitata. nec enim dixerim tam libenter armum iudicium,— etsi est apud eundem :

> nihilne ad te de iudicio armum accidit ?—

156 quam centuriam, ut censoriae tabulae locuntur, fabrum et procum audeo dicere, non fabrorum et procorum ; planeque duorum virorum iudicium aut

[1] tu meum *Vahlen* (*cf. Il. 9. 453*), tuum *A*, tu *L*.
[2] portentum *vulg.*, portentu *AL*.
[3] pavos *vulg.*, pavor *A M²*, pavox *FO¹*, pavor *O²*, panox *P*, panor *M¹*.
[4] omnibus neutris *L*, hominibus neutriq. *A*, omnibus nominibus neutris *Heerdegen*.

---

[a] Ennius, *Phoenix* 299 V.², *Remains*, i. p. 332.
> Ne'er to my bosom may you raise
> A son by you begot.
[b] *Ibid. Hectoris Lytra* 165 V.², *Remains*, i. p. 278.
> For of Aesculapius' sons. . .
[c] Pacuvius 80 R.³, *Remains*, ii. p. 200.
> Ye townsmen, ancient lovers of our line.

us do in the phrases *cupidos liberum* and *in liberum loco*, but as they, the Analogists, demand [a] :

> neque tu meum umquam in gremium extollas liberorum
> ex te genus

and again [b]

> namque Aesculapi liberorum.

But another poet [c] in the *Chryses*, not only says :

> cives, antiqui amici maiorum meum

which was customary, but somewhat harshly [d] :

> consilium socii, augurium atque extum interpretes:

and then continues [e] :

> postquam prodigium horriferum, portentum pavos;

but this genitive is certainly not usual in all neuter nouns. For I should never feel as free to say *armum iudicium*—although it is found in the same poet [f] :

> nihilne ad te de iudicio armum accidit ?—

as I would to say *centuria fabrum et procum*, using the language of the census records,[g] rather than *fabrorum et procorum*. I certainly never say *duorum virorum*

---

[d] *Ibid.* 81 R.[3], *Remains*, ii. p. 200.

> Comrades in counsels and interpreters
> Of auguries and victims.

[e] *Ibid.* 82 R.[3], *Remains*, ii. p. 200.

> When there came the portent's terror and the dread
> Of prodigies horrific,

[f] *Ibid.* 34 R.[3], *Remains*, ii. p. 176.

> Has no word reached your ears
> About the judgement of the arms ?

[g] The census of Servius Tullius.

trium virorum capitalium aut decem virorum
stlitibus[1] iudicandis dico nunquam. Atqui[2] dixit
Accius :

> video sepulcra dua duorum corporum

idemque

> mulier una duom[3] virum.

Quid verum sit intellego ; sed alias ita loquor ut
concessum est, ut hoc vel pro deum dico vel pro
deorum, alias ut necesse est, cum trium virum, non
virorum, et sestertium nummum, non sestertiorum
nummorum, quod in his consuetudo varia non est.

157   XLVII. Quid quod sic loqui : nosse, iudicasse
vetant, novisse iubent et iudicavisse ? Quasi vero
nesciamus in hoc genere et plenum verbum recte
dici et imminutum usitate. Itaque utrumque
Terentius :

> eho tu, cognatum[4] tuom[5] non noras?

post idem

> Stilponem,[6] inquam, noveras.

Sient[7] plenum est, sint[8] imminutum ; licet utare
utroque. Ergo ibidem :

---

[1] stlitibus *Muretus* (*e libro vetere*), litibus *AL*.
[2] atqui *vulg.*, et qui *L*, quid *A*, et quid *Heerdegen*.
[3] duom *Heerdegen :* duum *AL*.
[4] cognatum *AL*, sobrinum *Terence*.
[5] tuom *Heerdegen :* tuum *AL*.
[6] Stilponem *Donatus :* stilionem *F*, Stilbonem *OP*, stili-
ponem *A*, Stilphonem *εf, Terence*.
[7] sient *Heerdegen :* siet *L*, sin *A*.
[8] sint *Heerdegen :* sient *FO*, scient *P*, sin *A*.

iudicium, or *trium virorum capitalium,* or *decem virorum stlitibus iudicandis.* But what does Accius say? [a]

> video sepulcra duo duorum corporum

and again

> mulier una duom virum. [b]

I know what is correct, but sometimes I avail myself of the variation in usage, saying either *pro deum* or *pro deorum*; sometimes I follow necessity, saying *trium virum,* not *virorum,* and *sestertium nummum,* not *sestertiorum nummorum,* because in these cases there is no variation in usage.

Well, they forbid us to say *nosse, iudicasse,* and bid 157 us say *novisse* and *iudicavisse,* as if we did not know in this case that the full form is correct, and the shorter form customary. Terence therefore uses both [c]:

> eho tu, cognatum tuom non noras?

and later

> Stilponem, inquam, noveras. [d]

Sient is the full form, *sint* the shorter; you may use either. Therefore in the same author [e]:

[a] Accius 655 f. R.³, *Remains,* ii. p. 574.

> Two sepulchres I see, and bodies two they hold.

[b] Of husbands two, one wife.
[c] *Phormio* 384, 390.

> Sirrah, didst not know thy kinsman?

[d] You knew Stilpo, I say.
[e] A mistake. The author is unknown. Ribbeck³, *Trag. frag. inc.* 194 f., *Remains,* ii. p. 618.

> And afterwards, when these are dearly lost
> They learn how dear these were to them,
> And how great sovereignties must be retained.

quae quam sint cara[1] post carendo[2] intellegunt,
quamque attinendi magni dominatus sient.

Nec vero reprehenderim "scripsere alii rem" et
scripserunt esse verius sentio, sed consuetudini
auribus indulgenti libenter obsequor.

idem campus habet

inquit Ennius, et in templis : "IDEM PROBAVIT";
at isdem[3] erat verius, nec tamen eisdem[4] ut opimius ;
male sonabat isdem[5] : impetratum est a consuetudine
ut peccare suavitatis causa liceret. Et posmeridianas[6]
quadrigas quam postmeridianas quadriiugas[7] libentius
dixerim et mehercule quam mehercules. Non scire
quidem barbarum iam videtur, nescire dulcius.
158 Ipsum meridiem cur non medidiem ? Credo, quod
erat insuavius. Insuavissima praepositio est af,[8]
quae nunc tantum in accepti tabulis manet ac ne
his[9] quidem omnium, in reliquo sermone mutata est ;
nam amovit dicimus et abegit et abstulit, ut iam
nescias a'ne[10] verum sit an ab an abs.[11] Quid, quod
etiam abfugit[12] turpe visum est et abfer[13] noluerunt,
aufugit et[14] aufer maluerunt ? Quae praepositio

quae quam *sint* cara post carendo intellegunt,
quamque attinendi magni dominatus *sient.*

I should not criticize the form "scripsere" in *scripsere
alii rem,*[a] yet I feel that *scripserunt* is more correct,
but I am glad to follow custom which favours the
ear. Ennius says

idem campus habet [b]

and on temples we find *Idem probavit.*[c] But *isdem*
would be more correct, not *eisdem,* however : the
sound is too broad. *Isdem* had an unpleasant sound,
and so custom granted permission to err for the sake
of agreeable effect. Moreover I would rather say
posmeridianas quadrigas than *postmeridianas quadriiugas,* and *mehercule* than *mehercules. Non scire* seems
barbarous nowadays : *nescire* is pleasanter. Why is 158
meridiem itself not *medidiem* ? I suppose because it
would be unpleasant. There is a very harsh-sounding
preposition *af* which is now in use only in accounting,
and not universally there ; in ordinary speech it has
been changed ; we say *a-movit* and *ab-egit,* and *abstulit,* so that you might fail to realize whether *a* or *ab*
or *abs* is the correct form. Also it may be added that
ab-fugit seemed disagreeable and they disliked *ab-fer,*
and preferred *aufugit* and *aufer.* This preposition

---

[a] Ennius, *Annals* 213-214 V.[2], *Remains,* i. p. 82. Others
have written of the matter.
[b] Ennius, *Annals* 477 V.[2], *Remains,* i. p. 52. The same
plain holds.
[c] The same (official) approved. Cicero is unusually brief
here, and as a result there is a certain obscurity. He means
to say that the original form of the word was *isdem* (the
spelling *eisdem,* which he rejects, uses *ei* to represent long *i,*
but the *i* of *isdem* is short), and that this was changed to
idem for the sake of euphony.

praeter haec duo verba nullo alio in verbo reperietur.
Noti erant et navi et nari, quibus cum in praeponi
oporteret, dulcius visum est ignotos, ignavos, ignaros
dicere, quam ut veritas postulabat. Ex usu dicunt
et e re publica, quod in altero vocalis excipiebat, in
altero esset asperitas, nisi litteram sustulisses, ut
exegit, edixit ; refecit, rettulit, reddidit : adiuncti
verbi prima littera praepositionem[1] commutavit, ut
subegit, summutavit, sustulit.

159 XLVIII. Quid, in verbis iunctis quam scite insipientem non insapientem, inicum non inaecum, tricipitem
non tricapitem, concisum non concaesum. Ex quo
quidam pertisum etiam volunt, quod eadem consuetudo non probavit. Quid vero hoc elegantius,
quod non fit natura sed quodam instituto : indoctus
dicimus brevi prima littera, insanus producta, in-
humanus brevi, infelix longa et, ne multis, quibus in
verbis eae primae litterae sunt quae in sapiente atque felice, in[2] producte dicitur, in ceteris omnibus
breviter ; itemque composuit, consuevit, concrepuit,
confecit.[3] Consule veritatem : reprehendet ; refer
ad auris : probabunt ; quaere cur ita sit[4] : dicent
iuvare ; voluptati autem aurium morigerari debet
160 oratio. Quin ego ipse, cum scirem ita maiores
locutos ut nusquam nisi in vocali aspiratione uterentur, loquebar sic ut pulcros, Cetegos, triumpos,

[1] prima littera praepositionem *Maioragius :* primam litteram praepositio *AL.*   [2] in *addidit Stangl.*
[3] confecit *L, Gell.,* consuluit *A.*
[4] sit *Gell. :* se *AL.*

---

[a] Cicero is in error here ; the original form of the three
words showed the initial *g—gnoti, gnavi, gnari.*
[b] Probably the original form of the prefix was *red-* ; *cf.*
red-ire. Rettulit is from *re-t(e)tulit.*

will be found nowhere except in these two words. We had the forms *noti, navi* and *nari* ; when the syllable *in* was prefixed, it sounded better to say *ignoti, ignavi, ignari,* than to use the true form.[a] They say *ex usu* and *e re publica* because in the first phrase the preposition is followed by a vowel ; in the second there would be a certain roughness unless the *x* were dropped ; a parallel case is *exegit, edixit.* In the words *refecit, rettulit, reddidit* [b] the initial letter of the verb has changed the preposition, as is also the case in *subegit, summutavit, sustulit.*

Then the matter of compound words : how nicely 159 *insipientem* is substituted for *insapientem, inicum* for *inaecum, tricipitem* for *tricapitem, concisum* for *concaesum.* By analogy with the latter some desire to say *pertisum* which is not approved by usage.[c] Could there be a nicer discrimination than that shown in the following principle, established not by nature but by custom ? We say *indoctus* with the first letter short, *insanus,* with the first letter long, *ĭnhumanus,* but *īnfelix.* To be brief, words beginning with the initial letters of *sapiens* and *felix* lengthen the *i* in the prefix *in,* and in all other combinations it is short. Likewise *cŏmposuit, cōnsuevit, cŏncrepuit, confecit.* If you consult the strict rule of analogy, it will say this practice is wrong, but if you consult the ear, it will approve. If you ask the ear why, it will say that this is pleasant ; speech should gratify the ear. In my own case, 160 knowing that our forefathers did not use the aspirate except with a vowel,[d] I said *pulcer, Cetegus, triumpus,*

---

[c] Scipio Aemilianus said *pertisum*: Lucilius *apud* Fest. 273, Marx 964.

[d] *i.e.* only before an initial vowel, or between vowels; *humanus, nihil.*

Cartaginem[1] dicerem ; aliquando, idque sero, convicio aurium cum extorta mihi veritas esset, usum loquendi populo concessi, scientiam mihi reservavi. Orcivios tamen et Matones, Otones, Caepiones, sepulcra, coronas, lacrimas dicimus, quia per aurium iudicium licet. Burrum semper Ennius, nunquam Pyrrhum ;

vi patefecerunt Bruges,[2]

non Phryges : ipsius antiqui declarant libri. Nec enim[3] Graecam litteram adhibebant—nunc autem etiam duas—et cum Phrygum et Phrygibus dicendum esset, absurdum erat aut etiam in[4] barbaris casibus Graecam litteram adhibere aut recto casu solum Graece loqui ; tamen et Phryges et Pyrrhum aurium causa dicimus. Quin etiam, quod iam subrusticum 161 videtur, olim autem politius, eorum verborum, quorum eaedem erant postremae duae litterae quae sunt in optimus, postremam litteram detrahebant, nisi vocalis insequebatur. Ita non erat ea offensio in versibus quam nunc fugiunt poetae novi. Sic enim loquebamur :

qui est omnibu' princeps,

[1] pulchros ceteros (et cethegos *L*) triumphos carthaginem *AL*, om. *vulg.*
[2] Bruges *Victorius* : fruges *FPM*, phruges *O*, phry *A*.
[3] enim *AL*, unam *Stroux.*
[4] etiam in *Hoerner* : tam in *L*, tamen *A*.

---

[a] Instead of the more usual *pulcher, Cethegus, triumphus, Carthago.*
[b] Ennius, *Hectoris Lytra* 176 V.[2], *Remains*, i. p. 282. See also *ibid.* i. pp. 64, 100, for other examples of this form in Ennius.

The Brugians by force have broken open . . .

[c] The Greek Υ (upsilon) was at first translated by Latin *u* ;

Cartago[a] ; after a while,—a long while indeed—the reproof of the ear forced me to abandon the correct pronunciation ; I yielded to the people in the matter of usage, and kept the knowledge for myself.   However we say *Orcivius, Mato, Oto, Caepio, sepulcrum, corona, lacrima*, because the judgement of the ear permits it.   Ennius always says Burrus, never Pyrrhus ;

vi patefecerunt Bruges,[b]

(not *Phryges*) is the reading of the oldest manuscripts of the poet.   For in his day Latin had not adopted the Greek letter,[c] now they use two,[d] and since they had to say *Phrygum* and *Phrygibus*[e] the strange situation arose of using a Greek letter in a word with foreign endings, or of using the correct Greek form only in the nominative ; nevertheless we say *Phryges* and *Pyrrhum*,[f] following the dictates of the ear. Furthermore, though it now seems somewhat country- 161 fied, it was once considered refined to drop the last letter, if the word ended in the same two letters as *optimus*, unless a vowel followed.   Consequently this was not thought objectionable in verse ; now it is avoided by the " new " poets.   So we used to say :

qui est omnibu' princeps[g]

---

later the letter *y* was used for this sound.   The Greek aspirates *ph, th, ch*, were originally transferred to Latin as smooth mutes *p* (*b*), *t, c*.   [d] *y* and *z*.

[e]   The Greek forms of the genitive and dative were *Phrygon* and *Phryxi*; these would have sounded strange to Roman ears.   The nominatives *Phryx* and *Phryges* were sufficiently like Latin words to be adopted without change.

[f]   *i.e.* we are not consistent : *Phryges* is pure Greek, *Pyrrhum* uses a Greek letter and a Latin ending.

[g]   Ennius, *Ann.* 67 V.³, *Remains*, i. p. 24.   Who is chief of all.

non omnibus princeps et :

> vita illa dignu' locoque,

non dignus. Quodsi indocta consuetudo tam est
artifex suavitatis, quid ab ipsa tandem arte et doc-
162 trina postulari putamus ? Haec dixi brevius, quam
si hac de re una disputarem—est enim locus hic late
patens de natura usuque verborum—longius autem
quam instituta ratio postulabat.

XLIX. Sed quia rerum verborumque iudicium in
prudentia est, vocum autem et numerorum aures
sunt iudices, et quod illa ad intellegentiam referuntur, haec ad voluptatem, in illis ratio invenit, in
his sensus artem. Aut enim neglegenda fuit nobis
voluntas[1] eorum quibus probari volebamus[2] aut ars
163 eius conciliandae reperienda. Duae sunt igitur res
quae permulceant auris, sonus et numerus. De numero mox, nunc de sono quaerimus. Verba, ut
supra diximus, legenda sunt potissimum bene sonan-
tia, sed ea non ut poetae exquisita ad sonum sed
sumpta de medio.

> qua pontus Helles[3] supera Tmolum ac Tauricos[4]

locorum splendidis nominibus illuminatus est versus,
sed proximus inquinatus insuavissima littera :

[1] voluntas *Bake :* voluptas *AL.*
[2] volebamus *L,* videbamur *A,* nitebamur *Stangl.*
[3] helles *AP²M²,* hellus *FOP¹,* hellis *M¹.*
[4] supera *Baehrens :* superat tmolum (*Fε,* timolum *P,*
Thinolum *O*), ac (*P,* at *FO*) tauricos *L,* superadmolum
adauricos *A.*

---

[a] Lucilius 150 M. *Remains,* iii. p. 56. Worthy of that
life and station.

not *omnibus princeps*, and :

> vita illa dignu' locoque,[a]

not *dignus*. If custom, untaught, is such an artificer of sweet sounds, what have we a right to expect from art and study ? I have discussed this subject more 162 briefly than I should have done had I been treating this alone—for the subject of the nature and use of language is very wide—but at greater length than the plan of the work required.

To proceed, then—the decision as to subject-matter and words to express it belongs to the intellect, but in the choice of sounds and rhythms the ear is the judge ; the former are dependent on the understanding, the latter on pleasure ; therefore reason determines the rules of art in the former case, and sensation in the latter. We had thus either to neglect the favour of those whom we were striving to please, or find some art of winning it. Now there are two things which charm the ear, 163 sound and rhythm. We shall treat rhythm presently ; now we are discussing the subject of sound. As we have said above,[b] one should select the most euphonious words, but they must not be selected with particular attention to euphony as the poets do, but taken from the ordinary language.

> By Helle's sea beyond Tmolus and Taurica.[c]

The verse is embellished by the magnificent geographical names : but the following verse is spoiled by the repetition of an unpleasant letter[d] :

[b] §§ 80, 149.
[c] Ribbeck[3], *Trag. frag. incert.* 163, *Remains*, ii. p. 612.
[d] *f.*

441

finis frugifera et efferta[1] arva Asiae tenet.

164 Quare bonitate potius nostrorum verborum utamur quam splendore Graecorum, nisi forte sic loqui paenitet :

qua tempestate Paris Helenam

et quae secuntur. Immo vero ista sequamur asperitatemque fugiamus :

habeo ego istam[2] perterricrepam,
itemque[3]

versutiloquas malitias.

Nec solum componentur verba ratione sed etiam finientur,[4] quoniam id iudicium esse alterum aurium diximus. Et finiuntur aut compositione ipsa et quasi sua sponte aut quodam genere[5] verborum in quibus ipsis concinnitas inest; quae sive casus habent in exitu similis sive paribus paria redduntur sive opponuntur contraria, suapte natura numerosa sunt, 165 etiamsi nihil est factum de industria. In huius concinnitatis consectatione Gorgiam fuisse principem

---

[1] efferta *Lachmann :* ferta *LA²,* feria *A¹.*
[2] ego istam *Heerdegen :* ego ista *A,* istam ego *L.*
[3] itemque *Ernesti :* idemque *L,* fidem *spatium duarum litterarum A.*
[4] componentur . . . finientur *L,* componantur . . . finiantur *A.*
[5] aut quodam genere *vulg.,* ut quaedam genera *AL.*

---

[a] Ribbeck³, *Trag. frag. incert.* 164, *Remains,* ii. p. 614.
[b] Ribbeck³, *Trag. frag. incert.* 80, *Remains,* ii. p. 242. These lines of the passage are quoted in *De Oratore* 3. 219 :

qua tempestate Paris Helenam innuptis iunxit nuptiis,
ego sum gravida, expletis iam fere ad pariendum mensibus,
per idem tempus Polydorum Hecuba partu postremo parit.

At that season
When Paris joined Helen to a marriage—

He holds the fields, the fruitful, fertile meads of Asia.[a]

Therefore let us use the good old Latin words, 164 rather than the magnificent Greek ones, unless, perchance, one might be ashamed to have written the passage beginning

> qua tempestate Paris Helenam.[b]

No, let us rather imitate this latter style, and avoid the roughness of such lines as :

> habeo ego istam perterricrepam,

and

> versutiloquas malitias.[c]

But we shall use design not only in the collocation of words, but also in rounding off the sentence ; this was the second point on which we said the judgement of the ear is required. Sentences are rounded off either by the arrangement of words,— spontaneously, as it were,—or by using a certain class of words in which there is an inherent symmetry. If they have similar case-endings, or if clauses are equally balanced, or if contrary ideas are opposed, the sentence becomes rhythmical by its very nature, even if no rhythm is intended. It is 165 said that Gorgias was the first to strive for this sort

---

> No marriage that !—and I myself was big
> With child, the sum of months being nigh fulfilled
> For me to give it birth, in that same time
> Did Hecuba give birth to Polydorus
> In her last travail.
>
> Tr. by Warmington.

[c] *perterricrepam*, terribly-rattling, and *versutiloquas*, crafty-speaking, are strange un-Latin compounds, modelled on the Greek. Ribbeck[3], *Trag. frag. incert.* 142, 114, *Remains*, ii. pp. 626, 620. The woman's mine—that scare-rattle. Clever-worded rogueries.

accepimus ; quo de genere illa nostra sunt in Milo-
niana : " Est enim, iudices, haec non scripta sed nata
lex, quam non didicimus, accepimus, legimus, verum
ex natura ipsa arripuimus, hausimus, expressimus, ad
quam non docti sed facti, non instituti sed imbuti
sumus." Haec enim talia sunt ut, quia referuntur ea
quae[1] debent referri, intellegamus non quaesitum
166 esse numerum sed secutum. Quod fit item in
referendis contrariis ut illa sunt, quibus non modo
numerosa oratio sed etiam versus efficitur :

> eam quam nihil accusas damnas,—

condemnas diceret[2] qui versum effugere vellet—

> bene quam meritam esse autumas
> dicis male merere ?
> id quod scis prodest nihil ; id quod nescis obest.

Versum efficit ipsa relatio contrariorum. Idem esset
in oratione numerosum : quod scis, nihil prodest ;
quod nescis, multum obest. L. Semper haec, quae
Graeci ἀντίθετα nominant, cum contrariis opponuntur contraria, numerum oratorium necessitate ipsa
167 efficiunt, etiam sine industria. Hoc genere antiqui
iam ante Isocratem delectabantur et maxime Gorgias, cuius in oratione plerumque efficit numerum
ipsa concinnitas. Nos etiam in hoc genere frequen-

---

[1] ea quae *A*, ad ea quae *L*.
[2] diceret *L*, dixisset *A*.

---

[a] *Pro Milone* 10. The studied symmetry of this passage
can be only imperfectly rendered in English.
[b] Ribbeck[3], *Trag. frag. incert.* 200 f.

> Her whom you ne'er accused you now condemn ;
> Her merit once confessed, you now deny.
> From what you've learnt no real good accrues,
> But every ill your ignorance pursues.

> Tr. by Jones.

of symmetry. An example of it is found in the
following passage from my oration *In Defence of
Milo*[a] : "For this law, gentlemen of the jury, is
not written, but born ; we did not learn, receive and
read it, but we seized, plucked and wrested it from
Nature herself ; for this we were not taught, but
made ; we know it not by training, but by instinct."
The nature of this passage is such that, as the words
match those which they ought to match, we recognize that the rhythm was not studied, but was the
natural result of the thought. The same effect is 166
produced by balancing opposites, as in the cases which
produce not merely rhythmical prose but even verse :

> eam quam nihil accusas damnas— [b]

(one would say *condemnas* if one desired to avoid
verse)—

> bene quam meritam esse autumas
> dicis male merere ?
> id quod scis prodest nihil ; id quod nescis obest.

The juxtaposition of opposing ideas makes the verse.
It would likewise be rhythmical in prose : What you
know does not help ; what you do not know greatly
hinders. Clauses of this sort which the Greeks call
ἀντίθετα or "antithetical," in which contrasted ideas
are set off one against the other, necessarily produce
a rhythm in prose even if it is not intentional. The
ancients even before the time of Isocrates were 167
fond of this style—Gorgias particularly so ; in his
prose symmetry of itself frequently produces rhythm.
We, too, have made frequent use of this style, for
example in the fourth speech of the *Accusation*[c] :

[a] *In Verrem*, Actio Secunda, iv. 115.

tes, ut illa sunt in quarto Accusationis: " conferte hanc pacem cum illo bello, huius praetoris adventum cum illius imperatoris victoria, huius cohortem impuram cum illius exercitu invicto, huius libidines cum illius continentia : ab illo qui cepit conditas, ab hoc qui constitutas accepit captas dicetis Syracusas."

168   Ergo et hi numeri sint cogniti et genus illud tertium explicetur quale sit,[1] numerosae et aptae orationis.[2] Quod qui non sentiunt, quas auris habeant aut quid in his hominis simile sit nescio. Meae quidem et perfecto completoque verborum ambitu gaudent et curta sentiunt nec amant redundantia. Quid dico meas ? Contiones saepe exclamare vidi, cum apte verba cecidissent. Id enim exspectant aures, ut verbis colligetur sententia. " Non erat hoc apud antiquos." Et quidem nihil aliud fere non erat ; nam et verba eligebant et sententias gravis et suavis reperiebant sed eas aut vinciebant

169 aut explebant parum. "Hoc me ipsum delectat " inquiunt. Quid, si antiquissima illa pictura paucorum colorum magis quam haec iam perfecta delectet, illa nobis sit credo repetenda, haec scilicet repudianda ? Nominibus veterum gloriantur. Habet autem ut in aetatibus auctoritatem senectus sic in exemplis antiquitas, quae quidem apud me ipsum valet plurimum. Nec ego id quod deest antiquitati flagito potius quam laudo quod est ; praesertim cum ea maiora iudicem quae sunt quam illa quae

---

[1] quale sit *L*, quales sint *A*.
[2] orationis *L*, orationes *A*.

---

[a] *Cf.* § 149.
[b] Four—yellow, red, black and white, according to Pliny, *Nat. Hist.* 35. 50, and others.

" Compare this peace with that war, the arrival
of this praetor with the victory of that general,
this abandoned retinue with that invincible army,
the praetor's lust with the general's restraint ; you
will say that Syracuse was founded by its conqueror,
and captured by its governor."

Now that we have learned the nature of this kind 168
of rhythm, let us proceed to explain the third
topic [a]—the well-knit rhythm of prose. There are
some people who do not feel this, but I do not know
what sort of ears they have, nor whether they are
human at all. My ear, at any rate, rejoices in a
full and rounded period ; it feels a deficiency, and
does not like an excess. Why say " *my* ear ? " I
have often seen the whole assembly burst into a
cheer, in response to a happy cadence. For the ear
expects the words to bind the sentence together.
" This was not done by the ancients," they will
object. True, but they had almost everything
else ; they selected their words carefully, and produced many dignified and charming ideas, but they
paid too little attention to binding them together
or giving them fullness. " But that is just what I 169
like," they say. Suppose they prefer archaic painting which used only a few [b] colours to the perfection of modern art ; must we, then, go back to
the ancients and reject the moderns ? They pride
themselves on the names of their ancient models.
Antiquity does carry authority in the precedents
it furnishes, as old age does in respect of years ;
and this authority has great weight with me. I
do not demand from antiquity what it has not ;
rather I praise what it has, particularly because I
judge their excellence of greater concern than their

desunt. Plus est enim in verbis et in sententiis
boni, quibus illi excellunt, quam in conclusione
sententiarum, quam non habent. LI. Post inventa
conclusio est, qua credo[1] usuros veteres illos fuisse,
si iam nota atque usurpata res esset ; qua inventa
170 omnis usos magnos oratores videmus. Sed habet
nomen invidiam, cum in oratione iudiciali et forensi numerus Latine, Graece ῥυθμὸς inesse dicitur.
Nimis enim insidiarum ad capiendas auris adhiberi
videtur, si etiam in dicendo numeri ab oratore
quaeruntur. Hoc freti isti et ipsi infracta et am-
putata locuntur et eos vituperant qui apta et finita
pronuntiant ; si inanibus verbis levibusque sententiis,
iure ; sin[2] probae res, lecta verba, quid est cur clau-
dere aut insistere orationem malint quam cum sententia pariter excurrere ? Hic enim invidiosus
numerus nihil affert aliud nisi ut sit apte verbis
comprehensa sententia ; quod fit etiam ab antiquis,
sed plerumque casu, saepe natura ; et quae valde
laudantur apud illos, ea fere quia sunt conclusa
171 laudantur. Et apud Graecos quidem iam anni
prope quadringenti sunt, cum hoc probatur ; nos
nuper agnovimus. Ergo Ennio licuit vetera con-
temnenti dicere :

Versibus quos olim Fauni vatesque canebant,

mihi de antiquis eodem modo non licebit ? Prae-

---

[1] credo *L*, vero *A*, spero *Muther*.
[2] sin *P³y*, sint *AL*.

---

[a] Referring to the Greek orators.
[b] Ennius, *Ann.* 214 ff. V.², *Remains*, i. p. 82.

deficiency. There is, in fact, more good in words and ideas, in which they excel, than in a rhythmical sentence ending, which they lack. The rhythmical ending was a later invention, which I believe the ancients would have used if it had been known and employed in their day. We see that after its invention, all great orators[a] employed it. But the word "rhythm" (in Greek ῥυθμός) is invidious when it is said to be employed in judicial and forensic oratory. For it seems too much like a trick to catch the ear, if the orator in the midst of his speech is hunting for rhythms. Relying on this objection, those friends of yours themselves deliver broken and choppy sentences and upbraid those who produce rounded and finished periods. Their criticism would be justified if the words were silly and the ideas trifling ; but if the subject-matter has merit, and the words are well chosen, why should they prefer to let the sentence limp or stop short rather than keep pace with the thought ? As a matter of fact this invidious rhythm does nothing except to form the words into a well-knit sentence. This occurs in the ancient orators, generally by accident, often because of the nature of the language ; and the passages in their speeches which are most highly praised are generally those which end rhythmically. In fact nearly four hundred years have passed since this became the approved style in Greece, but we have only recently recognized it. Therefore Ennius was permitted to say with a touch of scorn for the primitive :

> Verses which the Fauns and bards once sang.[b]

Shall I not have equal privilege to criticize the

sertim cum dicturus non sim : " ante hunc " ut
ille nec quae secuntur : " Nos ausi reserare "; legi
enim audivique nonnullos, quorum propemódum absolute concluderetur oratio. Quod qui non possunt,
non est eis satis non contemni, laudari etiam volunt.
Ego autem illos ipsos laudo idque merito quorum
se isti imitatores esse dicunt, etsi in eis aliquid
desidero, hos vero minime qui nihil illorum nisi
vitium secuntur, cum a bonis absint longissime.

172   Quodsi auris tam inhumanas tamque agrestis habent, ne doctissimorum quidem virorum eos move-
bit auctoritas ? Omitto Isocratem discipulosque
eius Ephorum et Naucratem, quanquam orationis
faciendae et ornandae auctores locupletissimi summi
ipsi oratores esse debebant. Sed quis omnium doctior,
quis acutior, quis in rebus vel inveniendis vel iudicandis acrior Aristotele fuit ? Quis porro Isocrati est
adversatus infensius ? Is igitur versum in oratione
vetat esse, numerum iubet. Eius auditor Theodectes,
in primis, ut Aristoteles saepe significat, politus
scriptor atque artifex, hoc idem et sentit et praecipit ;
Theophrastus vero isdem de rebus etiam accuratius.
Quis ergo istos ferat qui hos auctores non probent?
Nisi omnino haec esse ab eis praecepta nesciunt.

173 Quod si ita est—nec vero aliter existimo—quid, ipsi

ᵃ The correct form of the name is now known to be
Theodectas from *I.A.* ii²., 977 b, which is believed to rest
on the authority of Aristotle.

ancients, especially since I am not going to say:
" Before me," as he did, nor—to continue as he did
—" We dared to burst the gates." For I have read
and listened to not a few orators whose style was
almost perfectly rhythmical in its cadence; but those
unable to attain to this are not satisfied with not being
criticized; they even wish to be praised for their
failure. I, on the other hand, praise precisely those
whom they profess to imitate, and I am quite right
in doing so, although I find something lacking in
them ; but I have scant praise for these moderns who
imitate only the weak points of the ancients while
they are far from attaining to their real merits.

But if their ears are so unnatural and unculti- 172
vated, will they not be moved even by the authority
of learned men ? I forbear to mention Isocrates
and his pupils Ephorus and Naucrates, although
distinguished orators should be the best authorities
in the matter of the construction of the oration
and its artistic embellishment. But who ever ex-
ceeded Aristotle in learning or in acumen, in originality of thought or in subtlety of dialectic ? Who
again was a more violent opponent of Isocrates ?
Well then, Aristotle forbids the use of verse in an
oration, but requires rhythm. His pupil Theodectes,[a] a highly accomplished literary artist, as
Aristotle often says, has the same feeling and gives
the same instructions ; and Theophrastus is still more
explicit on the same subject. Who, then, can endure
those who will not accept these authorities ? It
may be, however, that they are quite ignorant that
such precepts were ever laid down by these men.
But if that is the case—and I can imagine no other 173
explanation—will they not accept the authority of

suis sensibus non moventur ? Nihilne eis inane
videtur, nihil inconditum, nihil curtum, nihil claudicans, nihil redundans ? In versu quidem theatra tota
exclamant, si fuit una syllaba aut brevior aut longior;
nec vero multitudo pedes novit nec ullos numeros
tenet nec illud quod offendit aut cur aut[1] in quo
offendat intellegit[2]; et tamen omnium longitudinum
et brevitatum in sonis sicut acutarum graviumque
vocum iudicium ipsa natura in auribus nostris
collocavit.

174   LII. Visne igitur, Brute, totum hunc locum accuratius etiam explicemus quam illi ipsi qui et haec
et alia nobis tradiderunt, an eis contenti esse quae
ab illis dicta sunt possumus ? Sed quid quaero
velisne, cum litteris tuis eruditissime scriptis te id
vel maxime velle perspexerim ? Primum ergo origo,
deinde causa, post natura, tum ad extremum usus
ipse explicetur orationis aptae atque numerosae.

Nam qui Isocratem maxime mirantur hoc in eius[3]
summis laudibus ferunt, quod verbis solutis numeros
primus adiunxerit. Cum enim videret oratores cum
severitate audiri, poetas autem cum voluptate, tum
dicitur numeros secutus, quibus etiam in oratione
uteretur,[4] cum iucunditatis causa tum ut varietas
175 occurreret satietati. Quod ab his vere quadam ex
parte, non totum dicitur. Nam neminem in eo
genere scientius versatum Isocrate confitendum est,
sed princeps inveniendi fuit Thrasymachus, cuius

---

[1] cur aut *L*, curat ut *A*, curat aut ε, *Heerdegen*, anquirit
aut *Stangl*.
[2] offendat intelligit *L*, offendit intelligat *A*.
[3] eius *L*, omnis *A*.
[4] uteretur *A*, uteremur *L*, *Rufinus* (*Gram. Lat. 6. 573*).

their own senses ? Do they never have the feeling
that something is lacking, that a sentence is harsh,
mutilated, lame or redundant ? People do in the
case of poetry, for the whole audience will hoot at one
false quantity.[a] Not that the multitude knows
anything of feet, or has any understanding of rhythm ;
and when displeased they do not realize why or with
what they are displeased. And yet nature herself
has implanted in our ears the power of judging
long and short sounds as well as high and low pitch
in words.

Do you wish me then, Brutus, to discuss this 174
whole topic in greater detail than has been done
by those authorities who have handed down to us
these and other rules, or can we be content with what
they have said ? But why do I ask this question
when your scholarly letter enables me to see that
this is exactly what you want ? First, then, let us
discuss the origin, then the cause, next the nature,
and finally the use of prose which is well knit and
rhythmical.

The enthusiastic admirers of Isocrates extol as
the greatest of his accomplishments that he was the
first to introduce rhythm into prose. For when he
observed that people listened to orators with solemn
attention, but to poets with pleasure, he is said to
have sought for rhythms to use in prose as well,
both for their intrinsic charm and in order that
monotony might be forestalled by variety. Their 175
claim is only partly true. We must grant that
nobody showed greater skill in this style than Isocrates, but the inventor was Thrasymachus. All

---

[a] I take *una syllaba* as nominative, following Lenchantin
de Gubernatis, *Boll. di filol.* xxix. (1922–23), pp. 139–141.

omnia nimis etiam exstant scripta numerose. Nam, ut paulo ante dixi, paria paribus adiuncta et similiter definita itemque contrariis relata contraria, quae sua sponte, etiamsi id non agas, cadunt plerumque numerose, Gorgias primus invenit, sed eis est usus intemperantius. (Id autem est genus, ut ante dictum est, ex tribus partibus collocationis alterum.)

176 Horum uterque Isocratem aetate praecurrit, ut eos ille moderatione, non inventione vicerit. Est enim ut in transferendis faciendisque verbis tranquillior sic in ipsis numeris sedatior. Gorgias autem avidior est generis eius et his festivitatibus—sic enim ipse censet—insolentius abutitur; quas Isocrates, cum tamen audivisset adulescens in Thessalia senem iam Gorgiam, moderatius temperavit. Quin etiam se ipse tantum quantum aetate procedebat—prope enim centum confecit annos—relaxarat a nimia necessitate numerorum, quod declarat in eo libro quem ad Philippum Macedonem scripsit, cum iam admodum esset senex; in quo dicit sese minus iam servire numeris quam solitus esset. Ita non modo superiores sed etiam se ipse correxerat.

177 LIII. Quoniam igitur habemus aptae orationis eos principes auctoresque quos diximus et origo inventa est, causa quaeratur. Quae sic aperta est, ut mirer veteres non esse commotos, praesertim cum, ut fit, fortuito saepe aliquid concluse apteque dicerent. Quod cum animos hominum aurisque pepulisset, ut intellegi posset id quod casus effudisset cecidisse

---

[a] Isocrates in *Philippus* 27 describes these tricks of style as ποικιλίαι.

[b] *Philippus* 27.

his work shows even an excess of rhythm. Furthermore Gorgias, as I said before, was the first to employ clauses of equal length, with similar endings, and with antithesis, which, by their very nature, generally have a rhythmical cadence even if this is not intended, but he used these devices somewhat immoderately. (However, as has been said before, this is the second of the three heads under arrangement of words.) Both Gorgias and Thrasy- 176 machus were predecessors of Isocrates, so that his superiority to them was not in originality but in adaptation. For as he is more moderate in the use of metaphor and in forming new words, so he is more restrained in his rhythms. But Gorgias is too fond of this style, and uses these "embroideries" [a] (his own word for it) too boldly. All these Isocrates used with still greater restraint, in spite of the fact that he was a young man when he had studied with the aged Gorgias in Thessaly. Moreover, Isocrates himself as he grew older—he lived to be nearly a hundred—had gradually relaxed the extreme strictness of his rhythm, as he says in his address to Philip of Macedon,[b] written in his ripe old age ; in this he says that he was less attentive to rhythm than had been his custom. This indicates that he had corrected, not only his predecessors, but also himself.

Since as I have said we consider these men just 177 named as the authors and inventors of well-knit prose, and the origin has been discovered, we must now seek for the cause. This is so obvious that I wonder the ancients did not notice it, especially since, as will happen, they often accidentally produced well-knit, rhythmical sentences. When this struck the minds and ears of men and they could appreciate that the product

iucunde, notandum certe genus atque ipsi sibi
imitandi fuerunt. Aures ipsae[1] enim vel animus
aurium nuntio naturalem quandam in se continet
178 vocum omnium mensionem. Itaque et longiora et
breviora iudicat et perfecta ac moderata semper
exspectat ; mutila sentit quaedam et quasi decurtata,
quibus tanquam debito fraudetur offenditur, pro-
ductiora alia et quasi immoderatius excurrentia,
quae magis etiam aspernantur aures ; quod cum in
plerisque tum in hoc genere nimium quod est offendit
vehementius quam id quod videtur parum. Ut igitur
poeticae[2] versus inventus est terminatione aurium,
observatione prudentium, sic in oratione animadversum est, multo illud quidem serius sed eadem
natura admonente, esse quosdam certos cursus
conclusionesque verborum.

179 Quoniam igitur causam quoque ostendimus, naturam nunc—id enim erat tertium—si placet explicemus;
quae disputatio non huius instituti sermonis est sed
artis intimae. Quaeri enim potest, qui sit orationis
numerus et ubi sit positus et natus ex quo et is unusne
sit an duo an plures quaque ratione componatur et
ad quam rem et quando et quo loco et quemadmo-
180 dum adhibitus aliquid voluptatis afferat. Sed ut in
plerisque rebus sic in hac duplex est considerandi via,
quarum altera est longior, brevior altera, eadem etiam
planior. LIV. Est autem longioris prima illa quaestio

---

[1] aures ipsae enim *Friedrich :* aures enim *L,* ipse enim *A.*
[2] poeticae *Goeller,* poetica et *L,* poetae *A ; seclusit Jahn,*
in poetica *Schütz.*

---

[a] In this sentence Cicero aims to show how highly technical
the discussion will be, not to give an outline ; one point
456

of chance had a pleasing effect, they might have been expected to note the general character of the phenomena and reproduce their own success. For the ear, or rather the mind which receives the message of the ear, contains in itself a natural capacity for measuring all sounds. Accordingly it distinguishes 178 between long and short, and always looks for what is complete and well proportioned : certain phrases it feels to be shortened, mutilated as it were, and is offended by these as if it were cheated of its just due ; others are too long and run beyond reasonable bounds ; the ear rejects these still more ; for in this as in most things excess is more offensive than deficiency. Accordingly, just as in the realm of poetry verse was discovered by the test of the ear and the observation of thoughtful men, so in prose it was observed, much later to be sure, but by the same promptings of nature, that there are definite periods and rhythmical cadences.

Having explained the cause, we may now, if you 179 will, discuss the nature of rhythm ; that was, as you recall, the third point. The exhaustive treatment of this topic, however, is out of place in such an informal discussion, and belongs rather in a highly technical treatise. For we might inquire *a* what prose rhythm is, where it is used, and what its origin is ; whether there is only one, or two or more, and on what principles it is constructed ; why, when, where and how it is used to produce some pleasurable effect. But, as is generally the case, there are two ways of 180 considering this question, one longer, the other shorter and at the same time easier. The first step

(*natus ex quo*) has already been taken up under *origo* ; others are left to the fourth subdivision (*usus*)—(Kroll).

sitne omnino ulla numerosa oratio ; quibusdam enim
non videtur, quia nihil insit in ea certi ut in versibus,
et quod ipsi qui affirment esse eos numeros, rationem
cur sint non queant reddere. Deinde, si sit numerus
in oratione, qualis sit aut quales et e poeticisne
numeris an ex alio genere quodam et, si e poeticis,
quis eorum sit aut qui ; namque aliis unus modo aliis
plures aliis omnes idem videntur. Deinde, quicumque sunt sive unus sive plures, communesne sint omni
generi orationis—quoniam aliud genus est narrandi,
aliud persuadendi, aliud docendi—an dispares numeri
cuique orationis generi[1] accommodentur ; si communes,[2] qui sint ; si dispares, quid intersit et cur non
aeque in oratione atque in versu numerus appareat.
181 Deinde, quod dicitur in oratione numerosum, id
utrum numero solum efficiatur an etiam vel compositione quadam vel genere verborum ; an sit[3] suum
cuiusque, ut numerus intervallis, compositio vocibus,
genus ipsum verborum quasi quaedam forma et lumen
orationis appareat, sitque omnium fons compositio ex
eaque et numerus efficiatur et ea quae dicuntur orationis quasi formae et lumina, quae, ut dixi, Graeci
182 vocant σχήματα. At non est unum nec idem, quod
voce iucundum est et quod moderatione absolutum et
quod illuminatum genere verborum ; quanquam id

---

[1] generi πε, genere L, generis A.
[2] communes Manutius : omnes L, omnis A.
[3] sit Lambinus : est AL.

in the long way is to consider whether there is such a thing as rhythmical prose at all ; for some think there is not, because there is nothing definite about it as there is in verse, and because the supporters of rhythm cannot render a reason for its existence. In the second place, if there is rhythm in prose, what is its nature, whether it have one or many forms ? Does it consist of the rhythms of poetry, or does it belong in a different class ? If it is the rhythm of poetry, what type or which types are used ? For some think only one is used in prose, others several, still others think that all are used. Again, whether there be one or more, are they used equally in every kind of prose—for there is one kind of prose for narrative, another for persuasion, another for exposition—or are different rhythms adapted to each kind of prose ? If the same rhythms are used indiscriminately, what are they ? If different rhythms are used, what is the distinction, and why is rhythm not so obvious in prose as in verse ? Then again, is 181 this rhythmical effect in prose produced solely by rhythm or also by a certain harmonious arrangement and by the character of the words ? Or does each have its own peculiar field, so that rhythm appears in time intervals, harmonious arrangement in sounds, and the character of the words appear as a certain beauty and embellishment of style ? Is harmonious arrangement the source of all and does this produce rhythm and the so-called figures and embellishments of style, which, as I have said, the Greeks call σχήματα or "figures"? But as a matter of fact 182 these three are not identical—I mean what is pleasant in sound, what is regulated by rhythmical law, and what is embellished by the form of expression,

459

quidem finitimum est numero, quia per se plerumque
perfectum est ; compositio autem ab utroque differt,
quae tota servit gravitati vocum aut suavitati. Haec
igitur fere sunt in quibus rei natura quaerenda sit.

183 LV. Esse ergo in oratione numerum quendam non
est difficile cognoscere. Iudicat enim sensus ; in quo
est inicum quod accidit non agnoscere, si cur id
accidat reperire nequeamus. Neque enim ipse versus
ratione est cognitus, sed natura atque sensu, quem
dimensa ratio docuit quid acciderit.[1] Ita notatio
naturae et animadversio peperit artem. Sed in
versibus res est apertior, quanquam etiam a modis
quibusdam cantu remoto soluta esse videatur oratio
maximeque id in optimo quoque eorum poetarum
qui λυρικοὶ a Graecis nominantur, quos cum cantu
184 spoliaveris, nuda paene remanet oratio. Quorum
similia sunt quaedam etiam apud nostros, velut illa
in Thyeste :

> quemnam te esse dicam ? qui[2] tarda in senectute

et quae secuntur ; quae, nisi cum tibicen accessit, orationis sunt solutae simillima. At comicorum senarii
propter similitudinem sermonis sic saepe sunt abiecti,
ut nonnunquam vix in eis numerus et versus intellegi

---

[1] acciderit *AL*, accideret *Madvig*.
[2] qui *A*, quin *L*.

---

[a] Ennius, *Thyestes*, frag. 348 V[2], *Remains*, i. p. 350.

Who, pray, are you, who in slow old age . . . ?

[b] The metre is bacchius ($\smile \underline{\;\;} -$), but this metre is treated
so freely by the Roman poets that it is difficult to identify.
The line scans

quēm nám t(e) ĕs|sĕ dícăm | quī tárd(a) ĭn | sĕnéctū(te).

although the latter is akin to rhythm, because in itself it generally has a certain finished quality. But harmonious arrangement differs from both because it is wholly concerned with the dignity and charm of words. These are the lines along which the nature of rhythm should be investigated.

It is, then, not hard to recognize that there is a 183 certain rhythm in prose. For the decision is given by our senses ; and in such a case it is unfair not to acknowledge the occurrence of the phenomenon, even if we are unable to discover its cause. Verse itself, as a matter of fact, is not recognized by abstract reason, but by our natural feeling : later on theory measured the verse and showed us what happened. The art of poetry, therefore, arose from observation and investigation of a phenomenon of nature. But in poetry the presence of rhythm is more obvious, although in certain metres, if the musical accompaniment be taken away, the words seem to lack rhythm ; this is particularly true of the best of the poets whom the Greeks call " lyric " ; deprive them of the musical accompaniment and almost nothing but bare prose remains. We have something like this at 184 times in Latin poetry ; this, for example, from the *Thyestes* : [a]

> quemnam te esse dicam ? qui tarda in senectute

and the rest of the passage ; unless accompanied by the pipe, it is exactly like prose.[b] But the senarii of comedy are often so lacking in elevation of style because of their resemblance to ordinary conversation that sometimes it is scarcely possible to distinguish

This assumes that the following word began with a vowel. If not it would be necessary to read *senecta* with Bothe.

possit.   Quo est ad inveniendum difficilior in oratione
185 numerus quam in versibus.   Omnino duo sunt quae
condiant orationem, verborum numerorumque iu-
cunditas.   In verbis inest quasi materia quaedam, in
numero autem expolitio.   Sed, ut ceteris in rebus,
necessitatis inventa antiquiora sunt quam voluptatis.
186 Itaque et Herodotus et eadem superiorque aetas
numero caruit nisi quando temere ac fortuito, et
scriptores perveteres de numero nihil omnino, de
oratione praecepta multa nobis reliquerunt.   Nam
quod et facilius est et magis necessarium, id semper
ante cognoscitur.   LVI.   Itaque translata aut facta aut
iuncta verba facile sunt cognita, quia sumebantur e
consuetudine cotidianoque sermone ; numerus autem
non domo[1] depromebatur neque habebat aliquam
necessitudinem aut cognationem cum oratione.
Itaque serius aliquanto notatus et cognitus quasi
quandam palaestram et extrema liniamenta orationi
187 attulit.   Quodsi et angusta quaedam atque concisa
et alia est dilatata et diffusa oratio, necesse est id
non litterarum accidere[2] natura, sed intervallorum
longorum et brevium varietate ; quibus implicata
atque permixta oratio quoniam tum stabilis est tum
volubilis, necesse est eius modi naturam numeris
contineri.   Nam circuitus ille, quem saepe iam diximus, incitatior numero ipso fertur et labitur, quoad
perveniat ad finem et insistat.

Perspicuum est igitur numeris astrictam orationem

---

[1] domo *Victorius et* " *antiqua scriptura* " *apud Lambinum :*
modo *AL,* eo modo *Heerdegen,* de medio *Stroebel.*
[2] accidere *vulg.,* accedere *FPO²,* accredere *O¹,* accipere *A.*

rhythm and verse in them. All the more difficult, then, to discover the rhythm in prose! There are, 185 speaking generally, two things which lend flavour to prose, pleasing words and agreeable rhythms. Words furnish a certain raw material which it is the business of rhythm to polish. But here as in other lines of activity the discoveries arising from necessity were of earlier origin than those prompted by pleasure. Therefore Herodotus and writers of his 186 age and of earlier times had only accidental and unintentional rhythms, and the early theorists have left for us many precepts about diction, but absolutely nothing about rhythm. For what is easier and more necessary is always learned first. Consequently metaphors, coined words and compounds were easily understood because they were taken from the customary speech of the day. But rhythm was not ready-to-hand, and had no necessary connexion or kinship with prose. Accordingly it was noted and understood somewhat late; it brought as it were the athletic training in graceful movement, and added the finishing touches to prose style. Therefore if one passage is constrained and choppy, 187 and another is diffuse and flowing, this cannot proceed from the nature of the letters, but from the varied arrangement of long and short intervals; and since prose, which is an intertwining and blending of these intervals, is at times sedate, and at times rapid, such a phenomenon as this must depend on rhythm; for the period, *i.e. circuitus*, as I have already termed it repeatedly, is carried along by the rhythm in a vigorous movement until it comes to the end and stops.

It is clear, then, that prose should be bound or

CICERO

188 esse debere, carere versibus. Sed hi numeri poeti-
cine sint an ex alio genere quodam deinceps est
videndum. Nullus est igitur numerus extra poeticos,
propterea quod definita sunt genera numerorum.
Nam omnis talis est ut unus sit e tribus. Pes enim, qui
adhibetur ad numeros, partitur in tria, ut necesse sit
partem pedis aut aequalem esse alteri parti aut
altero tanto aut sesqui esse maiorem. Ita fit aequalis
dactylus, duplex iambus, sesquiplex paean ; qui
pedes in orationem non cadere qui possunt ? Quibus
ordine locatis quod efficitur numerosum sit necesse
189 est. Sed quaeritur quo numero aut quibus potissimum sit utendum. Incidere vero omnis in orationem
etiam ex hoc intellegi potest, quod versus saepe
in oratione per imprudentiam dicimus. Est id
vehementer vitiosum, sed non attendimus neque
exaudimus nosmet ipsos—senarios vero et Hip-
ponacteos effugere vix possumus ; magnam enim
partem ex iambis nostra constat oratio. Sed tamen
eos versus facile agnoscit[1] auditor ; sunt enim

---

[1] agnoscit *FA*, cognoscit *OPf; fortasse* ignoscit *Heer-degen.*

---

[a] It has frequently been noted that Cicero's treatment of
the rhythm of prose in the succeeding sections gives an
inadequate account of the actual use of rhythm in his
orations. The literature on the ancient theory and practice
of rhythmical prose is enormous ; merely as an introduction
the reader is referred to Norden, E., *Die antike Kunstprosa,
Anhang II.*; Zander, C. M., *Eurythmia, vel Compositio
Rythmica Prosae Antiquae*, Leipzig, 1910–1914 ; de Groot,
A. W., *A Handbook of Antique Prose-rhythm*, Groningen,
1919 ; and to two works by Th. Zielinski, *Das Clauselgesetz
in Ciceros Reden*, Leipzig, 1904, and *Der constructive
Rhythmus in Ciceros Reden*, Leipzig, 1914 (=*Philologus*,
Supplementband xiii.).
[b] Ancient rhythm depended on the length of syllables.

restricted by rhythm, but that it should not contain
actual verses.[a] The next question is whether these 188
are the same as the rhythms of poetry, or of a different
kind. We may be sure there are no rhythms other
than those used by poetry, because the kinds of
rhythms are strictly limited. They all fall into one
of three classes. For the foot, which is employed in
rhythms, is of three types ; it divides into two equal
parts, or one part is twice as long as the other, or half
again as long. Examples of these are, respectively,
the dactyl, the iambus, the paean.[b] How can these
feet fail to occur in prose ?[c] And when they are
arranged in a systematic order the effect must be
rhythmical. However, the question is raised as to 189
which rhythm or which rhythms it is most desirable to use. All of them may occur in prose, as
appears from the fact that we often make verses
unintentionally in delivering a speech. This is very
reprehensible, but we do not notice or listen to ourselves ; as a matter of fact it is almost impossible to
avoid senarii and Hipponacteans, for our speech
consists largely of iambi.[d] The auditor, however,
recognizes these verses readily ; for they are of the

In the usual notation ⌣ stands for a short syllable and – for
one twice as long. The dactyl was – ⌣ ⌣ (2 : 2), the iambus
⌣ – (1 : 2), and the paean ⌣ ⌣ ⌣ – or – ⌣ ⌣ ⌣ (3 : 2 or
2 : 3).
  [c] Because many words are exactly in one of these forms.
  [d] The senarius consisted fundamentally of six iambi

⌣ _́ ⌣ _́ ⌣ _́ ⌣ _́ ⌣ _́ ⌣ _́.

As substitutions and resolutions were freely allowed, the line
(as often in Plautus) nearly resembles prose. The Hippo-
nactean (scazon or choliambic) differed from the senarius by
having the penultimate syllable long.

⌣ _́ ⌣ _́ ⌣ _́ ⌣ _́ ⌣ _́ – _́.

usitatissimi ; inculcamus autem per imprudentiam
saepe etiam minus usitatos, sed tamen versus :
vitiosum genus et longa animi provisione fugiendum.

190 Elegit ex multis Isocrati libris triginta fortasse
versus Hieronymus Peripateticus in primis nobilis,
plerosque senarios sed etiam anapaestos[1] ; quo
quid potest esse turpius ? Etsi in legendo fecit
malitiose ; prima enim syllaba dempta ex primo
verbo sententiae postremum ad verbum primam
rursus syllabam adiunxit insequentis sententiae :
ita factus est anapaestus is qui Aristophaneus nominatur ; quod ne accidat observari nec potest nec
necesse est. Sed tamen hic corrector in eo ipso
loco quo reprehendit, ut a me animadversum est
studiose inquirente in eum, immittit imprudens ipse
senarium. Sit igitur hoc cognitum in solutis etiam
verbis inesse numeros eosdemque esse oratorios qui
sint poetici.

191 LVII. Sequitur ergo ut qui maxime cadant in orationem aptam numeri videndum sit. Sunt enim qui
iambicum putent, quod sit orationis simillimus ; qua
de causa fieri, ut is potissimum propter similitudinem veritatis adhibeatur in fabulis, quod ille dacty-
licus numerus hexametrorum magniloquentiae sit
accommodatior. Ephorus autem, levis ipse orator
et[2] profectus ex optima disciplina, paeana sequitur
aut dactylum. fugit autem spondeum et trochaeum.

---

[1] anapaestos *f*[3], anapaesta *L*, anapesti *A*, anapesticos *γ*.
[2] et *A*, sed *L*.

---

[a] Hieronymus of Rhodes, pupil of Aristotle. Some of his
criticisms of Isocrates are found in Dionysius of Halicarnassus,
Isoc. 13, and Philodemus, *Rhetorica* 1. 198 Sudhaus.

[b] That is for a careful orator to use an anapaestic line. A
senarius would not be so bad.

commonest sort ; but we often unwittingly insert
other verses, of less common type, but verses all the
same—a vicious practice, which is to be avoided by
looking far ahead. The eminent Peripatetic philo- 190
sopher Hieronymus [a] culled from the numerous works
of Isocrates some thirty verses, mostly senarii, but
also anapaests. What greater reproach than this is
possible ! [b] But he was unfair in his selection ; for he
cut off the initial syllable of the first word in the
sentence, and added to the last word the first syllable
of the following sentence, thus making the anapaestic
line called Aristophaneus.[c] It is impossible and
unnecessary to avoid instances like these. But the
high and mighty critic in the very passage in which
he criticizes Isocrates lets fall a senarius unwittingly, as I noted on careful examination of his
treatise. We may put it down as certain, then,
that there are rhythms even in prose, and that
those used in oratory are the same as those of
poetry.

The next point to consider, therefore, is which 191
rhythms are best suited to a well-knit prose. Some
favour the iambic as being closest to ordinary speech,
for which reason we find that it is chiefly used in the
drama because of the similarity to actual speech,
whereas the dactylic is better suited to the lofty
style of hexameter verse. Ephorus, however, a
polished [d] orator himself and a product of an excellent school, uses the paean or dactyl but avoids the

---

[a] The anapaestic tetrameter catalectic:

◡ ◡ ◡́ ◡ ◡ ◡́ ◡ ◡ ◡́ ◡ ◡ ◡́ ◡ ◡ — ◡ ◡ ◡́ —

[d] If we read *sed* with L instead of *et*, *lĕvis* must be read,
meaning " light," " inconsequential."

Quod enim paean habeat[1] tris brevis, dactylus autem
duas, brevitate et celeritate syllabarum labi putat
verba proclivius contraque accidere in spondeo et
trochaeo. Quorum[2] quod alter e longis constet,[3]
alter e brevibus, fieri[3] alteram nimis incitatam,
alteram nimis tardam orationem, neutram tempera-
192 tam. Sed et illi priores errant et Ephorus in culpa
est. Nam et qui paeana praetereunt non vident
mollissimum a sese numerum eundemque amplissimum praeteriri. Quod longe Aristoteli videtur
secus, qui iudicat heroum numerum grandiorem
quam desideret soluta oratio, iambum autem nimis
e volgari esse sermone. Ita neque humilem et[4]
abiectam orationem nec nimis altam et exaggera-
tam probat, plenam tamen eam volt esse gravitatis,
ut eos qui audient ad maiorem admirationem possit
193 traducere. Trochaeum autem, qui est eodem spatio
quo choreus, cordacem appellat, quia contractio et
brevitas dignitatem non habeat. Ita paeana probat
eoque ait uti omnis, sed ipsos non sentire, cum
utantur. Esse autem tertium ac medium inter illos
et ita[5] factos eos pedes esse, ut in eis singulis modus insit aut sesquiplex aut duplex aut par. Itaque
illi de quibus ante dixi tantummodo commoditatis
194 habuerunt rationem, nullam dignitatis. Iambus

---

[1] paean habeat *usque ad* in eodem sem- (*§ 231*) *desunt in A.*
[2] quorum *addidit Heerdegen.*
[3] constet . . . fieri *Ernesti :* constaret . . . fieret *L.*
[4] et *Lambinus :* nec *L.*
[5] et ita *Sauppe :* sed ita *L.*

---

[a] – – and ˇ ˇ. Cicero calls the latter *trochaeus* and uses
choreus for what is commonly called trochee.
[b] *i.e.* the dactyl (– ˇ ˇ).

spondee and tribrach. For as the paean has three
shorts and the dactyl two, he thinks that because of
the shortness and swiftness of the syllables the words
flow along more rapidly and that the contrary is true
of the spondee and tribrach.[a] As the one is composed entirely of long syllables and the other of
shorts, the latter makes the style too rapid, the
former, too slow, and neither has the due proportion.
However the authorities first mentioned are wrong, 192
and Ephorus is at fault. For those who neglect the
paean fail to see that they are neglecting the rhythm
which is pleasantest but at the same time most
stately. Aristotle held quite a different opinion ; he
thought the heroic measure [b] too lofty for prose, and
the iambic too close to ordinary conversation. That
is, he approves neither a low mean style, nor one too
lofty and bombastic, but will nevertheless have it
dignified, in order to arouse greater admiration in
the audience. The tribrach, however, which occupies 193
the same time as the trochee, he calls a cordax
because its shortness and brevity is undignified.[c]
He consequently approves of the paean, and says
all men use this rhythm without realizing what they
are doing; but that it is a third form midway between
the other two, and that these feet have the propor-
tions 3 : 2, or 2 : 1 or 2 : 2. The other writers whom I
mentioned above were thinking only of convenience,
and not at all of dignity. For the iambus and dactyl 194

---

[c] Cicero makes sad work of rendering Aristotle, *Rhet.* 3.
8, 4. He uses *trochaeus* in the sense of *tribrach* ($\smile$ $\smile$ $\smile$)
whereas Aristotle refers to the true trochee ($-$ $\smile$). A
second error is in the use of the word *cordax*. This was a
vulgar dance. What Aristotle really says is that the trochaic
measure is somewhat like the *cordax*, *i.e.* that it is a tripping,
dancing rhythm, inclined to be vulgar.

enim et dactylus in versum cadunt maxime; itaque
ut versum fugimus in oratione, sic hi sunt evitandi
continuati pedes; aliud enim quiddam est oratio
nec quicquam inimicius quam illa versibus; paean
autem minime est aptus ad versum, quo libentius
eum recepit oratio. Ephorus vero ne spondeum
quidem quem fugit[1] intellegit esse aequalem dactylo
quem probat. Syllabis enim metiendos pedes, non
intervallis existimat; quod idem facit in trochaeo,
qui temporibus et intervallis est par iambo sed eo
vitiosus in oratione, si ponatur extremus, quod verba
melius in syllabas longiores cadunt. Atque haec,
quae sunt apud Aristotelem, eadem a Theophrasto
195 Theodecteque de paeane dicuntur. Ego autem
sentio omnis in oratione esse quasi permixtos et
confusos pedes. Nec enim effugere possemus anim-
adversionem, si semper isdem uteremur, quia nec
numerosa esse ut poema neque extra numerum ut
sermo volgi esse[2] debet oratio—alterum nimis est
vinctum, ut de industria factum appareat, alterum
nimis dissolutum, ut pervagatum ac volgare videatur;
196 ut ab altero non delectere, alterum oderis—sit
igitur, ut supra dixi, permixta et temperata numeris
nec dissoluta nec tota numerosa, paeane maxime,
quoniam optimus auctor ita censet, sed reliquis
etiam numeris, quos ille praeterit, temperata.

---

[1] fugit π, fecit L.
[2] esse vulg., est L.

---

[a] The next two sentences are *not* a paraphrase of Aristotle,
though the following statement, *atque haec, quae sunt apud
Aristotelem,* might lead one to think they were.
[b] Metrically equivalent, for the long is equal to two shorts

are best adapted to verse ; therefore just as we avoid
verses in prose, so we must shun a succession of these
feet.   For prose is a different thing from verse and
utterly hostile to it ; the paean, however, is poorly
adapted to verse, and therefore prose welcomes it
gladly.   Ephorus,[a] however, does not recognize that
the spondee, which he avoids, is equivalent to the
dactyl, which he approves.[b]   For he thinks that feet
are to be measured by the number of syllables, not by
their intervals.[c]   He does the same with the tribrach,
which has the same time and intervals as the iambus,
but is bad in prose if placed last, because it is better
to have words end with a long syllable.   These
remarks of Aristotle about the paean are repeated
by Theophrastus and Theodectes.   My own feeling, 195
however, is that all kinds of feet are mingled and
jumbled together in prose, for we could not avoid
the critic's censure if we used the same feet all
the time ; for prose ought not to be rhythmical as a
poem is, nor entirely without rhythm as is the speech
of the vulgar—for one is too strict and confined, so
that it seems artificial ; the other is too loose, so that
it seems rambling and vulgar.   You would not like the 196
one and would hate the other.   Prose, then, as I have
said before, should be tempered by an admixture of
rhythm ; it should not be loose, nor wholly rhythmical ; the paean is to be the principal measure,
because that is the opinion of our greatest authority,
but we should combine this with the other rhythms
which he disregards.

(– – = – ⌣ ⌣) ; but the effect of a succession of spondees
is quite different from that of the same number of dactyls.
    [c] *i.e.* the intervals of time between the beginning of
successive syllables, or in other words, the *length* of the foot.

LVIII. Quos autem numeros cum quibus tanquam
purpuram misceri oporteat nunc dicendum est atque
etiam quibus orationis generibus sint quique accom-
modatissimi. Iambus enim frequentissimus est in eis
197 quae demisso atque humili sermone dicuntur, paean
autem in amplioribus, in utroque dactylus. Itaque[1]
in varia et perpetua oratione hi sunt inter se miscendi
et temperandi. Sic minime animadvertetur delectationis aucupium et quadrandae orationis industria ;
quae latebit eo magis, si et verborum et sententiarum
ponderibus utemur. Nam qui audiunt haec duo
animadvertunt et iucunda sibi censent, verba dico et
sententias ; eaque dum animis attentis admirantes
198 excipiunt, fugit eos et praetervolat numerus ; qui
tamen si abesset, illa ipsa delectarent minus. Nec
vero[2] is cursus est numerorum — orationis dico ;
nam est longe aliter in versibus—nihil ut fiat extra
modum ; nam id quidem esset poema ; sed omnis
nec claudicans nec quasi fluctuans et aequabiliter[3]
constanterque ingrediens numerosa habetur oratio.
Atque id in dicendo numerosum putatur, non quod
totum constat e numeris sed quod ad numeros
proxime accedit ; quo etiam difficilius est oratione
uti quam versibus, quod in illis certa quaedam et
definita lex est, quam sequi sit necesse ; in dicendo
autem nihil est propositum, nisi ut ne[4] immoderata

---

[1] itaque ε *et Rufinus*, ita *L.*
[2] minus. Nec vero *Heerdegen :* nec vero minus *L.*
[3] aequabiliter *Schütz :* aequaliter *L.*
[4] ut ne *Schütz :* aut ne *L.*

---

[a] The ancient purple was almost always a mixture of two
natural dyes from shell-fish.

Now we must discuss the proper combinations of these feet one with another (like the art of mixing the purple dye [a]) and also consider which are best fitted to each kind of speech. The iambus, for example, is most frequent in passages of a plain, simple conversational type ; the paean is used in 197 the more elevated style, and the dactyl in both. Therefore in a long speech with varying moods these rhythms must be mingled and blended. If this is done the audience will scarcely notice the striving for a pleasing effect, and the pains spent in polishing [b] the oration ; which will also be better concealed if we use weighty language and thoughts. For the audience notice these two things and find them pleasurable—the words and ideas I mean—and while they are intent and listening with admiration to these, the rhythm escapes their notice and slips by. However, if it were absent, their 198 pleasure in the words and ideas would be lessened. Yet, to be sure, this course of the rhythm—I mean in prose, for the case is quite otherwise in verse—is not such that there is nothing unmetrical; for that would be a poem ; but every passage which does not halt or waver, but advances steadily and uniformly is considered rhythmical. And in spoken prose, a passage is regarded as rhythmical not when it is composed entirely of metrical forms, but when it comes very close to being so. That is why prose is harder to write than verse, because in the latter there is a definite and fixed law which must be followed. In a speech, however, there is no rule except that the

[b] More literally, " squaring." The figure seems to be taken from masonry, squaring the stones to make them fit together.

aut angusta aut dissoluta aut fluens[1] sit oratio.
Itaque non sunt in ea tanquam tibicini percus-
sionum modi, sed universa comprehensio et species
orationis clausa et terminata est, quod voluptate
aurium iudicatur.

199   LIX. Solet autem quaeri totone in ambitu verborum
numeri tenendi sint an in primis partibus atque in
extremis ; plerique enim censent cadere tantum
numerose oportere terminarique sententiam.   Est
autem ut id maxime deceat, non ut solum[2] ; ponendus
est enim ille ambitus, non abiciendus.   Quare cum
aures extremum semper exspectent in eoque ac-
quiescant, id vacare numero non oportet, sed ad
hunc exitum iam[3] a principio ferri debet verborum
illa comprehensio et tota a capite ita fluere, ut ad
200 extremum veniens ipsa consistat.   Id autem bona
disciplina exercitatis, qui et multa scripserint et
quaecumque etiam sine scripto dicerent similia scrip-
torum effecerint, non erit difficillimum.   Ante enim
circumscribitur mente sententia confestimque verba
concurrunt, quae mens eadem, qua nihil est celerius,
statim dimittit, ut suo quodque loco respondeat ;
quorum discriptus ordo alias alia terminatione concluditur.   Atque omnia illa et prima et media verba
201 spectare debent ad ultimum.   Interdum enim cursus
est in oratione incitatior, interdum moderata ingressio,

---

[1] aut fluens *L*, ac fluens *Heerdegen*, aut diffluens *Reis*.
[2] ut solum *Bake :* id solum *L*.
[3] iam *Heerdegen :* tam *FP¹O¹*, tamen *O²P²*.

---

[a] The piper who played the accompaniment for lyric
verse, beat time with his foot.   On the meaning of *percussio*
see R. Wagner in *Philologus*, lxxvii. (1921), p. 307.

style must not be straggling or cramped or loose or
chaotic. Therefore it has no measures of rhythmical
intervals like those given by the piper,[a] but the whole
periodic form of the sentence is rounded out and
brought to a finish in a way which can be judged only
by the pleasure of the ear.

A frequent inquiry is whether rhythm is to be used 199
throughout the whole sentence or only at the beginning and at the end; there are many in fact who
hold that it is only at the end that a sentence should
be rhythmical. It is true that the end is the most
appropriate place, but not the only one; for the
period must be brought to a close gently, and not
with a sudden movement. Therefore, since the ear
is always awaiting the end and takes pleasure in it,
this should not be without rhythm, but the period
ought even from the very beginning to move toward
such a conclusion, and to flow from the start in such
a way that at the end it will come naturally to rest.
This will not be very difficult for those who have 200
been well trained, who have had extensive practice
in writing, and who, even if they speak extempo-
raneously, will produce something which resembles
a speech written down beforehand. The outline of
the thought is no sooner formed in the mind than
the words begin to muster; and these the mind, the
swiftest thing there is, immediately distributes so
that each one falls into its proper place in the ranks,
and the orderly line of words is brought to a close
now with one, now with another rhythmical figure.
And all the words both at the beginning and in the
middle should look to the end. For in oratory 201
sometimes the speed is swift, sometimes there is a
slow and steady progress, so that at the very be-

ut iam a principio videndum sit quemadmodum velis venire ad extremum. Nec in numeris magis quam in reliquis ornamentis orationis, eadem cum faciamus quae poetae, effugimus tamen in oratione poematis similitudinem. Est enim in utroque et materia et tractatio : materia in verbis, tractatio in collocatione verborum. LX. Ternae autem sunt utriusque partes, verborum : tralatum, novum, priscum—nam de propriis nihil hoc loco dicimus—collocationis[1] autem eae quas diximus : compositio, concinnitas, numerus.

202 Sed in utroque frequentiores sunt, in altero liberiores poetae ; nam et transferunt verba cum crebrius tum etiam audacius et priscis libentius utuntur et liberius novis. Quod idem non[2] fit in numeris, in quibus quasi necessitati parere coguntur. Sed tamen haec nec nimis esse diversa neque nullo[3] modo coniuncta intellegi licet. Ita fit ut non item in oratione ut in versu numerus exstet idque quod numerosum in oratione dicitur non semper numero fiat, sed nonnunquam aut concinnitate aut constructione verborum.

203 Ita, si numerus orationis quaeritur qui sit, omnis est sed alius alio melior atque aptior ; si locus, in omni parte verborum ; si unde ortus sit, ex aurium voluptate; si componendorum ratio, dicetur alio loco, quia pertinet ad usum, quae pars quarta et extrema nobis in dividendo fuit ; si ad quam rem adhibeatur, ad delectationem ; si quando, semper ; si quo loco,

---

[1] collocationis *Manutius :* collocationes *L.*
[2] non *addidit Ammon.*
[3] nullo *Goeller :* ullo *L.*

---

[a] § 149.
[b] " These " apparently refers to words and rhythms.

ginning you must consider how you wish to end the sentence. This is no less true of the other ornaments of prose than of rhythms, since we are doing the same thing as the poets, but in prose we avoid the semblance of poetry. For in both prose and poetry it is a question of material and treatment : by material I mean the words, by treatment, the arrangement of the words. There are three parts in each section : in words we have metaphors, new formations and archaisms (for I need not mention words used in their " proper " sense); under the heading of arrangement the topics are, as we have said,[a] euphony, symmetry and rhythm. The poets, 202 however, are more assiduous in both and take greater liberties in the former ; they employ metaphors more frequently, and also more boldly, and use archaisms and new words more freely. The same is not true of rhythm, in which they are constrained to yield to necessity, as it were. However, we can appreciate that in prose and poetry these [b] are not greatly different, nor utterly unconnected. Consequently rhythm is not so conspicuous in prose as in verse, and what is called rhythm in prose does not always arise from metre, but at times from either the symmetry or the structure of the language.

Wherefore if the question be asked, which rhythms 203 are used in prose, the answer is, " all, but one is better suited to one part and one to another." The place ? In all parts of a phrase. What is the origin ? In the pleasure of the ear. The method of construction ? This will be discussed elsewhere, since this is a matter of practice, and that is the fourth and last topic of our discussion. For what purpose is it used ? To give pleasure. When ? Always. In what

in tota continuatione verborum ; si quae res efficiat
voluptatem, eadem quae in versibus, quorum modum
notat ars, sed aures ipsae tacito eum sensu[1] sine arte
definiunt.

204   LXI. Satis multa de natura ; sequitur usus, de quo
est accuratius disputandum. In quo quaesitum est
in totone circuitu illo orationis, quem Graeci περίοδον,
nos tum ambitum, tum circuitum, tum comprehen-
sionem aut continuationem aut circumscriptionem
dicimus, an in principiis solum an in extremis an in
utraque parte numerus tenendus sit ; deinde cum
aliud videatur esse numerus aliud numerosum, quid
205 intersit. Tum autem in omnibusne numeris aequaliter
particulas deceat incidere an facere alias breviores
alias longiores, idque quando aut cur ; quibusque partibus, pluribusne an singulis, imparibus an aequalibus,
et quando aut istis aut illis sit utendum ; quaeque inter se aptissime collocentur et quo modo, an omnino
nulla sit in eo genere distinctio ; quodque ad rem
maxime pertinet, qua ratione numerosa fiat oratio.
206 Explicandum etiam est unde orta sit forma verborum
dicendumque quantos circuitus facere deceat deque
eorum particulis et tanquam incisionibus disserendum
est quaerendumque utrum una species et longitudo
sit earum anne plures et, si plures, quo loco aut
quando quoque genere uti oporteat. Postremo
totius generis utilitas explicanda est, quae quidem

---

[1] sensu $M^2\pi$, sensum L.

[a] Clauses shorter than a sentence.

place ? Throughout the whole period. What produces the pleasure ? The same phenomena as in verse ; theory sets down the exact measure of these, but without theory the ear marks their limits with unconscious intuition.

But enough concerning the nature of rhythm ; the 204 next topic is the use, and this must be treated in greater detail. The question here is whether rhythm is to be used throughout the whole of that rounded form of expression which the Greeks call the "period," and to which we apply the terms *ambitus*, *circuitus*, *comprehensio*, *continuatio*, or *circumscriptio*, or whether it is to be used only at the beginning, or at the end, or in both places. In the second place, since rhythm seems to be one thing, and a rhythmical quality another, what the distinction is. Thirdly, 205 should the period be divided into equal *cola* [a] in all rhythms, or should some be shorter and some longer ; and when should this be done and why ? Which *cola* are to be used for rhythmical effect, several or only one, the unequal or the equal ones, and when should we use one and when the other ? Which rhythms are combined most aptly, and how is it done ; or is there no distinction on this point ? And most important of all, in what manner does prose become rhythmical ? We must also explain the origin of the regular 206 pattern of language ; we must discuss how long it is appropriate to make the periods, and about their *cola* and *commata*,[b] and we must inquire whether these have one form and length or several, and if several, where, when and what kind should be used. Finally we must explain the utility of the whole business of rhythm—a subject with wide implica-

[b] Phrases shorter than the colon.

patet latius ; non ad unam enim rem aliquam sed
ad pluris accommodatur.

207   Ac licet non ad singula[1] respondentem de universo
genere sic dicere ut etiam singulis satis responsum
esse videatur.   Remotis igitur reliquis generibus
unum selegimus hoc quod in causis foroque versatur,
de quo diceremus.   Ergo in aliis, id est in historia et
in eo quod appellamus ἐπιδεικτικόν, placet omnia
dici Isocrateo Theopompeoque more illa circumscriptione ambituque, ut tanquam in orbe inclusa
currat oratio, quoad insistat in singulis perfectis
208 absolutisque sententiis.   Itaque posteaquam est nata
haec vel circumscriptio vel comprehensio vel continuatio vel ambitus, si ita licet dicere, nemo, qui
aliquo esset in numero, scripsit orationem generis
eius quod esset ad delectationem comparatum re-
motumque a iudiciis forensique certamine, quin
redigeret omnis fere in quadrum numerumque sententias.   Nam cum is est auditor qui non vereatur. ne
compositae orationis insidiis sua fides attemptetur,
gratiam quoque habet oratori voluptati aurium
209 servienti.   LXII. Genus autem hoc orationis neque
totum assumendum est ad causas forensis neque
omnino repudiandum ; si enim semper utare, cum
satietatem affert tum quale sit etiam ab imperitis
agnoscitur ;   detrahit praeterea actionis dolorem,
aufert humanum sensum auditoris,[2] tollit funditus
veritatem et fidem.

    Sed quoniam adhibenda nonnunquam est, primum
videndum est quo loco, deinde quam diu retinenda
210 sit, tum quot modis commutanda.   Adhibenda est

----

    [1] singula *Bake :* singulas res *L.*
    [2] auditoris *Heerdegen :* auctoris *P,* actoris *FO.*

tions; for it relates to many subjects and not to one alone.

It is possible, without answering each individual 207 question, to discuss the whole subject in such a way as to give a complete enough answer to the several problems. Therefore, putting aside other forms of oratory, we have selected for our discussion that used in law-court and public assembly. In the other forms, to be sure, that is in history and epideictic oratory, as it is called, it is desirable to have everything done in the periodical style of Isocrates and Theopompus, so that the language runs on as if enclosed in a circle until it comes to an end with each phrase complete and perfect. Consequently, since the invention of 208 this style—call it *circumscriptio* or *comprehensio*, or *continuatio*, or *ambitus*, if you will—no one worth counting as an author has written an oration designed for entertainment and alien to the court room and the contests of public life without shaping nearly all his sentences in the mould of rhythm. For since the listener is not one who is afraid that he will be deceived by the tricks of an artistic style, he is grateful to the orator for ministering to the pleasure of his ear. But this style of prose is not to be taken over 209 bodily into forensic speeches, nor is it utterly to be rejected. If you use it constantly, it not only wearies the audience, but even the layman recognizes the nature of the trick: furthermore, it takes the feeling out of the delivery, it robs the audience of their natural sympathy, and utterly destroys the impression of sincerity.

But since this style is to be used at times, we must consider where to introduce it, how long to keep it up, and how it may be varied. Rhythmical style is 210

igitur numerosa oratio, si aut laudandum est aliquid
ornatius, ut nos in Accusationis secundo de Siciliae
laude diximus aut in senatu de consulatu meo, aut
exponenda narratio, quae plus dignitatis desiderat
quam doloris, ut in quarto Accusationis de Hennensi
Cerere, de Segestana Diana, de Syracusarum situ
diximus. Saepe etiam in amplificanda re concessu
omnium funditur numerose et volubiliter oratio. Id
nos fortasse non perfecimus, conati quidem saepissime sumus ; quod plurimis locis perorationes nostrae voluisse nos atque animo contendisse declarant.
Id autem tum valet, cum is qui audit ab oratore
iam obsessus est ac tenetur. Non enim id agit, ut
insidietur et observet, sed iam favet processumque
volt dicendique vim admirans non anquirit[1] quid
reprehendat.[2]

211 Haec autem forma retinenda non diu est, non[3] dico
in peroratione, quam in se[4] includit, sed in orationis
reliquis partibus. Nam cum sis eis locis usus quibus
ostendi licere,[5] transferenda tota dictio est ad illa quae
nescio cur, cum Graeci κόμματα et κῶλα nominent, nos
non recte incisa et membra dicamus. Neque enim
esse possunt rebus ignotis nota nomina, sed cum verba
aut suavitatis aut inopiae causa transferre soleamus,
in omnibus hoc fit artibus ut, cum id appellandum sit

[1] anquirit *π*, inquirit *f*, adquirit *FP*, acquirat *O*[1], acquirit
O[v].

[2] reprehendat *vulg.*, prehendat *Of*, prendat *FP*ε.

[3] non *Sauppe :* nec *L.*

[4] in se *Kroll :* ipse *L.*   [5] licere *π*, liceret *L.*

[a] *In Verrem,* Actio Secunda ii. 2.

[b] This speech is not extant. For an account of it see
Epist. ad Att. 1. 14, 4.

[c] *In Verrem,* Actio Secunda iv. 106-108, 72-79, 117-119.

[d] The Latin words are literal translations of the Greek

to be used, then, in an ornate laudatory passage such as my praise of Sicily in the *Accusation*[a] or my speech before the senate on the subject of my consulate.[b] It is used, too, in telling a story which calls for dignity rather than pathos, as, for example, the passages in the fourth *Verrine*[c] about the Ceres of Henna, the Diana of Segesta, and the site of Syracuse. Often also in amplification every one would grant that the language is poured out with fluent rhythm. We may not have brought this to perfection, but we have repeatedly made the attempt. Many passages in our perorations show that we desired and attempted this. It is effective when the audience have been won and held by the speaker; they no longer are intent on watching or catching him, but are now on his side, and wish him success; overcome with admiration for the vigour of his oratory, they do not seek points to criticize.

This style should not be maintained for a long 211 time; I do not mean in the peroration which falls entirely into it, but in the rest of the speech. For when you have finished the passages in which I have shown it is permissible, the whole style must be altered to the forms which, as the Greeks call them *commata* and *cola*, I am inclined to think we might properly call *incisa* and *membra*.[d] For names cannot be known if the things they represent are unknown; but since we are wont to use words figuratively either to add charm or because of the poverty of the language, it happens in all arts that

terms. *Incisa* is here used for the first time in this sense: *membrum* had already been used to translate the Greek κῶλον in Auct. *Ad Heren*. 4. 26. He means that the long involved rhythmical period is to be abandoned for shorter sentences.

quod propter rerum ignorationem ipsarum nullum
habuerit ante nomen, necessitas cogat[1] aut novum
facere verbum aut a simili mutuari.

212   LXIII. Quo autem pacto deceat incise membratimve
dici iam videbimus ; nunc quot modis mutentur com-
prehensiones conclusionesque dicendum est.   Fluit
omnino numerus a primo tum incitatius brevitate
pedum tum proceritate tardius.   Cursum contentiones
magis requirunt, expositiones rerum tarditatem.
Insistit autem ambitus modis pluribus, e quibus unum
est secuta Asia maxime qui dichoreus vocatur, cum
duo extremi chorei sunt, id est e singulis longis et
brevibus.   Explanandum est enim, quoniam[2] ab aliis[3]

213 eidem pedes aliis vocabulis nominantur.   Dichoreus
non est ille quidem sua sponte vitiosus in clausulis,
sed in orationis numero nihil est tam vitiosum quam
si semper est idem.   Cadit autem per se ille ipse
praeclare, quo etiam satietas formidanda est magis.
Me stante C. Carbo C. f. tr. pl. in contione dixit his
verbis : " O M. Druse, patrem appello "—haec
quidem duo binis pedibus incisim ; dein membratim :
" tu dicere solebas sacram esse rem publicam "—haec

214 autem[4] membra ternis ; post ambitus : " quicumque
eam violavissent, ab omnibus esse ei poenas persolu-

---

[1] cogat *vulg.*, cogit *L.*
[2] quoniam *Stangl :* quod iam *Rufinus*, quod *L*, *cf.* § 105.
[3] ab aliis *Rufinus :* ab illis *L.*
[4] autem *Piderit :* item *L.*

---

[a] Here, as in § 193, Cicero uses *choreus* for the more usual
trochee.   The ditrochee would be scanned $\stackrel{\_}{}\;\smile\;\stackrel{\_}{}\;\smile$.

[b] [O] Mārcĕ | Drūsĕ ‖ pătr(em) ăp|pĕllō
    "O Marcus Drusus, father of the dead, on thee I
    call."

[c] Tū dī|cĕrĕ sŏ|lēbās ‖ sācr(am) ēs|sĕ rēm | pūblĭcăm
    " You were wont to call the state sacred."

when we have to name something which had had no
name because the thing itself was unknown, we are
compelled to invent a new term or to use a metaphor.

We shall presently see the fitting way to speak in 212
cola and *commata* ; now we must explain how many
methods there are of varying the periods and rhythmical clausulae. In general the rhythm flows onward from the beginning, sometimes faster if the
feet are short, sometimes slower if they are long.
A vigorous dispute requires speed, exposition requires a slower rhythm. The period may end in
several ways ; Asia prefers the one called ditrochee in
which the last two feet are trochees, each composed of
a long and a short. (We have to make this explanation because the same feet receive different names
from different people.)[a] Surely the ditrochee is not 213
of itself vicious in the clausula, but in prose rhythm
nothing is so vicious as to keep the rhythm always
the same. In itself it has a splendid cadence ;
therefore we have all the more reason to fear satiety
or monotony. I was standing in an assembly when
the tribune of the people, Gaius Carbo the younger,
spoke in these words : *O Marce Druse, patrem appello*
—here two *commata*, each consisting of two feet[b] ;
then in *cola* : *tu dicere solebas sacram esse rem publicam* ;
this has *cola* of three feet each[c] ; then followed
the period : *quicumque eam violavissent ab omnibus* 214

The division given above seems the only possible way of
making three feet in each colon. A modern theorist would
probably mark it as follows :

Tū | dícĕrĕ sŏ|lébās ‖ sācr(am) | éssĕ rĕm | públĭcăm.

This gives the cretic clausula which Cicero used so frequently.
Cicero was poor at analysis of rhythmical phenomena, but his
practice was excellent.

tas "—dichoreus ; nihil enim ad rem, extrema illa
longa sit an brevis ; deinde : "patris dictum sapiens
temeritas fili comprobavit "—hoc dichoreo tantus
clamor contionis excitatus est, ut admirabile esset.
Quaero nonne id numerus effecerit. Verborum
ordinem immuta, fac sic : "comprobavit fili temeritas": iam nihil erit, etsi temeritas ex tribus brevibus
et longa est, quem[1] Aristoteles ut optimum probat, a
215 quo dissentio. "At eadem verba, eadem sententia."
Animo istuc satis est, auribus non satis. Sed id
crebrius fieri non oportet ; primum enim numerus
agnoscitur, deinde satiat, postea cognita facilitate
contemnitur.

LXIV. Sed sunt clausulae plures, quae numerose et
iucunde cadant. Nam et creticus, qui est e longa et
brevi et longa, et eius aequalis paean, qui spatio par
est, syllaba longior, qui commodissime putatur in so-
lutam orationem illigari, cum sit duplex—nam aut e
longa est et tribus brevibus, qui numerus in primo
viget, iacet in extremo, aut e[2] totidem brevibus et
longa, in[3] quem optime cadere censent veteres ; ego
216 non plane reicio sed alios antepono. Ne spondeus

---

[1] quem *Rufinus :* qn͞a͞e *P,* quam *FO*[1], al. quem *O*[2], quem
⟨numerum⟩ *Stangl.*
[2] e *Rufinus : omisit L.*
[3] in *L : omisit Rufinus, seclusit Stangl.*

---

[a] (Saying) "that all who had harmed her had paid the
penalty."
[b] pĕrsŏ|lūtās.
[c] The rashness of the son demonstrated the wisdom of
the father.
[d] cŏmprŏ|bāvĭt. It is perhaps not unfair to think that
Cicero has exaggerated the effect of the rhythm. The
recent murder of the younger Drusus, a follower of Gaius

esse ei poenas persolutas [a] : this ends in a ditrochee,[b] for the quantity of the final syllable makes no difference ; then : *patris dictum sapiens temeritas fili comprobavit* [c] ; it was marvellous what a shout arose from the crowd at this ditrochee.[d] Was it not, I ask, the rhythm which produced this ? Change the order of the words and write it this way : *comprobavit fili temeritas*. The effect is now gone, although *temeritas* consists of three shorts and a long, the foot which Aristotle regards as the best ; but I disagree. "The words, however, are the same, 215 the thought is the same." That satisfies the mind, but not the ear. But this ending ought not to be used too frequently ; for first it is recognized as rhythm, next it wearies, and then when it begins to seem an easy trick, it is despised.

There are many clausulae which have a pleasing rhythmical cadence ; the cretic, for example, made up of a long, a short, and a long (– ◡ –) and its equivalent the paean (– ◡ ◡ ◡ or ◡ ◡ ◡ –) which takes the same time but has one more syllable ; and which is thought most convenient to insert into prose, since it has two forms : either it takes the form of a long syllable followed by three shorts, which is strong at the beginning, but weak at the end of a sentence ; or of three shorts and a long, which the ancients consider the best cadence. I do not ab- 216 solutely reject it, but I prefer others.[e] Not even the spondee is entirely to be discarded, although, Gracchus, undoubtedly lent an emotional tension which was partly responsible for the outburst.

[e] According to Wüst, *De Clausula Rhetorica*, p. 96, Cicero uses the cadence ◡ ◡ ◡ – rarely in his early speeches, and later abandons it entirely. See also T. Zielinski, *Das Clauselgesetz in Ciceros Reden*, p. 90.

quidem funditus est repudiandus, etsi, quod est e longis duabus, hebetior videtur et tardior ; habet tamen stabilem quendam et non expertem dignitatis gradum, in incisionibus vero multo magis et in membris ; paucitatem enim pedum gravitate sua et[1] tarditate compensat. Sed hos cum in clausulis pedes nomino, non loquor de uno pede extremo : adiungo, quod minimum sit, proximum superiorem, saepe etiam 217 tertium. Ne iambus quidem qui est e brevi et longa, aut par choreo qui habet tris brevis trochaeus[2]—sed spatio par, non syllabis—aut etiam dactylus qui est e longa et duabus brevibus, si est proximus a postremo, parum volubiliter pervenit ad extremum, si est extremus choreus aut spondeus ; nunquam enim interest uter sit eorum in pede extremo. Sed idem hi tres pedes male concludunt, si quis eorum in extremo locatus est, nisi cum pro cretico postremus est dactylus. Nihil enim interest dactylus sit extremus an creticus, quia postrema syllaba brevis an 218 longa sit ne in versu quidem refert. Quare etiam paeana qui dixit aptiorem, in quo esset longa postrema, vidit parum, quoniam nihil ad rem est, postrema quam longa sit. Iam paean,[3] quod pluris habeat syllabas quam tris, numerus a quibusdam, non pes habetur. Est quidem, ut inter omnis constat

---

[1] gravitate sua et *Rufinus*, et O^2, gravitatis suaet F, gravitatis suae PO^1.   [2] trochaeus *Rufinus, omisit L.*
[3] paean *Rufinus*, paeana *L.*

---

[a] This is nonsense. It is true that in verse the final syllable is "common," *i.e.* it may be long or short. This is possible because the rhythm of the line is fully established before the final syllable is reached. In prose rhythm, however, where the final foot is a principal, and at times the sole, source of the rhythm, changing the quantity of the

because it consists of two long syllables, it seems rather heavy and slow ; still it has a steady movement that is not without dignity, especially in *cola* and *commata* where the heaviness and sluggishness compensate for the small number of feet. (In mentioning these feet as used in clausulae, I am not speaking only of the last foot ; I include at least the next to the last, and often the one before that.) The iambus composed of a short and a long, or the equivalent of the trochee, the tribrach with three shorts which is equivalent in time but not in number of syllables, or even the dactyl composed of a long and two shorts if placed in the penultimate position, reaches the end of the sentence rapidly enough if the last foot is a trochee or spondee. For it makes no difference which is used at the close of the sentence. But these same three feet make a bad cadence if any of them is placed last, except when the final dactyl stands for a cretic ; for it never makes any difference whether the dactyl or cretic be used last, because even in verse the quantity of the final syllable is a matter of indifference. For this reason the one who said that the form of the paean with the last syllable long was better adapted to the cadence, did not realize the real situation, since the length of the final syllable has nothing to do with the case.[a] Some even hold the paean to be a rhythm and not a foot, because it has more than three syllables. It is in fact, as all the ancients agree—Aristotle, Theo-

last syllable changes the whole form of the cadence. Aristotle meant to have the last syllable long. *Cf.* also Quintilian, 9. 4, 93 : " When I consult my ear, I find it makes a great difference whether the closing syllable is really long, or a short taking the place of a long."

antiquos, Aristotelem, Theophrastum, Theodectem,[1]
Ephorum, unus aptissimus orationi vel orienti vel
mediae ; putant illi etiam cadenti, quo loco mihi
videtur aptior creticus.   Dochmius[a] autem e quinque
syllabis, brevi duabus longis brevi longa, ut est hoc :
" amicos tenes," quovis loco aptus est, dum semel
ponatur ; iteratus aut continuatus numerum apertum
219 et nimis insignem facit.   LXV. His igitur tot com-
mutationibus tamque variis si utemur, nec depre-
hendetur manifesto quid a nobis de industria fiat et
occurretur satietati.

Et quia non numero[3] solum numerosa oratio sed
et compositione fit et genere, quod ante[4] dictum est,
concinnitatis—compositione potest intellegi, cum[5]
ita structa verba sunt, ut numerus non quaesitus
sed ipse secutus esse videatur, ut apud Crassum :
" nam ubi lubido dominatur, innocentiae leve praesidium est " ; ordo enim verborum efficit numerum
sine ulla aperta oratoris industria—itaque si quae
veteres illi, Herodotum dico et Thucydidem totam-
que eam aetatem, apte numeroseque dixerunt, ea
scilicet[6] non numero quaesito sed verborum collo-
220 catione ceciderunt—formae vero quaedam sunt
orationis, in quibus ea concinnitas est ut sequatur
numerus necessario.   Nam cum aut par pari refertur
aut contrarium contrario opponitur aut quae simili-

[1] Theodecten *Rufinus*, Theodectum *L*.
[2] dochmius *Rufinus*, dochimius *L*.
[3] numero solum (*om*. numerosa) *f*, *omisit L*.
[4] ante *vulg*., aut *L*.
[5] cum *vulg*., quam *L*.
[6] scilicet (*i.e.* s') *Stangl* : si *L*, sic *Heerdegen*.

---

[a] Cretic combinations are common in Cicero, *e.g.* $-\cup-|-\asymp$.

phrastus, Theodectes, Ephorus—the one foot best adapted to the beginning or the middle of the sentence ; they think it is best at the close, too ; but here the cretic appears to me better.[a] The dochmius, however, composed of five syllables, short, two longs, short and a long, for example, *ămīcōs tĕnēs*, is fitted for any position, provided it is used only once. If repeated or used in a series it makes an obvious and too conspicuous rhythm. Therefore if we use these many different variations, what we are doing so studiously will not be plainly discovered, and satiety or monotony will be forestalled.

Furthermore, prose becomes rhythmical, not only by the use of rhythms, but also because of the arrangement of words and a kind of symmetry, as has been said before [b] ; by arrangement, I mean, when the words are so placed that the rhythm seems not to be planned but to come naturally ; in the following passage from Crassus for example : " *Nam ubi lubido dominatur, innocentiae leve praesidium est,*" [c] the order of the words produces a rhythm without any apparent effort on the part of the orator. Consequently if the early writers,—I mean Herodotus, Thucydides and all that period—wrote anything rhythmical, this was due, I am sure, not to purposeful rhythm, but to the arrangement of the words. Moreover, there are certain figures of speech which involve such a symmetry that rhythm is the necessary result. For when clauses are equally balanced, or opposite is set against opposite, or words are

Quintilian (9. 4, 63) tells us that Brutus disliked this clausula.
  [b] § 149.
  [c] Where passion rules, innocence is helpless.

ter cadunt verba verbis comparantur, quidquid[1] ita
concluditur, plerumque fit[2] ut numerose cadat—quo
de genere cum exemplis supra diximus—ut haec
quoque copia facultatem afferat non semper eodem
modo desinendi. Nec tamen haec ita sunt arta et
astricta ut ea, cum velimus, laxare nequeamus.
Multum interest utrum numerosa sit, id est similis
numerorum, an plane e numeris constet oratio:
alterum si fit, intolerabile vitium est, alterum nisi
fit, dissipata et inculta et fluens est oratio.

221 LXVI. Sed quoniam non modo non frequenter
verum etiam raro in veris causis aut forensibus cir-
cumscripte numeroseque dicendum est, sequi videtur, ut videamus quae sint illa quae supra dixi incisa,
quae membra. Haec enim in veris causis maximam
partem orationis obtinent. Constat enim ille ambitus et plena comprehensio e quattuor fere partibus,[3]
quae membra dicimus, ut et auris impleat et neque[4]
brevior sit quam satis sit neque longior. Quanquam
utrumque nonnunquam vel potius saepe accidit, ut
aut citius insistendum sit aut longius procedendum,
ne brevitas defraudasse auris videatur neve longitudo obtudisse. Sed habeo mediocritatis rationem;
nec enim loquor de versu et est liberior aliquanto
222 oratio. E quattuor igitur quasi hexametrorum
instar versuum quod sit constat fere plena comprehensio. His igitur singulis versibus quasi nodi[5]
apparent continuationis, quos in ambitu coniungimus.

---

[1] quidquid *vulg.*, quid quod *L.*   [2] fit *vulg.*, sic *L.*
[3] partibus *L*, senariis versibus *ex Quint. 9. 4, 125 et Diom.
Gram. Lat. 1. 466, 21 Stangl.*
[4] et neque *Heerdegen :* et neve *L.*
[5] nodi *L*, modi *Stroux.*

* § 211.

matched with words of similar endings, whatever is elaborated in this way generally has a rhythmical cadence. We discussed this form or type above with examples. This gives abundant opportunity to avoid always ending in the same way. However, these rules are not so strict and binding that we cannot relax them at will. It makes a vast difference whether prose is rhythmical, that is *resembling* definite rhythms, or is composed entirely of definite rhythms; if the latter occurs it is an intolerable fault; if the former does not occur, the style is disordered, unpolished, and vague.

But since in actual practice in court the rhythmical 221 period is certainly to be used not only not frequently, but even sparingly, we must, it seems, examine the nature of the *incisa* and *membra* which I mentioned above[a]; for these form the largest part of the speech in actual practice. The full comprehensive period consists of approximately four parts which we call *membra*, so as to satisfy the ear and not be too long or too short. However, it happens occasionally or rather I should say frequently that one must stop sooner, or continue farther in order to prevent the ear from being seemingly cheated by the brevity or wearied by the length. But I am considering the average; I am not discussing verse, and prose is somewhat less restricted in form. The full period, 222 then, consists of four members each approximately equal to a hexameter verse.[b] In each of these lines appear the binding knots which we unite in a

---

[b] The dactylic hexameter contains from twelve to seventeen syllables. Quintilian and Diomedes, quoting apparently from this passage, say four senarii. The number of syllables in the two lines is approximately the same.

CICERO

Sin membratim volumus dicere, insistimus atque,[1]
cum opus est, ab isto cursu invidioso facile nos et
saepe diiungimus. Sed nihil tam debet esse numerosum quam hoc, quod minime apparet et valet plurimum. Ex hoc genere illud est Crassi: "missos
faciant patronos; ipsi prodeant"—nisi intervallo
dixisset "ipsi prodeant," sensisset profecto se
fudisse[2] senarium; omnino melius caderet "pro-
223 deant ipsi"; sed de genere nunc disputo. "Cur
clandestinis consiliis nos oppugnant? Cur de perfugis[3] nostris copias comparant contra nos?" Prima
sunt illa duo, quae κόμματα Graeci vocant, nos incisa
dicimus; deinde tertium—κῶλον illi, nos membrum
—sequitur non longa—ex duobus enim versibus, id
est membris, perfecta est—comprehensio[4] et in
spondeos cadit; et Crassus quidem sic plerumque
dicebat idque ipse genus dicendi maxime probo.
LXVII. Sed quae incisim aut membratim efferuntur,
ea vel aptissime cadere debent, ut est apud me:
"domus tibi deerat? At habebas. Pecunia superabat? At egebas." Haec incise dicta sunt quat-
224 tuor; at membratim quae secuntur duo: "Incurristi amens in columnas, in alienos insanus insanisti."
Deinde omnia tanquam crepidine quadam com-

---

[1] atque *Stangl:* idque *L.*
[2] profecto se fudisse π, profectos (profecto *OP*) effugisse *L.*
[3] perfugis *f, Quint., Rufinus:* perfugiis *L.*
[4] est comprehensio *Lambinus:* comprehensio est *L.*

---

[a] The text is obscure, and possibly corrupt. The comparison seems to be made to four strands of flowers knotted
together to form a long garland.
[b] Let them dismiss their advocates; let them appear in
person.
[c] It scans – ´ | ⌣ ⌣ ´ | ⌣ ´ | – ´ | – ´ | ⌣ ´.

period.[a] But if we wish to speak in *membra*, we stop, and when necessary, easily and often turn off from a course which offends. However, it is in the nature of things that nothing is rhythmical to such a degree as this, which shows least and has the greatest effect. An example of this style may be cited from Crassus : *Missos faciant patronos, ipsi prodeant*[b]; If he had not paused after *patronos*, he would have recognized that he had made a senarius[c] : on the whole *prodeant ipsi* would give a better cadence,[d] but I am speaking of general principles now—*cur clandestinis consiliis nos oppugnant? Cur de perfugis nostris copias comparant contra nos?*[e] The first two[f] are what the Greeks call *commata*, we call *incisa*; the third[g] they call *colon*, we *membrum*; the last is a full period, not long—it consists of only two verses, that is *membra*—with spondaic cadence. Crassus generally spoke in this style, and that is the style which I myself chiefly favour. But if *incisa* and *membra* are used, they ought to have a proper cadence, for example, my own words[h] : *Domus tibi deerat? at habebas. Pecunia superabat? at egebas.*[i] Here are four *incisa*; the following falls into two *membra* : *Incurristi amens in columnas, in alienos insanisti.*[j] Then the whole passage is set, as

---

[a] $\underline{\ } \smile - | \underline{\ } -$. This is a favourite cadence with Cicero.

[e] Why do they attack us with secret plans ? Why do they recruit deserters from our ranks to use against us ? "

[f] *Missos faciant patronos*, and *ipsi prodeant*.

[g] cur . . . oppugnant.

[h] From the fragmentary speech in defence of Scaurus.

[i] Did you lack a house ? Yet you had one. Was there money left ? Yet you were in want.

[j] You have madly dashed against the columns ; you have raved wildly against strangers.

prehensione longiore sustinentur : " depressam, caecam, iacentem domum pluris quam te et quam
fortunas tuas aestimasti "—dichoreo finitur. At
spondeis proximum illud. Nam in his, quibus ut
pugiunculis uti oportet, brevitas facit ipsa liberiores
pedes ; saepe enim singulis utendum est, plerumque
binis et utrisque[1] addi pedis pars potest, non fere
225 ternis amplius. Incisim autem et membratim trac-
tata oratio in veris causis plurimum valet, maximeque eis locis, cum aut arguas aut refellas, ut nos[2]
in Corneliana secunda : " o callidos homines, o
rem excogitatam, o ingenia metuenda ! "—membratim adhuc ; deinde caesim : " diximus ", rursus
membratim : " testis dare volumus "—extrema sequitur comprehensio, sed ex duobus membris, qua
non potest esse brevior : " quem, quaeso,[3] nostrum
226 fefellit ita vos esse facturos ? " Nec ullum genus
est dicendi aut melius aut fortius quam[4] binis aut
ternis ferire verbis, nonnunquam singulis, paulo
alias pluribus, inter quae[5] variis clausulis interponit
se raro numerosa comprehensio ; quam perverse
fugiens Hegesias, dum ille quoque imitari Lysiam
volt, alterum paene Demosthenem, saltat incidens
particulas. Et is quidem non minus sententiis
peccat quam verbis, ut non quaerat quem appellet

---

[1] utrisque *Rufinus*, utriusque *L.*
[2] nos *Rufinus*, nostra *L.*
[3] quaeso ε, quasi *L.*
[4] quam ε, *omisit L.*
[5] quae *Rufinus*, quas *L.*

---

[a] A fallen, dark and prostrate home you thought more
valuable than yourself and your fortunes.
[b] āestī|māstī. īnsān|īstī.
[c] Frag. 2. Or.
[d] What shrewd men ! What ingenuity ! What dangerous
cleverness !

it were, on the foundation of a longer period: *Depressam, caecam, iacentem domum pluris quam te et quam fortunas tuas aestimasti.*[a] It ends in a ditrochee. But the previous sentence ended in spondees.[b] For in these phrases which should be used as little daggers, the very brevity causes the feet to be somewhat freer; often you must use one, more frequently two—to both of these a part of a foot can be added—hardly more than three. A speech formed 225 of *incisa* and *membra* is very efficient in actual practice, particularly in passages of demonstration or refutation, as in our second speech for Cornelius[c]: *O callidos homines, o rem excogitatam, o ingenia metuenda!*[d] So far it is in *membra*; then with an *incisum*: *Diximus*[e]; then again a *membrum*: *Testis dare volumus.*[f] Last comes the period, composed of two *membra*, the shortest possible form: *Quem, quaeso, nostrum fefellit ita vos esse facturos?*[g] There 226 is no style better or stronger than to strike with phrases of two or three words, sometimes with single words, and at other times with several, in the midst of which comes sparingly the rhythmical period with varying cadences. Hegesias[h] perversely avoids this, and while, he, too,[i] tries to imitate Lysias, who is almost the equal of Demosthenes, he hops about, cutting his style into little fragments. Moreover he errs no less in thought than in language, so that anyone acquainted with

[e] We have spoken.   [f] We wish to offer witnesses.
[g] Who of our number, I pray, failed to know that you would act thus?
[h] Of Magnesia, an orator of the third century, generally regarded as the chief of the "Asiatic" orators.
[i] A dig at the "Attici," who despised the "Asiatic" oratory, and set up Lysias as the model of pure style.

ineptum qui illum cognoverit. Sed ego illa Crassi et nostra posui, ut qui vellet auribus ipsis quid numerosum etiam in minimis particulis orationis esset iudicaret.

Et quoniam plura de numerosa oratione diximus quam quisquam ante nos, nunc de eius generis 227 utilitate dicemus. LXVIII. Nihil enim est aliud, Brute, quod quidem tu minime omnium ignoras, pulchre et oratorie dicere nisi optimis sententiis verbisque lectissimis[1] dicere : et nec sententia ulla est, quae fructum oratori ferat, nisi apte exposita atque absolute, nec verborum lumen apparet nisi diligenter collocatorum. Et horum utrumque numerus illustrat, numerus autem—saepe enim hoc testandum est—non modo non poetice vinctus verum etiam fugiens illum eique omnium dissimillimus. Non quin idem sint[2] numeri non modo oratorum et poetarum verum omnino loquentium, denique etiam sonantium omnium quae metiri auribus possumus ; sed ordo pedum facit, ut id quod pronuntiatur aut orationis 228 aut poematis simile videatur. Hanc igitur, sive compositionem sive perfectionem sive numerum vocari placet, [et][3] adhibere necesse est, si ornate velis dicere, non solum, quod ait Aristoteles et Theophrastus, ne infinite feratur ut flumen oratio, quae non aut spiritu pronuntiantis aut interductu librari sed numero coacta debet insistere, verum etiam quod multo maiorem habent apta vim quam soluta. Ut enim athletas nec multo secus gladiatores videmus

---

[1] lectissimis π, lectissime L.
[2] sint (i in ras.)P, sunt FO.
[3] et seclusit Lambinus.

---

[a] Rhet. 3. 8, 1.

him need seek no further for an example of ineptitude. But I have cited these examples from Crassus and from my own speeches so that he who will may judge by the ear alone what is rhythmical even in the smallest parts of an oration.

Since we have written more about rhythmical prose than anyone before us, we will now take up the practical value of this style. As a matter of fact, 227 the art of delivering a beautiful oration in an effective oratorical style is nothing else, Brutus—though you are by no means unaware of it—than presenting the best thoughts in the choicest language. Furthermore, there is no thought which can bring credit to an orator unless it is fitly and perfectly expressed, nor is any brilliance of style revealed unless the words are carefully arranged. And both thought and diction are embellished by rhythm—rhythm, however — I must say it again and again — not only not rigid like the rhythm of poetry, but even avoiding this and as unlike it as possible ; not that the rhythm of prose and poetry are not the same—and for that matter of all speech, and even of all sounds which we can measure by the ear—but the arrangement of feet makes the utterance resemble prose or poetry. Hence this must be used, call it composition, or finish 228 or rhythm as you will—this must be used if you wish to speak elegantly, not only, as Aristotle [a] and Theophrastus say, that the sentence may not drift along vaguely like a river (it should end, not because the speaker stops to breathe, or the copyist has placed a mark of punctuation, but because the rhythm brings it to a necessary close) but for the reason that the periodic sentence is much more forceful than the loose. For as we observe that boxers, and gladiators

nihil nec vitando facere caute nec petendo vehementer
in quo non motus hic habeat palaestram quandam,
ut quicquid in his rebus fiat utiliter ad pugnam idem
ad aspectum etiam sit venustum, sic orator[1] nec
plagam gravem facit, nisi petitio fuit apta, nec
satis tecte declinat impetum, nisi etiam in cedendo
229 quid deceat intellegit. Itaque qualis eorum motus
quos ἀπαλαίστρους Graeci vocant, talis horum mihi
videtur oratio qui non claudunt numeris sententias,
tantumque abest ut[2]—quod ei qui hoc aut magis-
trorum inopia aut ingeni tarditate aut laboris fuga
non sunt assecuti solent dicere—enervetur oratio
compositione verborum, ut aliter in ea nec impetus
ullus nec vis esse possit. LXIX. Sed magnam exercitationem res flagitat, ne quid eorum qui genus hoc
secuti non tenuerunt simile faciamus : ne aut verba
traiciamus aperte, quo melius aut cadat aut volvatur
230 oratio. Quod se L. Coelius Antipater in prooemio
belli Punici nisi necessario facturum negat. O virum
simplicem, qui nos nihil celet,[3] sapientem, qui
serviendum necessitati putet ! Sed hic omnino rudis ;
nobis autem in scribendo atque in dicendo necessitatis
excusatio non probatur ; nihil est enim necesse, et
si quid esset, id necesse tamen non erat confiteri.
Et hic quidem, quid hanc a L. Aelio,[4] ad quem scripsit
cui se purgat, veniam petit, et utitur ea traiectione
verborum et nihilo tamen aptius explet concludique

---

[1] orator *Bake :* oratio *L.*
[2] ut *Manutius :* ne *L.*
[3] celet ε, celat *L.*
[4] L. Aelio *Kroll :* Laelio *L.*

---

[a] Historian of the latter part of the second century. His
account of the second Punic War was dedicated to L. Aelius
Stilo (*Ad Heren.* 4. 18).

not much less, do not make any motion, either in cautious parrying or vigorous thrusting, which does not have a certain grace, so that whatever is useful for the combat is also attractive to look upon, so the orator does not strike a heavy blow unless the thrust has been properly directed, nor can he avoid the attack safely unless even in yielding he knows what is becoming. Consequently the speech of those 229 who do not form their sentences with a rhythmical cadence seems to me to resemble the movements of those whom the Greeks call ἀπαλαίστρους or "untrained in gymnastics"; and it is far from being true that—as those are wont to say who, from lack of teachers, or slowness of wit, or shirking from hard work, have failed of success—careful arrangement of words enfeebles speech : on the contrary without this it can possess no force or vigour. But a great deal of practice is required that we may avoid the errors of those who have attempted this style and failed ; words must not be transposed obtrusively for the sake of securing a better cadence or a more flowing rhythm. Lucius Coelius Anti- 230 pater *a* in the preface to his *Punic War* says he will not do this unless necessary. How naïve the man, to conceal nothing from us ! How wise, to recognize that he must bow to necessity ! But Antipater was altogether unskilled ; by men of our time, however, the plea of necessity is not accepted either in writing or in speaking ; for there is no necessity, and if there were, it would not be necessary anyhow to confess it. Certainly this man who asks indulgence from Lucius Aelius to whom he dedicates his work and in whose eyes he wishes to justify himself, not only transposes words, but also fails to fill out or round off his

sententias. Apud alios autem et Asiaticos **maxime**
numero servientis inculcata reperias inania quaedam
verba quasi complementa numerorum. Sunt etiam
qui illo vitio, quod ab Hegesia maxime fluxit,
infringendis concidendisque numeris in quoddam
genus abiectum incidant versiculorum[1] simillimum.
231 Tertium est, in quo fuerunt fratres illi Asiaticorum
rhetorum principes Hierocles et Menecles minime
mea sententia contemnendi. Etsi enim a forma
veritatis et ab Atticorum regula absunt, tamen hoc
vitium compensant vel facultate vel copia. Sed apud
eos varietas non erat, quod omnia fere concludebantur
uno modo. Quae vitia qui fugerit, ut neque verbum
ita traiciat, ut id de industria factum intellegatur,
neque inferciens verba quasi rimas expleat nec
minutos numeros sequens concidat delumbetque
sententias nec sine ulla commutatione in eodem
semper[2] versetur genere numerorum, is omnia fere
vitia vitaverit. Nam de laudibus multa diximus,
quibus sunt talia[3] perspicue vitia contraria.

232 LXX. Quantum autem sit apte dicere, experiri licet,
si aut compositi oratoris bene structam collocationem
dissolvas permutatione verborum; corrumpatur enim
tota res, ut et haec nostra in Corneliana et deinceps
omnia: " Neque me divitiae movent, quibus omnis
Africanos et Laelios multi venalicii mercatoresque
superarunt"—immuta paululum, ut sit: "Multi

---

[1] versiculorum *Jahn :* siculorum *L.*
[2] *a syllaba* -per *incipit A.*
[3] talia *Stroux :* alia *AL,* illa ε, *Heerdegen.*

---

^a II. Frag. 8. Or.

sentences more neatly for all that. In the case of
other writers, particularly the "Asiatics" who are
slaves to rhythm, you could find in them some silly
words inserted just to fill out the rhythm. Some also
in the vicious manner which stems from Hegesias,
cutting and breaking up their rhythms, fall into an
insipid style that resembles verselets. A third fault 231
is found in those leaders of Asiatic rhetoric, the
brothers Hierocles and Menecles, who are, in my
opinion, not at all contemptible. For although they
are far removed from the type of real speeches and
from the Attic norm, they compensate for this by
ease, or I might say, fluency. But they had no
variety ; nearly all their sentences ended in the same
way. The orator who avoids these faults, who does
not transpose words so that it seems to be done intentionally, who does not stuff in words as though to
fill up the cracks, who does not cut up and weaken
his sentence in his pursuit of short rhythms, who
does not use the same form of rhythm without variation, will avoid nearly all faults. For we have had a
great deal to say about the virtues to which such
vices are obviously opposites.

The importance of well-knit speech may be demon- 232
strated if you break up the well-ordered structure of
a careful orator by changing the order of the words :
the whole thing would be ruined, as, for example,
in the following words from my *Defence of Cornelius* [a] and the whole succeeding passage : *Neque me
divitiae movent, quibus omnis Africanos et Laelios multi
venalicii mercatorēsquĕ sŭpĕ|rārūnt* [b] : change this only
a trifle, so that it reads *multi superarunt mercatores*

[b] I am not moved by his wealth, in which many traders
and slave dealers have surpassed all the Africani and Laelii.

superarunt mercatores venaliciique": perierit tota
res. Et quae secuntur: "Neque vestis aut caelatum
aurum et argentum, quo nostros veteres Marcellos
Maximosque multi eunuchi e Syria Aegyptoque
vicerunt" verba permuta sic ut sit: "vicerunt
eunuchi e Syria Aegyptoque." Adde tertium:
"neque vero ornamenta ista villarum quibus L.
Paulum et L. Mummium, qui rebus his urbem Ita-
liamque omnem referserunt, ab aliquo video perfacile
Deliaco aut Syro potuisse superari"—fac ita: "po-
233 tuisse superari ab aliquo Syro aut Deliaco." Videsne
ut ordine verborum paululum commutato, isdem
tamen verbis stante sententia, ad nihilum omnia
recidant, cum sint ex aptis dissoluta ? Aut si alicuius
inconditi arripias dissipatam aliquam sententiam
eamque ordine verborum paululum commutato in
quadrum redigas, efficiatur aptum illud, quod fuerit
antea diffluens ac solutum. Age sume de Gracchi
apud censores illud: "Abesse non potest quin
eiusdem hominis sit probos improbare qui improbos
probet"; quanto aptius, si ita dixisset: "Quin
eiusdem hominis sit qui improbos probet probos
improbare!"

234　Hoc modo dicere nemo unquam noluit nemoque potuit quin dixerit ; qui autem aliter dixerunt hoc assequi non potuerunt. Ita facti sunt repente Attici ;

---

^a Neither raiment nor gold and silver plate in which our
ancient heroes, Marcelli and Maximi were outdone by many
eunuchs from Syria and Egypt.

^b Nor those ornaments of your villas, in which Lucius
Paulus and Lucius Mummius, who filled Rome and all Italy
with these treasures, could easily have been surpassed by
any slaver from Delos or Syria.

venǎlǐcǐ|íquě, and the whole thing is spoiled. Take the next sentence : *Neque vestis aut caelatum aurum et argentum, quo nostros veteres Marcellos Maximosque multi eunuchi e Syria Aegyptṓquě vī|cḗrūnt[a]* ; change this to *vicerunt eunuchi e Syria Aḗgȳ|ptṓquě* ; add a third example : *Neque vero ornamenta ista villarum, quibus L. Paulum et L. Mummium, qui rebus his urbem Italiamque omnem referserunt, ab aliquo video perfacile Deliaco aut Syro potuíssě sǔpě|rárī[b]* : Write it as follows : *potuisse superari ab al|íquṓ Sȳr(o) āut|Dḗlǐǎcō:* do you see that when the order of the words is slightly **233** changed, though the words are the same and the thought is the same, the whole sentence collapses, when its symmetry is destroyed? Or if you take some disordered sentence of a careless speaker and by slightly changing the order reduce it to shapeliness, that which was formerly loose and vague becomes elegant. Take this example from the speech of Gracchus [c] before the censors : *Abesse non potest quin eiusdem hominis sit probos improbare qui ímprŏbōs| prŏbět[d]* : how much more elegant if he had said : *Quin eiusdem hominis sit qui improbos prŏbḗt prŏbōs| ímprŏbārě.[e]*

No one was ever unwilling to speak in this way, and **234** no one who could ever refrained ; those who have adopted a different style, did so because they could not attain to this. And so they suddenly turned into

[c] Delivered in 124 B.C. by Gaius Gracchus to defend his return from a province without official recall. See Plut. *Gracchi* 23. 31.

[d] It is certain that the man who approves the wicked will disapprove of the good.

[e] It is to be noted that in these examples Cicero favours the clausula with the cretic basis, *i.e.* $\stackrel{\perp}{} \smile \stackrel{\perp}{}$ or $\stackrel{\perp}{} \smile \stackrel{\vee}{}$, followed by a trochee $\stackrel{\perp}{} \stackrel{\smile}{}$ or ditrochee $\stackrel{\perp}{} \smile \stackrel{\perp}{} \stackrel{\smile}{}$.

quasi vero Trallianus fuerit Demosthenes. Cuius non
tam vibrarent fulmina illa, nisi numeris contorta
ferrentur. LXXI. Sed si quem magis delectant soluta,
sequatur ea sane, modo sic ut, si quis Phidiae clupeum
dissolverit, collocationis universam speciem sustulerit,
non singulorum operum venustatem ; ut in Thucydide
orbem modo orationis desidero, ornamenta com-
235 parent. Isti autem cum dissolvunt orationem in qua
nec res nec verbum ullum est nisi abiectum, non
clupeum sed, ut in proverbio est—etsi humilius dictum est tamen simile est—scopas ut ita dicam mihi
videntur dissolvere. Atque ut plane genus hoc quod
ego laudo contempsisse videantur, aut scribant aliquid
vel Isocrateo more vel quo Aeschines aut Demosthenes utitur ; tum illos existimabo non desperatione
reformidavisse genus hoc sed iudicio refugisse ; aut
reperiam ipse eadem condicione qui uti velit, ut aut
dicat aut scribat utra voles lingua eo genere quo illi
volunt ; facilius est enim apta dissolvere quam
236 dissipata conectere. Res se autem sic habet, ut
brevissime dicam quod sentio : composite et apte sine
sententiis dicere insania est, sententiose autem sine
verborum et ordine et modo infantia, sed eius modi
tamen infantia, ut ea qui utantur non stulti homines
haberi possint, etiam plerumque prudentes ; quo
qui est contentus utatur. Eloquens vero, qui non
approbationes solum sed admirationes, clamores,
plausus, si liceat, movere debet, omnibus oportet ita

---

[a] A city in Caria, the home of the " Asiatic " orators
Dionysocles and Damas.

[b] He refers to the shield of the chryselephantine Athena by
Phidias. Not only the shield, but the entire statue was constructed so that it could be taken apart and put together
again easily. *Cf.* Plut. *Pericles* 31. 3.

"Attici"; as if Demosthenes came from Tralles![a]
Those famous thunderbolts of his would not have sped
with such vibrant power if they had not been whirled
onward by rhythm. If, however, anyone likes a
loose style let him by all means use it, but in the
manner of one who should take apart the shield of
Phidias : if any one ever takes it apart, he destroys
the beauty of the composition, but not the charm of
the several pieces.[b] In Thucydides, for example, I
miss only the periodic structure, the ornaments are
there. But when these "Attici" take a speech to 235
pieces in which both matter and words are mean, they
seem to me not to be taking apart a shield but, if I
may say so, untying a broom, as the proverb has it.
This is a homely expression, but expresses the
resemblance exactly. They may seem utterly to
despise this style which I praise, but let them write
something in the manner of Isocrates or Aeschines or
Demosthenes, then I shall grant that they have not
avoided this style out of despair, but on principle ; or I
myself will find some one willing to undertake the
task of writing or speaking in either Greek or Latin
in the style which they prefer ; for it is easier to
break up the well-knit sentence than to bind together
a loose one. To express my opinion briefly, the fact 236
of the matter is that to speak with well-knit rhythm
without ideas is folly, to present ideas without order
and rhythm in the language is to be speechless ; but
such a kind of speechlessness that those who use it
could be considered, not stupid, but on the whole
wise. If any one is satisfied with that let him be.
But the eloquent orator who ought to win not merely
approval, but admiration and shouts of applause, if it
may be, should so excel in all things that he would be

rebus excellat, ut ei turpe sit quicquam aut spectari
aut audiri libentius.

237   Habes meum de oratore, Brute, iudicium ; quod
aut sequere, si probaveris, aut tuo stabis, si aliud
quoddam est tuum. In quo neque pugnabo tecum
neque hoc meum, de quo tanto opere hoc libro asse-
veravi, unquam affirmabo esse verius quam tuum.
Potest enim non solum aliud mihi ac tibi, sed mi-
himet ipsi aliud alias videri. Nec in hac modo re,
quae ad volgi assensum spectet et ad aurium voluptatem, quae duo sunt ad iudicandum levissima, sed
ne in maximis quidem rebus quicquam adhuc inveni
firmius, quod tenerem aut quo iudicium meum diri-
gerem, quam id quodcumque mihi quam simillimum
veri videretur, cum ipsum illud verum tamen[1] in oc-
238 culto lateret. Tu autem velim, si tibi ea quae dis-
putata sunt minus probabuntur, ut aut maius opus
institutum putes quam effici potuerit aut, dum tibi
roganti voluerim obsequi, verecundia negandi scribendi me imprudentiam suscepisse.

[1] tamen *A*, tam *πf*, tum *ε*, um *F*, *omiserunt OP*.

ashamed to have anything else awaited with greater anticipation or heard with greater pleasure.

You have my judgement, Brutus, of what an orator 237 should be ; you will follow this if you approve, or keep your own, if you have a different one. I shall not quarrel with you over this, nor shall I ever assert that this ideal which I have championed so vigorously in this book is truer than yours. For it is possible that you may have one and I another, or that my own ideal might be different at different times. Not only in this matter which is concerned with popular approval and the pleasure of the ear, both of which are of little weight in forming a true judgement, but even on the most important subjects I have never found anything more substantial to hold to or use in forming my opinions, than what seemed most like the truth ; the truth itself is hidden in obscurity. If my argu- 238 ments find less favour with you, I would ask that you consider that a task was undertaken which could not be fulfilled, or that in my desire to yield to your request, my reluctance to refuse led me to write unwisely.

INDEX TO THE *BRUTUS*

Names of Persons [a]

(The numbers refer to the sections, indicated on the margins.)

[a] The general topics discussed in the *Brutus* may be surveyed in the Summary of Contents, pp. 14-17.

510

INDEX TO THE *BRUTUS*

515

INDEX TO THE *BRUTUS*

pleb. 126 B.C., son of preceding, author of a law, opposed by C. Gracchus, exiling non-citizens (*peregrini*) from Rome. It is referred to and condemned as inhuman by Cicero, *de Off.* 3. 47. *See note on* 109

D. Iunius Silanus, 240, cos. 62 B.C., father-in-law of Brutus, second husband of Servilia mother of Brutus

M. Iunius Silanus, 135, cos. 109 B.C.

T. Iuventius, 178, orator and jurist of the Marian period

Laelia, 211, daughter of C. Laelius, referred to as preserving the purity of speech of her father, and passing it on to her daughters

C. Laelius (Sapiens), 82-89 and *passim*, cos. 140 B.C., friend and associate of the younger Scipio Africanus

Lentulus, *see* Cornelius

Lepidus, *see* Aemilius

Libo, *see* Scribonius

Licinia, 160, a vestal virgin defended by Crassus

Liciniae, 211, daughters of Crassus the orator (granddaughters of Laelia) who still preserved the ancestral purity of speech

C. Licinius Calvus, 280, 283-284, orator and poet 82-47 B.C., leader of the group

of Roman Atticists, Int. pp. 3 and 4, and notes *ad loc.*

L. Licinius Crassus, 139-165 and *passim*, cos. 95 B.C., the most distinguished Roman orator before the period of Hortensius and Cicero

M. Licinius Crassus Dives, 233, 242, 308, 311, the triumvir, cos. 70 and 55 B.C., perished in the Parthian expedition, 53 B.C.

P. Licinius Crassus Dives, 77, cos. 205 B.C.

P. Licinius Crassus Dives, 281, 282, son of the triumvir, perished with his father in the Parthian expedition. *See note ad loc.*

P. Licinius Crassus Dives Mucianus, 98, 127, son of Mucius Scaevola, cos. 131 B.C.

L. Licinius Crassus Scipio, 212, son of the orator's daughter Licinia and P. Cornelius Scipio Nasica, praetor 94 B.C. He was adopted by his grandfather the orator

L. Licinius Lucullus, 81, cos. 151 B.C.

L. Licinius Lucullus Ponticus, 222, cos. 74 B.C., the well-known general, scholar, and dilettante, whose life is described by Plutarch. His name somewhat unfairly became a synonym for luxury

INDEX TO THE *BRUTUS*

Marcellus, *see* Claudius

C. Marcius Censorinus, 237, 311, of the Marian period

Cn. Marcius Coriolanus, 41, legendary character of early Roman history. His life by Plutarch the source of Shakespeare's play

L. Marcius Philippus, 166, 173, 186 and *passim*, cos. 91 B.C., ranked as orator next to Crassus and Antonius 173. *See note on* 166

Q. Marcius Philippus, 78, cos. 186 and 169 B.C.

C. Marius, 168, 224, general and popular leader, seven times cos. 107–86 B.C., native of Arpinum Cicero's birthplace

M. Marius Gratidianus, 168, 223, praetor 85 B.C.

C. Memmius, 136, trib. pleb. 111 B.C.

C. Memmius, 247, trib. pleb. 66 B.C., to whom Lucretius dedicated his poem

L. Memmius, 136, 304, brother of C. Memmius the trib. of 111 B.C.

Menecles, 325, leading figure of Asiatic type of oratory, brother of Hierocles of Alabanda

Menelaus, 50, Homeric type of brevity of speech

Menelaus Marathenus, 100, Asiatic rhetorician, teacher of C. Gracchus, from Marathus in Phoenicia. *Cf. note on* 104

Menippus Stratonicensis, 315, prominent orator and rhetorical teacher of Stratonicea in Caria, mentioned also by Strabo and Plutarch

Messalla, *see* Valerius

Metellus, *see* Caecilius

Q. Minucius Rufus, 73, cos. 197 B.C.

Molo, *see* Apollonius

Muciae, 211, daughters of Laelia and Q. Mucius Scaevola the Augur (cos. 117 B.C.)

Mucii, 252, mentioned as a family in which pure speech had been handed down from generation to generation

P. Mucius Scaevola, 98, cos. 175 B.C.

P. Mucius Scaevola, 108, son of the preceding, cos. 133 B.C.

Q. Mucius Scaevola, 101–102, 212, Augur, cos. 117 B.C., jurisconsult whose instruction Cicero sought, 306

Q. Mucius Scaevola, 115, 145, 147 ff., 194 ff. and *passim*, Pontifex, cos. 95 B.C., the most important Roman jurist before Servius Sulpicius (152)

L. Mummius Achaicus, 85, 94, cos. 146 B.C., destroyer of Corinth

Sp. Mummius, 94, brother of the preceding

Murena, *see* Licinius

521

INDEX TO THE *BRUTUS*

INDEX TO THE *BRUTUS*

INDEX TO THE *ORATOR*

(The numbers refer to the sections, indicated on the margins.)

529

531